GLADIATORS IN SUITS

TELEVISION AND POPULAR CULTURE

Robert J. Thompson, *Series Editor*

SELECT TITLES IN TELEVISION AND POPULAR CULTURE

GLADIATORS IN SUITS

Race, Gender, and the Politics of Representation in SCANDAL

Edited by
Simone Adams,
Kimberly R. Moffitt,
and Ronald L. Jackson II

Syracuse University Press

∞ The paper used in this publication meets the minimum requirements of the American National Standard for Information Sciences—Permanence of Paper for Printed Library Materials, ANSI Z39.48-1992.

For a listing of books published and distributed by Syracuse University Press, visit https://press.syr.edu.

ISBN: 978-0-8156-3622-9 (hardcover)
     978-0-8156-3640-3 (paperback)
     978-0-8156-5468-1 (e-book)

Library of Congress Cataloging-in-Publication Data
Names: Adams, Simone, editor. | Moffitt, Kimberly R., editor. | Jackson, Ronald L., 1970– editor.
Title: Gladiators in suits : race, gender, and the politics of representation in Scandal / edited by Simone Adams, Kimberly R. Moffitt, and Ronald L. Jackson II.
Description: First edition. | Syracuse : Syracuse University Press, [2019] | Series: Television and popular culture | Includes bibliographical references and index.
Identifiers: LCCN 2019016746 (print) | LCCN 2019018953 (ebook) | ISBN 9780815654681 (E-book) | ISBN 9780815636229 (hardcover : alk. paper) | ISBN 9780815636403 (pbk. : alk. paper)
Subjects: LCSH: Scandal (Television program) | Thrillers (Television programs—Social aspects—United States. | Thrillers (Television programs—History and criticism. | Political television programs—Social aspects—United States | Political television programs—History and criticism | African American women on television. | Race on television. | Women on television.
Classification: LCC PN1992.77.S33 (ebook) | LCC PN1992.77.S33 G58 2019 (print) | DDC 791.45/72—dc23
LC record available at https://lccn.loc.gov/2019016746

Manufactured in the United States of America

Contents

Contents | ix

Acknowledgments

SIMONE ADAMS: It takes a village to raise a child, but it also takes a village to publish a book. This book wouldn't exist without so many exceptional people, first and foremost our contributors who made this volume what it is with their sharp analyses of the cultural phenomenon that is *Scandal*. So much gratitude also goes out to my coeditors, Kimberly Moffitt, who had the idea for the panel that later became this book, and Ron Jackson, who readily jumped on board when we asked him to. I am so grateful to call these two brilliant scholars my colleagues and dear friends. We have shared many (academic) adventures together, and I am humbled that they let me in on our biggest adventure as of yet—becoming "Gladiators in Suits" in our own way. Thank you for your mentorship all along! I would also like to thank my husband, Matt Adams, who spent many hours helping to proofread this volume, and the rest of my family and lifelong friends (Nina Schabkar, Sabine Schatz, and Sandra Körbler in particular), who are patient with me when I am working instead of spending time with them. Next, I thank my mentors at Syracuse University, Rennie Simson (rest in peace) and Linda Carty for helping me forge my path in academia. Last but not least, immense gratitude goes to our fabulous acquisitions editor, Deborah Manion; our series editor, Bob Thompson; and everyone else at Syracuse University Press for helping to make this book a reality.

KIMBERLY R. MOFFITT: I am so grateful to reach this milestone with my coeditors who stimulate my intellect but are also great friends with whom to dine, theater hop, and laugh! I also acknowledge my husband, Noah Garrison, and our children, Niles and Kaya, who are my biggest critics, but also my greatest fans. I love you! Thanks to our contributors who have amassed a great piece of literature that will withstand time as others reflect back in the years to come on such a powerful body of work on television. I extend thanks to my University of Maryland, Baltimore County, Department of American Studies and the Language, Literacy, and Culture doctoral program for your belief and support of my scholarship. And finally, I want to express gratitude to my abundant circle of family, friends, and colleagues, too countless to name, but a special shout-out to my HU sister-docs and travel buddies (Clover Baker-Brown, Cherylann Charles-Williamson, Laura Dorsey-Elson, Diane Forbes-Berthoud, Heather Harris, and Sharnine Herbert) for encouraging me to press ahead.

RONALD L. JACKSON II: I am thankful for my coeditors and friends Simone Adams and Kimberly Moffitt for their friendship, genuineness, and brilliant intellects. I also owe a debt of gratitude to the contributors of this volume for your patience, wisdom, and lucidity. A special shout-out to John Jennings for his creative artwork that is the cover of this book. My mentors and influences are countless, but I must say I am grateful for the constant guidance of my mother, Sharon Prather; my father, Ronald L. Jackson Sr.; my wife, Ricci Jackson; my brother, Bruce Jackson; and good friends Brad Hogue, Carlos Morrison, Keith Wilson, Torrence Sparkman, Theo Coleman, Sam Burbanks, Ovie Mitchell, Barry Stewart, Ramone Ford, and Carson Trotter. Thank you for your undying support and love.

GLADIATORS IN SUITS

Introduction

SIMONE ADAMS, KIMBERLY R. MOFFITT,
AND RONALD L. JACKSON II

WE THE PEOPLE. The words of the US Constitution frame a larger-than-life-size portrait of a woman clad in a white blouse and flowing teal skirt, an outfit that bears resemblance simultaneously to Michelle Obama's likeness hanging in the National Portrait Gallery and to Lady Liberty standing tall in New York Harbor, both symbols of liberty and freedom in their own right. Awestruck, two little Black[1] girls look up at this woman who shares their skin hue and hair texture and who stands tall, almost defiant, looking right back at her onlookers, as if to remind them that they, too, are America. This is the final shot of the iconic (anti-)heroine Olivia Pope (played by Kerry Washington), in the series finale of the Emmy Award–winning political thriller *Scandal* (ABC, 2012–18), created by television powerhouse Shonda Rhimes.

We the People. Penned at the Constitutional Convention of Philadelphia in 1787 and amended twenty-seven times since then, the US Constitution, some have argued, is a "metaphor of enduring strength" of a country's survival (Ferguson 1987, 3). Yet, as has been shown time and again, government is not perfect. It comes with its own set of flaws, idiosyncrasies, and scandals. That's also the general premise of

---

1. Throughout the volume, we have chosen to capitalize the terms *Black* and *White* when they refer to racial identities.

I

this "art-imitating-reality" television drama, which portrays a fictional Washington, DC, complete with what (and who) it takes to keep the government running, all in an effort to "protect the Republic," one of the most quoted lines on the show.

We the People. The bold promise of the Constitution seemingly is that government exists to serve its citizens. All its citizens. From the start, *Scandal* is a show about representation. It features a diverse group of characters, racially and otherwise, who gather around the show's lead, a powerful crisis manager, who has a complex, initially extramarital, affair with the president of the United States, Fitzgerald Grant III (played by Tony Goldwyn). Not since the 1970s have viewing audiences seen an uncharacteristically powerful Black woman as a protagonist in a prime-time drama series on American network television (Smith-Shomade 2002; Mittell 2009; Cheers 2018). But for seven seasons, viewers have learned a great deal about the series' Black female lead and those interwoven in her complex world of politics and drama in the *Scandal* universe.

Olivia Pope is a formidable presence as a crisis-management expert, or "fixer" as known by some, who navigates the chaotic world "inside the Beltway." Together with her team of "Gladiators in Suits," she manages crises and makes the problems of Washington's political elite disappear, all while trying to hide her own scandalous affairs in and around the White House from plain sight. Her work carries the audience on a journey of mischief and mayhem, as her team at Olivia Pope & Associates (OPA) takes on what feels like one impossible case and looming scandal after another.

The show's powerful protagonist has a real-life inspiration, Judy Smith, a "corporate fixer" and head of the DC-based crisis-management and communications firm Smith & Company, who once served as special assistant and deputy press secretary to President George H. W. Bush and who also doubled as co–executive producer on *Scandal*. Unlike on the show, of course, Smith has not been involved in any public scandals of her own, but her website claims that she is "on speed dial for some of the highest-profile celebrities, politicians, and corporations in the world" ("Judy Smith" n.d.). Past clients include former White House intern Monica Lewinsky, former senator Larry Craig (R-ID), actor Wesley Snipes, celebrity chef Paula Deen, and many others. And while the series does take creative license to take the life of a crisis manager to a fictional level filled with elements of steamy love triangles, jaw-dropping plot twists, and other melodramatic elements that are well-tested recipes for success on prime-time television, *Scandal* showcases real Black female talent and agency on all levels. This becomes all the more clear after it was revealed that ABC originally wanted White actress Connie Britton for the show and Rhimes insisted on her protagonist being Black and played by Washington (Goldberg 2017).

In the show's seven-year run, Olivia Pope has become a bona fide cultural icon whose very identity is wedded to that of actress Kerry Washington and who was named as one of *Time* magazine's most influential fictional characters in 2013, ahead of, for example, *House of Cards'* ruthless megalomaniac Frank Underwood, or *Hunger Games'* girl power heroine Katniss Everdeen, and only second to *Breaking Bad*'s chemistry teacher turned drug lord Walter White (Brown 2013). Yet the "Alpha Gladiator" in charge is not the only icon on the show. Olivia Pope would be nothing without her team of devoted employees who—episode after episode—prove their loyalty and commitment to "saving the Republic," by any means necessary. Sometimes this effort goes to the extent of even reminding Olivia Pope why she is here, as her colleague Abby Whelan (Darby Stanchfield) does in "The Fluffer" (3.16): "You don't get to run. You're a Gladiator. Gladiators don't run. They fight. They slay dragons. They wipe off the blood and stitch up their wounds, and they live to fight another day. You don't get to run." Apart from Abby, who vacillates between the role of trusted confidante and fierce competitor, particularly after she takes on a job at the White House only to later come back to working for Olivia, the show's team of Gladiators—over the course of seven seasons—consists of Stephen Finch (Henry Ian Cusick) and Harrison Wright (Columbus Short), who both left the show after season one and season three, respectively; Quinn Perkins (Katie Lowes), who takes over the crisis-management firm when Olivia trades her white hat for the White House; Huck, a.k.a. Diego Muñoz (Guillermo Diaz); and, later in the show Charlie (George Newbern) and Marcus Walker (Cornelius Smith Jr.). All of them are used to "fixing" things, which is also code for hiding, lying, and deceiving—in short, ensuring that unwanted stories (and people) disappear. At the same time, they often are in need of "fixing" themselves, which is precisely why they ended up at OPA, as Huck explains to a tearful Quinn in the show's pilot: "Olivia Pope fixes things. That's who she is. You need fixing. I don't know your story. I don't need to know. We all have a story. Everyone in this office needs fixing. You're a stray dog, and Olivia took you in" ("Sweet Baby" [1.01]).[2] Yet although the show features a veritable scandal in almost every episode, which gets fixed in procedural crime-show fashion, *Scandal* would be nothing without the high-powered drama in and around the White House. Aside from the "complex interplay between desire, difference, and representation" (Warner 2015, 17) that dominates the interracial affair between Olivia Pope and then married White Republican president of the United States Fitzgerald "Fitz" Grant III, affectionately labeled as "Olitz" by the show's fans, the series explores the lives of First Lady and later first female president Melody "Mellie" Grant (Bellamy Young), Chief of Staff (and later vice president) Cyrus Beene (Jeff Perry), US Attorney General David Rosen (Joshua Malina), and intelligence operative and later National Security Agency chief Jake Ballard (Scott Foley), who also stands in as Olivia's second love interest. In a literal "third space," outside the immediate influence of either Olivia Pope or those in power at the White House, in other words, "above the pay grade" ("A Door Marked Exit" [3.10]) of even the president of the United States, is Olivia Pope's father, Eli "Rowan" Pope (Joe Morton). He is "Command" of the top-secret black-ops intelligence agency B613, and his piercing monologues reveal a complex take on Black masculinity, power, and racial identity throughout the show. His thundering speeches remind the viewer of the inherent fallacy of

---

2. Complete episode references (with original airdates) are found in the appendix of this volume.

believing in the rhetoric of "color blindness"[3] in America, as "a gritty counter-argument to [Olivia's] post-racial ideas about power and influence" (Thomas 2018). Or, to say it with showrunner Rhimes herself, "Olivia Pope was sort of the post-racial Obama world that everybody believed they were living in and Papa Pope is old school. He showed up and was like, don't you remember that everybody is inherently racist?" (quoted in Tillet 2018).[4]

All this makes for a complex and unique television drama whose style has been likened to Aaron Sorkin's, as Dodai Stewart from the women's blog *Jezebel* writes of the pilot, "Quick-paced, with Sorkinesque rapid-fire dialogue, smash cuts, tight shots and dynamic camera movements that make you feel like you're eavesdropping or engaging in surveillance on these characters, it's not about soapy navel-gazing as much as it is procedural with a twist. *CSI: DC*, with more money, power, and high heels" (2013). In another early review, television critic Emily Nussbaum of the *New Yorker* highlighted the show's similarities to *24* and *The West Wing*, two series that television scholars have often given the moniker of "quality TV" (Thompson 1996; McCabe

---

3. We recognize the term *color blindness* as being ableist, for "color-blindness, as a racial ideology, conflates lack of eyesight with lack of knowing," thus equating blindness with ignorance and reinforcing the stereotype of a disability as weakness or limitation (Annamma, Jackson, and Morrison 2017, 154). Scholars like Annamma, Jackson, and Morrison have suggested using the term *color evasiveness* instead. When we use the term *color blindness* in this volume, we refer to existing scholarship describing a social phenomenon that has become "racism without racists" (Bonilla-Silva 2018).

4. The series boasts an even longer list of supporting characters, including high-profile political figures like Vice President and later conservative TV host Sally Langston (Kate Burton) and family members of the main cast, such as Olivia's terrorist mother, Maya Pope (Khandi Alexander), and Cyrus's journalist husband, James Novak (Dan Bucatinsky). Notably, in "Allow Me to Reintroduce Myself" (7.12), the series features a powerful crossover episode between *Scandal* and *How to Get Away with Murder*, another ShondaLand production with a Black female lead. In this much-anticipated meet-up of the two protagonists, Olivia Pope helps Annalise Keating (Viola Davis) argue a case for judicial reform in front of the Supreme Court.

and Akass 2007): "Popping with colorful villains, vote-rigging conspiracies, waterboarding, assassinations, montages set to R&B songs, and the best gay couple on television (the president's chief of staff, Cyrus, and his husband, James, an investigative reporter), the series has become a giddy, paranoid fever dream, like '24' crossed with 'The West Wing,' lit up in neon pink" (2013). Unlike its popular predecessors, however, *Scandal*'s political world is one that strives for representational equality (Puff 2015), even though it is sometimes criticized for perpetuating the myth of a "post-racial" America (Vega 2013; Murphy 2017; and several chapters in this volume).

In spite of, or perhaps precisely because of, its flaws, *Scandal* has had success beyond measure as fans, who also call themselves "Gladiators." They tuned in for each of the seven seasons; had *Scandal* watch parties with Olivia's staple food and drink, popcorn and red wine; bought the fashion that was featured as the "Scandal Collection" at the Limited (Elliott 2014); caused the wineglasses featured on the show to be sold out for months on end (Sweeney 2014); and rushed to social media week after week to share their thoughts about the characters, outfits, one-liners, climactic moments, plotlines, and shocking cliffhangers in live-tweet sessions with Shonda Rhimes and the entire cast that often broke the Internet (John 2013). *Los Angeles Times* television critic Mary McNamara claimed that *Scandal* was "the show that Twitter built," and the savvy social media presence of both the show's creator and its biggest stars in the "age of convergence culture" certainly played a role in that phenomenon (McNamara 2013; Damico and Quay 2016). Reportedly, Kerry Washington even kept tweeting to her faithful fan base while going into labor with her daughter, Isabelle, during the airing of season three (Johnson 2015).

Filled with symbols and signifiers such as the "white hat," audiences are drawn into a world that is structurally familiar to them but politically distant. Although US citizens know the White House is the home of their elected president and his family, and is the nerve center of the free world, they are unfamiliar with the daily machinations of the US President's Office. So this show comes with a bit of intrigue, as it offers a glimpse behind the veil. The fascinating part is that this show is not the first TV drama to depict the White House, yet it is one of the most compelling because of how it resonates with what audiences actually see in the news week after week and for whom it chooses to represent the political players inside the Beltway. There are conspicuous moves in *Scandal* to represent a multicultural populace that includes marginalized group members in key positions. It mimetically shows the audience when those characters are right and wrong, kind and devious, bombastic and humble, scary and meek. Perhaps part of the magic of *Scandal* is that it shows marginalized people as normal rather than sets them apart from what is normal, all while subtly questioning this sense of "normalcy" and who gets to define it. It also shows the complexity of Black characters, in particular, who are intelligent, capable, loving, and savvy human beings, something that is often missing from other televisual and filmic representations in American popular culture (Bogle 2001; Smith-Shomade 2002; Gray 2004; Jackson 2006; Childs 2009; Neal 2013; Goldman et al. 2014; Leonard and Guerrero 2013). Its casual portrayal of this basic reality is partly what makes this show special. Its use of soul, jazz, and R&B music is another vehicle through which Black people are presented as conspicuously normal (Monk-Peyton 2015). These subtleties in cultural representation and others are explored in this edited collection, while maintaining a steadied focus on the way in which *Scandal* blurs the boundaries between what is real and what is diegetic.

Gladiators in Suits: Race, Gender, and the Politics of Representation in "Scandal" is a timely volume, just like *Scandal* is a timely show. It appeared on our TV screens at the height of the "Obama era" in early 2012, just a few months before President Barack Obama was about to be reelected, yet at a time when America was already past the illusions of the country being "post-racial" and the (painful) realization that "change" did not happen overnight (Squires 2014; Dyson 2016). Even more important, the show continued during and after the historically significant 2016 presidential election, which offered Shonda Rhimes and her team of writers at ShondaLand a unique opportunity to create a parallel universe to what was happening in and around Washington, DC, while *Scandal* was on the air.

Scandal offers a bit of historical significance, in its own right, as a television series. In its seven-year run as a hit prime-time TV program, *Scandal* taught us about the machinations that complicate US democracy. Although audiences were treated to what felt like an actual insider's glimpse into the White House and the general political process, the profoundly dramatic soliloquies of Olivia's father, Eli "Rowan" Pope, the steamy romance between Olivia and Fitz, and the traumatizing antics of Huck quickly reminded us this drama was, in fact, television. Arguably, what made this show so compelling throughout its 124 episodes was a seductive allure that drew audiences into its world. That seduction featured all the trappings of a great dramatic televisual narrative—love, sex, crime, betrayal, trust, and hope. It was able to remain relevant at a time when dozens of other television shows were being introduced and the "Netflix effect" turned video on demand and streaming into a significant threat to network television. Yet audiences of *Scandal*, who made "appointment television" popular again, were able to easily imagine themselves in the drama's private world because the nation's public world of politics appeared so similar. The narrative twists also spurred viewer interest. As you will read in this volume, the character of Olivia Pope was written with complexity, perhaps more so than any other Black female character in history.[5] She gets to be strong, fierce, confident, and bold with her take-charge persona, yet she crumbles in the domain of her love life and her seeming quest for power. This contrast often depicts her as not knowing what she wants or who she wants it from, but the fact that she is an (anti-) heroine who gets to command respect by day and make mistakes by night adds to the intrigue that viewers love about her. Salamishah Tillet calls her "one of the most memorable antiheroes . . . of television"

5. Olivia Pope paved the way for complex Black female lead characters such as Annalise Keating (Viola Davis) on *How to Get Away with Murder* (ABC, 2014–), Mary Jane (Gabrielle Union) on *Being Mary Jane* (BET, 2014–18), Cookie Lyon (Taraji P. Henson) on *Empire* (Fox, 2015–), and Issa (Issa Rae) on *Insecure* (HBO, 2016–), making *Scandal* break glass ceilings and thus become a unique artifact in the annals of television.

(2018). And as Shonda Rhimes said of her protagonist, "Writing Olivia Pope as the lead meant she got to be the lead and the lead is everything. She's the love interest, she's mean, she's kind, she's flawed, she's brilliant at her job. She makes mistakes. Equality is getting to be as screwed up and as messed up as all of the other leads on television" (quoted in Tillet 2018).

Part of the viewing pleasure of *Scandal* is to see the protagonist, who is idolized as not only "the good guy . . . [but] the best guy" in the pilot ("Sweet Baby" [1.01]), conflicted in her morality. It is even visible in her outfits: In the first five seasons, she wears white dresses, trench coats, and hats. Although she wears other neutral colors, the "white hat" becomes a symbolic mantra representing Olivia "standing in the sun" while making ethical choices even when it seems impossible to do so. In the last two seasons, as she becomes mired in Mellie's run for the presidency, romantically detached from Fitz, separated from the daily operations of OPA, and drawn into the clandestine mercenary operation B613, she switches to a red Fendi cape coat, along with other vibrant colors. This chromatic switch from white to red signifies a dramatic dialectic between good and evil. The choices Olivia makes when wearing red are seemingly more sinister, devious, and maniacal, at times. It seems the more determined her character becomes, the more vibrant the colors become. As we see throughout the series, Olivia evolves all the way until the end. This aspect is an utterly refreshing part of the series because of what it suggests about the human condition. We are always evolving. After seven seasons Olivia stands as an icon modeling for women everywhere that it is okay to be fierce, bold, sexy, in control, and occasionally reckless and still be loved and lovable. The cataclysmic conclusion of the show interrupts the familiar and demonstrates its raison d'être—problematizing the world in which we live and being willing to ask the hard questions so that we are left to grapple with the essence and character of our own humanity.

Fictionalizing American politics in drama series such as *The West Wing* (NBC, 1999–2006), *The Good Wife* (CBS, 2009–16), *House of Cards* (Netflix, 2013–18), *Madame Secretary* (CBS, 2014–),

Designated Survivor (ABC, 2016–18), and, of course, *Scandal* (ABC, 2012–18) has become increasingly popular with viewers. As Douglas Kellner maintains in the foreword to *Politics and Politicians in Contemporary US Television*, "TV series dealing with politics and TV movies portraying recent and even current events in U.S. politics have intensified during the Obama era" (2016, xix). A fictionalized Washington, DC, provides a televisual escape into a world with nuanced dramatic interpretations of reality and sexual escapades and, of course, an opportunity to voyeuristically gaze into seemingly private activities. Audiences' fascination with these types of shows begs several questions. Why are we so enthralled with *Scandal*? What does this popular TV show teach us about American culture, politics, and society—past and present? Where has the show reached milestones, and where are the missed opportunities that both critics and audience members alike have identified?

An edited volume on *Scandal* provides an opportunity to analyze the communication, politics, stereotypes, and genre techniques featured in the television series, while also raising key questions about the intersectionality of race, gender, sexuality, and viewing audiences. Our analyses center on a critical look at various members of *Scandal*'s ensemble cast, on the one hand, and an in-depth analysis of the show's central themes, on the other hand. Additionally, this volume contributes to the literature pertaining to femininity, masculinity, and representations of Black womanhood, as this series features a Black female protagonist in an overwhelmingly popular and powerful role seen as unprecedented since Diahann Carroll in the sitcom *Julia* (NBC, 1968–71) and Teresa Graves in the short-lived crime drama *Get Christie Love!* (ABC, 1974–75). Ultimately, the collection offers original and timely perspectives on the study of what certainly was one of America's most "scandalous" prime-time network television series, one that may have even spurred the creation of a new genre—the "hyperdrama" (Paskin 2014).

A host of fans and TV critics alike have taken to social and popular media to offer their perspectives on *Scandal*, and scholarly attention to the show has also produced some really interesting studies (see, for example, the special issue on *Scandal* in the March 2015 issue of the *Black Scholar*, titled "Scandalous"). On a larger scale, Rhimes's "meteoric rise to stardom," which includes ratings hits on ABC such as *Grey's Anatomy* (2005–), *Private Practice* (2007–13), *Scandal* (2012–18), *How to Get Away with Murder* (2014–), and *The Catch* (2016–17), is analyzed and explored from a critical/cultural perspective in Rachel Griffin and Michaela Meyer's collection, *Adventures in Shondaland: Identity Politics and the Power of Representation* (2018). Such scholarship is particularly important, given Rhimes's unique position as a media power broker and dominant cultural storyteller regarding issues of identity, specifically race, gender, and sexuality. Our volume is now able to travel deeper into the *Scandal* universe. It chronicles, contextualizes, and critically analyzes the show's novelties and transgressions on network television, offering full treatment of the nexus between television and the politics of racial and gendered representation.

The interdisciplinary scholarship presented here, then, is not categorized by season or episodes, topic, or theory. Yet we have productively gathered critical, cultural works that align with four thematic strands reflective of the series: part one, "Politics, Death, and Protecting the Republic"; part two, "Romance, Race, and the Erotic"; part three, "Sisterhood, Feminism, and Female Body Politics"; and part four, "Race, Gender, and the Politics of Respectability." Each of these sections contains chapters that—taken together—illustrate the myriad ways critical/cultural analyses can and need to be performed when it comes to a complex cultural artifact like *Scandal*, thereby creating a mosaic of approaches to thinking about the television series and its lead character, diverse cast, and viewing audiences. Chapters in this volume are simultaneously part of this larger critical dialogue and stand-alone essays in their own right. Contributions range from colleagues who have their "academic homes" in the fields of communication, English, sociology, Black and Africana studies, women's and gender studies, history, and others, yet whose work is decidedly interdisciplinary and intersectional. Chapters consider the role of race and gender in political discourse, interracial relationships and romance, feminism and queer theory, the impact and power of social media, and the complexities of audience research. *Scandal* amplifies concerns about all of these topics, and the authors in this volume encourage us to consider them all as we ponder whether "life imitates art" or "art imitates life" in this entertainment program.

In Defense of the Republic

The volume begins with part one, "Politics, Death, and Protecting the Republic," which problematizes our understanding of the Republic and its existence (or "death"). In particular, the chapters presented here explore the highly depoliticized environment created within a series that also highlights the troubled interactions between citizens and the nation-state in a post-9/11 America. Catherine R. Squires's work, "Olivia Pope, Citizen of Empire: Gendered Duties and Sacrificial Violence on *Scandal*," highlights this tension by illustrating how the series' plotlines surrounding Olivia Pope and her suitors fall within the parameters set by the hierarchies of American imperialism. Recognizing our troubled assumptions on issues of democracy, security, and the use of military force, this chapter suggests the vast contradictions regarding how political power is wielded in the United States.

In chapter 2, "Olivia Pope: 'Fixer' of Necropolitical Fallout," Nicholas Manganas illustrates how new modes of governmentality and corporate rationality are employed if the Republic is challenged. To that end, both life and death become potential options for the sake of championing the existence of the Republic, and Olivia Pope is its primary protector. Patricia Ventura explores another form of death in her chapter, "*Scandal:* A Melodrama of Social Death." Considering the historical events circumscribing her students' lives (for example, coming of age after 9/11 in a country shaped by the election of the first man of color as its president), Ventura investigates the position of the Black woman whose body has often been the brunt of the country's violent past and present. She concludes that *Scandal* offers a death or victimization that affects the series' White characters more often and, in fact, creates a space in which her Black female students can ultimately identify with a powerful Black heroine.

Part one concludes with Shantel Gabrieal Buggs and Ryessia Jones Russell's work, "The Power of Whiteness: Disciplining Olivia Pope." The use of the color white or whiteness as a practice is highlighted by Pope's adornment of a "white hat," her relationships with White men, and her expertise often expended to save the careers of White political figures. This chapter reveals how whiteness is utilized as a mechanism for policing or disciplining Pope's Black female body. This point is most apparent in the plotlines that constrain her behavior, her body, and her identity to fit into the expectation of Black women of the Republic.

What Is Love?

A major theme of the television series addresses the interracial interactions between *Scandal*'s Black lead female protagonist and the other characters, including the romance between Olivia Pope and the White male "leader of the free world." While race is implicitly referenced in the series, the overt presentation of these exchanges raises questions about the postrace narrative, racial hegemony, and power, as well as the "scandal" surrounding Pope's trysts. This becomes the foundation of part two, "Romance, Race, and the Erotic."

In chapter 5, "'Tangled Skeins': *Scandal*'s Olivia Pope and the Counternarrativizing of Black Female Enslavement," Ernest L. Gibson III offers an interpretation of the romance between Olivia Pope and President Fitzgerald Grant beyond the historical angle of enslaved Black woman and White slave master (read: Sally Hemings and President Thomas Jefferson). The author ultimately concludes that Pope may be reimagined as a "Gladiator in a Suit" constructed for the purpose of disentangling the haunted memory of Black enslaved women by the layered plotlines of the television series. Christopher A. House and Sean Eversley Bradwell in chapter 6, "'You're Nobody's Victim, Liv': The Scandal of Black Love and White Hegemony in *Scandal*," consider Black women's perspective of this relationship, utilizing audience-reception theory to gauge an understanding of the success of the series via Black Twitter. The authors suggest that Olivia Pope's love relationships offer viewers a deeper and radical reading of available and consumable Black love in the White House, revealing to us a negotiation of multiple meanings of a Black love story among the audience.

Chapter 7 by Kadian Pow, "Insider/Outsider: Olivia Pope and the Pursuit of Erotic Power," highlights the insider/outsider status of Olivia Pope. The character's portrayal is a queering of sorts in which her interior life is held in dramatic tension with the expectations of the Black female body she inhabits. Specifically, the chapter centers on Pope's "erotic power" but does so in a way to problematize her presence and highlight both the sexual and the asexual means in which her body is represented to audiences. This part closes with Kavyta Kay discussing the postracial elements of this interracial romance in "#Olitz: The Erotics of (E)Racing in *Scandal*." She proclaims that the discourse of color blindness is centered to make this relationship palatable and believable to its audience, yet race continues to be conveyed in complex ways without being named. As a result, race is then "(e)raced" and "re-raced" in the series, utilizing Pope's complex Black female sexuality—on the one hand, combating the one-dimensional, hypersexual woman and, on the other hand, negating the norms of White upper- and middle-class respectability.

We Stick Together

Uncategorically, *Scandal* instills a gaze that is quite feminine and centers the female experience for its viewers. As a result, the exploration of how women relate to one another and hence are represented is significant. In part three, "Sisterhood, Feminism, and Female Body Politics," we explore the relationships among key characters such as Olivia Pope and the woman whose (ex-)husband she is in love with (Mellie), as well as the representation of sisterhood among the other female "Gladiators." Issues of gender and power are considered to further understand the complexity of women who are portrayed as strong female characters. Tracey Owens Patton starts this section with an exploration of the "entangled" relationship of Olivia Pope and the (ex-)wife of her lover, Mellie Grant, in her chapter, "A Sisterhood of Strategic Convenience: Olivia Pope, Mellie Grant, and Their *Scandalous* Entanglements." While the series has highlighted the tension between these two women, rightfully so, another plotline reveals that the pair must, in fact, work collaboratively in order to maintain power. Viewers encounter the complicated dynamics of this cross-racial relationship and, in turn, come to understand more about the expectations of womanhood and sisterhood and how those entities are impacted by race, power, and socioeconomic differences. In chapter 10, "Female Gladiators and Third Wave Feminism: Visualizing Power, Choice, and Dialogue in *Scandal*," Lara C. Stache and Rachel D. Davidson continue to interrogate the theme of power. They analyze the intersection of empowerment and femininity among the three primary female Gladiators (Olivia, Quinn, and Abby), using the lens of a third-wave feminist rhetoric. And while tensions remain regarding choices women must make regarding work, life, and love, the authors note that the series offers key progressive steps forward in gender politics.

The next two chapters consider Black feminist thought as a framework to explore feminism and Black body politics. In "Nimble Readings: Black Women, Meaning Making, and Negotiating Womanhood through *Scandal*," Timeka N. Tounsel captures the voice of Black women interviewed about the representation of Olivia Pope. While the character is viewed as highly flawed, audience members navigate a nuanced practice where fictional performances of Black womanhood are read through the lens of aspiration. Ultimately, the viewers temporarily suspend reality in order to reject the "controlling images" cast upon Black women in media texts and instead embrace the fictional opportunities presented in *Scandal*. Kimberly Alecia Singletary adds to this discussion by suggesting *Scandal* visually engages the stereotypes of Black female sexuality and identity. Olivia Pope is seemingly in control of her being (and body) and uses that power to turn those "controlling images" on their heads. Again, we see the essence of human complexity reflected, and in this instance (and this television series) it appears in the form of a Black female protagonist.

Slayed by Respectability

Part four, "Race, Gender, and the Politics of Respectability" begins and ends with an exploration of how race both constrains and liberates its players, in particular in the world of politics. This final section of the volume also extends the gender conversation of the series to consider the manifestations of masculinity as well as the notion of queering our lived experiences. In chapter 13, "'It's Handled!': Critiquing the Politics of Respectability at the Intersection of Race and Gender in *Scandal*," Tina M. Harris, Myra Washington, and Diamond M. Akers demonstrate how the character of Olivia Pope is reflective of the racialized critique of Black women's bodies that has existed since American slavery; yet she counters it. In the end, the authors call for audiences to embrace a new thought paradigm that allows Black women to be seen as complex beings no longer inhibited by antiquated notions of otherness or respectability. In contrast, in an attempt to interrogate hegemonic masculinity, Will Howell, in his chapter, "Advocacy and Normalcy: The Politics of Same-Sex Marriage in *Scandal*," explores the same-sex characters of the series, James and Cyrus. He questions Shonda Rhimes's desire to write characters that "blow [that] box wide open" by contextualizing the rhetoric of heteronormativity in marriage-equality stories and other series' plotlines. Yet his conclusions suggest that Rhimes reinscribes texts and visuals that are quite "heteronormative" and, in fact, discipline all couples of the series who do not participate in marriage as an institution.

David Ponton III and Kelly Weber Stefonowich convincingly argue that there is, in fact, a crisis of masculinity, and it is reflected in the character of Fitz. Their work, titled "'He Exists Because I Say He Exists': The (Un)Making of Fitz's Manhood and the Enduring Adaptability of Hegemonic Masculinity," suggests that Fitz, even with assumed power before him, struggles with the embodiment of manhood and, as a result, often expresses frustration, anxiety, and insecurity. In the end, however, like men before him, he successfully redefines masculinity to fit his interpretation and, in turn, maintains the dominance of White maleness in power. Finally, in chapter 16, "'I Can't Fix This': Reflections on *Scandal*'s Racial Commentary in the 'Lawn Chair' Episode," the coeditors of this volume return to the topic of race as it relates to more contemporary social ills. Specifically, they engage in a conversation surrounding the responses to the politically charged episode "The Lawn Chair" of season four (4.14) that focused on police brutality and racial profiling. What is created is a space for the coeditors to offer both scholarly and personal commentary about this episode, while also entertaining the ways in which the viewing audience grappled with the burden of its impact. The conclusions drawn remind us that for the first time in the series, there was a developed plotline that willingly explored (and resolved) a pressing and contemporary issue affecting American society, yet such resolution is never that simple outside of ShondaLand.

It's (Not) Handled

Within the *Scandal* universe, there are arguably no simple resolutions, either. Cases in point are the complexities of the characters and their morally ambivalent (and often outright criminal) actions, the elements of corny soap opera fused with savvy political thriller, and the conflicted portrayals of (Black) femininity and masculinity, which can be both heralded for its progressiveness (for example, Pixley 2015; Puff 2015) and read as simultaneously paradoxical and problematic (Griffin and Meyer 2015). As Mia Mask notes in her introduction to the roundtable on *Scandal* in the special issue of the *Black Scholar*, published in March 2015, "Even in communities of color, folks are not certain whether Rhimes' *Scandal* is a progressive step in an anti-essentialist direction or a regressive move backward toward a reconstituted Jezebel-in-bed-with-Massa stereotype" (2015, 4). And even though Olivia Pope's catchphrase, "It's handled," gets continuously employed throughout the entire series, it is also painfully obvious that certain aspects, political and otherwise, cannot be as easily "handled" as others. As "Gladiators," the passionate and loyal fan base of the show was rooting for the complex ensemble cast for seven seasons, in large part because the show encouraged its viewers to engage in watching a powerful Black woman take control of "the most powerful country of the world." At the same time, the audience was able to take to social media and try to make sense of the mediated representations in the viewers' real lives, while engaging in direct conversations with those individuals who made and starred on the show. This volume started out as a panel discussion at the 2013 Convention of the National Communication Association in Washington, DC, doing just that—engaging in conversations. Our hope as editors is that this important book encourages readers—as the show's run on network television has ended but lives on in the world of streaming TV—to keep these important conversations going, not simply saying "It's handled" and moving on, but critically reflecting on how far we have come and how far we have yet to go.

References

Annamma, Subini Ancy, Darrell D. Jackson, and Deb Morrison. 2017. "Conceptualizing Color-Evasiveness: Using Dis/Ability Critical Race Theory to Expand a Color-Blind Racial Ideology in Education and Society." *Race and Ethnicity in Education* 20(2): 147–62.

Bogle, Donald. 2001. *Primetime Blues: African Americans on Network Television*. New York: Farrar, Straus, and Giroux.

Bonilla-Silva, Eduardo. 2018 [2003]. *Racism without Racists: Color-Blind Racism and the Persistence of Racial Inequality in America*. 5th ed. Lanham, MD: Rowman and Littlefield.

Brown, Ann. 2013. "It's Handled: Olivia Pope One of 2013's Most Influential Fictional Characters." *Madame Noire*, Dec. 20. http://madame noire.com/334344/home-entertainment-top-20-influential-african -american-women-television-ever-seen-list-top-20-influential-african -american-women-television-ever-seen/.

Cheers, Imani M. 2018. *The Evolution of Black Women in Television: Mammies, Matriarchs and Mistresses*. New York: Routledge.

Childs, Erica Chito. 2009. *Fade to Black and White: Interracial Images in Media and Popular Culture*. Lanham, MD: Rowman and Littlefield.

Collins, Patricia Hill. 2005 [1995]. *Black Feminist Thought: Knowledge, Consciousness, and the Politics of Empowerment*. New York and London: Routledge.

Damico, Amy M., and Sara E. Quay. 2016. *21st-Century TV Dramas: Exploring the New Golden Age*. Santa Barbara, CA: ABC-Clio.

Dyson, Michael Eric. 2016. *The Black Presidency: Barack Obama and the Politics of Race in America*. New York: Houghton Mifflin Harcourt.

Elliott, Stuart. 2014. "'Scandal' Inspires Clothing Line at the Limited." *New York Times*, Sept. 14. https://www.nytimes.com/2014/09/15/business /media/scandal-inspires-clothing-line-at-the-limited.html?_r=0.

Ferguson, Robert. A. 1987. "'We Do Ordain and Establish': The Constitution as Literary Text." *William & Mary Law Review* 29(1). Art.3: 3–25. http://scholarship.law.wm.edu/wmlr/vol29/iss1/3.

Goldberg, Lesley. 2017. "'Scandal' Hits 100 Episodes: Casting Secrets, Trump and a Battle over Abortion Revealed in Dishy Oral History." *Hollywood Reporter*, Apr. 11. http://www.hollywoodreporter.com/features /scandal-hits-100-episodes-casting-secrets-trump-a-battle-abortion -revealed-dishy-oral-histo?utm_source=Sailthru&utm_medium=email &utm_campaign=THR%20Breaking%20News_2017-04-11%2007 :00:00_MJang&utm_term=hollywoodreporter_breakingnews.

Goldman, Adria, Y., VaNatta S. Ford, Alexa A. Harris, and Natasha R. Howard, eds. 2014. *Black Women and Popular Culture: The Conversation Continues*. Lanham, MD: Lexington.

Gray, Herman. 2004. *Watching Race: Television and the Struggle for Blackness*. Minneapolis: Univ. of Minnesota Press.

Griffin, Rachel Alicia, and Michaela D. E. Meyer, eds. 2018. *Adventures in Shondaland: Identity Politics and the Power of Representation*. New Brunswick, NJ: Rutgers Univ. Press.

Jackson, Ronald L., II. 2006. *Scripting the Black Masculine Body: Identity, Discourse, and Racial Politics in Popular Media*. Albany, NY: SUNY Press.

John, Arit. 2013. "A Beginner's Guide to Tweeting about 'Scandal.'" *Atlantic*, Oct. 3. https://www.theatlantic.com/entertainment/archive/2013 /10/beginners-guide-tweeting-about-scandal/310340/.

Johnson, Zach. 2015. "Kerry Washington Live Tweeted *Scandal* While in Labor." *EOnline*, Mar. 26. http://www.eonline.com/news/639862 /kerry-washington-live-tweeted-scandal-while-in-labor.

"Judy Smith." N.d. JudySmith.com. http://www.judysmith.com/.

Kellner, Douglas. 2016. "Foreword: Television Criticism and Contemporary US Politics." In *Politics and Politicians in Contemporary US Television: Washington as Fiction*, edited by Betty Kaklamanidou and Margaret J. Tally, xii–xxi. New York: Routledge.

Leonard, David J., and Lisa A. Guerrero, eds. 2013. *African Americans on Television: Race-ing for Ratings*. Santa Barbara, CA: Praeger.

Mask, Mia. 2015. "A Roundtable Conversation on *Scandal*." *Black Scholar* 45(1): 3–9.

McCabe, Janet, and Kim Akass, eds. 2007. *Quality TV: Contemporary American Television and Beyond.* London: I. B. Tauris.

McNamara, Mary. 2013. "'Scandal' Has Become Must-Tweet TV." *Los Angeles Times*, May 11. http://articles.latimes.com/2013/may/11/entertainment/la-et-st-scandal-abc-social-media-20130511/.

Mittell, Jason. 2009. *Television and American Culture.* Oxford: Oxford Univ. Press.

Monk-Payton, Brandeise. 2015. "The Sound of *Scandal*: Crisis Management and the Musical Mediation of Racial Desire." *Black Scholar* 45(1): 21–27.

Murphy, Caryn. 2017. "'Stand Up, Fight Back': Race and Policing in *The Good Wife* and *Scandal*." In *Politics and Politicians in Contemporary US Television: Washington as Fiction*, edited by Betty Kaklamanidou and Margaret J. Tally, 47–60. London and New York: Routledge.

Neal, Mark Anthony. 2013. *Looking for Leroy: Illegible Black Masculinities.* New York and London: New York Univ. Press.

Nussbaum, Emily. 2013. "Shark Week: 'House of Cards,' 'Scandal,' and the Political Game." *New Yorker*, Feb. 25. http://www.newyorker.com/magazine/2013/02/25/shark-week/.

Paskin, Willa. 2014. "How to Get Away with Hyperdrama." *Slate*, Sept. 25. http://www.slate.com/articles/arts/television/2014/09/how_to_get_away_with_murder_review_viola_davis_show_is_the_latest_shonda.html/.

Pixley, Tara-Lynne. 2015. "Trope and Associates." *Black Scholar* 45(1): 28–33.

Puff, Simone. 2015. "Another *Scandal* in Washington: How a Transgressive, Black Anti-heroine Makes for New 'Quality TV.'" In *Transgressive Television: Politics and Crime in 21st-Century American TV Series*, edited by Birgit Däwes, Alexandra Ganser, and Nicole Poppenhagen, 103–26. Heidelberg: Universitätsverlag Winter.

"Scandalous." 2015. *Black Scholar* 45(1): 3–43.

Smith-Shomade, Beretta E. 2002. *Shaded Lives: African American Women and Television.* New Brunswick, NJ: Rutgers Univ. Press.

Squires, Catherine R. 2014. *The Post-racial Mystique: Media and Race in the Twenty-First Century.* New York: New York Univ. Press.

Stewart, Dodai. 2013. "Kerry Washington's *Vanity Fair* Cover Is Hot (and a Big Deal)." *Jezebel*, July 2. http://jezebel.com/kerry-washingtons-vanity -fair-cover-is-hot-and-a-big-d-645201828/.

Sweeney, Brigid. 2014. "How 'Scandal' Has Made This Crate & Barrel Item a Star." *Chicago Business*, Feb. 13. http://www.chicagobusiness.com /article/20140213/NEWS07/140219915/how-scandal-has-made-this -crate-barrel-item-a-star.

Thomas, Eric R. 2018. "The Emancipation of Olivia Pope." *Elle*, Apr. 20. https://www.elle.com/culture/movies-tv/a19871480/scandal-finale -recap-season-7-ep-18-over-a-cliff/.

Thompson, Robert. 1996. *Television's Second Age: From "Hillstreet Blues" to "ER."* New York: Continuum.

Tillet, Salamishah. 2018. "The Gladiators of 'Scandal' Leave the Arena." *New York Times*, Apr. 12. https://www.nytimes.com/2018/04/12/arts /television/scandal-finale-shonda-rhimes-kerry-washington.html.

Vega, Tanzina. 2013. "A Show Makes Friends and History: 'Scandal' on ABC Is Breaking Barriers." *New York Times*, Jan. 16. http://www.ny times.com/2013/01/17/arts/television/scandal-on-abc-is-breaking -barriers.html?pagewanted=all/.

Warner, Kristin J. 2015. "If Loving Olitz Is Wrong, I Don't Wanna Be Right: ABC's *Scandal* and the Affect of Black Female Desire." *Black Scholar* 45(1): 16–20.

PART ONE

Politics, Death, and Protecting the Republic

1 | Olivia Pope, Citizen of Empire

Gendered Duties and Sacrificial Violence on *Scandal*

CATHERINE R. SQUIRES

THE EPISODE "Happy Birthday, Mr. President" (2.08) features an argument between Olivia Pope and President Grant. Olivia compares their relationship to that of President Thomas Jefferson and Sally Hemings, whom he enslaved. Fitz takes her to task in the White House Rose Garden:

> FITZ: The Sally Hemings–Thomas Jefferson comment was below the belt.
> OLIVIA: Because it's so untrue?
> FITZ: You're playing the race card on the fact that I'm in love with you? Come on. Don't belittle us.
> OLIVIA: You own me. You control me.
> . . .
> FITZ: I love you. . . . I wait for *you*. I watch for *you*. . . . There's no Sally or Thomas here. You're nobody's victim, Liv. I belong to *you* . . .

Though Fitz dismisses the Hemings-Jefferson comparison because, as he insists, *he* belongs to Olivia, not the other way around, this chapter explores how the relationships between the major characters of *Scandal* have uncomfortable resonances with the imperial culture and political expectations of the eighteenth and nineteenth centuries. Specifically, I examine how the plotlines surrounding Olivia and her lovers are constructed well within parameters set by the hierarchies of American imperialism. Through its hybrid of soap-opera and espionage action genres, *Scandal* exemplifies the fraught relationships between citizens and the nation-state. Its portrayals of attacks on the press, violations of human rights, and revelations of domestic surveillance programs surface and trouble assumptions about democratic citizenship, intimacy, security, and the state's use of violence.

I read *Scandal* in order to examine its neo-imperial ideologies as well as to discern critical openings in the text. The show's sexually charged psychodrama and multicultural casting are suffused with contradictions that raise questions about how political power and violence are wielded in the United States. Indeed, audiences might conclude that no characters on *Scandal*—regardless of their status—can be trusted to abstain from severe, violent abuses of power that violate laws, interpersonal relationships, and bodies. *Scandal*'s protagonists are not just "flawed" (as TV critics like to put it when protagonists do bad things), they're criminals. Their few redeeming qualities, if one can call them redeeming, are their unwavering belief in true love and a deep sense of loyalty to their lovers and the United States of America, a nation they obsessively refer to as "the Republic." These qualities surface in the "sacrifices" suffered and recounted by the chief players at Olivia Pope & Associates (OPA), suffering endured in the name of the Republic and in the service of their preferred leaders, President Fitzgerald Grant III and his ex-wife and former first lady, Mellie Grant. Moreover, as they perform and elicit sacrifices, characters invoke a duty to protect the citizenry or the Republic or both from threats the public cannot know or learn about, lest the experts who deflect those threats be subjected to legal scrutiny, thereby undermining the state's authority to use stealth and preemptive deadly force.

Despite its multicultural casting, *Scandal*'s "Gladiators" fight to secure the position of White heterosexual chief executives.[1] Black and

---

1. The devotion to White heterosexual executive power continues in season five, when Olivia leaves the White House as Fitz's consort in order to regain her

Brown men, White gay men, and White and Black women scheme, lie, and murder to maintain the power of a White president in the name of the stability and integrity of the Republic, despite the fact that neither of the Grants is ethically worthy or popular enough to merit voter confidence. Neither of Fitz's electoral victories was clean: the first featured rigged ballot machines; the second required the assassination of his son to drum up voter sympathy and a last-minute surge at the polls. In the winter premiere for season six, we learn that Mellie didn't win the presidential election and can enter the White House only if murder charges stick against her elected rival. Fitz and Mellie have clear, present, and dangerous flaws in character and judgment that demonstrate neither is fit for the White House: he's an alcoholic, he murdered a Supreme Court justice to cover up voting fraud, and he allows himself to be blackmailed into a war; Mellie fakes a pregnancy to solidify her husband's reputation, and she allows Rowan Pope to murder the members of a grand jury to ensure her election to the Senate. These two are not paragons of democratic integrity and stability, let alone trustworthy lovers.

Scandal's love triangles expose these leaders' extreme flaws and how their fraught romantic relationships and political schemes exemplify (and attempt to justify) the violent excesses of American empire. In the process, I suggest that audiences can read the vicious, political soap opera of *Scandal* in ways that disrupt the fiction that violence committed in the name of the Republic is always necessary and unrelated to violence committed in "private" spaces. The show's depictions of extreme violence and the characters' justification of civil rights violations reinforce postracial and postfeminist norms that limit women and people of color to behind-the-scenes roles in the sustenance of empire. Moreover, the plot's obsessive insistence on the validity and

---

power behind the throne with a new White heterosexual presidential candidate: Mellie Grant. Likewise, scheming Elizabeth North uses her boy toy, Attorney General David Rosen, to get another White woman to run: Vice President Susan Ross ("The Candidate" [5.11]).

necessity of a President Grant to the survival of American democracy is constantly challenged by raw scenes of gross malfeasance within the White House and its intelligence agencies.

Whether intended or not, *Scandal* is ripe for reading against the hegemonic grain. Because *Scandal* filters the issues of national security and citizen sacrifice through the main characters' romantic and familial relations, significant spaces remain for audience members to question the validity of the expectations of sacrifice and the ends of those sacrifices. This reading troubles the ways that violence is normalized in the name of the state and security, particularly as that violence literally bleeds over into the (allegedly) loving relationships between Olivia, her paramours, and her father.

First, I situate *Scandal* within the context of recent broadcast TV translations of the White House and post-9/11 security anxieties. I draw on scholarly analyses of *The West Wing* and *24* to situate *Scandal* in terms of its "realistic" renderings of the Washington political scene (including ripped-from-the-headlines plots), the soap opera–like romantic entanglements that drive plot, and its imagination of how "real" politics and security issues are handled, unbeknownst to the assumed-to-be naive (or gullible) public. Second, I summarize key aspects of feminist theory that grapple with the continuing legacy of imperialism, outlining racist and sexist parameters of citizenship and sacrifice that are dramatized in *Scandal*'s portrayals of love, sex, betrayal, and power. Third, I analyze moments in the series that illustrate how violence committed in the name of the Republic and violence that occurs in romantic, "private" relationships overlap and resonate with each other. Reading the show through feminist, anti-imperialist lenses gives us critical means to reconsider the melodramatic "pleasures" of the show as opportunities to question and denormalize the imperial regimes of patriarchal violence and authority the characters are, ostensibly, willing to risk their happiness, their careers, even their lives to sustain. As the series continues over seven seasons, mounting losses and abuse experienced by Olivia and her team of "Gladiators" leave the characters and the audience asking whether these spectacular sacrifices were made for the right reasons.

Scandal and Its Predecessors

Scandal premiered in 2012 with a splash: its fabulous main character, Olivia Pope, was ostensibly inspired by the career of Judy Smith, a Black female "fixer" in Washington, DC, who rescues the reputations of compromised politicos. As *Los Angeles Times* reviewer Mary McNamara summarized, "Olivia Pope isn't just a crisis manager, she's The Crisis Manager, a woman of supernatural energy, insight and influence, . . . willing to stare down Russian thugs and law enforcement officials alike, capable of summoning swaths of information at her fingertips and the president on her cellphone, all while keeping her white trench coat perfectly belted and pristine" (2012).

Pope runs her crisis-management agency, OPA, with a crew of savvy employees who refer to themselves as "Gladiators" (an eerily imperial nickname). All of Pope's staff members owe her their lives or livelihoods (revealed in flashbacks), or both, and show her intense loyalty. Olivia's crew includes Huck, a Latino savant who is a former spy from the top-secret, shadowy extralegal intelligence agency B613. Huck can hack into Central Intelligence Agency (CIA) systems and ATM machines with ease, piloting his boss through the backchannels of power by accessing databases, security cameras, cell phone signals, and other illegal strategies to help their clients, who range from White House insiders to everyday folks caught in the crossfire of politics. Huck is also portrayed as hopelessly *addicted* to bloody interrogations and revenge killing.[2]

Thus, *Scandal* has a lot in common with recent hit shows that imagine what *really* happens when our government makes decisions about national security, such as NBC's *The West Wing* (1999–2006),

---

2. During the course of season two, Huck becomes more and more violent as he deals with his job requirements. His colleague and protégée, Quinn, discovers that he goes to Alcoholics Anonymous meetings, using the urge to drink as a metaphor for the urge to kill and torture (for example, "Beltway Unbuckled" [2.04]). His visits align with his reentry into torture and murder, and he admits to the AA group that he has "fallen off the wagon" after he commits these crimes.

Showtime's *Homeland* (2011–present), and Fox Network's *24* (2001–10). Like *The West Wing*, *Scandal* is preoccupied with "spin" in politics, but unlike that show, *Scandal* is not awestruck by the government employees who write policy papers and speeches to help the president sell his ideas: OPA's crew of spin doctors, ex-spies, and hackers dig up dirt, kidnap witnesses, seduce and bribe ex-boyfriends, and try to lead the press down blind alleys to deflect attention from the crimes and misdemeanors committed by their clients—including the president.

In this light, *Scandal* is more like *24* and *Homeland*: it presents audiences with an (imagined) insider's view of how security apparatchiks protect us in top-secret fashion from extreme threats. These shows portray the United States as a nation encircled "by barbaric enemies, of being lethally imperiled" at all times, necessitating extensive surveillance and secret deployments of violence (Downing 2007, 78). Like *24*'s Agent Jack Bauer, Pope and her associates possess almost supernatural instincts and unlimited access to technological power, as well as the grit to employ illegal surveillance, torture, and murder when "necessary" to keep the public "safe" from imminent (or imagined) harm. These shows justify the use of extreme violence and extralegal action by insisting that there is no time for legal procedures or public debate; rather, as Downing concludes, the "prime virtues extolled in these situations are decisiveness, the readiness to opt for the least worst outcome, *and the moral courage to swallow one's own moral scruples*" for an assumed greater good (77).

Finally, Pope, her team, and their adversaries juggle their intimate lives—intimacies often directly entangled with the politicians they serve—while striving to save the day, just as Bauer negotiated the trials and tribulations of his damaged relationship with his wife and as CIA agent Carrie Mathison of *Homeland* battles her attraction for a terrorism suspect, as they race against the clock to save the United States of America. These intimate entanglements provide additional opportunities for audiences to sympathize with the protagonists, humanizing them with backstories audiences can access when these characters commit extreme, extralegal violence. As such, these shows are examples of what Andersen termed "militainment" (2006), where audiences are entertained by realistic portrayals of military or covert action, portrayals often assisted by script and technical consultations with the Pentagon (Vavrus 2013). Because of this insistence that we must justify any means for the end of "keeping the nation safe," I suggest we view *Scandal* as a "story of empire."

Stories of Empire

Chandra Mohanty observes that imperial powers have always been bolstered by culture, particularly storytelling culture. At the turn of the twentieth century, the representatives of empire were "salesmen and planters," whereas contemporary conveyors of empire "may be corporate executives and security personnel" (2006, 8). These executives include media owners and producers, storytellers who transmit their wares through multinational media, corporations that are themselves heavily invested in the power and prestige of American empire (Vavrus 2013). These imperial actors provide media narratives that normalize the hierarchies and relationships that underpin empire. "Each of these groups of imperial actors . . . tell very particular stories—not just of political economy and territorial control but also of the gender and the color of empire, of racialized patriarchies and heteronormative sexualities of empire at different historical junctures. These stories (and others like them) necessitate mapping a landscape where corporate cultures of power, domination, and surveillance coincide with a politics of complicity in the academy and elsewhere" (Mohanty 2006, 8).

My reading of *Scandal* follows Mohanty's project, mapping how the "language of imperialism and empire" is adopted in a popular television text, articulated with romantic entanglements and particular gendered notions of patriotic duty and sacrifice. Whereas Mohanty wrote about how certain Western feminists deployed rhetoric to "save Afghan women" in ways that justified American military intervention in the Middle East, I am concerned with how *Scandal*'s love triangles mix with national security hysteria to justify fantasies of empire, legitimizing illegal surveillance, torture, racism, and misogyny in the name of preserving the global dominance of the United States, "the Republic."

Scandal engages in imperial storytelling, re-creating moments in the West Wing that echo, replicate, and normalize the use of military force and mass surveillance technologies. We watch President Grant with his advisers in a darkened room, viewing the live video feed of a special-ops raid to find terrorists—a scene reminiscent of photos released of President Obama and aides watching the SEAL team assassinate Osama bin Laden. Likewise, audiences are invited to watch current and former B613 agents, such as Huck, track and then torture "bad guys" in service to the Republic. But the spectacular violence done in the name of the state is never contained to just punishing the "bad guys." As Veena Das explains, violence is unstable: "The reality of violence includes its virtuality and its potential to make and unmake social worlds" (2008, 283). Violence always threatens to spill over into the intimate world, even as the state claims that its use of violence in the outside world will be used only to maintain order and stability so we may "go about our lives." State-sanctioned violence is always simultaneously spectacular and mundane, part of an assumed "social contract" we, as citizens, consent to with the state (Das 2008).

The imperial social contract requires a particular set of sacrifices that are gendered and anchored in the origin stories of nation and empire. Das observes that when we speak of the "birth" of the nation or "blood and treasure" spent to secure its borders, these metaphors signal the sacrifices citizens consent to undertake for the nation and the expansion of empire. These sacrifices align with heteropatriarchal norms. Women and men are called on to engage in "giving life to the nation and dying for the nation," normalizing death and violence "as part of gendered belonging to the nation-state." Women give life by bearing and rearing children to become good citizens and providing comfort to men at home. Men die for the nation, in its defense during war or in order to expand the territorial reach of the empire. "Thus sex and death, reproduction and war, become part of the same configuration of ideas and institutions through which the nation-state sets up defenses to stave off the uncertainty emanating from dangerous aliens and the ravages of time" (Das 2008, 285).

The story lines of *Scandal* trace how women and men make a host of gendered and raced sacrifices "willingly" to defend the nation, sometimes with a dash of cynicism, other times with a crushing sense of disappointment. In so doing, the plot resonates with Mohanty's argument concerning the operations of imperialism: "The argument I am making here is very simple: imperialism, militarization, and globalization all traffic in women's bodies, women's labor, and ideologies of masculinity/femininity, heteronormativity, racism, and nationalism to consolidate power and domination" (2006, 9).

Scandal provides audiences with spectacular, titillating narratives and dramatic displays that, while sometimes disturbing, frame the trafficking of feminine and feminized bodies[3] as a necessary element of maintaining American power, power symbolized by a White male president. In a similar vein, Victor Mendoza outlines how popular culture as well as legal and military discourses "support the management of intimacy . . . a crucial linchpin in the biopolitics of empire" (2015, 2). Thus, the dominance of US heteropatriarchal empire rests not only on military might but also on ideologies of "racial-sexual governance" that are legible in cultural texts.

The sacrifices that play out within the rubrics of racial-sexual governance are portrayed as vital—if sometimes stomach churning—to the survival of the Republic and as a *chosen fate*. *Scandal*'s characters participate in the recurrent, unequal sacrifices demanded by the state, and theirs is portrayed as a willing sacrifice, whether the price is emotional or physical, whether the exchange is violent, erotic, or nurturing, in a public or intimate setting—or a toxic mix of all of the above.[4]

---

3. The feminized body of Cyrus's partner, James, is literally trafficked in season three, when Cyrus and Mellie discover Vice President Sally Langston's husband, Daniel Douglas, is gay. They set James up to be caught in a sexual liaison with Daniel Douglas in order to take damning photos to blackmail Sally, Fitz's electoral rival ("Vermont Is for Lovers, Too" [3.08]). Later, James is literally sacrificed when Jake murders him to keep Fitz's fixed election secret ("Kiss Kiss Bang Bang" [3.14]).

4. In "Boom Goes the Dynamite" (2.15), Abby is revealed to be the former "trophy wife" of a powerful politician who beat her severely. Olivia helped her escape

I now turn to examples from *Scandal* that demonstrate the raced and gendered imperial relations of intimate sacrifice. First, I examine the show's main love triangle: President Grant, Mellie Grant, and Olivia Pope. Second, I look at other entanglements involving Olivia, the president, her other suitor (secret B613 agent Jake Ballard), and Olivia's father, Eli (a.k.a. Rowan), the leader of B613. When they use the tools at their disposal to make sacrifices—of laws, morals, bodies, even their own spouses—it is unclear if these sacrifices are beneficial for their stated aims for the Republic, let alone their own intimate goals for happiness or solace.

Olivia and Mellie: Making Sacrifices for Male Empire Builders

The first season of *Scandal* revealed that First Lady Mellie Grant has known about Fitz and Olivia's affair for a long time. However, Olivia calls it off (temporarily), leaving the president without his paramour and confidante as he navigates his first term. But his infidelities don't end: the first scandal to be "fixed" by OPA is that Fitz slept with an intern. In the season one finale, "Grant for the People" (1.07), Fitz declares that he will resign, allowing him to step away from the job that compels him to stay married rather than divorce and marry Olivia. Alas, Olivia rejects his plan: she wants Fitz to remain president because she believes in him. Instead, she schemes with Mellie to repair his public image. The women's discussion of their plan is fraught with disturbing imperial-era race and gender roles.

Mellie asserts an employer-employee/mistress-servant relationship with Olivia. She makes clear distinctions between their public and

---

the marriage, but her husband was neither prosecuted nor publicly exposed as an abuser. When Pope & Associates is asked to vet an acceptable wife for a promising up-and-coming male candidate, Abby is upset that Olivia might put another woman in a loveless marriage just to support a political career. In the end, they select a mate for their client, and she is portrayed as being aware and unfazed about a marriage that is a highly managed political deal.

private roles in relation to the president and then excoriates Olivia for not "doing her job" for the president.

> MELLIE: I'm the first lady. There are sacrifices. There's a price, and for a time, that was fine. You and I wanted the same thing—Fitz in the Oval [Office]. We were on the same team, you and I. And everything was fine. I just don't understand what happened.
>
> OLIVIA (confused): What happened?
>
> MELLIE (yelling): You let that girl get into his pants! You left the team, Liv! You fell down on the job! . . . I do my job. I smile, and I push him. And I make sure he has what he needs. *I do my job.* Why couldn't you do yours?

Mellie Grant is a woman scorned, but she is also politically savvy: she wants to be in power. Mellie's "job" is to keep her husband in the Oval Office; this requires her to tolerate his affairs. This sacrifice of her expectations of fidelity requires Olivia's "consent" to stay hidden as she "does her job" by giving the president "what he needs." Olivia, then, is a vehicle to help Mellie keep Fitz in the White House and reinforce her position as first lady. The "wrong" kind of woman, Amanda—a White intern who wouldn't keep quiet about her affair with Fitz—is now threatening Mellie's position because Olivia "left the team." Olivia's refusal to continue sacrificing her body and emotions to satisfy Fitz's needs—and by extension Mellie's—makes Mellie angry, but also crafty.

The women work out a solution. They decide to pretend Mellie is pregnant, hold a press conference announcing the good news to sway public opinion back to their corner, and have Fitz quickly get her pregnant. Olivia agrees that the expectant-couple "narrative" will quash the intern story and repair the image of the president as the head of a stable White heterosexual family in the White House. Mellie and Fitz regain their first-family image and reinforce their stature by reproducing for the nation. Mellie sacrifices, again, by "giving life to the nation," buttressing the facade of White heteropatriarchal stability. The White first lady is the proper vessel for the next generation of leaders of empire, not Olivia, who is left to stay in her place behind the scenes, even if she is allowed in Fitz's bed. This "sacrifice" of Olivia's happiness with her lover is repeated in "White Hat's Back On" (2.22), when Olivia again suppresses her desire for a public relationship with Fitz because it is more politically savvy to have the president run for reelection with his wife by his side.

Mellie is portrayed as a stereotypical upper-class White woman who marries not for love, but for power. Despite the fact that she is a lawyer, and by all accounts smarter and more capable than her husband, she plays the role of wife and mother as the price to pay to be part of empire. Whereas men pledge their allegiance to the empire by implicitly agreeing to die on the battlefield, women are expected to perpetuate empire through childbearing, sexual comfort, and other forms of domestic support of men (Das 2008, 285–86). The audience discovers in season two that Mellie and Fitz's marriage was first and foremost a match made by White patriarchs looking to create a powerful alliance. In a harsh, revealing conversation, the president compares their courtship to a commercial transaction: "My father . . . had this thing about breeding. . . . Your blood was blue. Mayflower blue. D.A.R. blue. . . . Old money meant something to Big Jerry. And you have breeding. You're a thoroughbred racehorse. . . . It was a merger. It was just shy of prostitution. They sold you to me. They made a deal, and they shook hands. I often wonder, did you know what was happening?" ("Molly, You in Danger, Girl" [2.18]).

As in plantation society of the nineteenth century, sons and daughters were paired according to their *fathers'* plans for power and prestige. Mellie sacrifices her desires for a loving relationship in order to remain close to power. Indeed, the president's chief of staff, Cyrus Beene, repeatedly reminds Mellie that her "job" is to convince the media and the public that her marriage is solid; she must sacrifice her legal career, and, most important, she must not complain about or expose her husband's infidelities.[5]

---

5. This type of exchange happens in many episodes, but is perhaps most troubling in the flashbacks that include her encounters with Big Jerry on the campaign trail in "Everything's Coming Up Mellie" (3.07).

But Mellie's compliance with and proximity to patriarchal power do not protect her. The violence associated with state power spills over into intimate space. During a flashback in season three ("Everything's Coming Up Mellie" [3.07]), we meet Fitz's father, "Big" Jerry Grant. After the men argue, Jerry has a late-night conversation with Mellie, where he reveals how he used his political clout in Congress to orchestrate a cover-up to protect Fitz's career. After this admission, Big Jerry rapes Mellie, and she fears he may have impregnated her.

Thus, Jerry Grant picked Mellie out as a suitable mate for his son, Fitz, but Big Jerry's prerogative as an imperial patriarch extended to her body. Mellie stays silent about the assault to secure Jerry's support for Fitz's campaign. Jerry's connections will secure Fitz's rise to power, but at a considerable cost to Mellie: she attempts suicide and endures years of depression and avoidance of sexual intimacy. Fitz accuses her of frigidity and subjects her to other humiliations, which she endures in the service of maintaining their family image to the public. She "consents" to these sacrifices to keep her man in power.

"Loving" and "Saving" Olivia

Despite her political connections, Olivia faces multiple precarious situations. The president and his aides repeatedly use force and coercion to bring Olivia to serve the president. In "Hunting Season" (2.03), Secret Service agents literally grab Olivia, force her into a car, and drive her to the countryside where the president is on a duck-hunting jaunt.

> OLIVIA: What is your problem?
> FITZ: What is *my*—I *don't* have a problem.
> OLIVIA: Then why are Secret Service agents physically removing me from my home at five in the morning?
> FITZ: Because they do what I say. . . . Why are you helping Artie Hornbacher?
> OLIVIA: . . . I don't discuss my clients with you.
> FITZ: You don't discuss *anything* with me anymore.
> OLIVIA: Are you angry that I haven't been taking your phone calls or because I'm helping Artie Hornbacher?

FITZ: I am angry because you are committing treason.

OLIVIA: To my country or to you?

FITZ: Oh, come on! This isn't personal!

OLIVIA: I am standing in the middle of a forest in God knows where, so you can yell at me? That feels personal.

Then Fitz pushes her against a tree and begins kissing her. Olivia pushes him away, declaring, "I am not yours."

Fitz uses the Secret Service, the CIA, and other agencies to monitor Olivia's movements, mixing national security, surveillance, and sex over and over again. In "A Woman Scorned" (2.20), the president has his military buddy, Jake, follow her everywhere and threatens her with arrest should she protest this surveillance and "protection."

OLIVIA (on the phone with the president): You cannot have me followed everywhere I go.

FITZ: Yes, I can.

OLIVIA: No, you can't . . . (hands phone to Jake)

JAKE (on the phone with the president): Of course, sir. I don't think that'll be necessary, sir. Well, yes. Yes, sir. I will keep you informed. Thank you, Mr. President.

OLIVIA: Well?

JAKE: Well, what?

OLIVIA: What did he say?

JAKE: He said that if you don't let me protect you, he will have the U.S. attorney obtain a material witness warrant and have you taken into custody and put in a cell, where you will be safe from harm.

Jake's assignment to "protect" Olivia is particularly disturbing not only because of the president's threat of prison. In the episode prior to this phone call, Olivia discovered that Jake was spying on her and had seduced her under false pretenses. As she tried to escape him, he restrained her with such force that she was knocked unconscious. When she came to in a hospital bed, he was standing over her and told her to lie to the president about who put her in the hospital ("Seven Fifty-Two" [2.19]).

Coercion haunts nearly all of Olivia's "consenting" moves in and out of the White House. Like Hemings, Olivia is not in complete control of her intimate life.[6] The show frames the president's violations of Olivia's privacy, mobility, and bodily integrity as "for her own good" or for the "good of the Republic." Ostensibly, for example, Jake "saved her" from an assassin. Likewise, all of the dirty work Jake does with B613 to keep truths about Fitz and his allies out of the public eye is deemed for "the good of the Republic."

Jake, unbeknownst to the president and Olivia, is under orders from her father, Rowan Pope. Rowan assigned Jake to seduce Olivia to cause a rift between her and the president. Her father finds Fitz unworthy of his daughter and because he is in charge of "protecting the Republic": a Black mistress threatens the image of stability in the White House. But as he does his job, Jake falls in love with Olivia, which leads to the entrance of the next player in the game: Olivia's father.

Who's Your Daddy? Patriarchs Battling for the "Power" of Olivia's Love

Rowan Pope, head of B613, is revealed as Olivia's father as he rescues her from a swarm of paparazzi. He excoriates her for her relationship with the president and predicts the White House will not protect her; she is disposable to them, but not to him, her father. He offers to send her to a private island to ride out the scandal, but she refuses. In subsequent episodes, she comes to believe (erroneously) that he was responsible for her mother's death. Fitz has Rowan incarcerated in a secret prison. The president interrogates Rowan himself and graphically describes his sexual relations with Olivia to try to get under her father's skin: "I'm screwing her, you know. Your daughter . . . The things I could tell you. About the way she tastes. She's quite a girl.

6. In season five, Fitz had White House and Secret Service staff empty Olivia's apartment and move her into the White House, ostensibly as a show of "love" and "protection" after they make their relationship public ("Rasputin" [5.08]).

Talented" ("A Door Marked Exit" [3.10]). Here Fitz asserts dominance over Rowan's incarcerated body *and* Olivia's body to try to
humiliate her father, a grimy rehashing of the ways White colonial
patriarchs tortured men of color by sexually abusing their sisters, wives,
and daughters, knowing the men had no legal or social recourse. The
resonance with White patriarchal racist abuse of men and women of
color continues when it becomes clear that Rowan is not guilty of
the particular crime for which he was extralegally apprehended, like
countless other men of color falsely accused by the state.

Once Rowan enters the fray, plots revolve around which man *possesses* Olivia's true love and loyalty or who has unlimited access to her
body. Jake and Fitz fight to be number one in her heart and bed;
they bait each other over who last slept with her, touched her, and so
on, peppering disagreements over rendition and torture with taunts
that detail how they last pleasured her. Her father tries to convince
Olivia that these "boys" will never really stand by her, will dispose of
her, and she should lean on her father for real protection. The three
men use their relations with Olivia to jockey for dominance over each
other, to be the ultimate patriarch. They insist they are working to
protect her *and* the nation as they steamroller the Constitution, torturing, murdering, and incarcerating citizens with abandon.

The theme, that whoever possesses Olivia is the most powerful
man in the world, reaches its apex in season four. Olivia is kidnapped
by mercenaries who know the president will do anything to get her
back: they threaten to kill her unless he sends troops into West Angola
("Run" [4.10]). Fitz acquiesces, desperate to get his mistress back. In
captivity, Olivia tries to get control of the situation by convincing the
ringleader, Ian, that he will win more money and influence if he "sells
her" on the open market, since the criminal world now knows Olivia
can be used to manipulate the president of the United States. Ian
agrees and has a crew of hackers literally put her up for auction on the
"dark Web" ("Where's the Black Lady?" [4.11]). But commodifying
herself is no safety valve: though she hopes her colleagues at OPA will
win the auction, her hopes are dashed: another mercenary executes
Ian and vows to sell Olivia only to the nastiest enemy of the United

States he can find. Olivia is back on the auction block, just as Sally Hemings would have been if Thomas Jefferson had chosen to sell her. Olivia has become a trafficked woman, her worth determined by a market controlled by men.

Protection predicated on a woman's perceived "value" for a man, and her willingness to endure sacrifices, does not provide safety for Olivia or Mellie, let alone less central female and feminized characters on the show. When women fail to adhere to patriarchal rule, a man's duty to protect them can quickly convert into anger at them for breaking the imperial "contract." Indeed, in the case of Olivia's abduction, the narrative arc strongly suggests that she was captured because she rejected her father in favor of her lovers. In "The Last Supper" (4.08), Olivia, Jake, and Fitz lure Rowan to a restaurant with the promise of reconciliation with his daughter, all the while surrounding the building with paramilitary troops ready to capture him. Over dinner, Rowan reveals that he anticipated the plan and that she will soon hear the sounds of ambulances arriving to take away the bodies of the men she thought would be capturing him. He concludes with a lecture that subtly predicts her imminent imperilment: "You know what they would have done to me. . . . A trial, an execution. You were going to let them to that to me. After all I've done to protect you from them. I tried, Olivia. I tried my best. For the first time in your life, you are on your own. You think the world is so terrible with me in it? Wait till you see what it's like without me." Days later, she is kidnapped from her apartment while Jake is preoccupied by disrobing for sex. Had she not broken faith with her father, would she have been spared the kidnapping? Would the world be a better place with the ruthless leader of B613 reigning over a vast extralegal security and surveillance network?

Olivia seems to be pondering this question while in captivity and after she is returned home. On the auction block, she is "bought" by Russian gangsters, not OPA or the president. It turns out the Russians are working with her ex-employee Steven, who calls in a favor to rescue Olivia via purchase. Interestingly, at the end of season one, Steven counseled Olivia to let go of Fitz, to not hope or trust that the president would ever commit to her. "It's always on you. . . . You can't have him," he said ("Grant: For the People" [1.07]).

The president rushes to see Olivia after her time in captivity, but she rejects him.

> FITZ: Liv—
>
> OLIVIA: Let go of me.
>
> FITZ: I went to war for you. For you!
>
> OLIVIA: I have been riding and dying for you! I fixed an election for you! Sacrificed everything to keep you in office. We all did! Cyrus, James, Jerry, Harrison, Mellie—every one of us! I was your mistress because you needed me.
>
> FITZ: And I was willing to give it all up for you—
>
> OLIVIA: Which is exactly the problem! . . . Everything we did, I did, all of it—if you gave up the presidency . . . what did I do all this for?! . . . I've sacrificed to get you here, to keep you here, so you could be the best, so you could make history. . . . And then, when the true test came along, when I was taken because of you, you go to war? You sent thousands of innocent soldiers into harm's way, some of them to their deaths, for one person.
>
> FITZ: I had to save you!
>
> OLIVIA: You didn't save me! I'm on my own! ("No More Blood" [4.13])

It seems that Olivia has had a revelation: the president has been exposed as unworthy of all the sacrifices she made in his name. Olivia's intimate experiences with the gendered, raced power of US empire expose the instability of the violence justified in the name of the Republic. *Scandal*'s fantasies, one might say, "simultaneously conceal and attest to the limits of colonial surveillance and . . . U.S. imperial self-identification" (Mendoza 2015, 9).

Closing Thoughts

After her kidnapping, Olivia changes. She suffers from post-traumatic stress disorder; she keeps a gun with her in her apartment. Her personality shifts; she is harsher to her employees and friends when they displease her. In the winter finale of season five, she ends her now public relationship with the president. She chafed against the feminine expectations of being his consort, seeing the role as a reduction in "real" power. But even as she rejects Fitz, she returns to her "partnership" with Mellie, scheming with the senator to make a run for the Oval Office. But Mellie, not Olivia, will be representing the nation. A White woman with the right "bloodlines" is poised to be the president, and Olivia takes her place in the background, managing and manipulating behind the curtain ("It's Hard Out Here for a General" [5.10]).

Scandal's major plotlines follow the contours of American empire. The normalization and forgiveness of violence, the justification of broad surveillance powers, lies, crimes, and secrets as necessary elements of political *and* romantic life—these are the imperial stories *Scandal* communicates with soap-opera flair. The show tells a specific story of empire to us, and it suggests that, in particular, feminized bodies are not safe, even if they are (allegedly) loved and cherished by powerful men. As Liv told Fitz, she's on her own: after all her sacrifices, Olivia's only hope for security is to become the imperial patriarch, not just support them. Over time, Olivia warms more and more to implementing and following masculine, violent forms of power in multiple episodes in seasons four and five. For example, she pushes Cyrus Beene to resist pressure to resign after he is caught with a prostitute:

OLIVIA: So they're mean-girling you in the press, they're calling you names that hurt your little soft spots deep inside? Well, so what? That's how it is. . . . [G]row the hell up because that is how it is! The Cyrus Beene I know doesn't hide in his half-empty closet and wet his pants like a little bitch baby. The Cyrus I know is a patriot. He bites the bullet, and he does what it takes to serve the Republic at all costs. So, I want to know . . . who are you, Cy?

CYRUS: Liv—

OLIVIA: Who are you, Cy?!

. . .

CYRUS: I am one of the most powerful men in the world.
OLIVIA: Who are you?!
CYRUS: I am one of the most powerful men in the world!!
OLIVIA: Oh, yeah? So, you're not a bitch baby?
CYRUS: I run this country. I'm nobody's bitch baby. ("Where the Sun Don't Shine" [4.09])

Cyrus, a gay White man, and Olivia, a heterosexual Black woman, goad each other on, insisting that they are bosses, not bitches. Taunting him with misogynist, feminizing insults, Olivia communicates and wields her understanding of power: it is realized through the practices and violent White heteromasculinity. It is hard and aggressive and devalues those individuals who dare to admit they feel pain or shame, people who need to have time to heal after sacrifices have been exacted from their flesh, rather than bite the bullet.

Olivia's embrace of violent masculinity as the only real source of power—not persuasion, not outsmarting the competition—accelerates after her abduction. The imperial power she serves (and craves) depends on someone to do savage work, to make good on threats, to make someone else the "bitch baby." Whereas before she would employ Huck or Jake or others to inflict pain—so long as they didn't tell her the details or "go too far"—in season five, Olivia begins to participate in both the physical and the psychological violence that underwrites imperial power.[7] This reaches its climax in the episode "Thwack!" (5.17), when former vice president Andrew Nichols blackmails Mellie. Huck kidnaps Andrew, taking him to a secret White House bunker. Olivia tries to get her best friend and former employee, Abby Whelan, to help her, but they are at odds and clash over tactics, which makes Olivia livid.

Olivia tries to bribe Andrew, but he responds with taunting. He declares he's outfoxed her, just as he did when he orchestrated her

7. For example, when the team discovers that her new lover, Russell, is really working for Rowan, she lures him to her bedroom to allow Huck and Quinn to abduct and torture him ("A Few Good Women" [4.21]).

kidnapping. While he jeers, she has flashbacks to being held hostage by his mercenaries.

> ANDREW: Always surprised me how much you went for. $2 billion, was it? Wonder what I'd get now if I . . . put you back on the open market . . . I mean, now that you're not the president's side piece, now that you're just a novelty act. . . . What's an aging porn star go for?
> . . .
> You've got nothing to offer me. I already got everything I wanted. Everything I needed and deserved—revenge! I got revenge.
> OLIVIA: You. You think you get revenge?! You don't get revenge! That's mine! That's mine! Mine!

As she shouts at him, she picks up a metal chair and bashes Andrew over and over again, splattering herself, her clothes, and the walls with his blood and brains. When Abby enters the room later, Olivia seems to be in a daze, but then turns on Abby, completely lucid.

> ABBY: Liv are you okay? Liv.
> OLIVIA: In one hour, you will issue a press release saying former Vice President Andrew Nichols is dead. That means you will have one hour to find Lillian Forrester and convince her that there is no story. . . . Never cross me again. ("Thwack!" [5.17])

Abby looks at her, shocked and disturbed—then obeys the order.

A few episodes later, in the midseason finale, Jake also realizes that Olivia has changed. Though she has "saved" him from her father's clutches, Olivia uses him to ensure Mellie's campaign success: she schemes to get Jake on the ticket as Mellie's vice presidential pick. He rejects the idea and tries to convince Olivia that, now that he's safe (supposedly) from Rowan, they can live a normal life away from the White House.

> JAKE: The world is ours now. We can literally do whatever the hell we want!
> OLIVIA (yelling): Put the tie on!
> JAKE: That's real power, Liv. Not this other crap.

OLIVIA: I have not gone through what I've gone through, worked
twice as hard for half as much, only to end up living an unimpres-
sive life! Mediocrity is not an option for me! I don't want that, and
neither should you!

JAKE: I see. . . . I've gone from being his bitch to yours. ("That's
My Girl" [5.21])

The midseason finale title, "That's My Girl," suggests that Olivia
has become her father's daughter. As Rowan watches Mellie's nomina-
tion on television, he chuckles at Jake standing by her side and sighs,
"That's my girl." Olivia has fully absorbed his definition of hard power.
Emasculating Jake, accepting violence and murder as par for the course
of empire, Olivia has arrived, battle scarred and keen to stay on top.

Did audiences cheer or squirm when Olivia murdered Andrew
or as she put Jake in check? Did they yearn for the days when Liv
declared OPA would not do "wet work," that she and Jake would
"walk in the sun," free of the darkness of B613? The drastic, violent
turn in her personality and actions across seasons four and five is hard
to watch, hard to accept from a protagonist who initially saved the day
by outsmarting the "bad guys." As Abby looks agog at her friend, now
a murderer, and as the promise of a romantic "happily ever after" is
vaporized for Olivia and her paramours, the audience has many reasons to tally the real cost of the sacrifices "the Republic" extracts from
even its most favored agents. There seems to be no pleasure, just grim
determination to be the boss, not the bitch.[8]

References

Andersen, Robin. 2006. *A Century of Media, a Century of War*. New York:
    Peter Lang.

8. In the final season's penultimate episode, "Standing in the Sun" (7.17), Olivia
works to convince her fellow schemers that it is time to tell the truth about their
crimes and bring down B613 in order to resuscitate US democracy. While it reduces
the problems of empire to a single shadow agency, it is interesting that the show is
ending with a disavowal of the tools that built the master's house, so to speak.

Das, Veena. 2008. "Violence, Gender and Subjectivity." *Annual Review of Sociology* 37: 283–99.

Downing, John. 2007. "Terrorism, Torture and Television: *24* in Its Context." *Democratic Communiqué* 21(2): 62–82.

McNamara, Mary. 2012. "There's Always a Crisis." *Los Angeles Times*, Apr. 5. http://articles.latimes.com/2012/apr/05/entertainment/la-et-Scandal -20120405.

Mendoza, Victor. 2015. *Metroimperial Intimacies: Fantasy, Racial-Sexual Governance, and the Philippines in U.S. Imperialism, 1899–1913.* Durham, NC: Duke Univ. Press.

Mohanty, Chandra T. 2006. "U.S. Empire and the Project of Women's Studies." *Gender, Place and Culture* 13(1): 7–20.

Vavrus, Mary D. 2013. "Lifetime's *Army Wives*; or, I Married the Media-Military-Industrial Complex." *Women's Studies in Communication* 36(1): 92–112.

2 | Olivia Pope

"Fixer" of Necropolitical Fallout

NICHOLAS MANGANAS

OLIVIA POPE is haunted by the specter of death. There is no doubt that the role of "Livvie" raises many questions to do with gender, race, and sexuality in the contemporary United States of America. But in this chapter, my objective is to situate the role of Olivia Pope in an entangled space of, on the surface, depoliticized politics. What is surprising about *Scandal* is how a show purporting to be about politics began its initial seasons in such depoliticized fashion. Indeed, this idea was most likely a commercial decision made by the creators of the show in order to appeal to viewers across the political spectrum. Over the course of the first five seasons, however, politics slowly crept into the story arcs. The extravagant plotlines of the series—the extraofficial B613 organization, Cyrus Beene's political maneuvering, Pope's mother's "terrorist" misadventures—all point to new modes of government surveillance and corporate rationality that are deployed in managing violence and social conflicts. In the *Scandal* universe, no conflict is tolerable that challenges the supreme requirements of "the Republic." Since the show's inception, the survival of "the Republic" has superseded personal relationships, destroyed lives, and been placed above all competing interests. In this chapter I posit that the *Scandal* universe is a necropolitical universe where necropolitics regulates life through the perspective of death. Olivia Pope, in this sense, is a "fixer" of the necropolitical fallout of the championing of "the Republic."

In *The Power of Death*, Ricarda Vidal and Maria-José Blanco argue that although we tend to push all thought of death aside, death is everywhere, on blood-spattered movie posters or grisly crime-fiction book covers (2005, 1). In the fictionalized *Scandal* universe, we cannot deny that as viewers, we are fascinated by the unrelenting images of death and killing that the show provides on an almost weekly basis. But although the "reality" of killing in *Scandal* is graphic, it is mediated and controlled by a fictional frame that heightens its dramatic impact on audiences while curiously lessening its political impact. As Judith Butler (2010) argues, making sense of or providing a narrative for what is going on always involves the operation of a frame. In this chapter I argue that *Scandal* is framed by necropolitics. Since the publication of Achille Mbembe's article "Necropolitics" in 2003, necropolitics has become a growing area of study. Necropolitics is an analytical approach that allows one to bring into view the fact that "making life live is . . . a lethal business" (Dillon 2008, 167). In this chapter my aim is to uncover *Scandal*'s necropolitical universe and explore Olivia Pope's role in "fixing," that is, hiding, such "lethal" business. The men in Olivia Pope's life (her father, Command; her lovers, President Fitzgerald Grant and Captain Jake Ballard; her friend and mentor Cyrus Beene; and her protégé Huck) are all imbued with the power of life and death. These characters constantly decide which lives are worth living and which are not. As spectators we identify with Pope's moral preoccupations with their, and sometimes her own, actions. By using the concept of necropolitics as a frame, this chapter argues that *Scandal* remarkably bears witness to a terror that is never really a final political objective. Yet it is the very blurring of lightness and darkness, of good and evil in the *Scandal* necropolitical universe, that provides the show with scope to engage with what it means to be human in a universe where saving the Republic at any cost underpins our system of government.

Dragging Everyone into the Light

As the series evolved, B613 slowly became one of the central drivers of drama on *Scandal*. At first, B613 was portrayed as a dark, shadowy organization with powers even beyond the White House and the president's purview. Such an organization reflects society's deep-rooted fears of not only government but those unnamed, faceless men who pull the strings, decide political outcomes, and direct the course of history. There is a long tradition of portraying shadowy organizations on American television, and *Scandal* at first played along with the conventions. But whereas the faceless men in shows such as *The X-Files* (Fox, 1993–2002, 2016–18) kept their mysterious aura, leaving viewers unsure of the truth, motivations, and justification for such shadowy organizations, *Scandal*, in a matter of just a few episodes, made B613 a protagonist of the show. In doing so, *Scandal* unmasked the faceless men and spelled out clearly the justification for B613's existence: to save "the Republic" at all costs. In the *Scandal* universe, there may be moral ambivalence, but there is no moral ambiguity. There is no counternarrative that challenges the core of B613's foundational claim: maintaining the people's faith in the American system of government justifies the killing of innocents.

On the surface, *Scandal* is exactly about moral ambivalence. Week by week, Olivia Pope, the white-hatted heroine, "fixes" scandals and crises as they come up, and she wears her moral concerns on her sleeve. When she or her mentor Cyrus Beene, President Fitzgerald Grant's chief of staff, goes too far, they rue what they have become and question their humanity. But the very fact that she calls her team "Gladiators" points to her concern about injustice and to her self-positioning as a defender of the underdog. When, in a rare moment of weakness, she questions the point of it all, the point of democracy, freedom, and patriotism when there are no white hats, her father, Eli "Rowan" Pope, tells her that there is a point: "If there are no more white hats, if the deck is always stacked, and if everyone you love is a monster, there is, in fact, someone worth saving. Who? Everyone! Everyone is worth saving! Even the monsters. Even the demons. . . . In the face of darkness, you drag everyone into the light. That is the point. At least, I like to think that is the point of you" ("Kiss Kiss Bang Bang" [3.14]). Olivia Pope's role as a "fixer" is thus two-toned. In one sense, she is the light, dragging everyone into the light with her. In another, she is darkness, since almost everybody she loves is a monster. Her father's speech telling her that there is a point to it all would almost be heartwarming if it were not for the fact that her father is Command, the head of the B613 organization. The father-daughter relationship as portrayed in *Scandal* likewise reflects the light-and-darkness divide. As much as Pope attempts to stay in the light, her father's darkness clouds her world. But the dark cloud that palls over her does not just come from her father. Her long-running affair with President Fitzgerald "Fitz" Grant is also tinged with darkness. She committed an original sin by rigging his election. Olivia Pope took a bite of the apple and thus got her lover elected, showing, in the process, how she, herself, is capable of corrupting the system. Her embroilment in the "Defiance" scandal that got Fitz elected was, in a way, justified as a means of saving the Republic. President Grant is portrayed as an honest, heartfelt politician with genuine concern for the welfare of Americans. The first and second seasons of *Scandal* provided its viewers only a limited sense of President Grant's policy positions or ideology. As the show progressed, we saw President Grant lobbying for equal pay for women, gun reform, and eventually the "Brandon Bill" in season four. Despite *Scandal*'s limited engagement with such issues, however, the show genuinely assures its audience that only President Grant could fulfill the role and duties of office so fittingly, and thus the terrible scandal of "Defiance" was justified in order to put him in his rightful place.

Olivia Pope's dark cloud gets bigger when Captain Jake Ballard enters her world. At first sent to spy on her by her father, we soon learn that Ballard works for the B613 organization and soon forms a relationship with her. His darkness impinges on Pope's world when he becomes, for a time, Command, replacing her father. In one of his first acts as Command, he kills three people, including James Novak, Pope's friend and Cyrus Beene's husband. When Pope accuses Ballard of taking three innocent lives, including a friend of hers, Jake responds: "Bad things happen to good people all the time" Of course, he justifies his actions by saying he was protecting the Republic: "I keep this country running. I do what needs to be done!" ("Kiss Kiss Bang Bang" [3.14]). But unlike Pope's father, Ballard is also two-toned like

Olivia. He has a light, but it was the reality of being Command, of protecting the Republic, that darkened him.

Apart from these three key men who surround Pope, her father and her two lovers, the other people she loves are similarly tainted by the murkiness of their everyday lives as fixers. Her friend and mentor Cyrus Beene repeatedly delves into criminal activity and morally hazardous situations in order to keep President Grant in office, situations that usually need the cooperation or "fixing" of Olivia Pope & Associates. Another mentor, Justice Verna Thornton, tried in season two to have President Grant killed in order to correct the original sin of rigging his election. In the end, it was President Grant who killed Verna, tainting himself in his struggle to maintain power. Even Pope's mother operates in darkness. Not only is she a terrorist, but she is also a depoliticized terrorist: "Terrorists use violence to advance their convictions," she says. "God, country. And since I am not burdened by those, I'm more of a facilitator. I don't make bombs, I make money" (3.14).

Pope's protégé Huck, another former B613 agent, is portrayed as a sadistic killer who enjoys torturing his victims, a trait that an even newer protégée, Quinn, seems to share. But Quinn's and Huck's darkness is tamed by their allegiance to Pope, by the fact that they are her Gladiators. In fact, in Olivia Pope's world, the only people she loves who are not "monsters" are her two other Gladiators Abby and Harrison and her sometimes professional nemesis David Rosen.[1] While Abby takes on the role of a Greek chorus, reminding Pope of her principles, of what her white hat stands for, the darkness in Pope's world leads to Harrison's death. David Rosen, on the other hand, mirrors Pope's character. Though they share a defiant sense of justice, Rosen is not willing to enter into the darkness that envelops Pope's world, although sometimes he himself is unwillingly dragged into it.

---

1. This changes somewhat in season six, when we see Abby as chief of staff becoming "seduced by money and power" (Stanchfield quoted in Abrams 2017), and thus getting involved in some "monstrous" activities herself (for example, "A Traitor among Us" [6.07] and "A Stomach for Blood" [6.08]).

In short, in the *Scandal* universe, there are no faceless men controlling history. They have a face. They are Olivia Pope's friends and family.

Despite the seriousness of *Scandal*'s drama, the show does not shy away from soap-opera conventions. Alison Willmore in *IndieWire* argues that *Scandal*'s open embrace of the soap-opera format has actually "freed it up to feel more relevant than its higher-end cable counterpart *Homeland*." As *Scandal* never has to worry about maintaining "credibility," the show exists, according to Willmore, "in a cynical, just-alternate universe in which the country may be large, but the group of people that matter are an attractive oligarchy of self-serving psychopaths, even our allegedly white-hatted heroine." Willmore points to the B613 organization as a case in point. Rowan Pope's limitless power as Command might be exaggerated but echoes, she argues, the claims of ignorance from the president and the Senate Intelligence Committee that greeted the National Security Agency spying revelations revealed in 2013. Willmore's argument that *Scandal* has a much bleaker view of power and governmental institutions than Showtime's *Homeland* (2011–) is sound. *Homeland* represents the point of view from inside the Central Intelligence Agency, thus placing a fundamental trust in what its characters are doing and their perceptions of the world: "They've made some reckless decisions, but their hearts are in the right place." In *Scandal*, however, the B613 organization is seen from the "outside" and thus represents "a malignant force acting in a warped vision of what's right" (Willmore 2013).

I would now like to take Willmore's insight a step further and explore *Scandal*'s just-alternate universe using Michel Foucault's conceptualization of biopolitics. By exploring that "malignant force acting in a warped vision of what's right" in order to "drag everyone into the light," I argue that the *Scandal* universe goes even beyond biopolitics to the point where we can consider it a death-world, a necropolitical world, where "saving everyone" means saving no one.

"Bad Things Happen to Good People All the Time"

The politics of the *Scandal* universe revel in a number of different conceptualizations of power. The first kind of power *Scandal* delights in showcasing is sovereign power, as conceptualized by Michel Foucault. He argued that "for a long time one of the characteristic privileges of sovereign power was the right to decide life and death" (1978, 135). That right that was formulated as the "power of life and death" was in reality the right to "*take* life or *let* live" (136). Let us consider Rowan Pope's role as Command in the *Scandal* universe. As a kind of sovereign power, we can argue that Command has the power to take life (for example, Harrison and President Grant's son Jerry) and to also let others live, those whom he chooses to spare for the sake of his daughter, Olivia Pope. There are thus direct parallels between the role of Command in the *Scandal* universe and the traditional awe-inspiring sovereign power to which Foucault was referring.

Scandal toys with sovereign power in its representation of the omnipotent role of Command, whose seemingly unlimited power stretches beyond even the most powerful man in the world, the president of the United States of America. When Rowan Pope as Command is being interrogated by President Grant, he relishes refusing to share information with him: "That's a matter of national security, and it's above your pay grade, Mr. President" ("A Door Marked Exit" [3.10]). Likewise, when Captain Jake Ballard has the role of Command and is questioned by Grant, Ballard bites back: "I am Command, which means you don't tell me to do anything because I'm not your bitch. . . . I decide if America sleeps at night. I decide if America endures" ("Mama Said Knock You Out" [3.15]).

And in one of the most infamous scenes of the whole series, Rowan Pope belittles the president with his "You're a boy" speech. With staccato-inflected venom, he attacks: "You've been coddled and cared for, pampered and hugged. . . . You're a Grant! You've got money in your blood! You . . . are . . . a . . . boy!" (3.10). *Scandal* thus plays with this conception of sovereign power, where above everybody else there is one, and only one, sovereign power, an ultimate power with complete control over who lives and who dies.

Biopolitical power, which Foucault argues emerged in the nineteenth century, did not necessarily replace the sovereign power detailed above, but did reshape power relations since for the first time "life" emerged as the center of political strategies. "Wars," he argues, "are no longer waged in the name of a sovereign who must be defended; they are waged on behalf of the existence of everyone" (1978, 137). Biopolitics reveals that the power to preserve life at all costs is inevitably coupled with the need to determine what must die. Foucault does not argue that this new right replaces sovereignty's old right "to take life or let live," but that it is complemented by a new right: "to 'make' live and 'let' die" (2003, 241).

Let us return to our example above of Command in the *Scandal* universe. If we consider Command as a kind of sovereign power, his motivation to exercise the "power of life and death" is not limited to his own survival. Although it is true that Command has used violence to protect his privileged position as "Command" (after all, who would want to give up the ultimate sovereign power that his position affords?), his justification for the violence and death he inflicts lies precisely in the fact that he is protecting the existence of everyone. In order to save "the Republic," some have to die.

It is the very fact that in the *Scandal* universe all the key players have a higher motivation at stake, a will for the greater good, that makes *Scandal* biopolitical. So while a show like *Homeland* deals with a geopolitics of security, driven by the need to protect and defend the territory of the sovereign nation-state, *Scandal* deals with a *biopolitics* of security, geared toward constantly promoting and improving the conditions of a population through protecting the idea of "the state" or "the Republic" and the faith of the people who sustain it (Debrix and Barder 2012, 10). Although undemocratic, Command makes the decision that for humanity as a whole, it would be better to liquidate certain individuals.

The central lesson we can draw from Foucault's conceptualization of biopolitics, suggests Timothy C. Campbell, is that "one cannot manage life without managing death" (2011, 58). In *Scandal*, Willmore's "attractive oligarchy of self-serving psychopaths" also has to manage life by employing death (2013). Indeed, according to Campbell, biopolitics has become so "indebted to death . . . that we have less a biopolitics at our disposal than a thanatopolitics" (2011,

8). Although in the *Scandal* universe we can see the dance of sovereign and biopolitical power at play, this dance often tips into a kind of necropolitics,[2] where Olivia Pope, our heroine, is a "fixer" of the necropolitical fallout of the championing of the Republic. It is in the character of Olivia Pope where we can best see necropolitics inscribed. Pope's role in "fixing," or better still "hiding" the "lethal business" of a necropolitical world, is a "lethal business" that has the supreme objective of saving the Republic at all costs.

Framing Necropolitics

Achille Mbembe's groundbreaking article "Necropolitics," published in *Public Culture* in 2003, took Foucault's insights into biopolitics a significant step further. Mbembe argued that "the notion of biopower is insufficient to account for contemporary forms of subjugation of life to the power of death" (2003, 39–40). Instead, he argued that in the contemporary world, *necropolitics* was a more appropriate term to understand the "creation of death-worlds," which he defined as "new and unique forms of social existence in which vast populations are subjected to conditions of life conferring upon them the status of living dead" (40). It might seem odd to use Mbembe's conceptualization of necropolitics in an analysis of the *Scandal* universe. But we can glean an unsettling insight from Mbembe's "Necropolitics." He was particularly interested in exploring necropolitics in various modes of historical terror, such as slavery, apartheid, the Nazi death camps, and the colony. Yet he also sought to question how political systems propagate a particular narrative of history and identity whereby the system itself is sacralized. As we will see in my discussion below, the system of US government overseen by Command propagates such a narrative where the state itself is sacred and underpinned by the idea that the Republic has "a divine right to exist" (27), a right that must be protected at all costs.

2. The terms *thanatopolitics* and *necropolitics* are more or less interchangeable.

In *Homo Sacer*, Giorgio Agamben was likewise interested in exploring this transition from biopolitics to what he called thanatopolitics. Agamben posited that such a transition lies in the "indistinction" between life and death, or between making live and letting die. As Agamben puts it, "If there is a line in every modern state marking the point at which the decision on life becomes a decision on death, and biopolitics can turn into thanatopolitics, this line no longer appears today as a stable border dividing two clearly distinct zones" (1998, 122). In the *Scandal* universe, necropolitics can be found in this "indistinct space" between life's potential to thrive, on the one hand, and to proliferate death-worlds, on the other. In my discussion below, I am particularly interested in locating this "indistinct space" in *Scandal*'s necropolitical story arcs. My concern now is thus: How can we read necropolitics in the *Scandal* universe? How can we determine if the system itself has become sacralized? Where can we find that indistinct space between life and the potential of death? Judith Butler's conceptualization of "framing" is useful in discerning the underlying necropolitics at play in *Scandal*.

In *Frames of War*, Butler argues that frames shape our understanding of political violence. Although Butler is specifically writing about the frames that shape our understanding of war, framing is an act of interpretation and understanding. According to Butler, "There is no life and no death without a relation to some frame" (2010, 7). In *Scandal*, defending the Republic at all costs is the frame that makes it possible to think that ending life in the name of defending life is not only possible but even righteous. Butler argues, "If certain lives do not qualify as lives or are, from the start, not conceivable as lives within certain . . . frames, then these lives are never lived nor lost in the full sense" (1). The victims of *Scandal* are also not conceivable within the frame of protecting the Republic and are therefore not lost in the full sense. The frequent taking of life in the series is thus positioned by a frame that usually seeks to justify death in order to preserve life. And as Butler suggests, these acts of life and death very often "call into question" the very frame itself. Let us consider some examples from

Scandal where such frames help end some lives in the name of defending life (the Republic) and thus also call the frame into question.

When Cyrus Beene requires the new Command, Captain Jake Ballard, to "take care of" the problem of Vice President Sally Langston's murder of her husband, that is, eliminate the three people who could bring the scandal into the light, Beene elevates the interests of "the Republic" to near-God status in a life-affirming narrative: "The fate of the Republic may not hinge on me or Fitz or Mellie, but it does hinge on the American people continuing to believe that their elected officials are not murderers. Sure, maybe a war here, a dubious FDA approval there, but not *murderers*. . . . Faith in government will be dead. People will stop paying their taxes. Economic systems, institutions that have lasted for centuries will begin to falter while our enemies pounce on our crippled nation and hack away until the great American experiment is no more" ("No Sun on the Horizon" [3.13]). Ballard, as Command, takes Beene's narrative to heart and thus "takes care of the problem" by killing Beene's husband and one other. Indeed, Beene had no idea that "taking care of the problem" would lead to his husband's death. But his speech above, by arguing that "faith in government will be dead" is the frame that justifies even his own husband's death. There is no life and no death without this frame, and thus the victims' lives remain in that "indistinguishable" space between life and death. Of course, they are mourned on a personal level, but the frame of protecting the Republic creates the death-world where some must die in order to avoid the destruction of the great American experiment.

As President Grant's reelection campaign manager, Pope puts an end to Vice President Andrew Nichols's affair with Mellie Grant, in what can only be described as a kind of blackmail. Unable to escape Pope's cavalry at her disposal, Nichols retorts: "What's it like? . . . Being you? Cutting people's throats and calling it politics?" ("The Fluffer" [3.16]). Indeed, Nichols strikes at the heart of Pope's job description. By "fixing" a situation (for her client, for the Republic), she inevitably enters a darkness paralleling her father's taking-care-of-business approach. Pope does, however, question what her role is in the scheme of things, especially after the cunning remark her mother, Maya, made to her, calling her "the help": "I'd rather be a traitor than what you are, Livvie. Cleaning up those people's messes. Fixing up their lives. You think you're family, but you're nothing but the help. And you don't even know it" ("Mama Said Knock You Out" [3.15]). Coming after the 2011 film *The Help* and the public debate that film inspired about the racialized role of Black women in US history, Maya Pope's remark is one of the most insightful, yet troubling, commentaries in the whole series. Is Olivia Pope really no different from Aibileen Clark (Viola Davis) as portrayed in *The Help*? In a later conversation with Cyrus Beene, Olivia begs him: "Tell me we're not the help, Cyrus, that I am not some maid with a mop in my hand cleaning up messes whenever they ring the bell." Cyrus's reply is not comforting: "I'd be lying. You know the job, Olivia. You know what we do. . . . But somewhere in this head of mine . . . is my faint recollection that what we do is important. . . . Because it's not just that family you're putting back together. It's the whole damn country" (3.15).

Whereas Rowan Pope, as Command, executes his sovereign power by choosing who lives and who dies, Olivia Pope is the mop, the "help" who cleans up the mess, not a killer but an abettor.[3] So coterminous are Rowan's and Olivia's worlds that Maya Pope, a "terrorist," is refreshingly a free agent, unburdened by any quasi-moral logic of "saving humanity" or the Republic. Despite being a "terrorist," her world is lighter and simpler than the one that both Rowan and Olivia inhabit. The death-world that Rowan and Olivia share, what Willmore calls a "malignant force acting in a warped vision of what's right" (2013), is darker than the death-world of an international terrorist. As the *Scandal* story arc develops over the course of the series,

---

3. This, too, somewhat changes with plot developments in seasons six and seven, when Olivia Pope becomes Command, giving orders to kill as she sees fit to save "the Republic." Nevertheless, she remains in ([in]direct) service of the White House until the series finale, when she chooses to decline President Mellie Grant's offer to return as her chief of staff, telling Mellie she "spent more than enough time helping people clean up their messes" ("Over a Cliff" [7.18]).

Olivia Pope is increasingly self-aware of her role amid the politicking of death. In an exchange with President Grant, she tells him: "You want to pretend to be above what happens here. . . . Maybe you didn't realize what that means, how dirty and dark it is behind the curtain of power, the level of sins and the sacrifices committed in your name! . . . This is how it's always worked. There is no clean" ("No Sun on the Horizon" [3.13]). There is a self-realization in this little speech that was nonexistent at the beginning of the series. A few episodes later, President Grant's son is murdered, and "there is no clean" reads like a prescient foretelling:

> OLIVIA POPE: We're going to win the election now. They lost their child. America will rally behind them . . . A child is dead, and that's the first thing that popped into my head . . . How did we get like this? When did we stop being people?
> CYRUS BEENE: Were we ever people? Or did serving at the pleasure of the president just help us to shed our pesky skins and unmask us as the monsters we really are? ("The Price of Free and Fair Elections" [3.18])

Unmasking the "monsters" is arguably a key trope in *Scandal*'s overarching thematic concern of good and evil, of the evil humanity is capable of, an evil that even Olivia Pope has inside her.

Early in season four, President Grant finally tells Mellie that their son Jerry did not die because of a rare illness but was murdered in an act of terrorism. Mellie's reaction is surprising, but within the frame of *Scandal* aptly fitting because it gave her son's death meaning—her son died for the Republic: "I'm saying it wasn't random, it wasn't senseless. It had meaning. It had a point. I can't tell you how much better that makes me feel on some strange level, how much order that brings to things. . . . He died so that we could stay in this White House for four more years" ("The Key" [4.05]). What Mellie calls "meaningful," her son's death giving her and Fitz the White House for four more years, a revelation that horrifies Fitz, is precisely the "monster" in the room: life and death in *Scandal* are somewhat blurred, opaque, have meaning, and at the same time are meaningless. The fact that Jerry was the president's son justified the expenditure of his life. This fact provides Mellie solace because it justifies her very existence as first lady, her life's work to make her husband the president of the United States. But this same fact horrifies Fitz because it is proof of the way in which necropower functions to destroy persons who unwittingly enter into death-worlds, in this case by association. In this moment, Mellie is "unmasked"; we see the monster rear its ugly head in her justification of power. But her "unmasking" is also Fitz's "unmasking," since his presidency is the root of the evil, his occupying the Oval Office the key event that leads to scandal and death. So while Jerry's death is "meaningful" in that context, it is further meaningless in the sense that he died for no other reason than for the fact that he was the president's son.

Yet, of course, "evil" is best manifested in the *Scandal* universe by the omnipotent presence of Command, Olivia Pope's father. The frame in *Scandal* is personalized through the father-daughter relationship between Olivia and Rowan Pope. The tension in their relationship is palpable throughout the series, but in season four it is taken up a notch. Olivia increasingly realizes her father's destructive capacity and attempts to separate herself from him by betraying him. In the midseason finale, just before the ultimate betrayal, Rowan Pope's speech to his daughter while armed snipers are outside waiting for him is almost philosophical and addresses (in)directly the death-worlds that he, as Command, operates in: "What I've done, all that I've done, is because of you. . . . You have forsaken me . . . You wanted to stand in the sun, in the bright, white light. It blinded you . . . For the first time in your life, you are on your own. *You think the world is so terrible with me in it? Wait till you see what it's like without me*" ("The Last Supper" [4.08]; emphasis added). Rowan Pope's speech to his daughter is fascinating. On one level, he pits the struggle to save the Republic as a battle between "us and them," about being on the right or wrong side of history. Olivia Pope is torn between her lovers and her father, where she must choose between light and darkness. On another level, as Command, that omnipotent sovereign power, he outsmarts his daughter, President Grant, and

Captain Ballard and in the process "calls the frame into question" (Butler 2010, 9).

His final words, "You think the world is so terrible with me in it? Wait till you see what it's like without me," exceed the frame of saving the Republic at all costs and are the statement that troubles our sense of reality. Outside the frame, *Scandal* makes us question the operation of power and ask ourselves, can we indeed live without Command? What would a world without such a power look like? On the surface, *Scandal* might be about Pope & Associates "fixing" the problems of the Washington elite, but outside the frame *Scandal* troubles us with its symbiotic representation of life and death where, we, as viewers, put ourselves in Olivia Pope's shoes. Do we choose love or family? Light or darkness? Or is the light an illusion, something we can see only in the photographic image, an illusion that Command tricks us into thinking is really there? In a world without Command, is there a light at all?

In season five these questions are neither answered nor discarded but further complicated in delicious Freudian scenes that paint an existential crisis for Olivia Pope. "Is Olivia Pope a political savant or a woman so ambitious she would do anything to get where she wanted to go?" a journalist asks in the wake of the outing of her affair with Fitz ("Dog-Whistle Politics" [5.04]). Season five reads like a descent into hell for Olivia where she questions the extent to which she is her father's daughter:

> JAKE BALLARD: How does someone as brilliant and as accomplished as you not know what you are, who you are? . . . You are Rowan's greatest achievement. You have become exactly the woman he raised you to be—power-hungry, entitled, dangerous. And the beauty of it is, you don't even know it. ("Even the Devil Deserves a Second Chance" [5.07])

The list of events that Olivia either *triggers* or *fixes* is relentless in season five, and the producers are certainly brave for diminishing their heroine's white hat in such radical strokes on prime-time TV.

Olivia arranges for Mellie to release her father from prison in order to save herself from being implicated in Fitz's impeachment process. She was willing to "cross a line" by releasing dirt on the father of Vice President Susan Ross's child: "I am talking about replacing the white hat with a black skullcap," worries Quinn ("The Miseducation of Susan Ross" [5.16]). But it is her violent reaction to former vice president Andrew Nichols's attempt to blackmail the White House and leak the story that Fitz invaded West Angola to save her that shockingly unmasks her. The trauma she experienced during and post her abduction is so palpable that the audience almost rejoices as she smashes a chair on his face, over and over ("Thwack!" [5.17]). A watershed moment, the mask is further removed two episodes later when she tells Abby: "I made that Oval. I built that president. I had to walk away from the White House because of him. I want it back. I want my White House back. I earned it!" ("Buckle Up" [5.19]). By the end of season five, Olivia Pope is flirting with a sovereign power that she used to struggle against. She does not all of a sudden turn to the dark side. Rather, select scenes provide us a glimpse of an internal conflict. She still wears her white hat, as evidenced by her drive to "save" Jake from the clutches of her father. But when she has to perform a faux breakup scene in order to save him from her father "slitting his throat," her choice of words is telling: "Mediocrity is not an option for me!" ("That's My Girl" [5.21]). In the season finale, she finally liberates Jack by taking Huck's advice ("You can't take Command. You have to become Command"). And when she does exactly that, we are left to ruminate whether that becoming is real, whether indeed Olivia Pope is replacing her father.

We can thus see how terror and death circulate in Olivia Pope's relationships with the men in her life, relationships that are the catalyst for much of the drama in *Scandal*, for much of the killing. But even this fact does not taint the audience's affection for Olivia Pope. If we consider the framing of Olivia Pope in the *Scandal* universe, we can see plainly that Pope's relationships are a "poison," a malignant force that wreaks havoc in the name of what is right.

What is kept "outside" the frame is that the universe in which Pope "fixes" scandals is necropolitical as long as the ultimate objective is to save the Republic at all costs.

The transformation of Olivia Pope that we began to witness by the end of season five points to the troubling nature of overlapping death-worlds. Olivia Pope was once asked by her father to imagine a world without him. As viewers, we sit back fascinated at the thought that inside her lies a dormant version of "Command." By doing so, we also question to what extent a kind of Command lies in us. An uncomfortable question for some, but a pertinent one in an age of alternative facts and (hi)stories.

Conclusion: "Helen of Troy, the Face That Launched a Thousand Ships"

At a time when the United States is increasingly divided into red and blue states, when party-driven narratives circulate in the mass media, politics in *Scandal* is often relegated to the background, often inconsequential. We do know that President Grant is a Republican, but viewers are told little about what kind of Republican President Grant is, what he believes in, and why Olivia Pope would work and vote for him. President Grant is represented as a quintessential American hero, a president who has the interests of all Americans at heart. Likewise, we know just as little about Olivia Pope. Apart from her unrelenting sense of justice and fairness, we do not know what she believes in. Yes, she is in love with a Republican president, but her previous lover Senator Edison Davis was a Democrat. *Scandal*'s painstaking attempts to remain politically neutral cover much ground. By season four, it is almost a miracle that the audience knows that the president is in favor of gun control after his assassination attempt and that many in his party think him too liberal. *Scandal* thus meets Americans halfway. Yes, he is a Republican, but he is not very conservative. Yes, he is the quintessential American hero, but he also has a Black lover and an openly gay chief of Staff. The representation of politics in *Scandal* could thus not be any more different from another of its cable counterparts, *House of Cards* (2013–), which revels in interparty politicking and where scandals have a real effect on legislation and government policy. Week by week, Pope & Associates "fix" scandals, but we are never quite sure of the final political objective beyond political survival and the metanarrative of protecting "the Republic" at all costs. But it is *Scandal*'s surface of depoliticized politics that allows the show to play with the meaning of what it means to be "human," to unmask the "monsters," and to blur the line between life and death. As determined as Olivia Pope is to stand in the light, she is inevitably dragged back into the dark by the death-worlds that encircle her, occupying that space of indistinguishableness between life and death. She is, as Secret Service agent cum undercover B613 agent Tom Larsen suggests, "Helen of Troy, the face that launched a thousand ships" ("Baby Made a Mess" [4.07]).

References

Abrams, Natalie. 2017. "*Scandal*: Abby's True Allegiances Revealed." *Entertainment Weekly*, Mar. 30. http://ew.com/tv/2017/03/30/scandal-abby-mole-darby-stanchfield/.

Agamben, Giorgio. 1998. *Homo Sacer: Sovereign Power and Bare Life*. Stanford, CA: Stanford Univ. Press.

Butler, Judith. 2010. *Frames of War: When Is Life Grievable?* New York: Verso.

Campbell, Timothy. C. 2011. *Improper Life: Technology and Biopolitics from Heidegger to Agamben*. Minneapolis: Univ. of Minnesota Press.

Debrix, Francois, and Alexander D. Barder. 2012. *Beyond Biopolitics: Theory, Violence, and Horror in World Politics*. London: Routledge.

Dillon, Michael. 2008. "Security, Race and War." In *Foucault on Politics, Security and War*, edited by Michael Dillon and Andrew W. Neal, 166–96. Basingstoke: Palgrave.

Foucault, Michel. 1978. *History of Sexuality*. Vol. 1, *An Introduction*. New York: Vintage Books.

———. 2003. *Society Must Be Defended: Lectures at the Collège de France, 1975–76*. London: Allen Lane.

Mbembe, Achille. 2003. "Necropolitics." *Public Culture* 15(1): 11–40.

Vidal, Ricarda, and Maria-José Blanco. 2015. Introduction to *The Power of Death: Contemporary Reflections on Death in Western Society*, edited by Maria-José Blanco and Ricarda Vidal, 1–9. New York: Berghahn Books.

Willmore, Alison. 2013. "Why 'Scandal' Is Doing a Better Job of Channeling American Fears than 'Homeland' This Season." *IndieWire*, Nov. 5. http://www.indiewire.com/article/television/why-scandal-is-doing-a-better-job-of-capturing-american-fears-than-homeland-this-season.

3 | *Scandal*

A Melodrama of Social Death

PATRICIA VENTURA

THIS CHAPTER began as an attempt to understand the excitement my students at Spelman College, an all-women's historically Black college, shared with me when they first started watching the ABC-TV drama *Scandal*. As a melodrama produced by African American showrunner Shonda Rhimes about a powerful, brilliant, and beautiful African American heroine engaged in a torrid affair with the White US president, the surface-level appeal of *Scandal* comes from following the spectacular love life and career of its protagonist, Olivia Pope. But I would argue that *Scandal*'s deeper appeal—and an aspect that kept the show's core audience coming back through its seven seasons—derives from its implicit and explicit exploration of larger themes, particularly race and the operation of racism today as they intersect with gender and sexuality. The show gives these themes added resonance by crosscutting them with larger national political questions, especially concerning the powers and limits of government surveillance and the ethics of politically motivated violence.

These national political concerns are themselves products of two profoundly significant events circumscribing US political life in the twenty-first century. The first is the attacks of September 11, 2001, which drastically expanded the landscape of government surveillance and Americans' support for state violence. (In this regard, it is worth noting that the war in Afghanistan, the war most directly connected to 9/11, is the longest conflict in US history.) The other signal event is the election of Barack Obama in 2008, a milestone that changed the American discourse on race—making racism more overt even while enabling the contradictory assumption that the mere presence of blackness in the White House somehow signals the end of racism. I would maintain that *Scandal*'s appeal lies in great part in the unique ways the show both reflects and addresses this political-cultural environment. It does so by staging a series of reversals and reinterpretations that erode the usual expectations for representing racial and gender identity. The effect of the reversals is to shine a new light on the violence at the heart of American power, both today and in the past, and to demonstrate how violence enacted in the private sphere also manifests in the public.

In this chapter, I consider the unique position *Scandal*, as a melodrama, occupies in relation to violence. I contrast the program's representations of acts of brutality in Olivia's personal world with past depictions of violence against African American women. And I analyze the program's larger historical context, juxtaposing its presentation of state violence against depictions of state violence in other contemporary popular media. While spectacles of torture in other programs and films tend to stage violence as the product of a state of exception, thereby obscuring the physical brutality that is rooted in US history, I demonstrate that *Scandal* operates from an understanding of violence as constitutive of the nation, especially in the ways it impacts the lives of African Americans. In this regard, I explore *Scandal*'s representation of violence as a vehicle for understanding the program's perspectives on racial oppression generally.

Ambivalent Impulses

Historically, the African American woman has functioned as an iconic recipient of American structural brutality represented through spectacles of violence enacted on her body. As Saidiya Hartman's *Scenes of Subjection* argues, the ubiquity of the representation of African American women as recipients of violence makes such suffering mundane. Hartman memorably begins the text by contrasting her approach to that taken by Frederick Douglass in his *Narrative* that begins with the torture of Aunt Hester. Hartman explicitly identifies and then rejects a tradition around representing violence on Black women as a means for providing the audience "the opportunity for self-reflection" (1997, 4) or serving as a means for everyone else to experience what some might call "a bit of the other" in a kind of sadomasochistic fantasy. To call attention to the spectacle of brutality enacted on Black women's bodies, Hartman explains that she will not re-recount the violent story of Douglass's aunt or other spectacular acts of violence, but will instead investigate the mundane abuses in the bureaucratic corners of law or in the oppressive entertainment of minstrel performances.

Importantly, Hartman makes a further point, which is echoed in the current writing of other thinkers such as Jared Sexton (2010). For them, such spectacles of violence hide the more fundamental ethical lapse in US history that is rooted not in physical brutality toward African Americans, but in what Orlando Patterson (1982) has termed their "social death"—that is, the lack of recognition of their humanity by wider society—or what Hannah Arendt (1958) describes as being denied "the right to have rights." Outside of the category of human, the long-term result of brutalization and torture is the inscription of categories of people within a racial order. In this way, as Dorothy Roberts has shown, "torture produces race" itself (2008, 233).

Today, the representation of Black women's physical torture remains a spectacle reinscribing the category of race and continues to obscure a history of alienation of African Americans from the category of human. In short, it is clear that the United States is not done with slavery. The need remains to "take seriously the ways in which its logic of property, belonging, and family reshaped each and every one of those concepts irrevocably, as well as the lives of the subjects—black, white, native, Hispanic—who lived within this discursive logic" (Holland 2012, 31).

For its part, *Scandal* represents this discursive logic at the heart of American political life in its rather frequent depictions of abuse and torture. The show presents a new look at these structural problems not by refusing to depict the violence, brutality, and torture upon which American capital and the US government rely, but by changing the recipient of violence. *Scandal* has depicted the state's torture, abuse, and murder of a great many anonymous or minor characters. More noticeably, the list of those individuals who have suffered physical brutality at the hands of the state contains much of the featured cast, including some of the people closest to Olivia, Harrison, Huck, Jake, and Quinn, and a long list of supporting characters.[1] What is important to note, however, is that almost all of these victims are White, and despite the violence surrounding her, Olivia's physical body remains inviolable.

By depicting state violence through non-Black characters, the narrative is able to call attention to the brutality that lies at the heart of US capitalism without engaging in the more standard narrativized spectacle of violence meted out to African American women who serve as the occasion for everyone else to experience pity and thereby reach their fullest humanity. In the War on Terror era, the representations of the institutions built to mete out violence are different from those representations of previous centuries, and at least part of this difference is registered in *Scandal*, where it is the African American woman who benefits from the status quo even when she opposes the violence and surveillance apparatus that benefit her. As explained to her by Eli "Rowan" Pope, her godlike spy-chief father who violently eliminates most threats to the American power structure and by extension to his power, "You may choose to pretend that what you do and how you live are not made possible by what I do and how I live. I do my job so that fatty can watch reality TV, eat fast food, stare at the Internet, screw their husbands or their battery-operated products, and never use their teeny, tiny brains to think about the freedoms that I make possible! Never think about the democracy that I make possible. They

---

1. There is a long list of supporting characters physically brutalized or murdered in the name of protecting the state or the status of the administration, including Billy Chambers, Jerry Grant, Andrew Nichols, James Novak, Adnan Salif, Amanda Tanner, and Verna Thornton.

never think about it, so they sleep like babies at night" ("It's Handled" [3.01]). In this speech, as in the show generally, there is no illusion that state violence is occasioned only by states of exception. *Scandal* consistently and memorably represents the scope of violence required to maintain the regular operations of American life—not merely in an attempt to legitimize the violence, as in so much of dominant media discourse, but also to illustrate its destructive pervasiveness. In this way, the program maintains a certain ambivalence toward violence that is echoed in the equivocal position Olivia occupies vis-à-vis dominant power. She uses her insider status to erode the extralegal aspects of the United States' security and surveillance apparatus, even as she remains deeply committed to it.

Olivia's Body

Given her unique insight and ambivalent position as insider-outsider, Olivia lives with a great deal of fear, but she is not characterized by fear. She is not a fearful body, which is to say she does not characteristically do those things that fearful bodies do: make themselves compressed and small or try to make themselves invisible. It is here that Olivia's much-discussed wardrobe takes on another resonance beyond sheer eye candy, which certainly it is, to become an announcement of her determination to remain highly visible.[2]

In this way, the show counters its own frightening spectacles of violence with the hope of resistance and refusal that is presented not in the grand spectacles of so many Hollywood films where exposing the truth of corruption results in the vindication of the just and expulsion of the crooked. Here hope is found in small acts of resistance and small victories that become part of her regular work life. Thus, if the elder Pope is the embodiment of state violence and sub rosa power, Olivia embodies the resistance to them, at least in the show's first

---

2. As Kerry Washington explains, Olivia's well-tailored, soft-colored business suits in early seasons are part of her character's visual presentation of herself as a caring but effective power broker (Kamp and Diehl 2013).

several seasons, by trying to stop him and undermine his highly illegal branch of the Central Intelligence Agency as well as using her skills in other ways, such as helping good people get elected to office or to keep their jobs and by pushing Fitz to be a better president. But these acts can add up to only a termite strategy in the face of unmitigatedly violent forces hell-bent on maintaining their position. This asymmetry reflects a larger trend both in the actual US War on Terror and in the representation of state violence on TV generally where the number of scenes representing torture and sadistic torture has doubled since the terror attacks of September 11, 2001 (Hall 2013).

To reflect on just how *Scandal*'s presentation of state violence is unique, it is helpful to contrast it with other programs. When we consider post-9/11 programming about state violence and torture, the urtext is surely the Fox network series *24* (running from 2001 to 2010, with a sequel, *24: Live Another Day*, in 2014).

With its graphic depictions of savagery in the name of national security and its contrived ticking-time-bomb scenarios in which hero Jack Bauer has literally twenty-four hours to prevent a spectacular tragedy and thus uses any method possible to obtain information, *24* sparked a national discussion on the use of torture.[3] With self-declared fans as well placed as then vice president Dick Cheney, Supreme Court justice Antonin Scalia, and conservative radio icon Rush Limbaugh, *24* enjoyed the status of a kind of unofficial state ideology. Justice Scalia even cited the show as an example of why torture is a necessary legal option (Lithwick 2008), rejecting a body of legal literature refuting the legitimacy of the ticking-time-bomb scenario that is used to excuse any number of otherwise illegal and immoral actions (for example, see Luban 2005). Of course, just watching a few seasons of the program

---

3. Each episode covers the time span of one day, a chronology emphasized by a dramatic ticking clock on-screen that subtracts the sixty minutes of each hour-long episode, making up the twenty-four episodes of each season. The ticking clock even marks the actual time between commercial breaks, dramatically counting down the minutes until certain doom—or maybe just until the next instance when Jack can hurt someone.

itself could make the case against torture, as *24* devolved into self-parody through the increasing absurdity of the contrived circumstances created to instill a tension that could be released only in that hour's orgasmic scene(s) of torture. In this way, the program seems to act less as a statement about the need for uncompromising governmental agents and more of a kind of "collective catharsis" working to shore up the myth of American masculine authority that was damaged by 9/11 (Hall 2013, 268).

The show *24* is able to sustain a unique level of human-rights violation, both by creating a state of exception through its twenty-four-hours-until-doomsday framework and by avoiding the obvious pitfalls of representing torture as something White men do to Black bodies. The show presents a great variety of ticking-time-bomb scenarios occasioned by sociopaths from various racial and ethnic backgrounds— European, Arab, Hispanic. Indeed, the president in whose interest the torture is being committed is in the show's first seasons a Black man and in later seasons is succeeded by a White woman. In these ostensible recodings of the circumstances of torture, the show attempts, albeit lamely, to moderate the discussion of race and racism accompanying actual US torture in the so-called War on Terror by representing women and Black men—those persons who have traditionally been torture's victims—as today's beneficiaries of it. In this way, the audience is not forced to confront the underlying problem that the United States' War on Terror, which provides the occasion for all the sadistic violence, has shown itself to be a biopolitical race war (Ventura 2016).

What's more, the program doubles down on its ideological gamble of condoning torture by going a step further and representing the greatest victim of torture as Jack himself. Not only does he experience severe psychological trauma as his loved ones become increasingly alienated from him, and not only does his antiterror activity put him at great risk and subject him to intense physical abuse, but within the economy of the show perhaps even more painful than the bodily violence or the loss of loved ones is the psychic trauma Jack experiences. This trauma is caused by the fact that he has been forced by the evil actions of his victims to stoop to their level by committing evil acts of his own. The real criminal then is not Jack but the person who has vital information and forces Jack into becoming a torturer in order to obtain it. This predicament for cultural theorist Slavoj Žižek (2006) is the crux of *24*'s sadism—that the show presents Jack, not the people he tortures, as the narrative's true victim. Just as Adolf Eichmann, according to Hannah Arendt's account of his trial, saw himself as the true victim of the Holocaust because following orders and pursuing his duties required him to commit such horrible acts, Žižek sees the program positioning Bauer as the hero because he has allowed himself to become evil in the performance of his duties.

For its part, the economy of torture in *Scandal* operates differently. Torturers are not Jack Bauers or SS soldiers "ennobled" by doing the necessary dirty work of the state. They are not noble at all but scary, pathetic, and broken. *Scandal*'s torturers enjoy the pain they inflict and enjoy the power they possess, and in witnessing their pleasure both the characters and the audience see that they are psychically ruined by the reality that they have become brutal sadists. Unlike *24*'s ticking-time-bomb trope in which torture is allowed because of the exigency of the circumstances, *Scandal* represents violence as a fundamental part of normal operations of the state itself.

In the wake of *24*, as well as with the images from places like the Abu Ghraib prison in Iraq showing real-life human-rights violations of detainees held by American forces, torture has popularly become an expected part of today's mediated presentation of US covert operations. Indeed, the plot twists in the second decade after 9/11 center not on macho Jack Bauer types but on women agents forced to come to grips with the fact of torture. From the prominent scenes of torture in Kathryn Bigelow's *Zero Dark Thirty* (2012) to programs such as Showtime's *Homeland* (2011–19) and more forgettable programs such as CBS's *Madam Secretary* (2014–) or NBC's *State of Affairs* (2014–15), there is a kind of primal scene in which the White female agent protagonist has to overcome her personal emotions and opposition to torture because she wants the truth that will save American lives. But yet again, *Scandal* differs from other presentations of women in these unique positions because it does not show violence as a desperate response to unique circumstances that we all should accept because even women—the guardians of conscience and civilization by traditional heteronormative standards—have accepted it.

Scandal's protagonists refuse to excuse or be shocked by state violence and acknowledge the actual position that it occupies in US history—as standard operating procedure whose primary purpose is to enable those individuals in power to keep their power while degrading and psychically destroying both the victims of torture and those people who administer it. This attitude reflects a unique-for-TV historical awareness of the violent history of White treatment of subaltern populations in the United States. It refuses the dominant mythology that continues today to shape most presentations of state violence in American pop media—what Richard Slotkin (1973) characterizes as the "myth of regeneration through violence" that enables the forces of American social dominance to justify using savage techniques in the name of protecting and expanding the self-identified forces of civilization.

Instead, we see that state violence is endemic and cruel and ennobles no one. Indeed, all in the power structure have literal blood on their hands: as when Jake, the head of arguably the most powerful agency of government, B613, personally executes those persons who threaten the structure of unfair advantages the privileged enjoy (Jake kills James, a reporter, to prevent him from exposing a massive White House cover-up of murder), or when even the president, the embodiment of the nation itself, personally beats up suspects to elicit a confession (as Fitz does to Jake when he mistakenly believes Jake ordered the killing of his son).

Most important, in a program centered on a Black woman and in which violence is such a prominent narrative element, the protagonist is not the direct victim of physical violence. Olivia suffers—she is depressed, morose, scared, and psychologically scarred—but her body is not physically violated, even when she is kidnapped and imprisoned. In this way, Olivia's near untouchability brings a different kind of visibility to the United States' historic violence through its absence upon her body.

In this regard, we must consider the traditional narrative of beating that Hartman argues "readily lends itself to an identification with the enslaved . . . at the risk of fixing and naturalizing this condition of pained embodiment" (1997, 20). Consider in more specific terms the iconic brutality of torture upon Black women's backs—from Toni Morrison's former-slave protagonist Sethe in *Beloved* (1987) whose back looks like a "chokecherry tree" to the "horror" Solomon Northup describes at his and Epps's whipping of Patsey in *12 Years a Slave* (1853)[4] to the whip-mark scars permanently etched on the back of Kerry Washington's Broomhilda character in *Django Unchained* (2012).

These images force the audience to appreciate the humanity of the slave but do so by reinscribing her relative powerlessness. As such, they both compare and contrast with the representation of the scarred back in the episode "Where's the Black Lady?" (4.11), belonging not to an African American but a White woman, Elizabeth North, whose back Huck has shredded with some unseen instrument of violence from his torture toolbox in order to coerce her to help him recover the kidnapped Olivia. *Scandal*'s reversal is further enhanced by the uselessness of the information Elizabeth helps provide since Olivia in fact enacts her own escape plan: if her kidnappers had been working for the vice president who coerced the president to start a war as ransom for Olivia, she arranges with her kidnappers to sell herself on the black market in order to undercut the vice president's leverage. Though she is held in deplorable conditions, Olivia's body is never beaten, and she is never raped. In fact, she even taunts the kidnappers with their inability to hurt her. But whereas Olivia's body is inviolable, Elizabeth North, who as head of the Republican Party would seem to possess great power in one of the chief institutions preserving White privilege, actually becomes the embodiment of abuse and victimization. Olivia's trajectory in the episode—from an ungroomed captive resembling her Broomhilda character to well-dressed, coifed human trafficker jetting

---

4. The nineteenth-century slave narrative was famously turned into a movie in 2013 (directed by Steve McQueen) and won three Academy Awards.

in a private plane—contrasts drastically with the story of Elizabeth. And while Kerry Washington's Broomhilda and Olivia are, within their narratives, the inspiration for massive destruction wrought by lovers who want to free them from captivity, *Scandal* operates in a very different economy from *Django*. Here Olivia arranges for her own sale in order to find a way to free herself.

Thus, if violent capture, human trafficking, and back scarring have been signs of blackness in US history, the episode "Where's the Black Lady" and the program more generally turns that equation upside down. Here, we may well ask, just who is "the Black lady" if scarring has come to be a signifier of female blackness in slavery narratives and if it is Elizabeth who bears the scars administered by a White man in order to instill fear and compliance, while the putative "Black lady" sets up the conditions that will lead to her freedom? Such rewritings of torture and its victims denaturalize American racial and gender hierarchies, while highlighting the American historical use of torture to enforce those very race and gender hierarchies.

This same kind of reversal characterizes the reception of the war that the vice president demanded as a condition for keeping Olivia alive in the kidnapping narrative arc. When Olivia rejects the president's love of her as a rationale for starting a war, the final element of reversal has been instituted. Here, Fitz and Mellie Grant, two of the most powerful people in the world, signed on to starting a war in order to keep his mistress alive. For Olivia, their action represented a certain turning point. If in the past she experienced guilt and remorse about her relationship with Fitz because it was a personal weakness and a moral failing, the kidnapping and Fitz's response move their relationship beyond the private into a geopolitical global terrain. As an allegory, the shifting of the affair from personal failing to war crime highlights the larger terrain upon which the program's story lines operate; personal melodramas are repositioned as larger statements illustrating the instrumentalizing of human life both today and in the past.

Indeed, the story reaches beyond American history into classical mythology, rendering Olivia a latter-day Helen of Troy—a historical rewriting foreshadowed by Tom, the Secret Service agent who had previously likened Olivia to Helen in her great beauty and power over the president. But here she rewrites this mythical antecedent by rejecting the man who authorized the war in her name. If hers is the contemporary face that launched a thousand ships, or a carrier group, as it were, Olivia rewrites history by rejecting the privileges that allow her life to be spared at the cost of so many others. She rejects the president's proclamation of love.

In this kidnapping arc, as throughout the series, Olivia does not emerge unscathed, even though she does not experience physical brutality. The sadness and horror that are regular parts of her life play out affectively on her, and she suffers deep depressions that she tries to hide behind her resourcefulness and beauty. But she does not merely continue her life as if these acts were not occurring. Victims of violence reach out to her, finding her even when she escapes to an uncharted island on the other side of the globe—as when she responded to the call to deal with Harrison's murder—or leading her to a local Washington neighborhood to help an aggrieved father whose son was unjustly killed by a police officer.

Olivia in the Age of Obama

When Olivia responds to the plight of people in need, she never couches her response in terms of a consistent set of political positions. Oddly, in a series set in Washington, DC, in which politics features so prominently in the story line, Olivia seems to be nearly a blank slate politically. As she explains it, she is nonpartisan. For their part, both President Fitzgerald and President Mellie Grant are liberal Republicans, and through the reasonable presentation of their agendas, the show itself seems to endorse issues that are typically coded as liberal, such as gun control, equal pay for women, and women's right to access abortion. But Olivia herself seems to be invested in few particularly ideological positions, which actually brings her close to the real-life president Barack Obama.

Columnist Thomas Frank has argued that Democratic presidential nominees since Jimmy Carter have positioned themselves as outside ideology. In the case of Carter and Obama, they represented themselves as intelligent outsiders operating beyond the usual political arrangements. However, as Frank warns, "Being a 'blank screen' or the personal object of the enthusiasm of millions—these may play well when a candidate is unknown, but they are postures impossible to maintain as president . . . [and lead] inevitably to disappointment and disillusionment" (2014).

But where Frank's comparison between Obama and Carter falls apart is that as the first African American president, Barack Obama cannot truly be a "blank screen"—at least not at this historical juncture. He is imbued with meaning by virtue of his race and position as the first African American to occupy his office. So too Olivia Pope, as one of the most well-known African American protagonists on dramatic television, is imbued with meaning. Yet the meaning comes by virtue of her positionality as much as from any specific position she actually takes. Indeed, showrunner Shonda Rhimes created a program about a Black woman who is singularly placed in national events yet is representationally rich enough to feel familiar to the show's African American audience—even as *Scandal*'s producers assiduously avoid letting it be seen as a "Black show." Much of the media hype surrounding the program—for example, Kerry Washington's cover articles in magazines such as *Vanity Fair*, *In Style*, and *Parade*—discuss race and center on the fact that race is not a focus of the show. Here is a typical excerpt from *Vanity Fair*'s article by contributor David Kamp and Jessica Diehl:

> That Olivia has transcended her racial identity, and that *Scandal* has transcended pigeonholing as "a Black person's show" (and, for that matter, as a women's show), is a tribute to *Scandal*'s creator, Rhimes. We as a nation have not yet fulfilled the promise of being a post-racial society, of which Barack Obama's election was supposed to be an augury, but in ShondaLand race is almost an afterthought. Rhimes, herself an African American woman, commands an empire . . . [of programs] nonchalantly populated with smart, able people of both sexes and various races—more notable for the

sheer fact of their diversity than for any explicit discussion of race within their episodes. (2013)

Scandal is about race, but unlike the coverage of the show suggests, it is about race in more ways than the contemporary neoliberal context theorized by David Theo Goldberg (2009) in which race and racism can never be named as such. If we see *Scandal* in relation to the age of Obama, then we see the story of a post–civil rights narrative about the phenomenon of people whose racial background explicitly shapes their experiences in ways that they recognize as deeply meaningful and that they publicly own but that they speak about in new ways.

In a more critical perspective on the representation of race, Eduardo Bonilla-Silva and Austin Ashe deride ShondaLand productions as emerging from an "abstract liberal frame" that presents "racial issues in an abstract manner using the language of liberalism." They contrast Rhimes's programs, particularly *Grey's Anatomy* (2005–), with HBO's *The Wire* (2002–8) that they characterize as "dealing with the realities of race" (2014, 69) in its complex depictions even of stereotypical characters such as Black drug dealers and single mothers. These scholars maintain that representations such as the ones from ShondaLand are epiphenomena of what is commonly named the "new racism" that reproduces racial inequality by promoting the ideology of "color-blind racism," arguing further that the ideology operates optimally now that the United States actually has elected a Black president because "the new racial order works better in Blackface" (71).

Certainly, in the age of Obama, racial discourse did not utilize the same language it may once have. Indeed, the phrase "age of Obama" has become a term describing approaches for opposing racism and for addressing race that are different from previous critical contexts—perhaps the critical approaches that scholars such as Bonilla-Silva require to find resistance to racism legible at all. However, it was the presence of Obama as president that helped make racism legible in popular media discourses too long stuck in the mode of neoliberal racism that Goldberg identifies. The age of Obama enabled a discussion of structural racism made evident by the obvious contrast between what Obama's election was assumed to represent and the reality of structural inequality and social death for millions of African Americans.

Consider again the episode "Where's the Black Lady?" (4.11) that specifically names Olivia's blackness in the title. The episode demands that the audience recognize Olivia's race, especially in a key scene in which Rose, a friend of Olivia's neighbor, comes to the Olivia Pope & Associates offices in search of Olivia. "The Black lady she's still not here? . . . I need to talk to the Black lady. . . . [My friend] gave the Black lady her spare key." The repetition of "Black lady" emphasizes this description, and even Quinn starts to use the phrase.

Key to understanding the centrality of this scene is to consider that the visitor is played by Marla Gibbs, arguably most famous for being the outspoken housekeeper on *The Jeffersons* (1975–85). That sitcom of the early post–civil rights era was important because it staged larger cultural struggles with integration and comically opened the way for mediated redefinitions of Black identity. Despite Gibbs's brief appearance in *Scandal*, the scene creates a sharp generational contrast between Olivia and Gibbs's character who, besides signifying an older presentation of mediated African American identity as Florence on *The Jeffersons*, describes herself as "old" and speaks with the conversational privileges that the elderly enjoy of being allowed to talk bluntly without concern for the niceties of contemporary coded language: she simply describes Olivia as the Black lady who helps people. And in the bluntness of this presentation, Olivia's race is foregrounded, but it is foregrounded to be defined in new ways in a narrative arc that includes not only a White woman being scarred but also Olivia arranging to have herself sold at auction as a way to rewrite her imprisonment and free herself.

What we begin to see is that this show acts as a container for many different cultural impulses that lead us to confront racism, even if the show rarely uses the language or iconography associated historically with the topic. Racism is everywhere, and it is quotidian and so emerges in numerous ways beyond the stereotypical inner city.

Tellingly, Bonilla-Silva and Ashe accuse Rhimes of dodging the key racial issues in her promise that in ShondaLand productions, "We're not going to have a Black, drug-dealing single-mother selling crack." These critics take the lack of presentation of such problems as an unwillingness to confront "the realities of race" (69). However, it is fairer to say Rhimes has found other ways to present "the realities of race." If *Scandal* does not depict the social institutions that create crack-dealing single moms—such as inadequate schools or deindustrialized cities—the program does represent racial inequalities and gender struggle as part of the roadblocks that Black people and Black women specifically have to overcome. Consider here the phrase that Rowan forces Olivia to repeat as he excoriates her for having an affair with the president, "[You have to be] twice as good as them to get half of what they have" (3.01). The statement has become famous in social media as viewers revel in the familiar presentation of an African American dad's admonition to his child. And because the pronouns in this sentence are vague, they have taken on a broad resonance with many groups. For instance, they may well reference her gender as well as her race, and thus reflect the program's more complex understanding of intersectional social forces, thereby highlighting both the race- and the gender-based oppressions she must overcome. So, too, we learn that Olivia's neighbor and Rose (Marla Gibbs's character) were more than just friends, but they had to hide their love for each other their entire lives since "it was hard enough being Black, let alone Black and gay" ("The Testimony of Diego Muñoz" [4.15]).

Scandal's Racialized Queer Family Melodrama

In this rerouting of racialized discourse, *Scandal* is not unique. Indeed, Sharon Patricia Holland, for instance, argues that there is necessary work in conceptualizing race in terms of the erotic—what she describes as "the personal and political dimensions of desire" (2012, 32). This framework helpfully highlights *Scandal*'s presentation of race conflict, as in the example with Olivia's father above or, in another example, when Olivia describes herself as Sally Hemings to the president's Thomas Jefferson ("Happy Birthday, Mr. President"

[2.08]). In this way, *Scandal* redraws the political racial framework, but, as a melodrama, the political discourse emerges within the sphere of erotic and family relationships. And if, as scholars of melodrama such as Linda Williams argue, melodrama seeks "dramatic revelation of moral and emotional truths through a dialectic of pathos and action" (1998, 42), *Scandal* provides these revelations in the context of the Obama era.

If melodrama has traditionally (and unfairly) been dismissed as a depoliticizing form because it focuses on individualized actions and choices rather than larger social circumstances, this melodrama uses key reversals to rewrite real-life historical antecedents such as the Hemings-Jefferson affair and, in a more contemporary frame, Bill Clinton's presidency. After all, in a reversal of Clinton's affair with Monica Lewinsky, *Scandal* gives us this: a White male president who is willing to throw his presidency away for his African American mistress and who performs oral sex on *her* in the White House.

If their affair constitutes one of the program's central ways of framing race and reframing the parameters of race discourse, then we must consider the way in which the program reframes social death itself through its institutional form as B613. And B613 is the territory of Rowan Pope, the African American patriarch who refers to the president of the United States as "boy" ("A Door Marked Exit" [3.10]) and explains to his daughter, "I know more than you could possibly imagine about things of which you cannot dream" ("It's Handled" [3.01]). Here, Rowan has built his own world, both illustrating and at the same time reversing, pace Jared Sexton's reading of Fred Moten, "how black social life steals away or escapes from the law, how it frustrates the police power and, in so doing, calls that very policing into being in the first place" (2012, 23).

If such reversals rewrite the parameters of race and racism, they do not overlook the fact of racism existing both in the real world and in *Scandal*'s version of it. This point is clear throughout the series—not simply in the explicit moments such as those provided by the episode "The Lawn Chair" (4.14) that reenacts the wrongful death of Michael Brown in Ferguson, Missouri, in 2014. In this regard, we may well consider two finale episodes, season two's finale, "White Hat's Back On" (2.22), and the season-three midseason finale, "A Door Marked Exit" (3.10). In both of these episodes, a scandal has been created that blindsides each of the Popes—Olivia, in season two, who has to contend with the public release of her identity as the president's mistress, and Rowan, in season three, who finds himself imprisoned and chained in the Pentagon. In both cases, the Popes were caught off balance by the machinations of President Fitzgerald Grant—the man who embodies White privilege as the leader of a nation where whiteness remains a profoundly advantageous position and as a man whose life story is one of access and inherited wealth.

If he has the power establishment and a tradition of privilege and double standards protecting him, Olivia finds she must rely on her own wits and her team of Gladiators to help her. It is they who are there for her and become her queer family who share a life outside the conventional narratives of connection and heterosexual family centered on reproduction. So, too, not only is the conception of family rewritten, but so is the idea of home. It is certainly not a private space outside an ostensibly public world of work or politics that traditional ideologies of the domestic sphere may lead us to expect. Indeed, Olivia's home has an almost comic permeability, as any number of individuals enter surreptitiously—her dad, her boyfriends, her kidnappers. But this porousness only highlights the ways that *Scandal* erodes traditional expectations of separate public and private worlds, leaving both to be characterized by violence, depression, and great loss.

In such ways, *Scandal* uses the melodramatic settings of home and family to allegorize contemporary life and social death. The result is a confirmation, in a hyperbolic style, of course, of the complicated reality that African American women contended with even in the age of Obama. Now, in the post-Obama era defined by a Trumpist backlash against the progress Obama represented, popular media centering on Black women gains a different, and perhaps even greater, significance as part of a new era of cultural struggle.

References

Arendt, Hannah. 1958. *The Origins of Totalitarianism*. Orlando: Harcourt Brace.

Bonilla-Silva, Eduardo, and Austin Ashe. 2014. "The End of Racism: Color-blind Racism and Popular Media." In *The Colorblind Screen: Television in Post-racial America*, edited by Sarah Nilsen and Sarah E. Turner, 57–79. New York: New York Univ. Press.

Frank, Thomas. 2014. "We Are Such Losers." *Salon*, Oct. 26. http://www.salon.com/2014/10/26/thomas_frank_we_are_such_losers/.

Goldberg, David Theo. 2009. *The Threat of Race: Reflections on Racial Neoliberalism*. Malden, MA: Blackwell.

Hall, Amy Laura. 2013. "Torture and Television in the United States." *Muslim World* 103(2): 267–86.

Hartman, Saidiya V. 1997. *Scenes of Subjection: Terror, Slavery, and Self-Making in Nineteenth-Century America*. New York: Oxford Univ. Press.

Holland, Sharon Patricia. 2012. *The Erotic Life of Racism*. Durham, NC: Duke Univ. Press.

Kamp, David, and Jessica Diehl. 2013. "Ms. Kerry Goes to Washington: The First Lady of *Scandal* Speaks." *Vanity Fair*, Aug. http://www.vanityfair.com/style/2013/08/kerry-washington-scandal-cover-story.

Lithwick, Dalia. 2008. "How Jack Bauer Shaped U.S. Torture Policy." *Newsweek*, July 25. http://www.newsweek.com/lithwick-how-jack-bauer-shaped-ustorture-policy-93159.

Luban, David. 2005. "Liberalism, Torture, and the Ticking Bomb." *Virginia Law Review* 91: 1425–61. http://scholarship.law.georgetown.edu/facpub/148/.

Patterson, Orlando. 1982. *Slavery and Social Death: A Comparative Study*. Cambridge, MA: Harvard Univ. Press.

Roberts, Dorothy. 2008. "Torture and the Biopolitics of Race." *University of Miami Law Review* 62: 229–48.

Sexton, Jared. 2010. "People-of-Color-Blindness: Notes on the Afterlife of Slavery." *Social Text* 28(2): 31–56.

———. 2012. "Ante-anti-blackness: Afterthoughts." *Lateral* 1. http://lateral.culturalstudiesassociation.org/issue1/content/sexton.html.

Slotkin, Richard. 1973. *Regeneration through Violence: The Mythology of the American Frontier, 1600–1860*. Norman: Univ. of Oklahoma Press.

Ventura, Patricia. 2016. *Neoliberal Culture: Living with American Neoliberalism*. New York: Routledge.

Williams, Linda. 1998. "Melodrama Revised." In *Refiguring American Film Genres: Theory and History*, edited by Nick Browne, 42–88. Berkeley: Univ. of California Press.

Žižek, Slavoj. 2006. "Jack Bauer and the Ethics of Urgency." *In These Times*, Jan. 27. http://www.egs.edu/faculty/slavoj-zizek/articles/jack-bauer-and-the-ethics-of-urgency/.

4 | The Power of Whiteness

Disciplining Olivia Pope

SHANTEL GABRIEAL BUGGS
AND RYESSIA JONES RUSSELL

WHILE THE DISCUSSION regarding race, sex, and gender in *Scandal* emphasizes the portrayal of interracial relationships—specifically the love triangle between Olivia Pope, President Fitzgerald "Fitz" Grant III, and Captain Jake Ballard—the majority of Olivia's interactions are informed by whiteness. Olivia upholds various social norms as she engages in intimate relationships with White men, wears the "white hat," associates mostly with White colleagues, and consistently uses her resources to save the careers and lives of White political figures. In this chapter, we utilize content analysis and close reading to explore how whiteness emerges in *Scandal*; our analysis focuses on how whiteness is utilized as a mechanism for policing and disciplining the Black female body by assessing Olivia's relationships with several characters: Fitz, Jake, First Lady Millicent "Mellie" Grant, White House Press Secretary Abigail "Abby" Whelan, and Olivia's father, Eli "Rowan" Pope.

Whiteness, as a structural system of inequality rooted in legacies of patriarchal colonialism and capitalism, has served as a category of privilege in the United States since the nation's founding. Particular bodies—male, heterosexual, White, and financially secure—possess social and political power, maintaining a structural hierarchy where people of color and women are disenfranchised. This disenfranchisement relies upon *discipline*, the modern training, observation, and control practices that enable the creation of "docile" bodies (Foucault 1995). Olivia threatens the spaces intended for whiteness (Puwar 2004); because of the privilege required to gain access, Olivia is forced to prove herself worthy of occupying the White House. Olivia's blackness becomes particularly visible when it "underscores the White privilege of other *Scandal* characters or draws attention to the simmering inequity between Pope and her White counterparts" (Pixley 2015).

The relationships within *Scandal*'s universe utilize whiteness in different ways; we use them as a means of exploring three forms of discipline: sexual discipline, familial discipline, and gender discipline. These forms of discipline are not mutually exclusive, as they are sexualized, racialized, classed, and gendered. However, by breaking these disciplinary forms into categories, we can focus on particular aspects of Olivia Pope's relationships and how they work to surveil and constrain her behavior, her body, and her identity, as well as how these constraints might translate onto the bodies of the Black women who constitute the show's audience.

Color Blindness and the Control of Black Womanhood

The past several years have been a case study in the lack of representation, and recognition, of the performances of people of color in both film and television. Though privileged, aged White heterosexual men hold virtually all power, Shonda Rhimes and her peers are a respite from this power inequality and fodder for industry insiders and viewers to question the entertainment industry's color blindness. Color-blind ideology promotes the idea of equal opportunity and the notion that racism no longer exists or impacts the life chances of racial minorities. Color blindness allows Whites in particular to posit that they do not "see" race. Therefore, the dominance of color blindness in television has sustained contemporary racial structure(s) by making the "reality" of racial economic inequality, segregation, and discrimination invisible to mainstream (White) America. As Sarah Nilsen and Sarah E. Turner (2014) argue, the "color-blind screen" fails to challenge White racial apathy, instead perpetuating postracial ideals.

We take popular culture seriously because the media is a "necessary site for understanding racial ideologies" as it contributes to the (re)production and transformation of racial logics and discourses (Bonilla-Silva and Ashe 2014). The value of whiteness is protected through color-blind rhetoric, as the roles for people of color still tend to wax stereotypical, and diverse casts serve to support color blindness through "symbolic inclusion" (Bonilla-Silva and Ashe 2014). C. Richard King notes that shows centering exclusively on Whites have appeal because they "celebrate a vision of the heterosexual nuclear family with marked gender roles and a clear sexual hierarchy" (2014, 227). Whiteness as a social construction informs not only how we understand sexuality, gender, and family in the "real" world but also our fictional worlds.

Social concerns for sex(uality) are rooted in demands for bodily self-discipline (Foucault 1990). Because social power is exercised through sex, sex and sexuality become imbued with great importance. In television and film, interracial relationship story lines are often limited and never fully developed (Childs 2009). If interracial relationships are featured in side story lines, these relationships are often used to offer comic relief, cause conflict, provide some type of shock value, or highlight social and racial differences (Childs 2009). When interracial relationships occur, to justify the relationship the person of color is often described as someone who is extraordinary and transracial, while the White person is framed as someone who is good. Barbara Perry and Michael Sutton note that popular culture influences and reflects people's perceptions of interracial relationships. The current cultural emphasis on sex and sexuality—particularly around interracial relationships and same-sex relationships—hinges on concerns for "healthy" or proper sexuality. Although these depictions of interracial relationships are rare in television and film, when interracial relationships are displayed they tend to be portrayed as "inherently dangerous to 'racial purity'" and "unnatural" (Perry and Sutton 2006, 888). These portrayals reinforce hegemonic ideologies by reminding Blacks and Whites of the consequences of these relationships. Further, when considering the sexual scripts available to (heterosexual) women, desire and pleasure are considered optional, with women's sexual role framed as passive and acquiescing. For women of color, (hetero)sexuality is reframed and racialized as promiscuity or complete desexualization (hooks 1992; Spillers 2003; Collins 2005).

The images of Black women as Jezebels, "thots," and hoochies in television and film sexually exploit Black women, reinforcing hegemonic ideologies. These ideologies rationalize and legitimize the marginalization of Black women (Lundy 2018). Although shows like *A Different World* (NBC, 1987–93), *Living Single* (Fox, 1993–98), *Being Mary Jane* (BET, 2013–18), *Black-ish* (ABC, 2014–), *Chewing Gum* (E4/Netflix, 2015/2016–17), and *Insecure* (HBO, 2016–) provide positive depictions of Black women having emotional and intellectual value, these images are overshadowed by representations of Black women's physicalities and sexualities (Bailey 1988). Because these controlling images are hegemonic, it almost becomes impossible for Black women viewers to escape internalizing these negative stereotypes. Olivia Pope is an amalgam of Patricia Hill Collins's controlling images, at once embodying the "educated Black bitch," the desexualized "Black lady," and the hypersexual "freak." Olivia's relationships with Fitz and Jake engage a variety of sexual scripts, with Olivia both embracing and trying to reject gender and racial stereotypes. Black female sexuality, then, is limited by "appropriate" sex being understood through a White lens. This restricted definition is why bodies of color are considered literally and figuratively consumable and why Black women in particular are read as "selling hot pussy" (hooks 1992) rather than as sexual, agential beings.

As Hortense Spillers suggests, the Black family is viewed as having "no father to speak of," which is the "fault of the daughter, or the female line" (2003, 204). Olivia's entire familial dynamic relies on her overbearing father's disappointment in her, blaming their "failed" family on Olivia and her mother, Maya. Collins (2005) notes the class dynamic within contemporary notions of Black masculinity, where Black men oscillate between being read as "bad-boy" athletes and "criminals" who are defined by their physical strength, hypersexuality, and violence or as nonthreatening, desexualized sidekicks whose masculinity is in service to Whites. While Black fatherhood is rarely seen through the latter lens—to be a father implies being a sexual being— the assumed criminality or violent physicality of Black men perpetuates the notion that they are incapable of being fathers. Therefore, redeeming this image of Black masculinity forces an engagement with White familial norms. Eli Pope embraces the violence and criminality of masculinity but is also rendered relatively desexualized through his assimilation into White modes of being. In fact, Eli relies on norms of White masculinity to inform his relationship with Olivia. As Frantz Fanon argues, the greater the assimilation into whiteness, the closer one comes to "becoming a true human being" (2008 [1952], 2–3). In this case, the more closely the family comes to a "traditional" formation—based on a heteronormative, White patriarchal model—the more socially acceptable and functional it becomes.

American womanhood defaults to this "traditional" whiteness. It is not so much about "acting White" as it is about performing a particular classed heterosexual femininity. Frankenberg (1993) argues that whiteness is put forward as the "default" or "baseline" American; therefore, how we understand gender in the United States operates through our understanding(s) of whiteness. Historically, access to White womanhood depends on social distance from physical labor and hypersexuality; working-class European women could be rendered Black in the social imagination owing to their unsatisfactory performance of upper-class femininity (McClintock 1995). This legacy remains, even as mainstream second-wave feminist understandings of White middle-class womanhood have opened up opportunities for women to be viewed as competent and independent. Within this gender logic, White femininity is defined in opposition to masculinity; stereotypes and derogatory imagery are used to describe not only the men that White women engage with in interracial relationships (Frankenberg 1993) but also the women of color who are masculinized in order to shore up understandings of White womanhood (Collins 2005).

Olivia Pope and the Disciplinary Role of Whiteness

As the main protagonist in *Scandal*, Olivia deftly leads a highly competent team of Washington, DC's political and problem-solving "Gladiators." Olivia's character has a variety of relationships that are representative of color-blind logics and whiteness as normative; *Scandal* appears to succeed because it is viewed not as a "Black" show but rather as a show that happens to have a Black main character (Vega 2013). In discussing her role of Olivia Pope, Kerry Washington suggests that the show is successful because of White women's connection to her character. She mentions, "The fact that White women can see this woman of color as an aspirational character is revolutionary, I think, in the medium of television. I don't think White women would feel that way about Olivia if her identity as a *woman*, period, wasn't first in their mind" (Kamp and Diehl 2013). The fact that Olivia Pope was the first Black female major network lead in a drama series in nearly forty years,[1] and that the show does not explicitly deal with race, further illustrates the power of color-blind liberalism and meritocracy in informing the construction of compelling television characters. Though Olivia's connections to whiteness are made apparent throughout *Scandal*—particularly during the show's early seasons with her signifying of morality through an all-white wardrobe and the wearing of a symbolic "white" hat, illustrating how "purity" is central to the social identity of whiteness—our analysis here centers on seasons three through five's visual, sonic, and dialogic texts.

Sexual Discipline

Olivia's sexuality and body are presented as a form of "property" belonging alternatively to Fitz and Jake over the course of the show,

---

1. Kerry Washington's Olivia Pope has since been joined by the likes of Megan Good's Joanna Locasto (*Deception*, NBC) and Dr. Lara Vega (*Minority Report*, FOX), Nicole Beharie's Abigail Mills (*Sleepy Hollow*, FOX), Viola Davis's Annalise Keating (*How to Get Away with Murder*, ABC), Halle Berry's Dr. Molly Woods (*Extant*, CBS), Taraji P. Henson's Cookie Lyon (*Empire*, FOX), and Regina King's Aliyah Shadeed (*American Crime*, ABC), among others.

particularly in seasons three and four. Olivia's love triangle forces the audience to side with one of these men ("Team Jake" or "Team Fitz"), all while relying on a variety of tropes rooted in whiteness to demonstrate their worthiness. For instance, a dichotomy between Fitz and Jake is reinforced through Olivia's imagined "lives" with these two men: with Fitz, she desires "Vermont" and making jam from scratch ("Vermont Is for Lovers, Too" [3.08]), whereas with Jake, she desires to escape and "stand in the sun" ("The Price of Free and Fair Elections" [3.18]; "Randy, Red, Superfreak, and Julia" [4.01]). While there are obvious connections to whiteness in that Olivia's love interests are both White men, there are also symbolic connections. As of 2013, Vermont boasted a 93.8 percent non-Hispanic White population, with a home-ownership rate at 71 percent (US Census Bureau 2015). "Vermont" is a stand-in for White, middle-class, and traditional values, and Fitz reinforces these notions when he describes their possible future:

> OLIVIA: What is this place? Why am I here? Why the hell are we out here in the middle of the nowhere?!
>
> FITZ: This house is yours. Ours. I had it built for us. When it looked like there was a chance for us I bought the land, and I had it built. I couldn't really be mayor, but you can make jam. And there are bedrooms for lots of kids. [pauses] This was going to be you and me raising a family and growing old together in this house. It was supposed to be our house, Livvie. . . . I wanted you to see the dream. ("Vermont Is for Lovers, Too" [3.08])

As Olivia rushes across the room breathlessly, embracing Fitz and kissing him passionately, we are shown how much she, too, desires the "dream" in Vermont. It is the American dream, replete with land and home ownership, (heterosexual) marriage, multiple children, and growing old together. Olivia does not require more convincing than this speech, though moments before she was angry about being "summoned" and forced onto a helicopter.

By living in Vermont, Olivia would have her relationship with Fitz legitimized and eliminate ways the relationship imposes constraints.

As Fitz's mistress, Olivia is framed as a hypersexual Jezebel both within the show's universe and in the "real world." *Scandal's* media and political elites react scornfully to Olivia's multiple outings as Fitz's mistress ("White Hat's Back On" [2.22] "Heavy Is the Head" [5.01]), and real-world male audience members also deride female fans for idolizing a "hoe" and "side piece" (Bleu 2013). Viewers are treated to Olivia and Fitz eagerly engaging in intercourse in various corners of the White House or Olivia's signature lip quiver as she makes eye contact with Fitz. Olivia's entire relationship with Fitz is predicated on their sexual chemistry and phone calls rife with innuendo, as, up to season five, they had no opportunity to engage in a "proper" courtship. Olivia's attempts to end their relationship or make Fitz "earn her" ("Nobody Likes Babies" [2.13]) reify Fitz's entitlement to Olivia, demonstrated through summonses and his demands for Olivia's attention, body, and love. If Olivia will not come, Fitz will have the Secret Service collect her. If she tries to walk away, he will grab her to kiss her or force her into a closet to have sex. If she will not answer her phone, he will show up at her door. If she does not respond to his advances in the way he wants, he yells at her, warning her to "not dare" ("No More Blood" [4.13]) to tell him that they are over. Fitz operates under the assumption that Olivia will always want him, and Olivia tends to oblige. While kidnapped, Olivia assures her cell mate that the president would absolutely come to save her ("Run" [4.10]) and convinces her kidnappers to sell her to the highest bidder ("Where's the Black Lady?" [4.11]), demonstrating that Olivia recognizes her sexual value.

Alternatively, Olivia's relationship with Jake revolves around the notion of emotional and sexual escape. The "sun" invokes light, purity, and goodness, a direct contrast to Olivia's life in DC that became "dark" due to lies, corruption, death, and Olivia's derailed career. "Standing in the sun" with Jake allowed for an erasure of the circumstances that led to their being together, as well as Olivia's mistakes, especially in regards to fixing Fitz's election:

JAKE: Take me with you. Run away with me. Save me.

OLIVIA: [turns to face Jake] I am in love with someone else.

JAKE: You're leaving everything else behind. Leave that behind, too. Don't go alone. You don't have to be alone.
OLIVIA: [pauses] You want to stand in the sun with me.
JAKE: I want us to stand in the sun together. Will you do that? ("The Price of Free and Fair Elections" [3.18])

While Jake and Olivia fulfill the requirements of an upwardly mobile couple that mirrors Vermont, "standing in the sun" consists of living on a remote island and drinking rare, expensive red wine under the identity of Julia. In DC the relationship represents Olivia trying to escape her feelings for Fitz. When Olivia is first outed as the president's mistress, she avoids press scrutiny with a fake relationship with Jake ("No Sun on the Horizon" [3.13]). Fitz's control of Olivia being undermined by Jake allows the power struggle between these two White men for control of, and access to, Olivia's body and sexuality to become a major plot point for the show. This struggle over control of her body is clear in Jake's and Fitz's efforts to rescue Olivia from her kidnappers—Fitz was tempted into going to war, while Jake directed a fake drug raid and led the Gladiators in purchasing her freedom—but also in these two men's (un)spoken competition for Olivia's love.

Olivia's relationships are inherently messy and problematic: one man was married for virtually all of their relationship, while the other was initially hired to surveil and monitor her by her lover *and* her father. This situation creates unique circumstances through which her bodily autonomy and sexual autonomy are contained. Her disciplining is most evident through Fitz's attempts to monitor her movements via his political office, his use of Jake and his Secret Service personnel as tools to exert control, and his objectification of her to punish others. Fitz relishes in using his sexual access to Olivia to emotionally manipulate others; when he wanted to torture Eli, he reduced Olivia to a body in service: "I'm screwing her, you know. [pauses] Your daughter. Every chance I get. The things that I could tell you. About the way she tastes. She's quite a girl. Talented" ("A Door Marked Exit" [3.10]). Fitz believes that he can rattle Eli with allusions to what he has done, and what he *can* do, to Olivia. She is a tool for his political and vengeful use, which Fitz uses to manipulate Jake, Mellie, *and* Olivia, accusing Mellie of "not loving him" and "not being sexual" ("The Fluffer" [3.16]; "Flesh and Blood" [3.17]) and shutting Olivia down once she admits to him that she had been gone with Jake ("Like Father, Like Daughter" [4.04]).

However, Fitz is not the only one who uses his relationship with Olivia to hurt others. Jake, too, makes allusions to their closeness in order to repay Fitz for imprisoning him and beating him up: "That's one of our catchphrases, 'standing in the sun.' I'm not sure if you knew that. Probably not. It's from our time on the island together. Did Liv ever catch you up on that?" ("The Last Supper" [4.08]). Jake is smug here in his assertion that Olivia is his girlfriend, as it implies an officialness that Fitz and Olivia could not have at the time owing to Fitz's still being married. Jake even uses his relationship with Olivia to make her feel guilty: "We both know it's not my turn anymore. We both know we're not standing in the sun. We both know you're standing in the shade of 1600 Pennsylvania Avenue, and it's *his* turn. As long as we're back, it's always his turn, despite the fact that I'm the one you like to ride, that I'm the one that makes you moan, that I'm the one who reaches you in places . . . [whispers] that he can't begin to touch. Isn't that right? [storms out]" ("Randy, Red, Superfreak, and Julia" [4.01]). Jake's insistence about whose "turn" it is to have access to and, essentially, ownership over Olivia's body and affections fits within a heteronormative paternalistic frame that manipulates Olivia and reminds the audience of the power and privilege that are at stake in this love triangle. In fact, Jake's claims of sexual superiority continue after Olivia "chose" Fitz and became his "first lady." In a disconcerting exchange, Jake appears in Olivia's apartment one night ("The Fish Rots from the Head" [5.13]) after she followed him. He boasts about his new girlfriend and reminds Olivia of her place:

OLIVIA: [startled] What are you doing here?
JAKE: Giving you what you want.
OLIVIA: [glares with disdain] Giving me what I want?

JAKE: Well, you've been following me, right? Keeping tabs on me? [pauses while Olivia stares warily] I'm the head of the NSA. You don't get to keep tabs on me unless I allow you to.
OLIVIA: [nodding] I'm only going to ask you this one more time before I call the cops: Why are you here?
. . .
[Jake and Olivia stare silently]
JAKE: Of course, no one will ever do for you what I can do for you. [reaches across the bed between Olivia's legs]

Jake taunts Olivia by telling her to fight how "good" he is making her body feel, whispering that he "needs" her, when suddenly she stops him and demands to know what he is "up to." Jake also confronts Olivia about continuing to spy on him and his fiancée, inquiring, "Did you enjoy it, hmm? Watching us? . . . Did you get off when she got off?" ("I See You" [5.14]). Jake enjoys punishing Olivia for her desire of him and insinuates that he can satisfy her in ways others cannot. Further, his suggestion that Olivia "got off" infers sexual deviance. These exchanges render Olivia dysfunctional for her eagerness to have sex with Jake or to observe Jake having sex with his fiancée. Jake's tactics also convince Olivia to apologize and admit that she misses him, marking her as oversexed, illogical, jealous, and petty.

Jake's manipulation reminds viewers of how he fought with Fitz in the Central Intelligence Agency (CIA) bunker ("The Last Supper" [4.08]). Olivia does not counter Jake's claiming of her as his girlfriend; she instead calms him by reminding him that they stand in the sun together. Overall, Olivia spends most of the scenes where Jake and Fitz openly fight over her either away—during her kidnapping—or silent, interjecting only to tell them "enough." Olivia's body is the terrain they battle over; when Olivia is nicknamed Helen of Troy (the "face that launched a thousand ships"), it refers to the violence waged by Eli, Jake, and Fitz to "protect" Olivia. The never-ending fight between Fitz and Jake for access to Olivia and dominance over her sexuality is not wholly about who actually loves her more, but rather about each man's own masculinity and lust for political power.

Familial Discipline

Eli Pope often uses his military rank to command White men to surveil and discipline Olivia, his daughter. This surveillance allows Eli to
serve as the gatekeeper of Olivia's blackness and sexuality. Visible in
Eli's audience-rousing soliloquies is the concern that the Black middle-class family is under threat from the "pollution" (Julien 1992)
of interracial relationships: "You have forsaken me. Your father. Your
family. You wanted to stand in the sun, in the bright, white light. It
blinded you. Those . . . people that you've chosen over me, you do
not see who they are, what they want, how they see you. Those people
are not your people. They never will be. And you will never be one of
them" ("The Last Supper" [4.08]). Eli's determination of who is or
is not worthy of Olivia is rooted in the desire for Olivia to retain her
ladylike image. As Isaac Julien notes, "Crossing racial lines usually
results in punishment" (1992, 263). This punishment for tarnishing
the Black family is evidenced in Eli's handling of Olivia's multiple outings as the president's mistress, but also in the way he berates her over
choosing "them"—the "White boys" he deems unworthy.

To clear Olivia, a White woman staffer's name is leaked as Fitz's
alleged mistress ("Guess Who's Coming to Dinner" [3.02]). In a press
interview, Olivia announces that she will be representing the woman.
In order to thwart her plans, Eli visits Olivia in her office:

> ELI: I'm sure you realize by now that there is one thing I have a say
> over. If you ever wanna see Jake Ballard again, America will believe
> it was Jeannine Locke that had an affair with the president.
> OLIVIA: How do I know he isn't already dead?
> ELI: You don't! [chuckles]

Using Jake as leverage enables Eli to manipulate his daughter's actions.
Eli forces Olivia to save the White woman or the White man. In giving Olivia an ultimatum, Eli polices Olivia's sexuality and morality,
specifically her defense of the "defenseless." Further, the ultimatum
illustrates how Eli uses other bodies, namely, White male bodies, to
discipline Olivia when he is unable to physically discipline her himself.

Because Jake disobeyed Eli's orders regarding Olivia and slept with her, he is being held captive in "the hole." Because Olivia continued her affair with the president, Eli found another person to take the fall. Because Olivia disobeyed her father by not disappearing after her name was leaked, she is indirectly disciplined as people around her suffer. Although Eli's power is not literally revealed in this scene, it is implied when Olivia questions what Eli has done to Jake.

Eli's confirmation that Jake is being tortured leads to flashbacks of the beginning of Olivia and Huck's friendship. In these flashbacks, Eli expresses disdain for Olivia's ties to Huck, a former B613 member. He labels Huck a "paranoid schizophrenic, repeat offender" ("Guess Who's Coming to Dinner" [3.02]), using his authority as B613's Command to criminalize and dehumanize Huck and "defend" Olivia's purity. Olivia fails to follow her father's orders to end their friendship, putting the lives of Huck and her fiancé, Edison Davis, in danger. Olivia finds Huck badly beaten; as she tends to Huck, Eli calls to inform her of her fiancé's tragic car accident. Eli warns Olivia that when she gives the ring back, she should "let the guy down gently. Poor guy's been through enough." In causing the car accident, Eli reveals the lengths he will go to use military and state resources to control Olivia.

Throughout the series, Eli sabotages Olivia's personal relationships when they become threatening to his relationship with Olivia. As Command, Eli orders his agent to murder Fitz's oldest son in order to frame Maya Pope ("The Price of Free and Fair Elections" [3.18]). When Jake threatens to expose Eli for killing Harrison, an employee from Olivia Pope's crisis team and her best friend, as well as Fitz's son, Eli sends agents after Jake ("Inside the Bubble" [4.03]; "Like Father, Like Daughter" [4.04]) and frames him for the murder of Fitz's son. Yet Olivia also defies her father and intervenes to save both Jake and Fitz ("Baby Made a Mess" [4.07]; "The Last Supper" [4.08]):

ELI: You do not disrespect me! Ever. Do you understand? Can I make that any clearer? I am the one who protects the Republic. I am the one who protects you. Everything I do serves that purpose.

I have spent a lifetime keeping you safe from harm, a lifetime worrying about your fate, a lifetime making sure that the path in front of you was clear of debris, a lifetime shining their shoes so that you might always see your reflection at every turn. You do not see this. You do not believe this. You think I am some relic, some misguided, vicious dinosaur from my museum who attacks without thinking. Let me assure you, I am not. When I strike, it is precise and it is for a reason. You do not interfere. You do not get in the way. You never, ever choose one of them over me again. I won't have it. Is that clear?

OLIVIA: What's clear is that you seem to have wasted a lifetime doing all the wrong things.

ELI: Olivia. Against me, you will lose. (4.07)

Eli habitually uses his resources to surveil and eliminate Olivia's relationships—her mother, former lovers, and colleagues. Raising Olivia as a single parent, Eli prides himself on having provided Olivia with "the best," which is demonstrated in her educational achievements—attending St. Anne's Belfield School, Surval Montreux, Princeton, and Georgetown Law. In discussing Olivia's education, Eli uses the physical settings—in the form of boarding schools, private universities, and other spaces of privilege—to discipline Olivia's identity and her body. These institutions aid his efforts because these spaces employ "judges of normality"—teachers, military officers, doctors, and employers. Individuals enter these disciplinary spaces to undergo reform that both constrains and constructs docile bodies (Foucault 1995). Only when Olivia decides to leave these spaces of privilege does Eli use his covert government agency to punish her.

Gender Discipline

Olivia's interactions with White women in the show revolve around Olivia's failure to properly perform femininity or competency. This communicative posture is seen in Mellie's gendered insults—for example, "slut" or "whore"—and Abby's questioning of Olivia's authority. However, male characters also police Olivia's womanhood; when Olivia is named as Fitz's mistress, Eli attempts to convince his daughter to "disappear" and take on a different identity ("It's Handled" [3.01]). In fact, Eli warns Olivia that if she does not get on the plane, "the White House will destroy you." This response reinforces the notion that Olivia's womanhood renders her incapable of saving herself despite being "DC's fixer," demanding her silence and dependency.

When video of Fitz leaving Olivia's apartment is leaked, Olivia meets with Fitz and Mellie in the CIA bunker beneath the Pentagon:

MELLIE: I don't see what the problem is. It's the same plan as always. Fitz and I hold hands and smile at Oprah or Barbara Walters. We do what we always do—act happy. And we just deny it. Deny you.

OLIVIA: That would have worked before.

MELLIE: Before what?

FITZ: Before you got the bright idea to go on national television and tell the world I cheated on you.

MELLIE: You did cheat on me.

FITZ: That's not the point.

MELLIE: It's exactly the point.

FITZ: Not if you want to smile at Oprah.

MELLIE: I wouldn't need to smile at Oprah if you didn't screw your whore every chance you got. ("It's Handled" [3.01])

Mellie's initial solution is to publicly deny Olivia, more specifically Fitz's affair with Olivia. By denying the alleged affair, Mellie delegitimizes the relationship. Because Fitz no longer wants to hide his affair, Mellie calls Olivia a whore and reminds Olivia of her "lesser" womanhood, in addition to the many ways that she has degraded their marriage. These gendered insults distance Olivia from purity, despite her white attire, and recenter her affair with a married man. The affair also reflects on Fitz, who fails to uphold the traditional White family and fulfill the role of the White father. The affair caused damage to the first family, their placement in the White House, and their reputation in the Republican Party, as evidenced in the ways Fitz's leadership skills and morals are questioned because of his transgressions.

Later, Fitz attempts to convince Olivia and Mellie to "tell the truth." Mellie quickly objects, because "the truth does not work." Further, Mellie's role as a wife and a woman would be damaged. Confirming the affair marks Mellie as weak for staying with a man who "is in love with another woman." Additionally, Mellie's inability to sexually fulfill her husband undermines her role as a wife. To maintain Mellie's purity, Olivia's sexuality is policed. She is forced to play into racialized notions of gender: White women are sexually pure, modest, and respectable, while Black woman are promiscuous and rapacious. After realizing that she can never tell the truth about her relationship with Fitz, Olivia decides to tell "part" of the truth:

> OLIVIA: How many times did Fitz and I sleep together? Three? Five? How many would you be okay with?
> MELLIE: Two.
> OLIVIA: Okay. Fitz and I slept together twice. The first time was?
> FITZ: After I was elected. You didn't get the job because we were sleeping together. Might as well make sure nobody questions that. . . .
> MELLIE: Let's just say that the two of you got to talking, and one thing led to another. It was just sex. It didn't mean anything. And you felt terrible afterwards. And it didn't happen again until after you got shot.
> OLIVIA: Okay. So . . . twice. The first time was after the inauguration, and then the second time after the assassination attempt.
> MELLIE: You had sex once after you recovered from your gunshot wounds because you were feeling your mortality. Facing death. ("It's Handled" [3.01])

The negotiation of how many times Olivia slept with Fitz delegitimizes Olivia. Mellie shortens the time of the affair, making the affair purely sexual. The negotiation process reveals the control Mellie has over Olivia's body; Mellie is able to determine when and how Olivia sexually pleases Fitz. In selecting the narrative, Mellie suggests that Fitz engages in sexual activity with Olivia only when he is not acting as himself.

Though Olivia is considered the voice of "reason" in the show, Abby takes on this role in Olivia's fantasies. During her kidnapping and captivity ("Run" [4.10]), Olivia copes by (day)dreaming about her possible lives with Fitz and Jake. In the midst of her dream in Vermont, Abby challenges the trappings of a traditional upper-middle class, White, heterosexual womanhood:

> OLIVIA: I chose Vermont and this life with Fitz, I'm happy here.
> ABBY: That's the thing, Liv. You didn't. You didn't choose Fitz. You didn't choose this life.
> OLIVIA: Abby—
> ABBY: What? He resigned from office just like that, and poof, you're here? Where's Mellie? . . . Where are his kids? Where's the press that I'm betting would be swarming you on a daily basis if the President of the United States went all Wallis Simpson on America? And what? Now you make jam for a living? Really? Do you know how to use a Dutch oven? Do you know how to turn on a regular oven?

Here, Abby notes the illogical nature of Fitz's mistress being allowed to live in complete peace in Vermont, saving her most gendered and searing comments for the notion of Olivia engaging in the domestic activity of making jam. At the time, it was highly unlikely that Fitz would ever resign the presidency. Apparently, Olivia engaging in domestic activities is equally unfathomable. Here, Abby (as Olivia's subconscious) delegitimizes Olivia by attacking her implied failures in the kitchen, suggesting that she is also a failed woman. Later in this exchange, Olivia is deemed nonsensical:

> OLIVIA: For once I'm not trying to make sense. I'm not trying to be logical. I'm being happy—
> ABBY: Where's Jake?
> OLIVIA: [pauses, confused] I . . . don't know.
> ABBY: So, he rescues you and now—
> OLIVIA: Are you judging me?
> ABBY: Do you love him? And by "him," I mean either "him"—Jake or Fitz?

OLIVIA: [turns] Goodbye, Abby.

ABBY: [reaching for Olivia] Doesn't matter who you love. [grabs Olivia's arms] Look at me. Jake and Fitz can't help you. There is no man to rescue you. Do you hear me? No one. No one is going to help you. You are the only Gladiator in the place. You are all you've got. You have to rescue yourself! [storms off]

Why does Olivia's subconscious take the form of Abby? Though Abby is Olivia's closest friend, there are other key characters who could have appeared to give this speech. Abby making this speech harks back to previous moments when she has challenged and questioned Olivia, particularly her doubts that led then district attorney David Rosen to investigate Olivia ("Beltway Unbuckled" [2.04]). The reliance on a White woman to question Olivia's morality and her fantasy of "proper" domesticity evoke contemporary tensions between mainstream (White) feminism and Black feminism. Abby scolding Olivia about "no man to rescue her" is on the surface an empowering call to action. However, the warning also plays into racialized notions of gender. White women can reasonably expect to be saved if they are in trouble; however, strong, independent Black women must save themselves. In season five, Olivia pushes back against assumptions about her femininity when she is installed as a semi "first lady" following Fitz and Mellie's divorce, amid a media firestorm about her immorality and power-hungry tendencies.

After photos of Olivia and Fitz are leaked to the media ("Heavy Is the Head" [5.01]) and Olivia's subsequent admission ("Yes" [5.02]), the White House—via Abby—works diligently to discredit the affair. To "save" Olivia, Fitz agrees to an exclusive interview where he would confess his love for Mellie and denounce the cheating allegations ("Paris Is Burning" [5.03]). Abby pleads with Mellie to save the legacy of the Grant administration (as well as Mellie's hopes of gaining the presidency) but is rejected, making it impossible to save both Fitz and Olivia. As the president tries to salvage Olivia's reputation, Abby informs him that the only thing left to do is to let her do her job ("Paris Is Burning" [5.03]). Her job is to make Olivia a villain:

ABBY: Hello, everyone. There are a number of things we could discuss today, but I know there's only one thing you're really interested in, so, Ashley, I'll give you the honors.

ASHLEY: Is the president having an affair with Olivia Pope?

ABBY: You know I'm unable to speculate on tabloid gossip and rumor, Ashley. But you also know that Olivia Pope has a certain reputation here in Washington.

MARTIN: You're talking about the fact that Pope's been linked to several powerful men?

ABBY: It is certainly true that Ms. Pope has had a number of high-profile relationships, but as to their nature, you'd have to talk to Ms. Pope about that, Martin.

Exposure of Olivia's "high-profile relationships" allows Abby to suggest that Olivia has an insatiable appetite for sex, particularly sex with powerful men. Furthermore, by speculating about her reputation, Abby reveals her gendered control over Olivia's body, or at least the narrative(s) around how her body moves and operates. Her legitimacy as White House press secretary facilitates this portrayal of Olivia as promiscuous and predatory, thus saving Fitz's reputation.

Conclusion

Being a Black woman places Olivia Pope at the intersection of a variety of marginalized positionalities, even as she exhibits a great deal of privilege and social power. Olivia's racialized sexuality, role as a daughter, and gender blur the lines between the forms of discipline used to exert control over her. As much as Olivia's relationships constrain the possibilities for her behavior, her body, and her identity, there are also moments for Olivia to assert agency and engage in resistance. To assert her sexual agency, Olivia "chooses herself" despite wanting both Vermont and "the sun" ("Where the Sun Don't Shine" [4.09]). She also resists her father's manipulation and micromanaging by "shooting" Eli—not realizing her father had removed the bullets from the gun—demonstrating that she was not dependent on Jake or Fitz. Olivia further claims her agency when she decides to rescue herself from her kidnappers ("Run" [4.10]). After her first escape attempt—out of the bathroom window—is thwarted, Olivia quickly comes up with another plan. Olivia is able to knock one of her kidnappers unconscious in order to obtain his gun and keys to unlock the doors. Olivia even shoots another kidnapper, revealing that she is capable of handling a "man's toy." Further, in one of season five's most pivotal moments, Olivia takes control of her body and makes the choice to have an abortion, as well as ending her relationship with Fitz, lest she lose her career ("Baby It's Cold Outside" [5.09]).

Yet Olivia internalizes the disposability of women of color's bodies. When she berates Fitz for going to war over her ("No More Blood" [4.13]), she reaffirms notions that Black women can be sacrificed for the nation while also critiquing Fitz's ineptitude and wasting her efforts to get him elected. Additionally, Olivia performs unpaid labor above and beyond her sexual and emotional service, unlike the plethora of White women political staffers and journalists whom Fitz parades around the White House once he becomes single again ("Wild Card" [5.12]). Abby may be his "work wife," but she is also a paid employee who earns the trust that enables her to usurp the position of chief of staff ("I See You" [5.14]). Olivia's only benefit from "fixing" White House political crises or advising Fitz on policy is her adjacency to power and the enhancement of her reputation; though her position provided her with social and political capital, she is denied financial compensation for her efforts. This dynamic becomes even more problematic considering the lengths to which Olivia went to sacrifice her career in the first place for Fitz ("Dog-Whistle Politics" [5.04]), as well as her campaign of "redemption" in order to save Fitz from embarrassment and impeachment ("You Got Served" [5.05]).

Olivia's complexity and the ways her experiences are not wholly separate from "real" life make us consider how the constraints that Olivia experiences are translated onto the bodies of the Black women who make up a major part of *Scandal*'s audience. Because Black bodies are continuously watched, there is little room for mistakes. Puwar terms this "the burden of representation," the pressure to be "seen to represent the capacities of groups for which they are marked and visible" (2004, 62). She further notes that the "consequent burden attached to being one of the minority" makes people "feel the pressure to do the job well, in order to show that non-white people can also do the work" (62–63).

The images on our television screens help define who "we" are as women, as workers, as mothers, and as friends. Olivia illustrates the possibilities of Black (heterosexual) womanhood (Iton 2010; McKnight 2014; Pixley 2015): financial independence, successful career, political and social power, and, of course, being capable of sexual desire *and* being desired by others. In this sense, she is like her (mostly heterosexual) counterparts in "ShondaLand"—Miranda Bailey (*Grey's Anatomy*), Naomi Bennett (*Private Practice*), and Annalise Keating (*How to Get Away with Murder*)—who are flawed but driven, ambitious, powerful, beautiful, and stylish. Olivia and her fellow Black female leads must be "perfect enough to not reflect poorly" while also "realistic enough to be recognizable," with blackness at the center of what informs their actions (Pixley 2015, 31). Though these characters demonstrate the consequences suffered on the way to achieving their power, the conflicts that Olivia, Miranda, and Annalise cope with every Thursday night are likely a result of Rhimes's own perceptions of what comes with success. In Rhimes's 2014 commencement speech at Dartmouth, she warns that success in one area means failure in another:

> Whenever you see me somewhere succeeding in one area of my life, that almost certainly means I am failing in another area of my life. . . . If I am killing it on a *Scandal* script for work, I am probably missing bath and story time at home. If I am at home sewing my kids' Halloween costumes, I'm probably blowing off a rewrite I was supposed to turn in. If I am accepting a prestigious award, I am missing my baby's first swim lesson. If I am at my daughter's debut in her school musical, I am missing Sandra Oh's last scene ever being filmed at *Grey's Anatomy*. If I am succeeding at one, I am inevitably failing at the other. That is the tradeoff. That is the Faustian bargain

one makes with the devil that comes with being a powerful working woman who is also a powerful mother. You never feel a hundred percent OK; you never get your sea legs; you are always a little nauseous. Something is always lost. . . . Something is always missing.

In many ways, Rhimes is her characters; as a middle-class Ivy League–educated woman, she navigates the ways whiteness influences every aspect of our society, especially the entertainment industry. As *Scandal* pushes the narrative of the "flawed" female protagonist, pressing the consistent message that women can have successful, competent careers but also messy personal lives, we wonder if the more problematic notions around race, gender, and sexuality can be surmounted, that this discipline and surveillance can be avoided or, perhaps, subverted.

References

Bailey, Cameron. 1988. "Nigger/Lover: The Thin Sheen of Race in 'Something Wild.'" *Screen* 29(1): 28–43.

Bleu, Diva. 2013. "Scandalous Behavior: Why Do Black Men Hate Olivia Pope?" *Sinuous Magazine*, Oct. 24. http://www.sinuousmag.com/2013/10/scandal-hate/.

Bonilla-Silva, Eduardo, and Austin Ashe. 2014. "The End of Racism? Colorblind Racism and Popular Media." In *The Colorblind Screen: Television in Post-racial America*, edited by Sarah Nilsen and Sarah E. Turner, 57–79. New York: New York Univ. Press.

Childs, Erica Chito. 2009. *Fade to Black and White: Interracial Images in Popular Culture*. Lanham, MD: Rowman and Littlefield.

Collins, Patricia Hill. 2005. *Black Sexual Politics: African Americans, Gender, and the New Racism*. London: Routledge.

Fanon, Frantz. 2008 [1952]. *Black Skin, White Masks*. New York: Grove Press.

Foucault, Michel. 1990. *History of Sexuality*. Vol. 1, *An Introduction*. New York: Vintage.

———. 1995. *Discipline and Punish: The Birth of the Prison*. New York: Vintage.

Frankenberg, Ruth. 1993. *White Women, Race Matters: The Social Construction of Whiteness*. London: Routledge.

hooks, bell. 1992. *Black Looks: Race and Representation*. Brooklyn: South End Press.

Iton, Richard. 2010. *In Search of the Black Fantastic: Politics and Popular Culture in the Post–Civil Rights Era*. Oxford: Oxford Univ. Press.

Julien, Isaac. 1992. "Black Is, Black Ain't: Notes on De-essentializing Black Identities." In *Black Popular Culture*, edited by Gina Dent, 255–63. Seattle: Bay Press.

Kamp, David, and Jessica Diehl. 2013. "Ms. Kerry Goes to Washington: The First Lady of Scandal Speaks." *Vanity Fair*, July 15. http://www.vanity fair.com/style/2013/08/kerry-washington-scandal-cover-story.

King, C. Richard. 2014. "Watching TV with White Supremacists: A More Complex View of the Colorblind Screen." In *The Colorblind Screen: Television in Post-racial America*, edited by Sarah Nilsen and Sarah E. Turner, 219–36. New York: New York Univ. Press.

Lundy, April D. 2018. "Caught between a Thot and a Hard Place." *Black Scholar* 48(1): 56–70.

McClintock, Anne. 1995. *Imperial Leather: Race, Gender and Sexuality in the Colonial Contest*. London: Routledge.

McKnight, Utz. 2014. "The Fantastic Olivia Pope: The Construction of a Black Feminist Subject." *Souls* 16(3–4): 183–97.

Nilsen, Sarah, and Sarah E. Turner, eds. 2014. *The Colorblind Screen: Television in Post-racial America*. New York: New York Univ. Press.

Perry, Barbara, and Michael Sutton. 2006. "Seeing Red over Black and White: Popular Media Representations of Inter-racial Relationships as Precursors to Racial Violence." *Canadian Journal of Criminology and Criminal Justice* 48: 887–904.

Pixley, Tara-Lynne. 2015. "Trope and Associates: Olivia Pope's Scandalous Blackness." Special issue, "Scandalous." *Black Scholar* 45(1): 28–33.

Puwar, Nirmal. 2004. *Space Invaders: Race, Gender and Bodies Out of Place*. Oxford: Berg.

Rhimes, Shonda. 2014. "Shonda Rhimes '91, Commencement Address." Dartmouth College Commencement, June 8. http://www.dartmouth .edu/~commence/news/speeches/2014/rhimes-address.html.

Spillers, Hortense J. 2003. "Momma's Baby, Poppa's Maybe: An American Grammar Book." In *Black, White and in Color: Essays on American Literature and Culture*, 203–29. Chicago: Univ. of Chicago Press.

US Census Bureau. 2015. "State & Country Quick Facts—Vermont." Feb. 26. http://quickfacts.census.gov/qfd/states/50000.html.

Vega, Tanzina. 2013. "A Show Makes Friends and History: 'Scandal' on ABC Is Breaking Barriers." *New York Times*, Jan. 16. http://nyti.ms/18 VoQqY.

PART TWO

Romance, Race, and the Erotic

5 | "Tangled Skeins"

Scandal's Olivia Pope and the Counternarrativizing
of Black Female Enslavement

ERNEST L. GIBSON III

IF THERE IS ANYTHING remotely poetic about American history,
it is the inevitable nature of its inescapability. The irony, of course,
lies in its resistance to actualizing itself, to becoming, in fact, history.
Yet the precise moment that we understand how historical hauntings
operate—how they bask in the riddles of their own fictions—we come
closer to accepting the reality of blurred lines and elisions. Even more,
we learn, despite the academy's relentless insistence that history is a
field of study grounded in the objective archiving of this nation's past
realities (the beautiful and ugly alike), that history is a living organic
entity that has consistently fed off the erased and silenced subjects
tortured within its margins. We also learn that history's creativity
emerges from its ability to re-create and revision itself, to stave off
the possibility of its own erasure or eradication, to remind those individuals who attempt radical forgetfulness that it has yet to pass. This
understanding is the case with so many narratives surrounding race,
gender, and sexuality, but particularly more present within the narrative of intimacy, whether forced or consensual, between Black women
and White men. And somewhere within the muffled and messy scripts
of interracial intimacy are the smothered voices of the "American"
abject—the subalterns of the West whose voices have been systemati-
cally gagged by the instruments of patriarchy sharpened and grown

within the peculiar institution of slavery. Indeed, somewhere within the dark spaces of the American imaginary lies the forever-shackled Black female body—the reflection, or perhaps embodiment, of this country's greatest puzzle and most grotesque textuality. Fortunately, and it is at times a disturbing fortune, popular culture has a way of masking serious discourse or transformative discursive work within an ensemble of entertainment, within plots that seemingly span for sixty minutes one day out of a week during a given television series. It is here, within the crevices of the performative masks, where fiction touches reality ever so gently, where the present dares to dance with the undead past. It is here where history haunts, where the ghosts of old regimes lurk vividly within our midst, waiting for the moment when they might be rendered visible. It is here that Shonda Rhimes's *Scandal* seems to find its home, as with each passing episode Olivia Pope appears less like a new construction or a character played by Kerry Washington and more like a figure whom we have tried desperately to forget—the Black woman cast as slave.

In her 1861 slave narrative, *Incidents in the Life of a Slave Girl*, Harriet Jacobs relays the following while contemplating which name to give her christened child: "What tangled skeins are the genealogies of slavery!" (2000 [1861], 87). Writing more than a century and a half prior to Shonda Rhimes's debuting of her acclaimed TV series *Scandal*, Jacobs could hardly be thought to be imagining the futuristic tangles and technologies of power that would inevitably place her and Olivia Pope into some metaphoric genealogical tie. Nevertheless, Pope's characterization within the popular imagination forces readers and viewers of *Scandal* to revisit the ways in which Rhimes's Black female lead participates in the construction of a literary and historical counternarrative. From the earliest episodes, the scandalous and controversial interracial relationship between political fixer Pope and American president Fitzgerald Grant has generated both the painful remembrance of the power-riddled dialectical relationship between White male master and Black female enslaved subject and the perverse nostalgic recollection of an American moment in which the Black female body is always already the leading performer in what Saidiya

Hartman calls "scenes of subjection" (1997, 22). Additionally, while the question of genealogy—as it is posed within social media spaces, the privacy of home, and academic discussions—lingers upon the precipice of problematic readings of Olivia Pope as enslaved woman, it also encourages a provocative discoursing of the complex system of gender oppression and how Black women, whether fictional or real, are continually marked by a textuality of enslavement.

Placing *Scandal* in conversation with two slave narratives and mythologies highlights how Kerry Washington's character, Olivia Pope, directly and inadvertently *fixes* epistemic elisions while simultaneously precluding and precipitating certain readings of both Pope and her "genealogical" counterparts. The leaping and linking of temporality and genre mine the complex dynamics of power that have historically mired the situating of ideas of love and unrepressive intimacy within the heart(s) of interraciality. Furthermore, this dynamic theorizes the palimpsestic relationship between Rhimes's scripting of Pope's sexuality and Black female slave narratives. Ultimately, reading Olivia Pope through the lensed textualities of Sally Hemings and Linda Brent uncovers significant nuances about Pope's character while also offering an epistemological challenge to narrative mythologies of Black female enslavement. In this regard, Olivia Pope must be reimagined as a "Gladiator in a Suit" constructed for the purpose of *fixing*, counternarrativizing, and untangling the skeins that haunt the memory of Black enslaved women whose lives have prefaced and pretextured the layered scandals in Rhimes's fiction.

"An American Controversy"

In the episode "Happy Birthday, Mr. President" (2.08), the complexities of race and interracial tension existing between Olivia Pope and Fitzgerald Grant are both historicized and textualized as the result of Pope's provocative reading of their relationship. The episode, executed through a series of well-placed flashbacks, foregrounds the fragility of human relationships against the backdrop of political controversy. Although seemingly centered on the inauguration of Fitzgerald Grant, whose presidency is largely owed to Pope's clever manipulation of societal structures and psyches, as well as the attempted assassination of the recently installed president on the occasion of his birthday dinner, the episode's zenithal impact emerges from the script's evocation of "an American controversy" that is paradoxically problematic and constructive in its remembrance. A scene in which her presence, as a Black female subject, is simultaneously questioned and juxtaposed to iterations of White womanhood skillfully prefaces Pope's proclamation of a historic and controversial dialectic of race. Reporters, gathered to obtain information concerning President Grant's physical state, appear more concerned with why both Mellie Grant (the first lady) and Sally Langston (the vice president) are absented in various capacities. As the scene alludes to the vulnerability of both Mellie and Sally, the viewer is offered the visual of Olivia, poised and articulate, secure and efficient, as an emblem of female power. Through the subtle pairing of White female absence with Black female visibility, Rhimes colors the subsequent scene in a way that complicates the historical narrative. Flashing back, the viewer follows Olivia Pope and her signature walk as she awkwardly attempts to avoid talking with Grant within the White House hallways. To his persistent efforts at dialogue, she offers the consistent refrain "I'm busy," at which Grant attempts a more affectionate approach in uttering, "Olivia, I miss you" (2.08). It is this utterance, or perhaps, more accurately, the transparency within it, that succeeds in coaxing Olivia into dialogue. Her immediate response, "You walked her to my cabin door," is a perfectly scripted double entendre in that it recalls the moment at Camp David when Fitzgerald ushered his wife, Mellie, to Olivia's door without warning, as well as conjuring, albeit abstractly, the idea of slave quarters during the antebellum period. While ostensibly a stretch in reading, the choice of language here—via "cabin"—even as cabins indeed populate Camp David, serves to reconstruct both the aesthetics of slavery and the social laws governing interracial intimacy from the time.

Fitzgerald, a personification of a freedom affording White men the right to naïveté, security, and protection, verbally dismisses the "difficulty" of being together (owing to social constraints and racial proscriptions) by stating, "We are together. That's all that matters"

(2.08). His obliviousness to the complications of his "inappropriate" relationship with Olivia speaks to the privilege he inherits as a beneficiary in a system of patriarchy and his own immature understanding of how such a relationship endangers Olivia as mistress. Even more, the definitive "that's all that matters" emerges from a logic of submission traceable back to the peculiar institution and makes apparent, in the words of Saidiya Hartman (despite a somewhat differing context), "the entanglements of slavery and freedom and the dutiful submission characteristic of black subjectivity, whether in the making and maintaining of chattel personal or in the fashioning of individuality, cultivation of conscience, and harnessing of free will" (1997, 7). Through a Hartmanian lens, I am suggesting here that submission is one of the shared signs in the separate vocabularies of Black slavery and Black freedom. Fitzgerald expects not only for Olivia to engage him on his own terms, but that she would also submit to his reasoning and reading of the situation. Operating from the protective shell of his American White manhood, Fitz was never forced to grapple with the pervasive and consistent scripting of Black bodies as the inferior other. Consequently, and in spite of pre- and postemancipation temporality, he cannot understand the social limitations projected onto a twenty-first-century Black woman (Pope) who must readily acknowledge that "an amazing continuity belied the hypostatized discontinuities and epochal shifts installed by categories like slavery and freedom" (7). Even more, Fitzgerald's response confirms Sharon Holland's understanding of how "the dialectic produced from this dynamic imposes transcendent being for the one and historical meaning for the other" (2012, 52). Pope's response, an iteration of the burden she carries as racial "other"—the task to educate the proverbial "self" occupying a position of power—is loaded with a tone of emphatic disbelief at Fitzgerald's cluelessness and removes any question of how Grant and Pope are to be reimagined in this moment: "Really? Because I'm feeling a little, I don't know, Sally Hemings/Thomas Jefferson about all this" (2.08). Her utterance blurs genre, history, and temporality to the end of highlighting the inextricable rhetoric of slavery and freedom for bodies deemed Black. And it is precisely this moment, this daring allusion by Rhimes and her team, that extends the already controversial relationship between Olivia and Fitz into the messy annals of American history.

In *Thomas Jefferson and Sally Hemings: An American Controversy*, Annette Gordon-Reed relays how her fascinations over the Jefferson-Hemings controversy are grounded in a discourse pervaded by denial of such a relationship and, more particularly, stem from "the vehemence and the substance of those denials . . . because historians, journalists, and other Jefferson enthusiasts have in the past (and continue to do so today) shamelessly employed every stereotype of black people and distortion of life in the Old South to support their position" (1997, xvii). Gordon-Reed's fascination led to a thorough historical and scientific study of the relationship and serves as a treatment for epistemological sloppiness, as she carefully undoes the largest criticisms of the Jefferson-Hemings relationship and carves space for more than a possibility for its existence. For Gordon-Reed, "In order to sustain the claim of impossibility, or even to discuss the matter in those terms, one has to make Thomas Jefferson so high as to have been something more than human and one has to make Sally Hemings so low as to have been something less than human" (xviii). Gordon-Reed's fundamental concern—the racial politics that ascribe unequal value of differing human subjects—can arguably be aligned with the work of Rhimes and crew, as they explore how power dynamics and definitions of difference script human intimacy.

When Olivia Pope historicizes herself as Sally Hemings and Fitzgerald Grant as Thomas Jefferson, she uses mythology to *re-member* the ways in which her body is read alongside, in relationship to, or even under Grant's. Although her expression can be read as a response to the growing discomfort in the Black popular imagination, as it readily traces such a relationship back to the horrors of history, it must also be read as a strategic interfacing with the past to illumine the complex relationships of the present. Rhimes's *Scandal*, like Gordon-Reed's text, engages with discourses and discoursing subjects unable (read: unwilling) to see beyond the interplay of power and structure in Black female—White male relationships. Thus, when Pope makes legible the

fears, discomforts, and hauntings of *Scandal*'s audiences, she simultaneously encourages a nostalgic visitation while also pushing for a more
complicated reading of her person and her relationships. To be clear,
I argue that the utterance "I'm feeling a little, I don't know, Sally
Hemings/Thomas Jefferson about all this" (2.08) forces the viewer
to wrestle with the elements of power existing within the Pope-Grant
affair, knowing the results of which will engender a more fruitful conversation. Here is where Olivia Pope emerges as the puzzling subject
that is both *becoming* and *unbecoming*.

Becoming Sally Hemings

Despite the truth or falsity of the scandalous "American controversy" known as the Jefferson-Hemings relationship, it is clear that
the mythology pivots on questions of power, racial hierarchy, submission, intimacy, and the confines of interracial exploration within a
Western context. Pope's proclamation, then, is less an endorsement of
a particular historical truth and more a reflection of how her relationship might be viewed through lenses of power passed down from the
Hemings era. More than two centuries later, when the ideological and
legal topography of America's racial terrain has changed, Olivia Pope
as Black female subject still holds striking and disturbing similarities to her predecessor Sally Hemings. While problematic to conflate
Pope as Hemings, seeing how she is neither enslaved subject nor held
captive by the same legal constraints, their ontology bears the same
texture—a textuality of Black womanhood where the subject is written as powerless, hypersexed, beastly, unworthy of genuine human
affection, unnamed, emotionally underdeveloped, et cetera. Indeed,
the flamboyance of Pope's freedom does little to undermine how she
is perpetually "stained" by the shackling racial ink of history. As a
result, her relationship with Fitzgerald Grant opens itself to readings
where we can, as uncomfortable audience, see her *becoming*, "I don't
know, Sally Hemings."

According to both the historical folklore and the classical mythology, the relationship between Thomas Jefferson and Sally Hemings
ought to originate in the mid-1780s, when Jefferson travels abroad as

minister to France. It is perhaps perversely romantic or disturbingly poetic that this particular "scandal" begins in France's city of eternal love; nevertheless, it is also appropriate, for, as Gordon-Reed notes, "this story begins in Paris because it was there, some have alleged, that Thomas Jefferson and Sally Hemings began a relationship that lasted for thirty-eight years" (1997, 1). Centuries later, even as one meanders through historical works that argue for and legitimate the possibility of the intimate relationship, one thing remains clear—the discourse alone has engendered one of the most scandalous mythologies. Ironically, Olivia Pope is intimately tied to this mythology, as her subjectivity, especially as it engages intimately with a White male body in a position of power, is symbolically narrated by a history unwilling to acknowledge the promise of emancipation. Yet, despite the wish to have Pope read through the modern scripts of her own subjective writings, we learn much through this genealogical fettering.

A responsible reading of *Scandal*'s Olivia cautions against the convenient coupling of her with the historical Sally Hemings. While loosely based on Judy Smith, a leader in crisis management and chief executive officer of Smith & Company, Pope is a fictional character largely scripted from the imaginations of Shonda Rhimes and her writing collective.[1] Additionally, Olivia Pope's temporality prohibits the possibility of enslavement, therefore undermining any "fair" comparisons, as she is not regulated by the same social realities. More important, there are a series of small but significant details that obscure the neat mapping of Sally onto Olivia: Sally Hemings mothered six children, while Olivia Pope has none; Olivia Pope was formally educated, Sally not so much; Sally occupied the position of forced servant, whereas Olivia has the freedom of career. Then there are those abstract notions of voice, choice, and movement protected by law. Although the list can go on perpetually, it does abruptly stop, if only momentarily in the

---

1. One might argue for the unique phenomenon of how the West "skillfully" constructed Black bodies into enslaved subjects divested of a proximity to their natural essence, but that argument ought to be a discussion for a different essay.

public imagination, at the site where we must admit how inherently problematic it is to conflate the two figures. Considering this stance, Olivia's love partner is somewhat right in his frustrated objection to Olivia's evocation of Sally Hemings, though there are some elements his White male privilege prevents him from acknowledging.

After Pope's daring historical allusion to Sally Hemings, it is Fitzgerald Grant, and perhaps the virtual gasps of a questioning audience, who challenges the notion. For both Grant and the spectatorial critic, Pope's feeling like Sally Hemings is more than a simple historical reaching; it is also a problematic embodiment grossly distorting her reality and her inherited history. Grant expresses his objection in the garden scene of the same episode, proclaiming to a visually frantic and pacing Pope, "The Sally Hemings–Thomas Jefferson comment was below the belt" (2.08). The danger of conflation underscores Grant's utterance and addresses the more general mishandling of American history. However, his indignation is also compounded by the fact that he is, as he will later announce, connected to her by the deepest profundities of the heart. Yet while Olivia's face and vulnerability might communicate how she understands the danger of her initial expression, Rhimes and company are unapologetic in this evocation of history. Instead of allowing Grant to defuse the situation with a logic riddled by power and White male privilege, Olivia retorts, "Because it's so untrue." So simple a phrase must not be overlooked in this intense dialogue. Pope's questioning of "truth" in this situation forces viewers to consider the larger implications at play. Calm and convicted, Pope encourages, if not demands, a greater nuancing of her relationship with "Mr. President." This is not to say that it erases the potential hazards of the analogy; rather, it affirms that the writers or constructors of Pope are aware, on some level, of how expressions appropriating dark moments of history are always dangling precariously. Arguably, the goal is to get both Grant and *Scandal*'s viewers to move beyond the surface of this interracial affair. For Pope and this writer (admittedly with a firm reluctance), Olivia is not engaged in a racial cliché-ing of the relationship. She is not doing that which Fitzgerald believes—"You're playing the race card on the fact that

I'm in love with you? Come on. Don't belittle us. It's insulting and beneath you and designed to drive me away. I'm not going away" or "So this is about Mellie?" The reasoning here is logical. In the mind of Fitzgerald, Olivia's rationale is a non sequitur, as it seemingly negates their occupied temporal space (they are centuries removed from slavery), and it ignores a preexisting unavailability (he was married to Mellie prior to meeting Olivia). Even more, Olivia's mentioning of race seems to be a convenient recourse for the messiness of their situation. Fortunately, for the viewer, Olivia refuses the simplicity of logic. And, as if to remind the world just how illogical the narratives of history have been, Pope becomes or approximates a racial subjectivity resisted by both Fitzgerald Grant and the spectatorial viewer; in a sense, she reifies Hemings.

Olivia Pope's responses to Fitzgerald Grant's presumption that she is playing the race card or that her discomfort is reducible to matters of Mellie solidify those "tangled skeins" connecting her to enslaved women of her past. Countering the somewhat condescending idea that she would intentionally play the "race card" and subliminally confirming her subjective positionality in regards to Mellie, Olivia informs all those individuals in question about the implications of her allusion through her direct response to Fitz: "No, no, no! This is—I smile at her and take off my clothes for you. I wait for you. I watch for you. My whole life is you. I can't breathe because I'm waiting for you. You own me. You control me. I belong to you" (2.08). Hidden within the fabric of Olivia's frustration are the stitches of Black female enslaved subject. Like Sally Hemings's relationship to Mrs. Jefferson, Olivia's relationship to the first lady is constructed by technologies of power where the structures of race and racism force certain performances. Although Sally may not have genuinely felt the pressure to disguise her love for Thomas Jefferson (if one considers the possibility that an authentic love did not exist), she undoubtedly was forced to masquerade the truth of their intimacy to protect her life and her children's lives. Thus, the necessity to render the unlawful, dangerous, and taboo private draws a connection between Sally and Olivia. Olivia aims to make these dark realities or truths visible, to render legible the hidden aspects of interracial relationships riddled by power. Additionally, after addressing how the affair colors her relationship with a White woman in a position of power and marriage, she digs deeper to expose the layered elements directly shaping their relationship. The proclamations of "my whole life is you" and "You own me. You control me. I belong to you" all coalesce into a discourse of possession that eerily reeks of enslavement. I argue this point as the intentional and subconscious working of Rhimes's writers. On the one hand, they seem purposeful in erecting a narrative of possession that alludes to how enslaved people were considered property. On the other hand, such a narrative is so ingrained within the American national consciousness that it is readily present in all musings related to racial subjectivity. Regardless, Pope's transparency speaks to the complexity of their relationship and highlights the intricacies of power, which while presented as convenient justifications for interracial conflict are nonetheless very real factors and shapers of contemporary social relations. For Pope, and students of American race relations, the traces or stains of history are undeniably present despite the passing of time. And while the effort to rebrand or refashion the modern era with new racial scripts is honorable and constructive, as this scene magnifies, one must not do so at the expense of undermining the persistence of history or the messiness of the present.

Seemingly, in an effort to continue the discursive work captured by Olivia and Fitzgerald's garden dialogue, the episode refuses to allow the president to be subsumed by Olivia's logic. In a retort strongly worded to and aimed at undermining Pope's vulnerable professions of being caught within Grant's gravity, of being an agent whose autonomy is minimized by the throes of love, race, and power, Fitz repositions himself as object within the discourse of possession. Matching, if not exceeding, Olivia's emotional expression with his own poignant and sentimental anger, he emotes:

> You own me! You control me. I belong to you. You think I don't
> want to be a better man? You think that I don't want to dedicate
> myself to my marriage? You don't think I want to be honorable, to

be the man you voted for? I love you. I'm in love with you. You're the love of my life. My every feeling is controlled by the look on your face. I can't breathe without you. I can't sleep without you. I wait for you. I watch for you. I exist for you. If I could escape all of this and run away with you . . . There's no Sally and Thomas here. You're nobody's victim, Liv. I belong to you. We're in this together. (2.08)

The mise-en-scène framing this dialogue lends itself to the unavoidable subtext and the hidden complexities within their exchange. Temporally, under the cloak of darkness, we are to see this exchange as colored by secrecy, invisibility, and taboo. Also, the occurrence of this exchange at night and outdoors speaks to its social disallowance. Despite all of the passion existing between Olivia and Fitzgerald, it can exist only when relegated to the dark outdoors. However, the idyllic setting—a far-fetched rerendering of the Garden of Eden—antagonizes the darkness. The juxtaposition of paradisiacal emoting with violations of social mores outlines this labyrinth of love. Nevertheless, a careful reading of Fitzgerald's response, which is more soliloquy than dialogue, challenges the truths offered to the audience.

Fitzgerald's response to Olivia's pleading confession discloses his privileged subjectivity, a disregard for the difference between him and Olivia, and a strong tie to the benefits of White masculinity. Beginning with an inauthentic voice, he echoes Olivia's pronouncement of objecthood and refuses her the right to occupy the one space of privilege she holds in this relationship—"victim." Saidiya Hartman's theory on the "fungibility of the captive body" is particularly useful here, as it allows us to frame his usurpation of Pope's sentiments within the rhetoric of power. Using John Rankin's personal epistles, Hartman theorizes the complicated use of empathy to "rouse the sensibility of those indifferent to slavery by exhibiting the suffering of the enslaved and facilitating an identification between those free and those enslaved." She notes that while Rankin's intentions are well placed and meaning, as they aid in revealing the horrors and brutalities of slavery to an otherwise unaware population of people, they also flirt with the problematic, as they conflate the experiences of the enslaved with the experience of the "surrogate witness" (1997, 18). Thus, despite the benefits, "empathy in important respects confounds Rankin's efforts to identify with the enslaved because in making the slave's suffering his own, Rankin begins to feel for himself rather than for those whom this exercise in imagination presumably is designed to reach" (19). Herein lies the idea of the "fungibility of the captive body." It captures how the oppressed body's fungibility allows it to be replaced by those individuals not intimately connected to the oppression shaping its existence. That replacement, even if used to bring about social change or awareness, is but another form of violence against an already victimized entity. Understanding this notion, Grant's almost literal echo of Pope's declarations engages in an exercise of power grounded in what we might call the fungibility of the "less powerful" body. His subsumption of Olivia's feelings erases her possibility for victimhood or inequality. In fact, he ends his speech with a fiery denouncement of her ability to access that very position. In its place, he deflowers their rosy sentimental scene with a litany of interrogatives inadvertently highlighting his White masculinity while confirming his unavailability. By identifying that he wants to be a better man who is dedicated to his marriage, honorable, and the man she voted for, he reveals his desire to uphold the tenets of White patriarchy. Thus, after disavowing the truth of Olivia's position within the larger sociopolitical schema, he resituates her as the "thorn" responsible for his inability to adhere to the laws of American White masculinity. Subsequently, in an effort to shroud his caged status within the prison of prescripted manhood, he adapts Olivia's words to hide a vocal impotency caused by an inability to speak against his confinement. While standing on a promontory of fragmented possibility, uncertainty, and nebulosity, he utters the following: "If I could escape all of this and run away with you . . ." (2.08). Quiet in his expression is the declaration that he cannot leave the trappings of White manhood for the Black woman he claims to love. More unspoken is how his articulations spectacularly transport him and Olivia Pope into the antebellum period. In this moment, Olivia Pope seems to *become* Sally Hemings. She goes from free to enslaved, as the freedom defining her individuality and ensuring her agency is eradicated by a White male expression of empathy laden with power. Her emotional self's fungibility rescripts her as captive subject. And Grant's actions highlight how, "by exploiting the vulnerability of the captive body [Olivia] as a vessel for the uses, thoughts, and feelings of others [Fitzgerald himself], the humanity extended to the slave inadvertently confirms the expectations and desires definitive of the relations of chattel slavery" (Hartman 1997, 19). Olivia becomes exactly what she initially proclaimed to be—a piece of property "owned," "controlled," and "belonging" to a White male president, a White male master. And, as if to punctuate the certainty of this truth, he turns, walks away, and leaves a fractured Olivia alone within a garden whose beauty is faded by the darkness. Or perhaps more accurately, Olivia's blackness sets the stage for his departure, guaranteeing the only body free to walk away is the one occupied by Fitzgerald Grant. Given this fact, how can Grant's departure not be read as another signifier in Pope's process of becoming Sally? Does not his "right" to leave her within the/her darkness and her "responsibility" to stand helplessly gazing upon the dejected possibility scrawled upon his back reflect a power dynamic witnessed countlessly within slavery? Even more, does not the coupling of his mobility and her transfixion lead us back into the antebellum "dark" period of American race relations? Ironically, whether in a plantation-ed past or gardened present, Sally and Olivia *become* linked signs in a language of oppression. Fitzgerald Grant's departure within this intense exchange negates the idea of subjective equality, cements the nuances of power structuring their scandal, and allows for the fantastical imagining permitting re-ontologizing of Olivia Pope as Sally Hemings.

Although the promise of social equality or the radical potential embedded within humanitarian optimism might impact the ways in which the Pope-Grant relationship is understood within the popular imagination, an understanding of how differing racial bodies are exacted with different, and at times conflicting, significations ought to be considered for a fuller and more critical reading. The latter does two things: it magnifies the subtle distinctions imperative for an exposition of meaning, and it provides the reader or viewer the tools necessary to grapple with the layered discourses constructed (both intentionally and unconsciously) by the writers. More specifically, by understanding how Pope's Black female body is, at times, scripted antithetically to Grant's White male body, one might identify how, just as Fitzgerald is unable to "escape" all of the conscriptions of White America, Olivia is unable to "escape" the historical narrative marked upon her body. For me, Fitzgerald's blindness to the various "inescapabilities" present within their relationship points more sharply to the differences of their subjectivities and the schisms that lie therein. And though both parties warrant ontological wrestling, it is clear the burden of proof rests upon Olivia's shoulders, as she purports to feel disadvantaged in the imbalance the leader of the free world is either unable or unwilling to validate.

Playing with the *Darkness*

The president's usurpation of Pope's feelings prevents her the access to a particular subjective expression while also foregrounding his "performative" play with and in darkness. By "darkness" here, I am simultaneously evoking an allusion to Olivia Pope's racial demarcation by skin tone and complexion, along with the tabooed space of interraciality endemic to the American pre-emancipation past. I am interested in the degree to which Grant's transformation of Olivia Pope into a fungible emotional being involves and invokes the nostalgic racial performance played by Thomas Jefferson and Sally Hemings. I "imagine" his play (read: love) as a reification of the power and whiteness engendered by the construction and within the presence of blackness. Or, as Toni Morrison offers in *Playing in the Dark: Whiteness and the Literary Imagination*, I see Grant as an extension of the "figurations of impenetrable whiteness that surface in American literature whenever an Africanist presence is engaged" (1992, 32–33). Additionally, like those persons who "clamor, it seems, for an attention that would yield the meaning that lies in their positioning, their repetition, and their strong suggestion of paralysis and incoherence; of impasse and non-sequitur" (1992, 33), the power held by his somewhat unassuming whiteness requires, as Rhimes and company encourage out of the viewers, a concerted effort at deconstruction. If Morrison is right in her reading of American literature, which I argue she is, "because they appear almost always in conjunction with representations of black or Africanist people who are dead, impotent, or under complete control, these images of blinding whiteness seem to function as both antidote for and meditation on the shadow that is companion to this whiteness—a dark and abiding presence that moves the hearts and texts of American literature with fear and longing" (1992, 33). The argument here rests in the inescapable reality that despite intentionality or investment masked as love, the conditions of intimacy are always metascripted within a social system historically built upon profound ideas of race. Popular culture and the viewers who wish to flee the truth of the present moment, even if for sixty-minute segments, are plagued by acts of historical amnesia or relinquishing works for both comfort and entertainment. However, for Black bodies like Olivia Pope, even despite fictional medium, race is that unavoidable truth consistently bearing itself. To this end, Fitzgerald's utterances are but a reflection of the American longing to forget, to move past the hauntings of its past. While there is nobility, if not merit, in this desire, the simple wish for difference does not guarantee its appearance, and this reflection is the weight of Olivia's frustration—society does not afford her the space to suspend reality; she is never *granted* the privilege of a romance free from history. She is there to remind us "even, and especially, when American texts are not 'about' Africanist presences or characters or narrative or idiom, the shadow hovers in implication, in sign, in line of demarcation" (46–47). Therefore, as much as we wish to believe Fitzgerald and to indict Olivia (or Rhimes) for the ostensibly sloppy mishandling of a sensitive American narrative, we are pushed to meditate on how race is consistently reified and resketched, how the vestiges of the past re-present themselves as brooding hauntings. In this amorous entanglement as we see Olivia's blackness, we cannot help but see Fitzgerald's whiteness; as we see Pope's disadvantage, we cannot help but see Grant's privilege. And if for nothing else, juxtaposing Olivia's historical gaze and Fitzgerald's willful blindness, the viewer and reader of *Scandal* must seek to visualize and understand what the latter fails to do.

Fitzgerald Grant's objection to Olivia Pope's proclamation of victimhood reveals how the plight of African American womanhood is often overseen or rendered invisible in America. More specifically, it magnifies the eclipsing power of White masculinity, the privilege of blindness, and the dangers of the interracial dialectic. On the one hand, Olivia is dualistically tormented by a layered DuBoisian double consciousness. As both a racialized and a gendered subject, she must wrestle with the phenomenon captured by DuBois's theorization of how African Americans are psychically affected by the racial system: "It is a peculiar sensation, this double-consciousness, this sense of always looking at one's self through the eyes of others, of measuring one's soul by the tape of a world that looks on in amused contempt and pity. One ever feels his two-ness,—an American, a Negro; two souls, two thoughts, two unreconciled strivings; two warring ideals in one dark body, whose dogged strength alone keeps it from being torn asunder" (1995 [1903], 45). Reminding us of the dialectics of race, DuBois makes clear the rupture between Olivia Pope and Fitzgerald Grant—how Olivia comes to see and understand herself as Sally Hemings runs contrary to Fitzgerald's view, as the latter is never made to carry the burden historically guaranteed for the former. In a sense, the viewer is more privy to how their relationship is constricted by an ocular-ontological difference, or an inability to fully recognize or visualize each other's *quidditas*. However, as DuBois himself might have argued, such an inability more readily shows itself in those identified or identifying as White, for blindness, like prestige, was fundamentally a racialized privilege. Thus, the viewer sees what Fitzgerald cannot—Olivia Pope, as a Black woman, is simultaneously a modern and historical subject who, while a free Black woman far removed from the peculiar institution, can at any given moment *become* the enslaved women of her past. Perhaps the consideration of Olivia Pope as Sally Hemings augments the speculative realism of blackness as it encourages a reconsideration of the ways in which we come to know or read particular subjectivities. Or maybe the modern Black subject's inability to escape certain historical scriptings pushes us to rethink politics of identity and intersectionality. Either way, Olivia's self-perceiving as Sally and Fitzgerald's denial of such point to how the construction of Black womanhood requires greater interrogation.

"This Narrative Is No Fiction . . ."

What happens when we divorce ourselves from the constraints of genre in an effort to explore the hidden meanings of a particular text? What becomes of our reading of *Scandal* when we consider the aforementioned deconstructed exchange between Olivia Pope and Fitzgerald Grant as a metonym for the larger intentionality and aim of the series? How do we describe this particular narrative when we allow Pope to be refigured as a symbol or signifier of an older discourse? Inevitably and ultimately, the realization of discursive work being at play within the dialogics of Shonda Rhimes's hit political thriller *Scandal* compels us to rethink whether "fiction" adequately captures the series. By questioning the fictional aspect of the show, I do not mean to suggest that Kerry Washington is Olivia Pope or that Olivia Pope is Sally Hemings; however, I am interested in how the medium engages with, while expanding, a sort of postmodern and speculative realist blackness. Once we concede Pope as a subject marked and taunted by the same transcendental signifier responsible for Hemings, we open the door for new hermeneutics concerning racial identity in general and Black womanhood in particular. We also acquiesce to the temporary blurring of genre for the purpose of reaching new understandings of Black female existential complexity. But even more important, through critical forgiveness, we authorize Rhimes and company creative license, as we know the caverns of epistemological work require the risky bending of temporality and reality. We do so in the spirit of spectatorial prophets who believe in the inevitability of desired truths being discovered and revealed.

The profundity of *Scandal*'s subtext depends on the allowance of historical allusion and demands the audience's patience in the careful unfolding and delicate engagement with the narrative of Black womanhood. Indeed, to measure the full merit of the show, one must grapple with how Olivia Pope is constellated with not just Sally Hemings but also other enslaved or free women of color who had the unique displeasure of navigating all the structures and technologies of power present within a White male–centered enterprise. And while Rhimes has chosen Hemings's narrative to spearhead the discursive descent, there are others perhaps more apt. For instance, Olivia might have easily said that she was feeling a little "Linda Brent"—the pseudonym used by once enslaved Harriet Jacobs in her autobiographical novel, *Incidents in the Life of a Slave Girl* (1861).

In the preface to the novel, Jacobs begins by stating, "Reader be assured this narrative is no fiction" (2000 [1861], xix). Although anticipating how easily her northern readership would undermine the truth of her accounts, the statement resonates with the resistance expressed by Grant when Pope attempted to share her existential sentiments. Pope, caught between her extramarital affair with Grant and another White male of power, Jake Ballard, finds herself very much akin to Brent who, in an effort to maintain her moral purity and chastity within the system of slavery, found herself caught between her master, Dr. Flint, and her chosen "lover," Mr. Sands. The differences between these women and their complicated relationships are obvious, as Linda's movement is determined by the wish for purity and freedom, whereas Olivia is seemingly trapped within the throes of love. Nevertheless, the similarities rest in the machinations of power, how each woman, regardless of historical space, is up against a racial system of patriarchy in which Black women and Black womanhood are rendered abject and consistently denied. Sexual autonomy and agency connect these two women across histories and genre. Both are in search of a freedom to be loved in a sense, along with a right to their own bodies.

Linda Brent's pursuit of freedom lies in the ability to escape the unwanted advances of Dr. Flint; Olivia Pope's freedom lies in the opportunity to break away from the unhealthy tie to the married Fitzgerald Grant. Similarly, both women fail at finding these freedoms in Black men—whereas Dr. Flint prevents Brent's love with a Black man, the social and structural realities hinder the actualization of Pope's love with a Black man (neither had access to the power needed to save the respective women). Consequently, as readers, we must not devalue the significance of their vacillation between White men of means. When Jacobs tells her audience, "There is something akin to freedom in having a lover who has no control over you, except that which he gains by kindness and attachment" (2000 [1861], 59), she carves a textuality for the reading of Pope's situation. In the episode entitled "Snake in the Garden" (2.17), Jake examples the expression of "something akin to freedom" by giving Olivia the language articulating a subconscious desire. After trying to make sense of her own confusion, Jake interjects and offers the following: "You seem sad. And if you let me, maybe I can help you not be so sad. Because whatever happened to you, whoever happened to you, already happened. It's done. So maybe I can help you start fresh. Maybe I'm your do-over, 'cause you deserve a do-over." Immediately following his utterance, he kisses her, and the audience "sees" him as a possible medium toward her freedom from Fitzgerald. Again, it is not unlike Brent's circumstance, for Mr. Sands too erected himself as an opportunity for freedom. As Jacobs relays, "It chanced that a white unmarried gentleman had obtained some knowledge of the circumstances in which I was placed. . . . He became interested for me, and asked questions about my master. . . . He expressed a great deal of sympathy, and a wish to aid me" (2000 [1861], 58–59). Ironically, the differences in circumstances and compulsions do not erase the strong similarities in the narratives of Pope and Brent. If anything, students of history and popular culture more deeply understand the possibility for their genealogical linkage.

While the ties between Olivia Pope and Linda Brent are innumerable and make for a fascinating read, there is simply not enough textual space for its exploration within this chapter. For the reader who finds him- or herself curious, here are a few delineated items for further investigation: First, both Dr. Flint and President Grant offer the respective women cottages as gestures of love. Second, both women are chastised and temporarily disowned by their families for being caught within White-male love triangles. Third, both Linda and Olivia carry the burden of dealing with jealous wives and must navigate the precarious waters of negotiating relationships with White women. Fourth, both Black women are preoccupied and protective of those persons who are within their "care and custody" (Brent's investment in her children foreshadows Olivia's investment in her "associates"). Fifth, both rely on their intelligence to come out victorious in what Jacobs would call "competition[s] of cunning" (2000 [1861], 142). Finally, et cetera—the narrative can never fit within the pages allotted, the time frame for each episode, or the language employed. Most important, the juxtaposition creates a new discursive space for the negotiation of meaning and the exploration of Black female identity. A new exploration will allow students of American history and critics of popular culture to challenge how we theorize Black womanhood. As Sharon Holland highlights, "Whenever neoliberal thought wants to think about the body of color, this figure is deployed through a historical matrix that mires the racially embodied in one particular historical dynamic" (2012, 52). These women—whether Pope and Hemings, Pope and Brent, or Pope and any other signifier of Black female enslavement—prompt a reevaluation of subjectivity and coax more creative ways to wrestle with identity.

Undeniably, these women are linked by "tangled skeins," which are all scripted by narratives of oppression. And just as "Jacobs sees an extant networking of genealogical inheritance, [and] by pulling at these skeins . . . shows how complacent beliefs in the staying logic of patri(lineal) fictions . . . are laughable" (Smith 1996, 267), the coupling of these women gives birth to a series of counternarratives. These counternarratives work for all parties engaged, as we learn more about Olivia Pope and her actions through a revisitation of Hemings and Brent. However, and perhaps more significant, Pope's characterization gives us the opportunity to revisit and revise the narratives we have so easily ingested about women such as Sally Hemings and Harriet Jacobs. From Fitzgerald's love of her, albeit unhealthy and laden with power dynamics, we are required to survey the myriad possibilities of how love can exist within systems of oppression and slavery. In this regard, we might reimagine Sally Hemings as someone with the agency to beget attraction and love, as an enslaved Black woman whose master found something of greater merit in her than those elements reserved simply for property. Even more, we might discover within the matrices of love, scandal, power, and oppression a reservoir of freedom, power, and autonomy so easily eclipsed or erased by a preoccupation with White male power and privilege. Ultimately, if we trust Rhimes enough to critically engage her series, we are led to the point where we must detach our readings of Black female subjectivity from the narrative of the slave. This point is not to obscure the reality of slavery; rather, it is to encourage us to recognize the ontological truth of Black women—they were and are so much more than the history that marks their bodies; they were and are entities in and of themselves; they are complex beings that, while victims of histories of oppression, are also the recipients of love, attraction, and agency. Olivia Pope's plea within *Scandal* is clear—she wishes for Fitzgerald, the proverbial symbol of America (which implicates the viewer), to see and love her for who she is in essence. That love requires sacrifice, risk, and the selflessness necessary to read a person or a text exactly as it has been written.

References

DuBois, W. E. B. 1995 [1903]. *The Souls of Black Folk*. New York: Penguin.

Gordon-Reed, Annette. 1997. *Thomas Jefferson and Sally Hemings: An American Controversy*. Charlottesville: Univ. Press of Virginia.

Hartman, Saidiya. 1997. *Scenes of Subjection: Terror, Slavery, and Self-Making in Nineteenth-Century America*. Oxford: Oxford Univ. Press.

Holland, Sharon P. 2012. *The Erotic Life of Racism*. Durham, NC: Duke Univ. Press.

Jacobs, Harriet. 2000 [1861]. *Incidents in the Life of a Slave Girl*. New York: Penguin.

Morrison, Toni. 1992. *Playing in the Dark: Whiteness and the Literary Imagination*. New York: Random House.

Smith, Stephanie A. 1996. "The Tender of Memory: Restructuring Value in Harriet Jacobs's *Incidents in the Life of a Slave Girl*." In *Harriet Jacobs and "Incidents in the Life of a Slave Girl": New Critical Essays*, edited by Deborah M. Garfield and Rafia Zafar, 251–74. New York: Cambridge Univ. Press.

6 | "You're Nobody's Victim, Liv"

The Scandal of Black Love
and White Hegemony in *Scandal*

CHRISTOPHER A. HOUSE AND
SEAN EVERSLEY BRADWELL

IN A RHETORICAL MOMENT of Black love and the Obama White House, famed televisual writer, producer, and screenwriter Shonda Rhimes brilliantly captured imaginations with the sordid relationship of a different political power couple: President Fitzgerald "Fitz" Grant (Tony Goldwyn) and Olivia "Liv" Pope (Kerry Washington). At a first televisual reading, *Scandal* promotes status quo White hetero-male patriarchy that is intimately and simultaneously connected to the protection of White femininity, the availability of Black femininity, and the denial of Black masculinity. However, this chapter demonstrates beyond a surface-level analysis that *Scandal* rhetorically positions Black women viewers to engage in a deeper and more radical reading of Pope's relationship with Edison Davis (Norm Lewis), Jake Ballard (Scott Foley), Franklin Russell (Brian White), and Fitz Grant.

In this chapter, we employ Stuart Hall's (1980) framework of audience-reception theory to offer a more complicated explanation of how the show is a site of struggle for meaning for Black women and invariably contributes to the show's success—particularly with Black women. We argue that juxtaposing the reality of a readily available and consumable form of Black love in then president and first lady Obama, Rhimes may in fact be encouraging Black women viewers to engage in *oppositional* readings of White hegemony and Black love. We contend that it is precisely the recontextualization of Olivia's interracial relationships that calls forth such a radical reading. Our analysis highlights the ways that Rhimes may be using Olivia and Fitz to talk back to traditional statements from White hegemony—oppositional statements that reaffirm Black women's fuller agency and humanity. However, our examination of Black women audience responses to *Scandal* via Black Twitter (BT, a term that will be defined and contextualized later in this chapter) also reveals that Black women are engaging in multiple readings of the show.

Our study locates Black Twitter as a space of community for *Scandal*'s Black women viewers. Consequently, we explore how Black women are able to move beyond the actors and the acting in a way that allows them to view the show's dialogue as part of a larger conversation directly between Rhimes and Black women. Our findings suggest that Rhimes's scripting of the relationship between Olivia and her suitors holds meaning for Black women audiences in three important ways: Black women have a desire for a strong Black love story, that is, shared love between two Black people; Black women should "talk back" to White hegemony; and Black women want a new Black love story, that is, love relationships on their terms that are not bound by racial and economic boundaries. In conclusion, we speak to the implications of a new Black love story in which Olivia, who occupies a racialized and gendered space, wields tremendous interpersonal and structural power. Ultimately, we argue that Black women's ability to attribute meaning to *Scandal* from multiple decoding positions is liberating in that wider expressions of love may create critical spaces for Black women to wield enough power to have love on their own terms.

Contextualizing Twenty-First-Century Black Love: The Obama Era

Tears streamed down the faces of Black America as the world watched Barack and Michelle Obama, newly elected US president and first lady, take the Grant Park stage in Chicago on the evening of November 4, 2008. Months later, Barack and Michelle Obama slow-danced their way into the nation's highest elected office as Beyoncé Knowles sang Etta James's "At Last" for their 2009 presidential inaugural ball.

Consequently, President Barack and First Lady Michelle Obama became one of the most visible expressions of Black love in the world. The couple's infectious smiles and exchanges of love were captured on our televisions and ultimately captured the hearts of Black America. We attentively watched as this cool, fashionable, and now incredibly powerful Black couple moved to Washington, DC. Black love was in the house! Black love was in the White House! In such a historic political and social moment, the Obamas were a reaffirming picture of traditional African American family life and also provided an aspirational vision of what African Americans can attain (Inniss and Feagin 1995).

The image of Black love reflected in the Obamas stood in stark contrast to the sharp decline of African American marriages and the relationship realities of other Black Americans across the country (Chaney and Fairfax 2013). The palpable Black love shared between Barack and Michelle—for example, their fist bumps, hugs, private dinner dates, and other public displays of affection—was regularly discussed in the media and held up in Black America as an example of what a "healthy, fulfilling, and long-lasting relationship can look like" (Phillips, Brown, and Parks 2011, 147). This love, while remaining real, was less of a reality for more and more Black women. This is to say, as Phillips, Brown, and Parks (2011) contend, the husband-and-wife relationship of the Obamas became a source of hope for the future of African American relationships in the face of a pervasive public rhetoric that embodies the colloquialism "A good man is hard to find, and a good Black man is even harder to find." In this case, Michelle Obama had found her good man in Barack, and Black America loved how he loved her. Consequently, Barack's name took on a new meaning within the context of Black love relationships, Black masculinity, and the relationship prospects for Black women. "President Barack Obama's name has become shorthand for a Black man with integrity, character, and spirituality, one who loves and values his wife and makes his family a priority—in other words, the kind of man that many Black women had despaired of finding" (Scott 2009).

Given the long history of mediated stereotypes of Black identity, the mediated presentation of a real image of Black love shared between the Obamas provided a "psychic healing" to the aspirations of African American relationships (Desmond-Harris 2011, 164). The relational aspirations inspired by the Obamas is then best examined alongside an understanding of Black America's identification with the Obamas. It served as the primary means of persuasion that this type of Black love was attainable, especially for African American women (Phillips, Brown, and Parks 2011; Burke 1969). Black Americans do not so much identify with the Obamas in their present moment as Ivy League graduates who had a meteoric rise to power; rather, Black Americans identify with the Obamas' life story. In short, Black people identify with the struggle of Barack and Michelle Obama as they worked their way up to the top.

The Obamas represent a new moment in American history for Black love and political power. Black Americans could easily turn on their television and see real Black love and a political power couple in the White House yet still yearned for a Black love story on prime-time television. The first family highlighted the reality that "Black love is not by any means a mythical creature—seeing Black love on TV is" (Gordan 2015). Enter the 2012 premiere of *Scandal*—a show representing a new moment in television history as Olivia Pope's character gives audiences the first African American lead actress in a network drama since 1974.

Methodological and Theoretical Context

Scholars (Collins 2000 [1990]; Wanzo 2013; Bobo 1995) rightly maintain that in their struggle for self-definition, Black cultural producers like Rhimes create representations of Black women in popular culture that challenge historic, dominant, and oppressive televisual codes. Therefore, audience-reception theory is important to conceptualize and understand how Black women read and make meaning of *Scandal*. Hall theorizes three hypothetical positions from which audiences decode televisual discourses: dominant-hegemonic position, negotiated position, and oppositional position (1980, 142–44).

Applying Hall's theory of three possible decoding positions to our study strengthens our analysis of Black women *Scandal* audiences' complex understanding of a Black love story. Key to understanding Hall's theory of hypothetical positionality is Hall's concept of cultural hegemony: "Cultural hegemony is never about pure victory or about pure domination (that's not what the term means); it is never a zero-sum cultural game; it is always about shifting the balance of power in the relations of culture; it is always about changing the dispositions and the configurations of cultural power, not getting out of it" (1993, 106–7). Thus, negotiating the process of reading and meaning making allows for a recognition of how Black cultural products may at the same time reify and resist historically oppressive representations of blackness, in this case female representations.

Hall's (1993) concept of cultural hegemony provides us with a particularly helpful lens to examine Black women's responses to *Scandal*. That is, cultural hegemony recognizes how past representations of Black women come to bear on Black women's representations vis-à-vis Olivia's character in *Scandal*. Such an acknowledgment at the same time grants agency to Rhimes and other Black cultural producers to reflect alternative visions of Black women's lived experiences or what Pixley (2015) coins the "Super Trope." In using cultural hegemony as a critical lens through which to view *Scandal*, Hall enables us to escape an either-or binary reading of Black cultural products as either totally liberating or totally oppressive to Black women. Employing Hall's theory creates a rich conceptual space of study that is rife with contestation and contradiction (Hall 1993). Thus, we examine Black women as both cultural producers and at the same time cultural consumers and "Black authentic" representations like *Scandal* as a site of rhetorical struggle (Brown, Baldon, and Stanton 2012). Real or authentic Black cultural representations need not reflect the full range of realities of an entire group but rather, as Wanzo claims, "only represent *a* real that is recognizable to some portion of the audience" (2013, 375–76). Hence, cultural hegemony and audience-reception theories position us to more clearly comprehend the nuances and diversity of meaning found in Black Twitter as a virtual space of community for Black women's reception and readings of *Scandal*.

Black Twitter

Identifying Black Twitter as a space of community to employ audience-reception theory informs our appreciation of how Black women negotiate the meaning-making process in the viewing of *Scandal*. Researchers involved with the "Black Twitter Project" at the University of Southern California's Annenberg Innovation Lab defined Black Twitter "tentatively . . . as a discursive phenomenon in which individuals and groups use Twitter as a counterpublic space to engage in everyday talk about cultural, social, and political events that are important to Black communities both nationally and globally" (Annenberg Innovation Lab 2014). Ultimately, Black Twitter may best be described as a city, and "if Twitter were a city, Black Twitter would be the Black part of town. Everyone can observe it, but only certain users understand it enough to successfully navigate it" (@SYLVIAOBELL 2014, 40).

In short, BT appears to be a site of blackness—a location where blackness is affirmed as well as performed (Brock 2012; Sharma 2013). For example, BT's use of hashtags is already a familiar component of Black culture. Hashtags are "signifiers," and at the same time they signify. In fact, they are not hashtags; they become Blacktags—"a particular type of hashtag associated with BT users (mainly African Americans), because the tag itself and/or its associated content appears to connote 'Black' vernacular expression in the form of humor and social commentary" (Sharma 2013, 51). Stated differently, the conventions of performative blackness as well as sociopolitical blackness are effortlessly transferable to Twitter.

Beyond signifying (Brock 2012; Florini 2014), a major part of this digital mapping is Twitter's built-in translation of "call and response." Tweet. Reply. Tweet. Retweet. This call-and-response nature of Twitter dialogues may best be demonstrated by Rhimes herself. Rhimes actively tweets and responds to tweets—and frequently did so during live airings of the show. Up until the airing of the final episode of *Scandal*, the biography line for Rhimes's Twitter account read, "I make stuff up for a living. Remember, it's not real, okay? Don't tweet me your craziness."[1] However, there are plenty of times that more serious discourse is exchanged through her tweets and retweets. For example:

> @shondarhimes: The last image does me in. Because he's just somebody's baby. That's all. He's someone's child. #BlackLivesMatter???????????????????????? #*Scandal*???????????????????????? (March 5, 2015)?.

> @shondarhimes: Stop asking women questions about what they wear to cover the containers they carry their brains around in. #AskHer More. (February 22, 2015)

These conversations give insight into the intentionality behind the writing of *Scandal* and Rhimes's awareness of larger issues that influence messages of the show. They also demonstrate some of the engagement between Rhimes and Black women who consume *Scandal*. Everett notes that ShondaLand fans who engage in oppositional and negotiated readings of *Scandal* often turn to Twitter to "refashion" scenes of the show to "suit their own viewing pleasure" (2015, 38). We analyze this refashioning as part of Black women audiences' meaning-making processes described below, using several love scenes between Olivia and her male suitors.

Our use of BT as a data source is supported by research on social media usage rates. A 2014 Pew Research reports that 23 percent of all adults who use social media are active on Twitter. For Black adults who use social media, the percentage increases to 27 percent (the highest percentage reported among racial groups) and jumps to 40 percent when talking about Black and African American Twitter users between the ages of eighteen and twenty-nine (Smith 2014). To be certain, there is a great deal of concern in using Twitter or BT as a

---

1. Since then, Shonda Rhimes changed her Twitter bio to a reference to her TED talk and her website as well as the dialogue from a famous scene from the series finale, in which Mellie asks Olivia about her plans post working for the White House: "'What will you do instead?' [Mellie asks] 'WHATEVER I WANT' [Olivia replies]."

source of data. Blogger Tamara Winfrey Harris argues, "Watching Black folks on Twitter tells no more about African American culture than watching the forums at *Salon* or *Gawker* reveals about White culture. Attempting to assign deep cultural meaning to trending topics like #hoodhoe is a reflection of racial bias" (cited in Sharma 2013, 52). We argue the contrary and believe there is much to be learned from topics like #hoodhoe, but Harris's warning is instructive. The co-option and misinterpretation of "Blacktags" can lead to *reflections of racial bias*. This point is further complicated by the fact that BT is not exclusively Black, and many of the hashtags and "Blacktags" have multiracial contributors and multiracial connotations.

Still, while it is true that not everyone who participates in BT is Caribbean, African, or Black American, it is safe to say that without Caribbean, African, or Black Americans, BT would not exist. Sharma argues, "The complexity of online racial formations raises the question of whether adequate attention is being paid to the significance of the online environments that race exists in: how are both race and digital networks transformed in their mutual encounter?" (2013, 47). If read carefully, and selectively, then, BT can offer insights to critical aspects of Black culture, including BT's decoding and refashioning of *Scandal*.

Data Collection

For the purposes of this study, we watched *Scandal* as viewers throughout the entire first five seasons (2012–16). We observed each season for a second time for the purpose of coding and observation of the interpersonal interactions of Olivia and Edison, Olivia and Jake, Olivia and Franklin, and Olivia and Fitz. Additionally, we identified any conversation between other characters on the show in which references to the aforementioned relationships were made. We employed Owen's thematic analysis for relational communication in the selection and coding of key transcriptions discussed below. Selections were made using three criteria: repetition, "the explicit repetition of key words, phrases, or sentences"; forcefulness identified by "vocal inflection, volume, or dramatic pauses, which serve to stress and subordinate some utterances from others" (1984, 275); and Keyton's idea of recurrence, which is "present when at least two parts of a report may have the same thread of meaning" (2006, 41). We discussed the coded data, indexed data as categories emerged, and then later organized data into themes using the constant comparative method (Glaser and Strauss 1967). The most salient interactions are fully transcribed and discussed below.

Comparatively, our sampling of BT included researching the hashtag #Scandal and some combination of secondary hashtags and "Blacktags": #Blacklove, #bringbackEdison #Edison, #sallyhemings, #LivandFitz, #interracial, #Franklin, #Russell, and #TeamJake to name a few. We reviewed all the tweets that met that threshold to identify major themes and sentiments. We coded them for later retrieval and analysis; in doing so, key themes and tensions emerged as we discussed and synthesized the data. We also regularly followed live Twitter feeds during original broadcasts. Our reading of the coded material through Hall's audience reception theory guides the generalizations in this chapter. What follows are our findings of how Black women using BT may construct meaning from the show.

Analysis

Our findings reveal that Black women audiences made meaning of Olivia's relationships with Edison, Jake, Franklin, and Fitz in at least two distinct ways. First, Black women clearly expressed the need for a strong Black love shared between two Black people and the refusal of anti–Black love sentiments. Second, Black women expressed the desire and acceptance of a new Black love story that is inclusive of expanding their love prospects beyond Black men, challenging White hegemony within interracial relationships, and Black women championing a strong love of self. We address each in turn using selected representative BT tweets.

Black Love in Scandal

In the second season of *Scandal*, viewers meet Olivia's previous longtime love interest and former fiancé, Democratic senator Edison

Davis. Olivia and Edison lived together in Georgetown and in New York City from 2002 to 2006 ("Hunting Season" [2.03]). After three years of estrangement, Edison, the newly appointed Senate Intelligence Committee member, seeks to become reacquainted with Olivia ("The Other Woman" [2.02]). When President Fitz learns of the interaction between Edison and Olivia, he has Edison removed from the Senate Intelligence Committee. Consequently, Edison seeks out Olivia as a potential client in need of her help. At the same time, however, he begins to romantically pursue her ("Hunting Season" [2.03]). After several invitations, Olivia finally agrees to a date with Edison. In "Spies Like Us" (2.06), Edison confronts Olivia about the lack of intimacy in their relationship and says, "Invite me in. It's time. Because I am a man, and I don't play games, and you and I are very good together, so, so let me in now, or I walk away." While standing at her door listening to Edison, Olivia begins to sob. She then runs and embraces Edison. The two walk into her apartment, and she starts to undress him. Things take a turn for the worse in their relationship when Edison forcefully inquires into the nature of Olivia's past "serious boyfriend," Fitz. Edison then accuses her of being the president's mistress. Olivia responds, "In the past three minutes, you've called me a criminal, a whore, an idiot, and a liar, so this is pretty much the last time we'll be speaking. So, one, who I am or am not screwing, what I am or am not doing, is no longer any of your damn business" ("A Criminal, a Whore, an Idiot and a Liar" [2.11]).

Edison quickly apologizes and shortly thereafter proposes to Olivia for the third time. In a key scene from a later episode ("Nobody Likes Babies" [2.13]), Edison appears at Olivia's door to escort her to the funeral services for Supreme Court justice Verna Thornton (Debra Mooney) when they have this dialogue:

OLIVIA: I . . . I have your grandmother's ring. I kept it safe. Right here.

EDISON: I've given you this ring twice, and both times, you've given it back.

OLIVIA: Edison . . .

EDISON: Tell me you don't want to be married. Tell me that being a senator's wife is too much. Tell me that you don't want a family. Tell me why I've been wasting my time. Tell me something.

OLIVIA: I'm sorry. Edison, I'm really sorry. I could marry you. I could be a senator's wife. I'd probably be happy. I could probably give all this up and live in a country house and have babies and be normal. I could. But I don't want to. I'm not built for it. I don't want normal and easy and simple. I want . . . I want . . .

EDISON: What? What? What do you want, Olivia?

OLIVIA: I want painful, difficult, devastating, life-changing, extraordinary love. Don't you want that too?

The end of this conversation marks the end of a potential rekindling of the Olivia-Edison relationship and what viewers point to as the first possibility of *Scandal*'s Black love story, that is, love shared between two Black people. Rhimes is very clear, however, on the kind of reading she intended for audiences to engage in as they wrestled to make sense of the Olivia-Edison relationship. "You weren't supposed to be rooting for Edison. If you were rooting for Edison, I would be very surprised," Rhimes once said. Rhimes's intention is clear as to the symbolic value that Black women should assign to Edison's performance of Black masculinity and pedigree: "He's the guy you're supposed to want on paper. He has every single quality of a guy you should want. He's a United States senator, he's handsome, he's rich, he loves Liv, he wants to get married and settle down. Except he's not the guy that she wants. Period. That was the goal for him. He's a great guy for someone else" (Abrams 2013). Rhimes's intended audience reading position for Edison's character is fraught with contradiction and perhaps that fact accounts for Black female audiences' multiple readings of Edison.

Hall (1980) acknowledges that most audiences do not accept a cultural producer's desired reading position for them. The prospect of a Black love relationship between Olivia and Edison provided Black female audiences with more than one subject position from which to make meaning of the show. It is clear that some Black women read the demise of the Olivia-Edison relationship from an oppositional position that perhaps Rhimes never anticipated. Our first finding indicates that the absence of the Black love story, for many, equated to the show expressing anti–Black love sentiments.

Anti–Black Love Sentiments and Scandal

Immediately following the "A Criminal, a Whore, an Idiot, and a Liar" (2.11) episode, prominent Black media personality Star Jones took to Twitter to register her voice. Jones's comments are representative and instructive of how Black women arrived at an oppositional reading of Olivia's rejection of Edison:

> @StarJonesEsq: I love #scandal. @kerrywashington is ridiculously good . . . but I'd love to see #OliviaPope reject the unethical & immoral for a good brother! (January 26, 2013)

> @StarJonesEsq: I get POWER . . . I get POSITION . . . but @shondarhimes can the fierce powerful SINGLE sister pick the fierce powerful SINGLE brother? #Scandal (January 26, 2013)

From the number of tweets and retweets, we notice how other Black women reject Rhimes's intended subject position as the singular way to interpret Edison's character. From this position, we learn how some Black women read Edison and Olivia as representing the quintessential Black power couple and love relationship akin to the pre–White House Obamas. Thus, to deny Black women audiences an opportunity to see the Olivia-Edison love relationship materialize is to essentially deny Black women a long-overdue Black love story on television (Gordan 2015). Hence, Rhimes's decision to end the Olivia-Edison relationship was read in a way that said less about the meaning Black women attributed to Edison's character and more about the meanings they attributed to Rhimes:

> @writeonkiah: #Scandal will have you believing Black love really doesn't exist smh. I'm all for interracial, but damn! (April 10, 2014)

@writeonkiah: Shonda Rhimes doesn't write Black-on-Black love. Hollywoods afraid of that. Black people loving Black people: a dangerous thought #Scandal (February 5, 2015)

@sevenmarie: #Scandal was good at first but now the drama is redundant and I cant get over the fact that Shonda Rhimes hates Black love. (January 29, 2015)

These tweets illustrate how some Black women ascribed meaning to the lack of a Black love story between Olivia and Edison as Rhimes's personal attack on Black love. In other words, many Black women read Olivia and Edison simply not as characters in a television show, but rather understood them to be the voices through which Rhimes is actually speaking. Hence, the underlying message of these tweets is disappointment and anger given the nonexistence of *Scandal*'s Black love story. Our interpretations of Black women audience engagement with BT leads to the observation that Black women, in fact, desired a *strong* Black love story.

A Strong Black Love in Scandal

@SLIMMVIXEN: They Should have found Olivia Pope a better Black Love interest bcuz I would prolly keep telling Ole Buddy No too lol #Scandal (November 8, 2012)

@HomeGirlBlog: @matternalnagging lol. THANK you! He has zero machismo. NONE! I wanted @ScandalWriters to give us Black love but not this way. smh #Scandal (November 16, 2012)

@Shayadro: Edison's will be going bye bye! I like to see black love but I hate spinelessness! #Scandal (January 10, 2013)

In specifically looking at the tweets following three key episodes, "All Roads Lead to Fitz" (2.05), "Spies Like Us" (2.06), and "One for the Dog" (2.10), @HomeGirlBlog, @Shayadro, and @SLIMMVIXEN demonstrate how Black women make meaning of *Scandal* from a negotiated reading position. Here, we see how Black women viewers generally read Edison's performance of masculinity in a way that did not equate to an outright rejection of Black love by Rhimes. Rather, Black women's rejection of Edison's "respectable" performance of Black masculinity and compatibility with Olivia adds complexity to *Scandal*'s Black love story. Others read Edison's performance of Black masculinity as that which is easy to hate and as the type of performance of Black masculinity that is less than what Olivia, or good Black women, deserves. Such responses on Twitter lead to a particular insight into what the Olivia-Edison relationship meant to other Black women. Mainly, Black women wanted to see a Black love story but not just any kind of Black love.

Case in point is the controversial 2015 "The Lawn Chair" (4.14) episode where Olivia meets the Georgetown Law–educated Black community activist Marcus Walker (Cornelius Smith Jr.). Our findings illustrate a negotiated reading of Black women audiences that found Walker to be exactly the kind of Black man who would be a suitable love interest for Olivia:

> @AngieSikes: OMG! Could Olivia possibly date a single black male who is not afraid or infatuated with her? #Scandal #BlackLove #YeahRight! (March 5, 2015)

> @Salmoore: Olivia, please let this be your next boo. I need for there to be some strong black love #ScandalABC #Scandal (March 5, 2015)

> @Nokidizzle: I think Olivia is getting a Black love interest That standoff was a lot! #Scandal (March 6, 2015)

Throughout this episode, Black women infer that Marcus could not be intimidated, nor was he infatuated or easily controlled by Olivia—a performance of Black masculinity to be desired. Black women audiences' meaning-making processes involved role playing the part of Pope in her (that is, their own) love relationships (Wellbon 1992). Thus, Black women's responses to any Olivia-Marcus interactions raises the question whether Black women believe Edison is not a suitable partner for themselves or simply not a suitable partner for Olivia. The Olivia-Marcus relationship also never materialized, but Walker went on to join Olivia Pope & Associates in a subsequent season.

After Rhimes failed in previous episodes and seasons to give Black women either a Black love story or a strong Black love story, BT exploded when Franklin Russell (Brian White) and Olivia embarked on a whirl-wind romance late in season five ("Baby, It's Cold Outside" [5.09]). Our examination of the Olivia-Franklin trysts highlights how Black women derived meaning of this Black love relationship from multiple reading positions. For example, when read from a *preferred* position, some Black women expressed a renewed optimism at the possibility that Rhimes had finally given them what they have long waited for:

> @Anti_Intellect: The ancestors heard our calls. @shondarimes done finally gave Pope a Black Love interest again. #Scandal (March 19, 2015)

> @dreanabeana: Russell and Liv don't make sense to me, but I'm glad she's with a Black guy. #scandal (April 2, 2015)

From Olivia's opening dialogue with Franklin, other Black women engaged in an *oppositional* reading of the relationship, as many believe that this relationship ultimately reconfirmed Rhimes's anti–Black love trajectory:

> @Legallycam225: Russell and Olivia having "pretty brown babies"? Fandom, CALM THE FUCK DOWN! Shonda will shit on your dreams #Scandal (April 1, 2015)

> @tweetsbytris: Bruh . . . @shondarhimes HATES BLACK LOVE . . . but that's fine . . . Bitter is as bitter does, I guess #HTGAWM #Scandal #PrivatePractice #Greys (September 18, 2015)

While these responses mirror our earlier findings, we identified one additional way that Black women read the short-lived relationship between Olivia and Franklin, especially after audiences learn that Franklin is a member of B613 ("Honor Thy Father" [4.18]). The less than positive messages of Black love are further complicated when Black women audiences learn that Franklin's interest in Olivia is con-trived as part of his assignment given to him by Olivia's father, Rowan. Our study suggests that akin to how Rowan could predict how his daughter would respond to this Black male suitor, Rhimes may have similarly anticipated how her Black female audience would respond to the prospect of another Black love story. Black women audiences viewed Rhimes as the voice speaking through Rowan's character and felt that she had pulled a "Papa Pope" on them. That is, Rhimes was well aware that Black female audiences wanted a Black love story and may have played on those desires with the Olivia-Franklin story:

> @chanellshorter: Yall notice the slick shade of Papa Pope sending a black love interest for Liv lol. #scandal (April 2, 2015)

> @thedaintytravir: Papa pope set up that car accident with liv 1st Black bf. Member the senator. Now set up Russell . . . LIV DONE WITH THE COCO YALL #Scandal (April 2, 2015)

Maryann Erigha's identification of *Scandal* as a crossover show that simultaneously embraces and transcends blackness gives us a way to explain the three failed attempts at a Black love story being less about Rhimes's personal politics and more about the constraints of the genre. Erigha insightfully argues, "The cautionary tale for *Scandal* and Shonda Rhimes is that White audiences yet again influence what directions studios take with Black cultural products. They influence which programs stay on air and which are canceled" (2015, 14). By genre conventions, crossover shows must appeal to both Black and White audiences, yet the question remains is the presence of a Black love story (for example, Olivia-Edison, Olivia-Marcus, Olivia-Franklin) "too Black" for White audiences? Crossover appeal demands that whiteness is featured prominently. Through Pope's use of the Black male body and denial of a lasting Black love story, we believe that Rhimes was writing a love story for Olivia that was safe for White audiences. To be clear, we put forth that Rhimes was writing a love story that dabbles around the edges of Black love while remaining safe for White audiences. Simply put, Rhimes writes her television script for White folk while she live-tweets with Black folk.

Our final set of responses supports our final argument that Rhimes's attempt to satisfy the demands of a crossover genre while at the same time addressing Black women's reading of Olivia's love choices reflects the need for an expansion of Black women's love possibilities that goes beyond essentialist notions of Black love.

A New Black Love in Scandal

Black women are attaching a new meaning to Black love. For many, interracial relationships constitute a new Black-love framework. Comments made on Twitter by @lanaltry, @allymyvents, and @FilmFatale_NYC strengthen our understanding of Olivia's scripted love choice of Fitz over Edison as empowering Black women to challenge a definition of Black love shared between two Black people and only two Black people:

> @lanaltry: I love it, a white president having an affair with a Black lady, interracial couples are the new Black #Scandal (December 6, 2012)

> @allymyvents: I love the way this white man loves this black woman #Scandal (February 12, 2015)

> @FilmFatale_NYC: Forbidden love is the new black . . . Liv and Fitz #Scandal Rayna and Deacon #Nashville (October 10, 2012)

Perhaps such thinking is an unintended consequence of the strong image of Black love in the Obama era that served as a model while also constraining Black women to heteronormative love choices to only among men of their racial group (Phillips, Brown, and Parks 2011). Still, the popularity of *Scandal* among Black women should not be seen as an explicit endorsement of interracial relationships within wider American culture (Everett 2015).[2] Even so, in this context there is no getting around the fact that part of *Scandal*'s scandal is not just the story involving the Oval Office. Of course, there is the specter of an

---

2. For example, see the furor and controversy around the 2013 Cheerios "Good for Your Heart" commercial and its 2014 sequel, featuring an interracial family (Demby 2014).

illicit affair and the spectacle of an affair that includes the president of the United States. However, these scandals are significantly increased by the spectacular consumption of *Scandal*'s interracial illicit affairs (Watts and Orbe 2002).

This is to say, Black and White relationships have been legally designated scandalous since Virginia's colonial laws banning interracial relationships in 1662. Randall Kennedy writes, "Nothing more vividly reflects American racial pathologies than the tendency to use power, especially state power, to discourage interracial love" (quoted in Sollors 2000, 142). Pascoe takes this idea further by writing, "Laws against interracial marriage didn't prevent masters from having sex with slave women or having mixed-race children . . . Rather, they prevented masters from turning slaves they slept with into respectable wives who might claim freedom, demand citizenship rights, or inherit family property" (2009, 27).

In other words, interracial relationships were deemed to be illegal, and significant energy was spent to create "moral panic" (52). Rhimes is able to tell stories that use historical narratives as part of the audience's meaning-making process as Olivia's character embraces aspects of multiple enslavement tropes: the Jezebel, the Mammy, and the Sapphire. When such historical narratives may not be so obvious, Rhimes takes to Twitter to make the connections more explicit.

> @shondarhimes: Can't believe I need to say this: yes, I wrote "black woman auctions herself off" storyline on PURPOSE. I have heard of slavery. #Scandal????????????????????? (February 13, 2015)

> @shondarhimes: @wheeltnt @kerrywashington Then respectfully I must say that I am not sure you actually know who Sally Hemings is (June 12, 2014)

Overall, there was no shortage of negative responses to Olivia's seeming proclivity to be romantically involved with White men:

> @FunkyDineva: Olivia Pope will lay up with ANY white man that will hold her. A glass of wine and that pussy is yours #scandal (October 24, 2013)

@maylady84: Ughhhhhhhh OMFG. WHO IS THIS WHITE MAN OLIVIA?! SHIT. IM SO SICK YOU And THESE WHITE MEN SAVIORS! #Scandal (February 19, 2015)

However, this response is an easy reading of *Scandal*. Deeper analysis reveals that some Black women used a *negotiated* position to respond to and remake the visual codes and signifiers placed before them. In other words, Black women rejected ("countered") White male hegemony in interracial relationships and made meaning of the relationship in a way that expands a new Black love story and simultaneously appeals to crossover audiences:

@ShannonIrene: Scandal give me hope on interracial love (October 13, 2013)

A New Black Love: Talking Back

Notwithstanding, our analysis confirms that Black women were engaging in deeper, negotiated readings of the dialogue that clearly indicate an understanding of how Rhimes uses Olivia's relationships to challenge historical narratives and White hegemony. We argue that Rhimes encouraged an oppositional reading of the Olivia-Fitz relationship *against* the historical narrative of White hegemony. Perhaps the most compelling evidence is found in the episode "Happy Birthday, Mr. President" (2.08), when Olivia tells President Grant, "I'm feeling a little, I don't know, Sally Hemings/Thomas Jefferson about all this." This would be a precursor to a longer exchange later in the show, and Sally Hemings would become a trending topic on Twitter:

FITZ: So this is about Mellie?
OLIVIA: No, no, no! This is—I smile at her and take off my clothes for you. I wait for you. I watch for you. My whole life is you. I can't breathe because I'm waiting for you. You own me. You control me. I belong to you—
FITZ: You own me! You control me. I belong to you. You think I don't want to be a better man? . . . I love you. I'm in love with you. You're the love of my life. My every feeling is controlled by the look

on your face. I can't breathe without you. I can't sleep without you.
I wait for you. I watch for you. I exist for you. If I could escape all of
this and run away with you . . . There's no Sally and Thomas here.
You're nobody's victim, Liv. I belong to you. We're in this together.

Repeatedly, Fitz (and Jake for that matter) submits to Olivia. Given the
historical narrative that gets easily mapped onto *Scandal*'s characters,
the response from Fitz here warrants more attention (see also Ventura's
analysis in chapter 3 of this volume). Unlike the real bondage condition of Sally Hemings, in this inverting of the interracial ownership
narrative, Fitz boldly proclaims to Olivia that she, in fact, owns him.
"You own me. You control me. I belong to you." Here, an oppositional
reading of Rhimes's dialogue offers a direct challenge to the historical White male supremacist narrative regarding relationships between
Black women and White US presidents. The obvious reference to Sally
Hemings and Thomas Jefferson encourages a complex and dynamic
reading of the "modern-day" relationship between Fitz and Olivia.
Later in season five, Fitz chooses Olivia over his wife, Mellie. He dramatically serves Mellie divorce papers; moves his girlfriend, Olivia, into
the White House; and publicly announces his intentions to marry her
("Get Out of Jail, Free" [5.06]). Fitz does not seek to preserve his marriage with Mellie, that is, White hegemony. Nonetheless, it is Olivia who
ends the relationship. Olivia is in control, and Olivia decides the future
of the presidential love ("It's Hard Out Here for a General" [5.10]).

Taken together, Rhimes's intentions to talk back to White hegemony inform our understanding of the ways in which Black women
used a *negotiated* position to make meaning in ways that work with,
between, and around the visual codes. Said differently, Black women
read the numerous relationships in a way that empowers one to get
beyond the script of *Scandal* and identify what Shonda Rhimes—a
Black woman—may be speaking through her characters.

A New Black Love: "Choosing Me"

Our final analysis assists us in identifying how Rhimes's scripting of
Olivia's love interest addressed what Warner calls the "affect of desire"

that Black women may experience. In short, there is a painful irony between the commodification of Black women's bodies and a simultaneous historical devaluation. Warner's idea of affect of desire suggests that through this duality, Black women want to be desired. As evidence of her desirability, Warner postulates that as a sexual subject, Olivia "receives more oral sex than anyone on network television, Black or white. And she never asks" (2015, 18). Our findings point to what may be the most radical notion of the show, that is, a Black woman centering a love of self above any romantic relationship with a man.

In one critical scene where Jake attempts to get Olivia to choose to be with either him or Fitz, we locate a prime example of Olivia engaging in this radical notion of self-love. In the end, Olivia chooses to love herself:

OLIVIA: [dancing and laughing]

JAKE: Man, do I love you.

OLIVIA: I want Vermont with Fitz.

JAKE: Oh. Okay.

OLIVIA: I also want the sun . . . with you.

JAKE: So—

OLIVIA: I'm not choosing. I'm not choosing Jake. I'm not choosing Fitz. I choose me. I'm choosing Olivia. And right now, Olivia is dancing. I'm dancing, Jake. I'm free. Now, you can dance with me or you can get off my dance floor. I'm fine dancing alone. ("Where the Sun Don't Shine!" [4.09])

Black women audiences read Olivia's decision as a choice of Black women's agency. As one might imagine, "I choose me" is one of the more quotable lines from season four, and the phrase was tweeted and retweeted on BT:

@lifebyangie: You can dance with me or get off my dance floor #ichooseme #oliviapope #Scandal (November 20, 2014)

@kerrywashington: @ninaerynn: "I choose me." That is what every woman should choose. #Scandal #TGIT @kerrywashington #TeamMe (November 20, 2014)

@RLVgtc: "Now, you can dance with me, or you can get off my dance floor. I'm fine dancing alone."—#Scandal #TeamMe #Boom (November 21, 2014)

It is here that Rhimes channels a longer genealogy of Black feminist wisdom—self-love is an act of revolution. The tweeting of "I choose me" stands as an *oppositional* reading of White hegemony, as Olivia's declaration of "choice" is also a declaration of power, agency, and self-determination. Olivia chooses Olivia! Our analysis thus leads us to a final conclusion that Shonda Rhimes and Black women demanded a new Black love story—one where a Black-love reality includes choices for Black women.

Conclusion

We argue that discourses found on BT employ multiple theoretical positions in making meaning of *Scandal* TV viewing (Hall 1980). By employing *preferred*, *oppositional*, and *negotiated* positions, it is clear Black women audiences desired strong Black love stories; challenged dominant narratives about race, gender, and sexuality; and rhetorically created space for complex readings of new Black love stories.

Further, we argue that Rhimes used *Scandal* to talk about and speak against White hegemony and to talk about and promote the self-determination and agency of Black women. This form of agency included a wider range of options and opportunities—including a possible redefinition of Black love. Black women's ability to reframe the conversation of Black love is thus an act of agency, self-determination, and Black self-love, as Black women articulate a love that is not bound by racial or economic boundaries. It appears Shonda Rhimes was trying to rewrite an old truth—Black women's agency and self-determination are an ultimate act of Black love in the face of White hegemony.

References

Abrams, Natalie. 2013. "*Scandal*'s Edison vs. Jake! Who's Better for Olivia?" *TV Guide*, Mar. 6. http://www.tvguide.com/news/Scandal-edison-jake-olivia-shonda-rhimes-spoilers-1062356/.

Annenberg Innovation Lab. 2014. "Black Twitter Project." Sept. 5. https://declara.com/content/d1qWQd59.

Bobo, Jacqueline. 1995. *Black Women as Cultural Readers*. New York: Columbia Univ. Press.

Brock, André. 2012. "From the Blackhand Side: Twitter as a Cultural Conversation." *Journal of Broadcasting & Electronic Media* 56(4): 529–49.

Brown, Kennaria, Shannon Baldon, and Amber Stanton. 2012. "Getting It 'Right?': African American Women Reading Tyler Perry's Films." In *Interpreting Tyler Perry: Perspectives on Race, Class, Gender, and Sexuality*, edited by Jamel Santa Cruze Bell and Ronald L. Jackson II, 240–53. New York: Routledge.

Burke, Kenneth. 1969. *A Rhetoric of Motives*. Berkeley: Univ. of California Press.

Chaney, Cassandra, and Nichols C. Fairfax. 2013. "A Change Has Come: The Obamas and the Culture of Black Marriage in America." *Ethnicities* 13: 20–48.

Collins, Patricia Hill. 2000 [1990]. *Black Feminist Thought: Knowledge Consciousness, and the Politics of Empowerment*. New York: Routledge.

Demby, Gene. 2014. "The Cute Cheerios Ad with the Interraical Family Is Back." *CodeSwitch*, NPR, Jan. 30. https://www.npr.org/sections/codeswitch/2014/01/30/268930004/that-cute-cheerios-ad-with-the-interracial-family-is-back.

Desmond-Harris, Jenée. 2011. "The Obamas: Beyond Troubled Love." In *The Obamas and a (Post)Racial America?*, edited by Gregory S. Parks and Matthew W. Hughey, 163–65. Oxford: Oxford Univ. Press.

Erigha, Maryann. 2015. "Shonda Rhimes, *Scandal*, and the Politics of Crossing Over." *Black Scholar* 45(1): 10–15.

Everett, Anna. 2015. "Scandalicious: *Scandal*, Social Media and Shonda Rhimes' Auteurist Juggernaut." *Black Scholar* 45(1): 34–43.

Florini, Sarah. 2014. "Tweets, Tweeps, and Signifyin': Communication and Cultural Performance on 'Black Twitter.'" *Television & New Media* 15(3): 223–37.

Glaser, Barney G., and Anselm L. Strauss. 1967. *The Discovery of Grounded Theory*. Hawthorne, NY: Aldine.

Gordan, Taylor. 2015. "Hollywood Struggles to Commit to Black Love Stories Even as Prime Time Welcomes More Diverse Casts." *Atlanta Black Star*, Mar. 1. http://atlantaBlackstar.com/2015/03/01/Holly

wood-struggles-commit-Black-love-stories-even-prime-time-welcomes
-diverse-casts/.

Hall, Stuart. 1980. "Encoding/Decoding." In *Media and Cultural Studies*, edited by Meenakshi Gigi Durham and Douglas M. Kellner, 137–44. 2nd ed. Malden, MA: Wiley-Blackwell.

———. 1993. "What Is This 'Black' in the Black Popular Culture?" *Social Justice* 20(1–2): 104–14.

Inniss, Leslie B., and Joe R. Feagin. 1995. "The Cosby Show: The View from the Black Middle Class." *Journal of Black Studies* 25: 692–711.

Keyton, Joann. 2006. *Communication Research: Asking Questions, Finding Answers*. New York: McGraw-Hill.

Owen, William Foster. 1984. "Interpretive Themes in Relational Communication." *Quarterly Journal of Speech* 70(3): 274–87.

Pascoe, Peggy. 2009. *What Comes Naturally: Miscegenation Law and the Making of Race in America*. Oxford: Oxford Univ. Press.

Phillips, Clarenda M., Tamara L. Brown, and Gregory S. Parks. 2011. "Barack, Michelle and the Complexities of a Black 'Love Supreme.'" In *The Obamas and a (Post)Racial America?*, edited by Gregory S. Parks and Matthew W. Hughey, 135–62. Oxford: Oxford Univ. Press.

Pixley, Tara-Lynne. 2015. "Trope and Associates: Olivia Pope's Scandalous Blackness." *Black Scholar* 45(1): 28–33.

Scott, Megan K. 2009. "Women Seeking: A Man Like Barack Obama." Associated Press, June 17. https://www.today.com/health/women-seeking
-man-barack-obama-1C9411018.

Sharma, Sanjay. 2013. "Black Twitter? Racial Hashtags, Networks and Contagion." *New Formations* 78: 46–64.

Smith, Aaron. 2014. "African Americans and Technology Use: A Demographic Portrait." Pew Research Center, Jan. 6. http://www.pewinternet
.org/2014/01/06/african-americans-and-technology-use/.

Sollors, Werner. 2000. *Interracialism: Black-White Intermarriage in American History, Literature and Law*. Oxford: Oxford Univ. Press.

@SYLVIAOBELL. 2014. "Looking for Black Twitter?" *Essence*, June 11. https://www.essence.com/2014/06/12/looking-black-twitter.

Wanzo, Rebecca. 2013. "Can the Black Woman Shout? A Meditation on 'Real' and Utopian Depictions of African American Women on Scripted Television." In *African Americans on Television: Race-ing for Ratings*, edited by David L. Leonard and Lisa A. Guerrero, 373–89. Santa Barbara, CA: Praeger.

Warner, Kristin. 2015. "If Loving Olitz Is Wrong, I Don't Wanna Be Right: ABC's *Scandal* and the Affect of Black Female Desire." *Black Scholar* 45(1): 16–20.

Watts, Eric King, and Mark Orbe. 2002. "The Spectacular Consumption of 'True' African American Culture: 'Whassup' with the Budweiser Guys?" *Critical Studies in Media Communication* 19(1): 1–20.

Wellbon, Yvonne. 1992. "Calling the Shots: Black Women Directors Take the Helm." *Independent* 15(2): 18–22.

7 | Insider/Outsider

Olivia Pope and the Pursuit of Erotic Power

KADIAN POW

OLIVIA POPE was a long time coming for so many in the Black community who hungered for "positive" and "powerful" Black women on TV. Yet from the outset, the persistent and pervasive tropes of the Mammy, the Jezebel, and the Sapphire have shaped the discourse of the Olivia Pope character in relation to either intersectional oppression or Black resistance. Such critiques, though grounded in the long shadow of the African American experience, often reflect the tendency to interpret blackness primarily through the framework of the White gaze. These modes of seeing reductively define powerful depictions of Black feminine subjectivity as a function of political expressiveness that should explicitly advocate on behalf of a Black collective. While the publicness of Black identity will always matter, exclusive focus on it leaves little room to appreciate the force of desire as a valid and necessary way of engaging Black cultural subjects, particularly in Black texts (Tate 1998). Addressing the portrayal of Olivia Pope from a lens of representation, fraught with binary notions of good/bad, or positive/negative, proves too limiting. Instead, I am more concerned with how the character engages blackness and femininity beyond dominant, externally defined, and performative tropes of Black feminine social identity.

The portrayal of Olivia Pope as a Black subject is a perfect opportunity to look at the tensions of her (not necessarily sexual) inner impulses. Examining Black interiority as a necessary source of power upon which blackness (and femininity) draws is a way of queering the portrayal of Olivia Pope's character. It is the exploration into Olivia Pope as a being in pursuit of erotic power that this chapter intends to take on, including the ways in which her interior life is held in dramatic tension with the socially defined expectations of the Black female body she inhabits.

Unpacking Olivia

As a public relations expert, Olivia Pope always wants to put her best foot forward. No matter how embattled her interior self is, her exterior presentation is endlessly impeccable. *Scandal*'s season one promotional poster features a confident Pope staring directly out at a would-be viewer, projecting that she has everything under control and can confront any challenge that comes her way. The first time we meet Pope ("Sweet Baby" [1.01]), she is negotiating with Russian thugs to recover the infant of the US ambassador to Russia. Before the episode's end, the audience discovers Olivia's affair with the married White president of the United States, Fitzgerald Grant—a man with whom she has remained emotionally entangled in an on-off relationship throughout the series. The tension between Olivia Pope's public expressiveness—one that smooths appearances—and her tangled interior contradictions is set up as a significant and foundational part of her character from the very beginning.

I am not the only scholar who wrestles with the nonbinary complexity of Olivia Pope's character and *Scandal* itself. In 2015 the *Black Scholar* dedicated an entire issue to critical examination of the show. Film scholar Mia Mask notes that "Pope's life is full of contradictions and innumerable complexities, the likes of which we haven't seen in Black women's lives as represented in mainstream culture. Popular entertainment is merely a reflection of the contradictions within the zeitgeist" (2015, 4). The politics of identity within the Black American community is often fraught with incongruous desires that seek to cast off the shackles of a racist legacy that monolithically essentializes its ontology. But toward this effort, it also seeks to present a united show of resistance to counter this racist reductiveness. In the end, both attempts interpolate blackness primarily within a confining structuralist binary (for example, Black/White, inferior/superior). In other words, these White-defined stereotypes make it the responsibility of Black people to "fix" the image of blackness under the unforgiving gaze of whiteness.

In the autumn of 2014, the rigid confines created for Black characters vis-à-vis the White gaze were potently evidenced by *New York Times* TV critic Alessandra Stanley. Stanley's piece, which is meant to be celebratory,[1] begins, "When Shonda Rhimes writes her autobiography, it should be called 'How to Get Away with Being an Angry Black Woman'. . . . Be it Kerry Washington on 'Scandal' or Chandra Wilson on 'Grey's Anatomy,' [Rhimes's characters] can and do get angry. One of the more volcanic meltdowns in soap opera history was Olivia's 'Earn Me' rant[2] on Scandal" (2014). Stanley never mentions the frequent rage of many of *Scandal*'s White characters, female or otherwise, or the booming monologues of Black male character Eli "Rowan" Pope.[3]

It is not surprising that a mainstream publication like the *Times* would put a modern spin on old racism. Mia Mask, commenting on the Stanley article, observes that a similar problem persists in communities of color, as many are not sure if *Scandal* is "a progressive step in an anti-essentialist direction, or a regressive move backward toward a reconstituted Jezebel-in-bed-with-Massa-stereotype" (2015, 4). The

---

1. With the premier of *How to Get Away with Murder*, Shonda Rhimes became the first Black showrunner to have three television shows on the same night: *Grey's Anatomy* (2005–), *Scandal* (2012–18), along with *How to Get Away with Murder* (2014–) constitute American Broadcast Company's Thursday-night prime-time lineup, dubbed "Thank God It's Thursday," or TGIT. Two of three shows have Black female protagonists.

2. Stanley references a monologue from the twentieth episode of the second season, "A Woman Scorned."

3. Played by Joe Morton, a characterization that earned him an Emmy Award in September 2014.

uncertainty and distancing from Olivia Pope's representational image are evidenced in a 2016 Medium.com article by a longtime Black *Scandal* viewer, Torri Oats. In "The Genius of Repackaging Old Stereotypes," Oats writes, "With every utterance of the word 'whore', with every physical blow, with every emotional bruise, and with every open display of her sex life, *our* Olivia Pope was slowly disappearing. Once formidable and mighty, she has been reduced to a 'Jezebel', 'mammy' and . . . a voiceless 'domestic abuse victim.' To people like [Alessandra] Stanley, she is now palatable and 'in her place'; reinforcing stereotypes that are inextricably woven into the fabric of Black America" (2016). The "*our* Olivia Pope" comment denotes a gendered racial familiarity that comes with pride and representative expectation. Disappointed that Pope's character no longer feels like a reflection of her own Black femininity, Oats, by season five, derives shame from the character's journey. By placing the onus on Rhimes to represent Olivia in ways that make it impossible for White critics to stereotype, Oats neglects that Stanley avails herself of a well-worn tool of White supremacy: the controlling image of the Angry Black Woman (Collins 2000).

Some Black academics have consistently leveled a similar criticism of *Scandal* and the stereotypical representation of Olivia Pope's blackness over the life of the series (Maxwell 2013; Evans 2014; McClearen 2015; Erigha 2015). A self-identified feminist, Brandon Maxwell, wrote a now infamous piece for the *Feminist Wire* that epitomizes the pitfalls of a narrow representational reading of Pope's character:

> In most episodes Pope is little more than a political mammy mixed with a hint of Sapphire who faithfully bears the burden of the oh-so-fragile American Political System on her shoulders. . . . But to only portray Pope as a political mammy with a hint of Sapphire would be too obvious to viewers and would make her character even more noticeably flat. . . . [Enter Jezebel stage left.] When Pope is not gleefully maintaining the house or being overbearing, thus undesirable, she's in the back shed with massah—the Oval Office—Fitz where we realize she's actually quite desirable (see Season 1 Episode 1). . . . In spite of the crafty stereotype switching that occurs on a

weekly basis, the character of Olivia Pope is the ultimate amalgamation of three of the dominant media narratives about Black women [Jezebel, Sapphire and Mammy]. She seamlessly switches between each in ways that would lead us to believe she transcends them. In this way, *Scandal* very subtly tricks us into celebrating these images as opposed to being critical of them and demanding better. (2013)

Throughout the article, Maxwell is at pains to shoehorn Olivia Pope (and Shonda Rhimes by extension) into stale, off-the-rack stereotypes, going to lengths to avoid entertaining the intentionality of Pope's juxtapositions. His "feminist" analysis lacks self-reflexivity about the problems embedded within his own arguments. Coined by queer Black feminist Moya Bailey in 2010, *misogynoir* is sexism and anti-blackness specific to Black women. Maxwell's treatment of Pope borders on misogynoir, as he interprets Olivia to be an impotent object in all respects of her life. Career, sex, and the "oh-so-fragile" American political system all happen *to* her. There is no consideration of Pope as a subject imbued with agency, desires, and class privileges who navigates vortexes of power within a system that was never designed for her benefit.

It is not my wish to use this chapter as a rebuttal to Maxwell, as other scholars have done a fine job of that (Cooper and Lindsey 2013; Lane 2013; Pixley 2015). I use Maxwell and viewers like Oats to point out the limitations of the representational lens. Such a lens demands of Pope's portrayal a triumphant narrative that services a political and social agenda around the complexities of Black existence in America.

Maxwell and Oats point to the ideologies behind controlling images, which are continual sites of struggle (Collins 2004, 148) in the march toward progressive portrayals of blackness on TV. For Black people, struggle is a necessary part of the reality of progress. In *Hope Draped in Black: Race, Melancholy, and the Agony of Progress*, Joseph Winters notes that the history of Black people in America is laced with unfinished struggles. For him, unifying ideas of progress are fantastical constructions designed to buffer us from a reality filled with melancholy and loss for Black people (2016, 6). Winters points to Black literary tradition as one in which the necessity of ambivalence to the progress of the Black subject is engaged.

The view through the representational lens makes it impossible for the vagaries of Black interior life to express unsavory parts of selfhood, such as shame, putridness, submission, or any contradictory state of existence, without being thought of as less than human, less than Black (Quashie 2012). Olivia Pope is a site of struggle, and the characterization must be examined as such. Scholars like Maxwell (2013) and Gibson (chapter 5 of this volume) interrogate Pope's present temporality within a historical sexual politic of victimization and enslaved female bodies. Such examinations are broadly valid but leave so much intentionally obscured. For Black women–created TV characters like Pope, there is no long history of analysis in which to place her, for it is the first time that we have a Black woman auteur directing a story around a Black feminine subject lead. With Pope, Rhimes troubles the idea of a postracial character in the Obama era by imbuing her with fear, strategic withholding, attachment to childhood abandonment, post-traumatic stress disorder (PTSD), and other challenges that are specific to particularities of her Black experience. In the midst of all these struggles, Rhimes challenges the Pope character to thrive and love in the often violent American political sphere she operates. For Mia Mask, Pope's continued ability to "confuse, bewilder and deconstruct" as she evades easy categorization by skating between various discourses means there is work to be done in the culture (2015, 7). Olivia Pope's being-ness, as wrought by Shonda Rhimes, is not definitive but dynamic in the way novelistic characters tend to be.

Shonda Rhimes and the Tradition of Black Women Writers

I first consider Olivia Pope as a character in a novel after reading a blog post by Caribbean literature and cultural studies scholar Schuyler Esprit. She writes:

> Our perceptions of [*Scandal*'s] characters are meant to be ambivalent. [Shonda] Rhimes wants to create these tensions by making their flaws present and visible. But are they meant to make us decide

whether Rhimes SHOULD show characters like that or not? . . . NO. It's not our story to tell. And our politics of respectability, of wanting to see the perfectly radical narrative of Blackness conquering all White patriarchal evil is merely a desire that we haven't demanded from our real-life political officials, so why not let Rhimes write her work the way she wants. . . . Let's not keep saying "This is right or wrong." Let's ask more about "what does it mean?" (2013)

Television is, of course, a different medium that is fraught with compromising commercial interests that are separate from the literary world. Nevertheless, if we focus on storytelling, we can consider *Scandal* as a serial novel.[4] Doing so places Rhimes in the tradition of Pauline Hopkins, a Black novelist and playwright writing in the late nineteenth and early twentieth centuries. Hopkins uses the serial novel form and romance genre to explore race and other sociological themes in works such as *Hagar's Daughter: A Story of Southern Cast Prejudice* (1901–2).[5] Rhimes openly admits to using Olivia Pope's character to explore similar themes in the twenty-first century, tweeting, "Can't believe I need to say this: yes, I wrote 'Black woman auctions herself off' storyline on PURPOSE. I have heard of slavery.[6] . . . We've been writing about the dynamics of race, gender and power over here at #Scandal for 4 seasons. All Gladiators know that."

Esprit's (2013) assertion of ambivalence in Rhimes's characters is related to literary critic Caresse A. John's (2011) analysis of strategic ambivalence found in the Black women protagonists of Nella

---

4. An American literature major at Dartmouth College who endeavored to be Nobel Laureate Toni Morrison when she grew up, Shonda Rhimes later realized that there can be only one Morrison but that she (Rhimes) could walk in Morrison's footsteps by telling her stories in prime-time TV (Rhimes 2015, 79–80).

5. Though *Hagar* has since been published as a complete novel, it was first serialized in the African American periodical the *Coloured American Magazine*.

6. A fourth-season story line generated a lot of controversy. Rather than remain trapped for three years, a kidnapped Olivia stealthily convinces her captors to sell her on the "dark Net," knowing that a digital footprint would leave a trail facilitating her rescue ("Where's the Black Lady?" [4.11]).

Larsen's novels *Quicksand* (1928) and *Passing* (1929). John uses feminist standpoint theory (FST) to analyze the use of ambivalence in Larsen's work. A standpoint is an understanding of one's social location in relation to the world and that one's place is influenced by sociopolitical contexts that are themselves dynamic (John 2011, 96). Standpoints can be achieved over and over again. Both individuals and collectives can achieve standpoints, but one must first self-define in order to define in relation to others. It is that inward turn toward self-examination inherent in achieving a standpoint that interests me about Olivia Pope. Writing during the time of the Harlem Renaissance (1919–29), Larsen was in a precarious position, given the politics of the era. She battled with the competing interests of telling the story of a Black woman with sexual desires (interiority) and the restrictions of Black middle-class respectability (exteriority) (McDowell 1986 in John 2011, 100). Given some earlier cited critiques of Olivia Pope, Rhimes is still battling with similar constraints.

In writing about the baggage and the biases we bring with us when judging an artist's work, Alice Walker, in her essay "Saving the Life That Is Your Own," writes that Black women often have to be their own models and fearlessly push against narrow views to find the larger perspective and common thread (1983).[7] Besides Walker, Shonda Rhimes follows in the tradition of other Black female writers such as Toni Morrison, Audre Lorde, Zora Neale Hurston, Nella Larsen, and Marita Bonner. All of these women in their works pushed to expand the boundaries of Black feminine identity, reflecting specific struggles of their era. With Shonda Rhimes exploring this novelistic approach to character on TV, we get in Pope a multidimensional being whose life "[reflects] the emotional breadth, psychological depth, diasporic range and multivalent variance that exist among us as a people"

---

7. Walker would know. The 1985 film based on her best seller *The Color Purple* (1982) opened to controversy from those filmgoers who claimed it to be an assault on the Black male image that would be used to form stereotypes against them (Penrice 2010). Twenty-five years later, the film is an undisputed classic.

(Mask 2015, 7). It is in the pockets of life that Shonda Rhimes excels with this character. At the points of vulnerability, there is space to stretch the boundaries of Black femininity, exploring the power of Olivia's interiority and all the contradictions of her being-ness.

Desire and the Queering of Black Subjectivity

Scandal and Olivia Pope's character are not polemic. Rhimes gives the audience both the glossy facade and the messy interior. Examining Pope's Black womanhood as one in pursuit of the erotic means that we read her power as one coming from a deeply feminine place (Lorde 1984). This place is also a queer one. As a verb, "to queer" means to trouble something or to make that thing strange by exploring its limits, boundaries, and biases. Queering is an act that peers beneath the surface of something, looking for its elasticity and points of vulnerability in which to transform one's ongoing relationship to it (Glickman 2012). Queering, like achieving a feminist standpoint, is not a permanent place of arrival but an evolving state of dynamic tension. Such a means of engaging blackness can seem antithetical in comparison to representational types of analysis, which emphasize the public performativity of identity.

African American studies scholar Kevin Quashie (2012) offers a queer take on examining Black subjectivity that, partly, takes inspiration from Lorde's use of the erotic (1984) and works of other Black women. Quashie uses the term *quiet* to queer the interior contours of Black identity. Born deep within, *quiet* can be a literal quiet as well as "raging and wild, . . . a place of desire and anxiety [that] holds all that is" (2012; Kindle loc. 1727). As a small example, we can look to the variations in pattern of Olivia's silent pacing. It is back and forth when she is thinking, circles when she is worried.[8] The latter type is specifically tethered to her emotional anxieties concerning Fitzgerald Grant

---

8. In a season-two flashback scene between Olivia and Fitz in the Rose Garden, Fitz reveals the patterns of her silent pacing ("Happy Birthday, Mr. President" [2.08]).

and the conflict their relationship poses to her professional responsibilities as a crisis manager ("Beltway Unbuckled" [2.04], "I'm Just a Bill" [4.19], and "The Fish Rots from the Head" [5.13]). This act is not performative; it is a private (or quiet) reflection of the character's internal conflicts.

To consider only Olivia's representational image would be to create a human subject wholly called into being by social discourse. By emphasizing the vagaries of Olivia's subjectivity, Shonda Rhimes is returning what Quashie calls the "complexity of the inner life to its rightful place," thus forming a variegated understanding of Black feminine cultural identity. An expansive look at the Black feminine subject that constitutes Olivia Pope requires a queer positionality that examines her quest for internal satisfaction as a valid source of power and preoccupation. Because the erotic is primarily about interiority, my analysis will focus on Olivia Pope's relationship with others and self. We can look at three aspects of Olivia's pursuit of the erotic: seeking a deep love defined by spiritual connection, contending with challenges to the pursuit of satisfaction, and saving the life that is her own.

The Contradiction of Being:
Olivia Pope's Pursuit of Erotic Power

Marriage is not a pseudonym for love, but with 60 percent of college-educated Black women between the ages of twenty-five to thirty-five having never been married (Brookings Institution 2015),[9] how Shonda Rhimes engages the marriage issue for Olivia is worth examination for what it indicates about the character's desires and fears. Olivia has twice rebuffed marriage proposals, from two different men: Edison Davis and Fitzgerald Grant. In episode thirteen of season two ("Nobody Likes Babies"), Olivia rebuffs Senator Edison Davis, her Black lover at the time (see House and Bradwell, chapter 6 of this volume). The monologue Olivia gives is an erotic statement concerned with the quest for satisfaction. Olivia tells Edison she could become

9. The findings were published in 2015, but the data set is from 2012.

part of the nice, respectable future he paints. The only impediment is her lack of desire, and their lack of deep connection ("I want . . . life-changing, extraordinary love. Don't you want that, too?"). The senator does not accept it as reason enough for her refusal to marry. Black feminist writer Kimberly Springer in "Queering Black Female Heterosexuality" notes that in a culture bent on convincing Black women that someone else's wants are our needs, asserting our own wants and needs is both a queer and a radical act (2008, 85). That claim builds on Lorde's ideas that rejecting that which requires settling for the conventional and the convenient is not radical at all but a grave responsibility to the self (1984, 58). In refusing marriage on the grounds of desire, Olivia shows a responsibility to an autonomy of which so many of her ancestors could not avail themselves.

The sixth episode of season five ("Get Out of Jail, Free" [5.06]) finds Olivia turning away from a Fitzgerald Grant literally on bended knee. Just as Edison asked what it is Olivia wants, Fitz does the same. The words do not form for Olivia. The "dreams" and "goals" she professed to have had two seasons prior ("We Do Not Touch the First Ladies" [3.12]) have not yet been vocalized, let alone realized. During her kidnapping ("Run" [4.10]), Olivia dreamed quixotically of a future with Fitz in Vermont. In it they are married, he is the mayor of Burlington, and she makes jam. Olivia is even joyful, a rare emotion for such a melancholy character. However, that dream is not her own; Olivia parroted a fantasy Fitz soothingly sold to her before and after he reveals the house he built for her ("Vermont is For Lovers, Too" [3.08]). This dialogue from "Guess Who's Coming to Dinner" (3.02) is the basis of Olivia's dream during her captivity:

> FITZ: Somewhere . . . In another life, in another reality . . . We are married and we have four kids, and we live in Vermont, and I'm the mayor, and . . .
>
> OLIVIA: And I make jam.

The dream Olivia has is not her organic vision for the future. It is a comforting balm for a woman who thought death inevitable at the time. Lacking that internal compass for her future puts Olivia's rejection of marriage—something that requires building on a shared vision with someone else—into perspective. If dreams point the way to freedom (Lorde 1984, 38), then the lack thereof translates to a fear of the same. We still have not heard Olivia articulate a vision for her own future, a seemingly deliberate contrast to many other characters on the show, none of whom are Black women.

An interrogation into Olivia's pursuit of the erotic as a source of power necessitates that we queer her biggest and most persistent impulse toward that end: the relationship with Fitzgerald Grant. If peering at this relationship through the long shadow of slavery, Black female sexuality becomes defined in relation to a powerful White maleness that is capable mostly of brutality (Springer 2008, 79) or ownership (see Buggs and Jones Russell, chapter 4 of this volume; and Gibson, chapter 5 of this volume). This view casts Olivia as the victim in a cautionary tale about Black women's manipulation as sexual objects. A more generous view interprets the Olivia and Fitz relationship within the framework of a Black love in which primacy is given to the desires and choices of the Black woman (see House and Bradwell, chapter 6 of this volume). The Olitz[10] relationship provides tension and motion that does not ebb in a linear, upward trajectory. Theirs is a dynamic that is, at times, beautiful and, at other times, painful and uncomfortable (Pavela[11] 2014b), not least for the dark historical comparisons it inspires in viewers (Warner 2015). Such a tension accepts that multiple truths exist simultaneously, awkwardly, and in contradiction to one another (Quashie 2012).

Olivia, too, has experienced tremendous struggle because of what this Olitz relationship exposes in her—an unresolved tension between the woman she presents to the world and an embattled one fighting to embrace authentic connection. Queering Black female heterosexuality

10. A neologism that combines Olivia's and Fitz's names, often used by fans ("#Olitz"). The portmanteau was made canon in *Scandal*'s final season ("Day 101" [7.03]) and is analyzed in more detail by Kavyta Kay (chapter 8 of this volume).

11. *katrinapavela.tumblr.com* is the author's blog.

means to do what is "contrary, eccentric, strange, or unexpected" (Springer 2008, 86). In this way, queer becomes a positional stance that is active in the continuous tense because it allows for exploration and movement. Analyzing the genesis of the Olivia and Fitz relationship from this positionality reveals their connection as an interior impulse for both, not a lonely need for sexual sensation.

Before their first sexual congress, Olivia and Fitz stand in a hallway, spending nearly a full minute peering into each other's eyes in silence, searching to confirm a shared feeling. That search is an act, arguably, more erotic than any sexual sensation. The moment of crossing the sexual precipice is presented as a pivotal one for Olivia, one that is quietly considered, but actively decisive. Before walking to Fitz's hotel room, Olivia stands in front of her own door and says, "This is me" ("The Trail" [1.06]). She then remains quiet in the pregnancy of the pause, her back to Fitz, who implores her to go inside her room. We see her eyes dance and imagine what is happening inside her. Alice Walker (2006) says "the pause" is the moment when something major is accomplished and wisdom requires us to stop and reflect; it is something to be embraced, not feared, in moving forward. Crossing that precipice, for Olivia, means putting her reputation at risk. The consequences for rejecting controlling images (Collins 2000) are often more inflexible for Black women, as Springer notes when she writes "from 'mammy' to jezebel,' Black female sexuality is defined in relation to white maleness, and as such serves as a cautionary tale about black women's sexuality unbound. What we face is a huge, but not insurmountable obstacle to 'yes'" (2008, 79). Olivia bravely surrenders to the erotic and to a curiosity to know herself through connection with Fitz (Pavela 2013)—even momentarily.

This erotic preamble takes place in the liminal space of a hallway (the second in the same episode). It is significant in that hallways are spaces that facilitate movement from one place to the next. In order for Olivia to advance her desire, she has to shift toward Fitz's room. Fitz follows her lead. Olivia moves herself from a place of self-denial, shutting out history and convention, to one that relishes a moment of selfish satisfaction. The luggage she and Fitz wheel behind them is a symbolic nod to the emotional and racialized consequences they bring with them into this illicit, interracial union.

In "Baby Made a Mess" (4.07), Rhimes gives us a moment of eroticism that is quite unusual for network television. Fitz details, over the phone, an erotic episode wherein he is the one in control, driving Olivia into a state of sexual craving, one for which she begs. Alone in her bedroom and aroused, Olivia "luxuriates in the wild possibilities of the interior" (Quashie 2012, Kindle loc. 532). Unbuttoning the public Gladiator armor (a cape), Olivia puts her hand over her heart and begins massaging the top of her breast in response. Audre Lorde comments that the erotic focuses on the depth of feeling rather than the act of doing (1984, 54). Fitz's words only have power because Olivia decides they do (Pavela 2014a). Kimberly Springer, in writing about the portrayal of Black female heterosexuality, says the predominant images in popular culture are ones where that sexuality is victimized or deviant (2008, 81). Here, Rhimes portrays Olivia as a Black woman who chooses to embrace her own craving. Taking matters into her own hands, so to speak, is completely in line with her professional behavior in the rest of the episode.

Rhimes uses Olivia's responsiveness to Fitz in nonromantic ways, too. In the latter half of the fifth season, Olivia teeters on the edge of sanity several times. Her laser focus on winning the Republican presidential primary for her client finds Pope willing to risk all of her past principles. When her Gladiators cannot help her, they stage an intervention for Fitz to reason with her ("The Miseducation of Susan Ross" [5.16]). Later, Olivia loses control and murders the man responsible for her kidnapping, in a PTSD-fueled rage over his political obstruction and misogynoir-ist insults. It is Fitz whom she calls to literally pick her up, spackled with blood, off the floor ("Thwack!" [5.17]). None of these things takes place within the confines of their tumultuous romance.

Olivia's impulse toward Fitz is not a result of insecurity, desperation, or a fixation with whiteness. It is based in the abundance of the connection she feels with him, one that is frightening in its capaciousness, its embers stubbornly refusing to wane. It is an erotic connection, one that is contradictory because it is Olivia's greatest source of joy and pain. Having left a divorced Fitz, Olivia confesses to his ex-wife, Mellie, that her leaving was out of fear of commitment ("The Candidate" [5.11]), but continues to pursue nonromantic closeness with him. As the seat of understanding, the "erotic is a measure between the beginnings of our sense of self and the chaos of our strongest feelings" (Lorde 1984, 54). This deep love has proved incapable of "fixing," for there is no external solution for that which comes from deep within her. Every attempt Olivia has made to deny, run, or hide from that love she harbors proves just how immense and persistent the feeling remains until the very end of the series ("Over a Cliff" [7.18]).

Suppressing the Erotic: Olivia's Relationship with Her Father

Olivia's public and private expressiveness is frequently at odds with the needs and goals of her overbearing father, Rowan. Rhimes portrays this relationship with grand operatic pathos wrapped in comic book tropes. A traumatic origin story, pseudo-superpowers, white-knight heroism, super-secret spy organizations, and "l'homme fatales" (Jake Ballard and Franklin Russell) sent to woo the heroine while working for the absent father figure (Harris 2015), the relationship between Olivia and Rowan is not your average Black family narrative! But beneath the iron-fist parenting and lengthy monologues, Rowan is a father who will stop at nothing to ensure that his Black daughter is an American success story. Imbuing Olivia with a more privileged upbringing than most Black women, Rowan says he raised her to feel "fully entitled to own the world as much as any White man"[12] ("Dog-Whistle Politics" [5.04]).

---

12. Reported as being said to one of Rowan Pope's coworkers during Olivia's childhood before sending her off to boarding school at age twelve.

In the third season's first episode ("It's Handled" [3.01]), Olivia's name is revealed as Fitz's mistress to the media.[13] Dutiful protector Rowan comes to rescue Olivia from a herd of reporters. In response to her refusal to be sent away, Rowan sexually shames her for having "raised [her] skirt" to a powerful man. Olivia is disparaged for allowing her inner impulse to compromise the public perception of her Black excellence, itself constituted in opposition to White supremacy. Lorde reminds us that women who follow the directive of their inner impulses seek to live life on their own terms, a kind of empowerment that makes them dangerous (1984, 55). Olivia must go because Rowan sees *her* as the danger to the social order. The past is ever present, so this moment between father and daughter is governed by the specter of the fears associated with African American women in the early twentieth century, which Collins describes as: "(1) rampant and uncontrolled female sexuality; (2) fear of miscegenation; and (3) independent Black female desire" (2004, 71). Lorde (1984) goes on to note that women are encouraged by the male world, through vilification and devaluation, to distrust this nonrational knowledge as a guiding principle in their lives. Rowan's concern is not with sex itself; it is that Olivia did not use it as a transactional tool in exchange for a plum cabinet position (secretary of state or chief of staff). Rowan does not consider the possibility that Olivia's relationship with Fitz is connected to pleasure, only to amassing political power.

ROWAN: You have to be what?

OLIVIA: Twice as good.

ROWAN: Twice as good . . . to get half of what they [White people] have.

Olivia cowers like a child under Rowan's booming baritone. A familiar refrain drilled into many a Black child's head, "Twice as good to

---

13. The audience later finds out that Fitz released Olivia's name in a bid to save their relationship, and Rowan knew it would happen. It is unclear if Olivia, to this day, knows that Fitz was responsible.

get half as much" emphasizes achievement in order to gain traditional forms of power and respect. The pursuit of this goal has been a historical means of survival for Black people in the dominant White, heteropatriarchal, capitalist hegemony that is the United States. On closer inspection, the imperative to be twice as good while possessing the capacity of one human is a dehumanizing endeavor. Professional success and achievement are admirable, but it is not as if Olivia was lacking those things when we meet her. It is her father's exacting standards for which she has sometimes fallen short. But, as Collins notes, African American survival depends, in part, on resisting hegemonic gender ideologies that interpret strength and power in the framework of domination (2004, 201). The question is will the cost for achieving standards defined by someone else cost Olivia to lose core parts of herself?

In the second half of season five, Rhimes puts Pope on a path leading away from the erotic, in a strategic move designed to ultimately convince the character of its value. Divorced from her interior life, or, perhaps reflecting its darker state, Olivia redecorates her apartment in darker tones, eschews white to swath herself in bold primary colors, and increases her drinking. More significant is the shift in her relationships. Pope reengages in a sexual, but nonromantic, association with Jake Ballard, even after she knows he is seeing another woman. As he is the original B613 agent cum l'homme fatale (Harris 2015) that Rowan sends to sexually entrap his own daughter,[14] Jake can be read as a psychosexual extension of Olivia's preoccupation with engaging her father in dysfunctional ways. Most notable is that Rowan becomes the primary influence in Olivia's life, planting the very seed that leads Olivia on a narrow, exclusive quest for political power: "You can either stand there like a 12-year-old and lecture me about morality, or worse, rat us out in the name of justice or you can take your cue from [me and Jake] and get yourself some power. Real power. 1600 Pennsylvania

---

14. Rowan, in a quintessentially misogynoir-ist move to divert Olivia's erotic impulse toward Fitzgerald Grant, sends Jake Ballard on a seduction mission after studying Olivia from afar. This mission takes place in the second half of season two.

Avenue power. You think you have that now, but you're standing on the sidelines, screaming at the referee like a sad, drunk parent at a high school football game. If you're okay with that, by all means. But I know my daughter . . . and I know that won't suffice" ("It's Hard Out Here for a General" [5.10]). The model for power Olivia is given is singular, externally defined, and decidedly male.

The character of Pope is defined by her motherlessness,[15] made more potent through the overwhelming influence of patriarchy in her life. The trope of motherlessness is often used individually and collectively in Black novels of the post–Reconstruction era to reify African American experiences of separation (from Africa), loss of identity, and melancholy that are deeply tied to subject formation (Bergman 2012). Moreover, the loss of the mother renders a lacuna character's endeavor to fill through association with White patriarchal America, which can never be realized because Black people are denied full citizenship (ibid.) I argue that Olivia's turn away from the erotic and toward political dominance and control of an American empire[16] is connected to this trope of motherlessness. It implicates both Olivia and Rowan as victims of White patriarchy's unfulfilled promise to Black Americans for their loyalty to the nation.

For several seasons, Rowan has endeavored to subvert Olivia's desire to define herself, attempting to compel her into submission under his father-knows-best authority. He wields control over her professional movements in order to retain the primacy of his (secret) power in the world at large, but primarily in Olivia's world, and on the back of her labor. On the one hand, it is impressive to see a father so dedicated to his daughter's success. However, this quest comes

---

15. Pope's mother (a spy) was imprisoned by her father when she was twelve. Rowan tells Olivia her mother is dead. Decades later, Olivia learns the truth. Mother and daughter reunite for several brief periods, but their relationship remains fractured and plagued by themes of imprisonment.

16. At the end of season six, Olivia takes on the role of both chief of staff and Command of B613, a role from which she forces her father to retire.

with the infliction of much emotional trauma, something with which Olivia finally confronts her father:

> OLIVIA: You think there's a soft, chewy center in here. You do think that. And for the life of me, I can't figure out why. You gave me a dead mother, a life in boarding school, then you told me everything I knew was a lie. You took away the only man I ever truly loved. You killed his son. You consistently erased my hopes—
> ROWAN: Mnh-mnh.
> OLIVIA: My dreams, my ambitions. You taught me the only constant worth holding on to is the Republic. You made me in your own image. "The apple doesn't fall far from the tree. Poison though it may be." Remember that?—
> ROWAN: Mm.
> OLIVIA: I am just as you made me. That ray of light you think I am isn't a warm campfire, Dad. It's a blowtorch. ("Something Borrowed" [7.07])

Patricia Hill Collins notes that in the past, Black men and women were more likely to recognize each other's full humanity in opposition to a system that dehumanized them both (2004, 253). However, the post–civil rights era makes it increasingly clear that patriarchy within Black communities adversely affects Black women. For Audre Lorde, the "fear that we cannot grow beyond whatever distortions we may find within ourselves keeps us docile and loyal and obedient, externally defined, and leads us to accept many facets of our oppression as women" (1984, 58). Olivia speaks directly to the ways in which her identity has been forged in a crucible of motherlessness and patriarchal domination, one that encouraged her to fill the void through national loyalty. What it has produced is a woman who thwarted an interior life of satisfaction for the constant that is the violence of the Republic. Implicit in Olivia's soliloquy is the driving force of fear used to affix Olivia to a national politic and away from community. Fear is an effective means of control used to guarantee loyalty and obedience. The structure of Rowan's relationship with his adult daughter, especially the emphasis on Olivia's obedience through manipulation, makes embracing her erotic power that much more challenging. But as a Black woman, how does Olivia distinguish herself as more than the manifestation of her father's dreams?

"I Choose Me": Saving the Life That Is Her Own

In season three, Olivia, encouraged by Rowan, is compelled to bring everyone into the light as her purpose in life because "everyone is worth saving" ("Kiss Kiss Bang Bang" [3.14]). Given this burden, Olivia becomes the mule that Zora Neale Hurston describes: "So the white man throw down de load and tell de nigger man tuh pick it up. He pick it up because he have to, but he don't tote it. He hand it to his womenfolks. De nigger woman is de mule uh de world so fur as Ah can see" (1937, 44). Being externally defined causes one to conform to needs that are not based on one's humanity (Lorde 1984, 58). Under the weight of so many demands, expectations, and guilt, Olivia flees Washington ("The Price of Free and Fair Elections" [3.18]), leaving everything and everyone (save Jake) behind. She retreats to an off-the-grid island, near Zanzibar, arranged by Rowan. Away from the Republic, she ceases to be Olivia Pope, adopting "Julia Baker" instead.

Many interpreted Pope's departure as a moment of acquiescence, a giving up. Where is the strong Black woman? She is tired. Kevin Quashie (2012) notes that vulnerability and doubt foster agency in the same ways that being sure and indisputable does. Olivia recognizes and yields to her own fragility by fleeing the environment that has produced it. To yield, Quashie says, is not a show of surrender or display of weakness. In giving up one thing, something else is embraced. Olivia's retreat from Washington can be understood as an embrace of her own fragility and a refusal to be the Strong Black Woman.

In the pivotal ninth episode of season four ("Where the Sun Don't Shine"), Olivia is heard saying that she chooses herself rather than choosing between either Jake or Fitz. It was perceived by viewers as a feminist moment of self-assertion and self-love (see House and Bradwell, chapter 6 in this volume). However, I contend that the moment is hollow because the character's journey is interrupted by a kidnapping that happens moments later. The kidnapping story line is itself important, as Rhimes uses it as a narrative device to juxtapose Olivia's value as an object of patriarchal nation building with the intrinsic value of her Black feminine subjectivity.[17] The controversial overtones of slavery are obvious and intended.[18] Olivia is stripped down so that she is impelled to draw upon that which is internal as a source of power. It is through dreaming that her subconscious recalls a pipe ring in the bathroom, which she uses to initiate her escape from captivity. The rest of the series seems to follow Pope's meandering trajectory toward self-discovery and what it truly means to choose herself.

Scandal's fifth season is explicitly enmeshed with the varied meanings and value of power for many of the characters. In the fourteenth episode, Olivia is interrogated by Quinn about changes in her behavior over the past year. For a woman who uses withholding as a weapon of interior defense, her reply is revelatory:

> I was kidnapped! Do you know what that means? They took everything from me, everything, my freedom, my dignity! And I could have just quit. I could have laid down and died, but I didn't. I took my life back! I stood up! And a year after being sold on the auction block, I was sitting in the Oval with the president of the United States, and I was running the country! I'm selfish because I can be. I'm selfish because, for a week of my life, I lost that right, and I never, ever, ever want to feel that way again. I don't owe anyone anything! It's my turn! Mine! ("I See You")

Olivia emphasizes her choice to persevere rather than recoil in death and interprets "choosing me" to mean the right to selfishness. It is powerful and refreshing to hear a Black woman own this attitude, especially noting that this is the same woman who was compelled to

17. Vice President Nichols hatches the kidnapping scheme as revenge against Fitzgerald Grant, who declares war to save Olivia's life, sending thousands to their deaths. Rhimes also forces Olivia to fight for her own freedom.

18. Rhimes's tweets explaining her intentions were quoted earlier in this chapter.

retreat from service to everyone else at the end of season three out of self-preservation.

But the arc of this pendulum swing cultivates an Olivia Pope who is deliberately insulating herself away from the emotional pain of her losses and compromised mental state. This results in her reconfiguring power in neoliberal, individualistic terms. Consequently, she begins coveting dominance associated with White patriarchal power to the detriment of nearly everything else, even the lives of the people she loves.[19] By the final season, Olivia is consumed with protecting the political "empire" she has built ("Something Borrowed" [7.07]). Such power is the exact kind Rowan importuned Olivia to pursue in "It's Handled" (3.01) and thereafter. With the knowledge that his "baby girl" is running the Oval Office, Rowan is finally able to delight in Olivia's success, near gleeful that such power was derived through romantic manipulation of her White male lover: "You stood on the mountaintop. The ring of fire was around *you*. You played [Fitz] like a fiddle. You held power in your hands. You were power. You had the Oval. My baby had the Oval. You were running the place, and he was clueless" ("It's Hard Out Here for a General" [5.10]).

Through Pope's conversations with other women, Rhimes indicates Olivia's ability to articulate solutions to the internal conflicts of others that she cannot yet resolve in herself. In "The Candidate" (5.11), Pope tells Mellie that the power she has inside herself is something to rely upon. Later, Olivia warns Abby about the corrupting influences of the Oval Office: "You're a good person. You're just standing too close to the Oval. You can feel the power, and you want it. Everyone does. But don't . . . Don't let that place corrupt you. . . . Once you take your white hat off, it's gone. You will no longer be you. And the thing is, being a big dog isn't as great as it seems. Be a better person" ("I See You" [5.14]). In Olivia's words to Abby, Rhimes cleverly hides her intention for Pope's character in the final season. It

19. Olivia risks the life of her pregnant former associate Quinn Perkins in an attempt to out-Command her father.

is Abby, the other Gladiators, and Fitz who intervene in Olivia's life to save her from corrupting influences ("The People v. Olivia Pope" [7.10]). Through recultivating these love connections, Olivia comes to relinquish a thankless loyalty to the Republic ("I think I've spent more than enough time helping people clean up their messes") and reclaims her time by choosing herself ("Over a Cliff" [7.18]).

In the brief period of Reconstruction, formerly enslaved women attempted to live and define, in confining political circumstances, full public and interior lives, which were denied to them for so long. In *Out of the House of Bondage*, historian Thavolia Glymph explains that after emancipation, Black women "pursued citizenship, land ownership, femaleness (denied through white patriarchy), and private leisure time" (2008, Kindle loc. 4105). Most important, notes Glymph, was the right to determine for themselves what all of this meant, including reprioritizing their lives around themselves and their families. These acts of reclaiming a self had far-reaching political and socioeconomic consequences. The echoes of such self-determination manifest in Rhimes's work. Olivia is free to pursue an interior life that is not conjured through public or representational roles and a private identity that is not constituted through the need for her labor (Pavela 2017).

Conclusion

Olivia Pope is a constellation of contradiction, the vagaries of whose humanity push against social expectations of Black womanhood. The pursuit of the erotic is ultimately about the search for reconciliation within the self, which brings satisfaction (Lorde 1984). As a Black woman whose public persona wields immense power in a White, privileged, elite world, Olivia Pope still has to contend with various controlling forces (individuals and systems) attempting to co-opt her existence for their own needs. At a Paley Center event in March 2016, when answering a question about Olivia's breakup with a divorced Fitz, Shonda Rhimes answers, "Olivia is on a journey and Olivia has been on a journey since we started. It's interesting to me that her primary story is a romance—that's what [the audience sees]—because to me, her primary story has been discovering herself. I'm happy that you have fallen in love with Fitz because that is the journey that Olivia went on. . . . [S]he went on the fantasy and she realized that the fantasy was not real. That does not mean that she does not love Fitz. That does not mean Fitz does not deserve love. It just means that Olivia does not know who she is yet" (quoted in Wagmeister 2016). Rhimes does allow the character, through self-reflection and strategic yielding, to reach a place of reconciliation, brimming with the possibilities of a full life.

Having analyzed Pope's character using themes of Black women's literary traditions, what is clear is Rhimes's purposeful use of contradiction, loss, repetition, agony, and vagary to lead Olivia's character toward self-realization. Agony and progress, as Joseph Winters argues, are inextricably linked for Black people, and literature is a space in which to "articulate hope draped in black. This awkward hope is a response to a culture attached to narratives of progress and eager for a world in which painful racial memories will be left behind, forgotten, or converted into an affirmation of the status quo" (2016, 23–24). Olivia will likely not feel she has satisfactorily progressed until she can reconcile the specters of painful memories and fears that haunt her. Rhimes's 2016 statement reflects what Audre Lorde calls the search for belongingness (1984), which is the fight to exist in the fullness of one's self. That position is the embodiment of the erotic. We are all social beings who have to live in the social world, the various intersecting hegemonies of which govern the structures of our existence. Yet we still exist in our individual bodies and are driven by needs and desires that are defined from within. Those proclivities are not always filtered through acceptable modes of social existence.

References

Bergman, Jill. 2012. *The Motherless Child in the Novels of Pauline Hopkins.* Baton Rouge: Louisiana State Univ. Press.

Brookings Institution. 2015. "Single Black Female BA Seeks Educated Husband: Race, Assortative Mating and Inequality." Social Mobility Memos. Apr. 9. http://www.brookings.edu/blogs/social-mobility-memos/posts /2015/04/09-race-assortative-mating-inequality-reeves.

Collins, Patricia Hill. 2000. *Black Feminist Thought*. New York: Routledge.
———. 2004. *Black Sexual Politics: African Americans, Gender and the New Racism*. New York: Routledge.
Cooper, Brittney, and Treva Lindsey. 2013. "Love in a Time of Scandal." *Feminist Wire*, Feb. 11. http://www.thefeministwire.com/2013/02/10180/.
Erigha, Maryann. 2015. "Shonda Rhimes, *Scandal*, and the Politics of Crossing Over." *Black Scholar* 45(1): 10–15. doi:10.1080/00064246.2014.997598.
Esprit, Schuyler. 2013. "If *Scandal* Were a Novel . . ." TheAcademicGladiator.tumblr.com, Feb. 19. Deleted post preserved at https://getpocket.com/a/read/302803814.
Evans, Lydia. 2014. "Representations of African American Political Women in Scandal." *Pepperdine Journal of Communication Research* 2, art. 4. http://digitalcommons.pepperdine.edu/pjcr/vol2/iss1/4.
Glickman, Charlie. 2012. "Queer Is a Verb." In *Momentum: Making Waves in Sexuality, Feminism, and Relationships*, edited by Tess Danesi, Dee Dennis, and Inara de Luna. Selected essays by 2012 (conference) speakers advocating change in current sexual dialogues, Sept. 10.
Glymph, Thavolia. 2012. *Out of the House of Bondage: The Transformation of the Plantation Household*. Cambridge: Cambridge Univ. Press.
Harris, Malcolm. 2015. "Super Women and the Rise of l'Homme Fatal." *Al Jazeera America*, June 1. http://america.aljazeera.com/opinions/2015/6/super-women-and-the-rise-of-lhomme-fatal.html.
Hopkins, Pauline E. 2000. *Hagar's Daughter*. London: [X Press].
Hurston, Zora N. 1937. *Their Eyes Were Watching God*. Philadelphia: J. B. Lippincott.
John, Caresse A. 2011. "Strategic Ambivalence: A Feminist Standpoint Theory Reading of Nella Larsen's Novels." *Feminist Formations* 23(1): 94–117.
Lane, Nikki. 2013. "A Reply to 'Olivia Pope and the Scandal of Representation' by Brandon Maxwell." Blog, Feb. 11. http://thedoctorlane.com/2013/02/a-reply-olivia-pope-scandal-of-representation/.
Larsen, Nella. 2010. *The Complete and Unabridged Fiction of Nella Larsen*. Blacksburg, VA: Wilder.
Lorde, Audre. 1984. "Uses of the Erotic: The Erotic as Power." In *Sister Outsider: Essays and Speeches*, 53–59. Feminist Series. Freedom, CA: Crossing Press.

Mask, Mia. 2015. "A Roundtable Conversation on Scandal." *Black Scholar* 45(1): 3–9.

Maxwell, Brandon. 2013. "Olivia Pope and the Scandal of Representation". *Feminist Wire*, Feb. 7. http://thefeministwire.com/2013/02/olivia-pope -and-the-scandal-of-representation/.

McClearen, Jennifer. 2015. "Gladiator in a Suit? *Scandal*'s Olivia Pope and the Post-identity Regulation of Physical Agency." In *Feminist Erasures: Challenging Backlash Culture*, edited by Kumarini Silva and Kaitlynn Mendes, 150–63. Basingstoke: Palgrave Macmillan.

Oats, Torri. 2016. "The Genius in Repackaging Old Stereotypes." *Medium*, Feb. 9. https://medium.com/@TorriOats/the-genius-is-in-repackaging -old-stereotypes-dbabc2c03bdc#.megxfra23.

Pavela, Katrina. 2013. "Desire Unbound; or, Why Olivia Pope Is Not Your Jezebel." *katrinapavela.tumblr.com* (blog). http://katrinapavela .tumblr.com/post/60779555663/updated-desire-unbound-the-sense -and-sexuality-of.

———. 2014a. "Olivia Pope Touched Herself and It Was Everything. Here's Why." *katrinapavela.tumblr.com* (blog). http://katrinapavela .tumblr.com/post/102291690541/olivia-pope-touched-herself-and -it-was-everything.

———. 2014b. "Scandalous Reflections: Queering the Black and White of Olivia and Fitz's Relationship." *katrinapavela.tumblr.com* (blog). http:// katrinapavela.tumblr.com/post/101074716629/scandalous-reflections -queering-the-black-and.

———. 2017. "Olivia Pope: When Keeping It Real Goes Wrong (#Scandal S7)." *katrinapavela.tumblr.com* (blog). http://katrinapavela.tumblr.com /post/166545026019/olivia-pope-when-keeping-it-real-goes-wrong.

Penrice, Ronda Racha. 2010. "'The Color Purple' 25 Years Later: From Con- troversy to Classic." The Grio, Dec. 17. http://thegrio.com/2010/12/17 /the-color-purple-25-years-later-from-controversy-to-classic/.

Pixley, Tara-Lynne. 2015. "Trope and Associates." *Black Scholar* 45(1): 28–33.

Quashie, Kevin. 2012. *The Sovereignty of Quiet: Beyond Resistance in Black Culture*. New Brunswick, NJ: Rutgers Univ. Press.

Rhimes, Shonda. 2015. *Year of Yes: How to Dance It Out, Stand in the Sun and Be Your Own Person*. Farmington Hills, MI: Thorndike Press.

Springer, Kimberly. 2008. "Queering Black Female Heterosexuality." In *Yes Means Yes! Visions of Female Sexual Power and a World without Rape*, edited by Jaclyn Friedman and Jessica Valenti, 77–92. Berkeley, CA: Seal Press.

Stanley, Alessandra. 2014. "Wrought in Rhimes's Image." *New York Times*, Sept. 18. http://www.nytimes.com/2014/09/21/arts/television/viola-davis-plays-shonda-rhimess-latest-tough-heroine.html?_r=0.

Tate, Claudia. 1998. *Psychoanalysis and Black Novels: Desire and the Protocols of Race*. New York and Oxford: Oxford Univ. Press.

Wagmeister, Elizabeth. 2016. "Shonda Rhimes on Fitz Learning about 'Scandal' Abortion: 'Does He Have To? A Woman Made a Choice about Her Body.'" *Variety*, Mar. 15. http://variety.com/2016/tv/news/scandal-abortion-shonda-rhimes-reaction-fitz-olivia-1201731223/.

Walker, Alice. 1983. "Saving the Life That Is Your Own." In *In Search of Our Mothers' Gardens*. San Diego: Harcourt Brace Jovanovich.

———. 2006. "All Praises to the Pause." In These Times, Nov. 22. http://inthesetimes.com/article/2906.

Warner, Kristen. 2015. "If Loving Olitz Is Wrong, I Don't Wanna Be Right: ABC's *Scandal* and the Affect of Black Female Desire." *Black Scholar* 45(1): 16–20.

Winters, Joseph R. 2016. *Hope Draped in Black: Race, Melancholy, and the Agony of Progress*. Durham, NC: Duke Univ. Press.

8 | #Olitz

The Erotics of (E)Racing in *Scandal*

KAVYTA KAY

THERE ARE A MULTITUDE OF BLOGS, websites, and social media platforms under which the hashtag "Olitz" commands a considerable online presence and that explicitly discuss the eroticism and the "undeniable chemistry" between Olivia and Fitz. Using this compelling fusion as a basis for this chapter, I explore the complex interplay of meanings and the discursive practices of race inherent in their erotics. Even though at first glance, the initial moral position is to condemn Olivia in her role as the mistress, we learn via flashback how the love story between Olivia and Fitz develops, and the latter's estranged marriage to First Lady Mellie is revealed as one of political convenience. While a large part of the popularity of the show is attributed to creator Shonda Rhimes's writing and the successful branding of the show through social media practices such as screening countdowns, sharing behind-the-scenes clips, trending hashtags, and the cast live-tweeting fans on Twitter while they are watching an episode, the love affair between Olivia and Fitz has taken center stage for the audience for most of the show's run. What has also been a long-standing narrative from the point of view of the fans is how *Scandal* has been profoundly silent on the issue of race, particularly in the portrayal of Olitz. Sex and sexuality are an integral part of how we experience race as a lived concept so that the show making scarce mention of them, save for a few references that graze the surface, could be read as a purposeful attempt to portray a postracial imagination where difference is present but irrelevant. Color blindness—the notion that race no longer matters in American society (Wise 2010)—serves as the dominant framework for *Scandal*, and while the ostensible desire to move beyond race as a central trope has never been denied, this articulation of postracialism has in turn drawn much criticism and consternation from fans and scholars alike. It could be discerned that Olivia's raced and gendered sexuality works silently and steadily throughout the show, in a way that challenges one-dimensional, stereotypical depictions of Black women on-screen, and it gradually unravels in the eroticized Olitz relationship.

Theorization of Erotics

Extending beyond the act of sex, I critically engage with erotics as irretrievably entangled with the politics of difference and also as concerned with heightened, painful, and pleasurable feelings associated with sex, sexuality, and seduction. Much scholarly work on sexuality and the erotic has been done in terms of a "natural" sameness and exoticized difference, as Valerie Amos and Pratibha Parmar discuss in their essay "Challenging Imperial Feminism" (1984). This gendered orientalist framework was typical of imperial-colonial constructions, which marked certain female bodies as mainstream (respectable, good, contained, ordered) and others as deviant (excessive, threatening, promiscuous, immoral). In terms of the erotic, Gayle Rubin's (1984) groundbreaking text orders sex acts through the concepts of the charmed circle versus the outer limits of sexual practice and a hierarchical system of value with married, heterosexual, and reproductive couples at the top of the erotic pyramid, while unmarried, heterosexual, as well as lesbian and gay couples are located in an area of contest. Within sexuality studies, Rubin's intellectual legacy continues to animate new work on the specificities of desire and the intersectionality in which gender, race, and class may produce forms of desire. In understanding Black women in popular culture, Rubin's sex hierarchy does not fully take into account the cultural construction of gender and race, but it does offer one way of problematizing the good/bad sex dichotomy that is crucially oppressive to minorities. The Black female body is a complex identity and cannot be constrained by narrow Eurocentric definitions and visual media, as mediated by a White, Western lens, which had done little to reformulate representations of this subject as the sexed, raced, and eroticized other.

If Audre Lorde conceives of the erotic as "a lens through which we scrutinize all aspects of our existence, forcing us to evaluate those aspects honestly in terms of their relative meaning within our lives" (1984, 57), this perspective is one that does not necessarily translate within American visual culture, where the fetishization of Black female and male bodies tends to follow a universalized notion of gender and race. The extent to which contemporary television shows the complexities of raced desire in everyday practice without delving into a Black-White polarity is significantly limited. I make the claim that race is tied to notions of blackness, particularly in visual culture, and while the strategy of (e)racing is deployed to, in a sense, give blackness erotic life that does not indulge stereotypes, ultimately the erotics of *Scandal* involves itself in the sticky terrain of racial practice. To reiterate, in my engagement with erotics, I do not simply mean the sexual encounters between the two protagonists but also include moments of pleasure and pain, agony and ecstasy, the simple "Hi" exchange, the "one-minute" pauses, the dances, literal and figurative.

For Simone de Beauvoir (2011 [1949]), quite simply, the erotic allows women to possess their own sexuality. Joan Morgan positions another dimension to the erotic in her formulation of "pleasure politics" as a space that "includes Black women's variegated sexual and non-sexual engagements with deeply internal sites of power and pleasure" (2015, 40). In some ways, I contend that this space is what Shonda Rhimes has attempted to craft in the characterization of Olivia Pope. While it could be said that Olivia has to provide a certain narrative (middle class, highly educated) to legitimize her body's presence in the political playground, the question arises if it runs the risk of treating race as essence rather than one narrative among multiple on blackness or Black womanhood or both. Feminists rarely pay much attention to desire, fantasy, or sexuality, and psychoanalytic theory, which dominates theories on desire, has a tendency to restrict its critical analysis to a single axis of differentiation, which is gender. It could be said that Olivia Pope, a fictitious character in which we are accorded a realm of fantasy to achieve both racial equality and eroticism, stands at this bifurcation of positions in which Black womanhood is defined through White social mobilities, on the one hand, and through desire and erotics, on the other. To go back to the former, in the context of millennial visual and media culture, does this position signify Black subjectivities as racialized beings within a framework in which they do not "sell out" or "have to work twice as hard to get half of what they have" ("It's Handled" [3.01])? If race is a tangible, visible mark on the body—both under and on the surface of the skin—that is ineffaceable, how does it figure in the imaginary of the American nation and television-viewing audience? If television has long been a medium that has neglected to think about and imagine the complexities of Black bodies, then can we read *Scandal* as a cultural text that makes the sticky terrain of race appear in its presentation of a counternarrative that reveals how whiteness works?

At first glance, the analysis of a prime-time network television show in order to engage with critical race theory might read as a frivolous proposition, but I posit that Rhimes's conceptualization of Olitz through an erotic lens works to overtake exasperating static visual representations of the Black female body in spite of her ambiguous approach. In arguably the most meticulous Black feminist engagement with the erotic, "Uses of the Erotic," Audre Lorde proposes that we discern this from the pornographic when she says, "We have often turned away from the exploration and consideration of the erotic as a source of power and information, confusing it with its opposite, the pornographic. But pornography is a direct denial of the power of the erotic, for it represents the suppression of true feeling. Pornography emphasizes sensation without feeling" (1984, 54). While it could be argued that there is another type of feeling that derives from a primal instinct in place of emotional connectedness, in my view Lorde's is one of the most critical feminist statements of the twentieth century and bears relevance even in contemporary times where discussions of pornography and perceived freedom dominate popular cultural representations in opposition to notions of feeling, pleasure, and sensuality—terms that are rarely attributed to modern Black women's sexualities. Whether conscious or not, this permutation is fairly evident in the character of Olivia, and I turn to the relationship of Olitz to explore these erotics of race and sexuality and how this on-screen coupling works to "(e)race" and "re-race," as in to "erase race" and "reinscribe race."

The Origins of Olitz

If social media is about selling illusions, then the small screen, in recent years, has become about screening sex, at least with a broader focus than a simply pornographic one. One example is the television series *Zane's Sex Chronicles* (Cinemax, 2008–10), which follows the erotic lives of four female friends, and Issa Rae's *Insecure* (HBO, 2016–). Admittedly, the television industry in the United States is pushing more boundaries and making greater strides in depictions of sexuality and eroticism compared to the film industry. For example, much like *Scandal*, its contemporaries and counterpart shows such as *House of Cards* (Netflix, 2013–), *The Good Wife* (CBS, 2009–16), and *Ray Donovan* (Showtime, 2013–) feature risqué and raunchy erotic scenes with complex characters as plot drivers more than for the sake of titillation. Yet although there is a vast spectrum of research studies concerning representations of sex in commercials and music videos, there are limited studies analyzing how sex is represented on television, which is ironic given the "mainstreaming of sex" (Attwood 2009) and porn-saturated era in which we are living. There is even less by way of sustained, systematic analyses of erotics or what may be interpreted as the myriad ways in which one is invited to contemplate sex through practices and feelings. Seduction and sensuality as well as sex constitute what I will collectively refer to as erotics, and I suggest here that it is developed in the conceptualization of Olitz as both fantasy and fiction, hate and love, physical and psychic, pain and pleasure. To come back to this demarcation of sex and erotics on-screen, Ariel Levy is one of the few writers to pick up on this point when she describes sexualization as "a desperate stab at free-wheeling eroticism in a time and place characterized by intense anxiety" (2005, 199). If it is true that "we need to surround ourselves with caricatures of female hotness to safely conjure up the concept 'sexy'" (198), then it could be said that the sketching of Olivia works to wonderful effect in challenging this notion. This point is particularly revealed in her erotics as we see how her love story is not simply a sex romp but a slow, gradual development punctuated with stormy moments.

From the outset of *Scandal*, the main audience interest has been the on-again, off-again hummingbird pulse of the relationship between these two lead characters. On social media, the division between #Olitz and #Olake (a reference to Olivia's other love interest Jake) played out with both teams facing backlash at various junctures in the show. The choice between Fitz and Jake is an oft-discussed and heated topic on a range of platforms such as Facebook, Twitter, Vine, and Tumblr, with some "Gladiators" (the name given to *Scandal* fan enthusiasts) divided between Olivia "living in Vermont" with #Team-Fitz or "standing in the sun" with #TeamJake. Yet while race and racial dynamics are not explicitly used as a central trope in the show's narrative, sex and erotics are. Over the course of the seven seasons, in addition to subplots ranging from political conspiracies to murder and illegal activities, we see a number of sex scandals "handled" by Olivia and her crisis-management team, discreetly and successfully. Her own scandal, however, remains unfixed. Olivia makes regular attempts to end the relationship throughout the earlier seasons and does not enjoy her role as well as being on the receiving end of Mellie's "whore" insults, but Fitz is determined to keep her at all costs, at one point even jeopardizing his presidency by deciding to divorce his wife. The love triangle between Olivia, Fitz, and Mellie takes on a fourth player later on in the show in the form of Captain Jake Ballard, a high-ranking military officer deployed to protect Olivia and who later becomes her lover. While the love triangle, or square, traverses a rocky terrain throughout the show, the romance with Fitz remains one of the most central and intriguing themes of *Scandal*.

The erotic moments between them have ranged from a sexual tryst in the Oval Office, face-off moments, and simple embraces. Going back to the beginning of their relationship, in the opening episode of season one we begin to get glimpses of their history through Olivia's distraught reaction after learning the president used the affectionate nickname "Sweet Baby," previously used with Olivia, on a White House intern. Through this exchange, she comes to the realization that Fitz did indeed have an affair with the intern, Amanda Tanner, and when she confronts him in the Oval Office, he moves away from the overhead cameras and corners her. In this charged moment, he leans in very closely and asks her to "look at me" while she, still distraught, asks him about Amanda. He reveals at this point that he loves her, and when she walks away, he goes toward her and kisses her passionately. They are interrupted by the arrival of the chief of staff, Cyrus Beene, who—at first taken aback by the encounter—reveals to Olivia that he was unaware of their affair. The following subplot revolves around the drama-filled managing of the intern's coming out publicly with the story. This story line happens amid a series of stolen glances, sleepless nights, veiled comments between Olivia and Fitz, his admission to Cyrus that "Liv is the love of my life" ("Dirty Little Secrets" [1.02]), repeated declarations of love to Olivia during a dance sequence at the state dinner, and efforts by Cyrus to keep Fitz and Olivia apart. However, it is not until further on in the season that we get a more detailed picture of how Olitz evolved ("The Trail" [1.06]), with the multiple layers that make up this pairing, and how (e)racing and (re)racing takes place in their encounters.

Erotic Encounters, Act 1

Olivia first makes contact with Fitz during his campaign for the presidency where she is highly critical of his lackadaisical strategies. His initial reaction is to fire Olivia for her candor, but he quickly apologizes to her when she overhears his comment and walks away. This interaction is their first face-to-face encounter, and while it is a brief one, he is visibly drawn to Olivia in that moment when staring into her eyes. It also becomes evident that the relationship between Fitz and Mellie is cold and distant, which Olivia in her professional capacity as a media-relations consultant seeks to spin in order to appeal to the voters. While at the forefront we see media strategizing, spin, and "handling" taking place in a political setting, in the background the relationship between Fitz and Olivia is slowly evolving. The second development we see is in the elevator scene where the two are riding alone. Very slowly, he sidles closer and closer to Olivia, who turns very slowly toward him, and their fingertips graze. When the door opens and Fitz leaves, Olivia is left alone in the elevator, somewhat shaken by that erotically charged moment. Both are drawn to each other, and even though their moments are brief and gentle, they are loaded. Perhaps one of the most well-known examples of this is the "one-minute" scene, the first of which we see when Fitz flirts openly with Olivia at her desk and then takes her outside in the hall for privacy. Wrestling with his attraction to her, he says, "I'm married. I'm running for president. I can't . . . But just stand here with me, for one minute" ("The Trail" [1.06]). Olivia at this point does not want to explore this attraction but acquiesces to his "one-minute" request, which becomes a trademark of Olitz, as he moves in closer and they stare into each other's eyes intently. In the darkness of the campaign bus, Olivia takes a seat next to Fitz, who is still wrestling morally with both his marriage when he says, "I'm sitting here complaining to you about my wife, which is sleazy and low and not fair to you and the oldest trick in the book" (1.06), as well as his now obvious attraction to Olivia when he follows up on this statement with "What kind of a coward was I to marry her and not wait for you to show up?" They hold hands for the rest of the bus journey. Upon reaching their hotel destination, Olivia is about to enter her room, and Fitz prods her to enter and "forget this ever happened." After a brief deliberation, she walks to his room farther down the corridor, and they both enter, after which he seductively instructs her, "Take off your clothes," finally giving in to their passion. Up until this point, there is a gradual buildup of sexual tension, and we are teased with "Will they or won't they?" questions, particularly given the dilemmas of position and politics. In this scene, however, passion trumps all of these, and Olivia and Fitz consummate their desires in a sensual and steamy depiction.

What follows is a scene cut to present day, where Fitz is in Olivia's apartment at daybreak, discussing the Amanda Tanner scandal. Before he exits, he requests her for "one minute," and we see the pair embracing on the couch, sentimental and gentle, and a sad exploration of a desire that has shifted course somewhat but remains very much present. In this touching scene, no words are spoken, and we see how their attraction is not solely physical but works on a number of levels: psychic, professional, emotional, energetic. Indeed, the emotional life of Olivia is rich and complex, as we see over the course of the show through the relationships she shares with her father, mother, Cyrus, and her coworkers Abby, Huck, Harrison, Marcus, and Quinn. These relationships are far from being one-dimensional, as various ebbs and flows, and peaks and troughs, challenge these dynamics in a multitude of ways. Another shade comes to the fore for #Olitz when the Amanda Tanner scandal threatens the president to step down, a notion that Fitz is not averse to, as it gives him the option to divorce his wife and finally be with Olivia. Surprisingly, Mellie blames Olivia and not on moral grounds: "You left the team, Liv! You fell down on the job! You broke his heart, and you left him open and vulnerable and helpless" ("Grant: For the People" [1.07]). In an unconventional turn of events, the wife accuses the "mistress" for not performing her role and letting a "girlfriend" enter the fold. The binary of wife/mistress is complicated at this juncture, and the uniting of the husband and the wife by the mistress, in the public eye and much to Fitz's chagrin, sees the exit of Olivia, given the complexity of the relationship(s).[1]

Erotic Encounters, Act 2

With Mellie newly pregnant in the opening of season two, Olitz has now taken a different turn. No longer able to meet in person, their

---

1. The gender stereotypes are turned with Olivia and Mellie, and this point is developed further in season five when Olivia ends up working as Mellie's campaign manager and later her White House chief of staff.

relationship is punctuated by late-night phone calls, long silent pauses, and a push-and-pull dynamic. Fitz finally calls it off for good after Olivia's repeated requests. This breakup affects both, and the next dramatic plotline to challenge their relationship is when Fitz is shot and lies in a coma for four episodes. When he does eventually awake, the first person he calls is Olivia. However, when he finds out that she was complicit in rigging the election to win in his favor, we see the dark side of Fitz emerge. He tells Olivia not to wait for him: "Screwing your mistress is one thing. But marrying her? It's political suicide" ("Nobody Likes Babies" [2.13]). After the harsh breakup that evidently signaled the end of Olitz, we see how Fitz unravels with his increased drinking habits and erratic behavior toward Cyrus and Mellie. Their next encounter is ten months after at the christening of Cyrus and his husband's adopted baby. During this entire event, they stare at each other intently. When Olivia is about to leave, Fitz follows her and pulls her into an electronics closet, and they have sex. Up until this point, the framing of the intimate scenes between these two draws on various techniques to evoke an eroticism that entices viewers in a seductive manner. The music, for instance, accompanying the Olitz scenes acts as a sort of commentary in a scene void of all verbal communication, with the closet sex scene being set to Stevie Wonder's "I Don't Know Why I Love You" ("Whiskey Tango Foxtrot" [2.14]). When Mellie threatens to expose Fitz on national television unless he commits to his family and Olivia tells him, in a quote embraced as empowering by fans, "If you want me, earn me," he waits out Mellie's deadline at Olivia's apartment, earning her, showing her that he is committed to her regardless of the severe consequences were Mellie to execute her threat ("A Woman Scorned" [2.20]). In this scene, they unite to the tune of Marvin Gaye's "You're All I Need." There are also moments of tenderness and romance, when, for example, Fitz tells Olivia, "I have learned only one thing. That I cannot exist without you. That I cannot breathe without you. That the man I am without you is—I'm nothing. I'm nothing. And you are everything. And I need you to give me another chance. I demand another chance. We're worth another chance" ("Seven Fifty-Two" [2.19]).

The staging, music, and stirring performances by Kerry Washington and Tony Goldwyn are layers of the proverbial scandalous cake, but the power of the writing gives the show an erotic quality that viewers have responded to in their consumption of the show and subsequent conjugation on social media. The pleasure derived within Olitz seems a particularly apt symbolic space for the pleasure Gladiators derive from the show.

Season three sees Olitz steep into murky territory as the death of Fitz's son, details of Mellie's rape, and the criminal sides of Olivia's parents emerge. There are very few Olitz moments, notwithstanding the more in-depth Vermont episode where Fitz reveals a house he built for them, with the long-term goal of living there after his presidency. We know at this point that they share a complicated relationship, but what is also discernible at this juncture in the show is how Fitz approaches Olivia. While the latter proclaims her love much later in their relationship and we do not see her declare it as frequently as Fitz, he is seen as at times dominating, aggressive, and emotionally blackmailing. One example is during a hunting trip when Fitz, having learned that Olivia is in contact with her ex-fiancé, Edison, summons her. In a heated argument where his jealousy is apparent, he aggressively kisses her and pushes her up against the tree in front of his two Secret Service agents. She eventually pushes him away. Another example is in "Baby Made a Mess" (4.07), when he attempts to get her to come to the Oval Office and slowly describes over the phone what he would do to her sexually. Interestingly, the themes of submission and empowerment were brought up by some fans who were polarized on this question of how a powerful woman like Olivia could be debilitated by a man in power and serve as an object of his pleasure (Ehrenreich 2013). This notion is one that she alludes to in an argument with Fitz, when she quips, "What else do you need? What service can I render for you today? Am I here to stroke your ego? Am I your cheerleader? Am I here to wipe your tears? Am I your nanny? . . . Or maybe I'm here to make you feel hot and manly and ready so you're not jealous of your wife's boyfriend" ("The Fluffer" [3.16]). The balance of power shifts continuously but is not recognized as such, and the onus is placed more on perceived submission rather than her sexual freedom, whether with Fitz or Jake. The reliance on long-standing tropes of Black female sexuality is in a way broken down by Olivia, but the vast majority of social media commentaries foregrounded Olivia's role as an object of sexual desire with very few exploring how Fitz and Jake serve, at various points, as objects of female pleasure.

The politics of respectability and morality is another theme that has continually dominated analyses of the show but is defied by Olivia. A case in point is her refusal of ex-fiancé Edison's marriage proposal, which promised the heteronormative family, but she declines this narrative because it does not accord her the happiness that she is searching for and trying to understand. Another case in point was the top trending Internet meme in which an African American couple is seen in an argument, and the top half is captioned "Chicks be like I hate infidelity," and in the bottom half a close-up intimate shot of Olitz captions "But on Thursdays be like Awww," a nod to the show's broadcast every Thursday. Through an array of social media practices, a Black feminist cultural critique emerges addressing and challenging certain narratives. In the case of Olitz, it signals that the binaries of good/bad, moral/immoral, and respectable/deviant are not an adequate way of looking at relationships in the contemporary age and that the shifting, contingent nature of the power relations between women and men are complex and multilayered. While to have a more nuanced understanding of binary oppositions is not without its own difficulties, as we have seen in the reactions to Rhimes's color-blindness framework, avoiding old categories can mean creating new ones. For instance, being a feminist in one's professional life does not necessarily cross over to one's personal life. From a theoretical point of view, Joan Morgan engages in an insightful critique of the failure of venerated Black feminist scholars to reinterrogate interventions such as intersectionality and the erotic with "the temporal, cultural specificity reflected in contemporary US black women's ethnic heterogeneity, queerness and the advent of digital technologies and social media" (2015, 38).

In short, Black women's lived experiences as linked to pleasure should not be negated. I make a slightly bold claim that Morgan's conceptualization of pleasure politics as building community based on feminist support is embodied in Olitz, a pairing that is both desired and debated by Black feminists in these online communities. Notwithstanding, there is general agreement that Olivia's racialized sexuality contributes to a more complex depiction of Black woman-hood who does not have a "right" or "wrong" identity, as we often see her navigating both, and to that end Rhimes has created a celebrated character in television, a cultural location in which Black women's bodies continue to be racially inscribed and replete with images of hypersexual "bad-girl" Black femininity.

The Race(y) Connection

The show itself relies on a "strategy of *(e)racing*" in which "a black character, for example, is cast into a fictional world with other (mostly white) characters where race is apparently not a concern. But in an attempt to contain all of the racial meanings signified by the actor's *already raced* body, the character is sketched as everything that 'blacks are not'—as civilized, rational, superior, good—as 'white'" (Hunt 2005, 4; emphasis in the original). This notion is somewhat problem-atic in the context of the United States, particularly given the history of race relations and against a backdrop of social and legal barriers to interracial marriage. For the majority of American history, legal institutions placed barriers on selection of marital partners through antimiscegenation laws—for example, the state of Virginia's Racial Integrity Act of 1924 made it "unlawful for any white person in this State to marry any save a white person, or a person with no other admixture of blood than white and American Indian" (Wadlington 2003, 54). In the landmark 1967 Supreme Court case of *Loving v. Virginia*, the petitioners, Richard Loving, a White man, and Mildred Jeter, a woman of color, successfully defeated the interracial mar-riage ban, and this case went on to be cited as one having long-lasting implications. The complexity of race was of significance in this case as race, politics, bodies, and intimacies intersect and continue to do so in diverse ways.

And this complexity is what we see in the erotics of Olivia Pope's sexuality, a Black woman in an affair with a White man. Crucially, however, the mode of (e)racing employed by Rhimes also makes room for "re-racings" (Crenshaw 1997), that is, reinscribing race, especially in the context of the interracial relationship of Olitz. This point was discussed at a roundtable published by the *Black Scholar* in which the question arose if it is "a progressive step in an anti-essentialist direction or a regressive move backward toward a reconstituted Jezebel-in-bed-with-Massa stereotype" (Mask 2015, 4).

Eduardo Bonilla-Silva refers to this particular presentation in media as "abstract liberalism" in which race is framed "in the language of liberalism, whites can appear 'reasonable' and even 'moral,' while opposing almost all practical approaches to deal with de facto racial inequality" (2014, 76). In response to the critique of Olivia's blackness hardly figuring in any of the story lines, Shonda Rhimes says, "It's a lovely weapon in our arsenal to use, in the sense that if people are going to be stupid enough to reduce it to nothing but that, then why not use it as a weapon to get what Olivia needs?" (Kamp and Diehl 2013). On one hand, one concurs that it is reductionist to read a cultural text solely on the lines of race, yet it could be argued that the show does, in some ways, do exactly that. For instance, in a flashback in "Happy Birthday, Mr. President" (2.08), where Olivia is reeling with shame after almost being caught by Mellie at Camp David and feeling resentment at being a booty call summoned at Fitz's will, she draws on the "Sally Hemings–Thomas Jefferson" racial reference to both express her anger and wound Fitz. When they meet later in the White House garden, this anger is quickly dissolved by his rebuttal that playing the race card was "belittling and insulting." This exchange is often cited as one of the few explicit examples where one is forced to consider race as an effect by drawing on the secret sexual relationship between President Thomas Jefferson and his mixed-race slave girl Sally Hemings (for a detailed analysis of this pivotal scene, see chapters 5 and 6 of this volume). This history is not elaborated on any further, however, and for those viewers not familiar with this Jefferson-Hemings relationship, the reference becomes a mere mention rather than a potential avenue for critically engaging with racial dynamics, past or present. This point is significant because in that moment Olivia is hinting at being controlled, being a victim, yet is retaliated with: "You own me! You control me. I belong to you . . . You're nobody's victim, Liv." This scene, though short, is underlining enslavement both at the political level and at a personal level with this idea of ownership and control. While Fitz and Olivia are talking about it in terms of affect, it is an interesting choice of words, considering their associations with slavery. Another example that brought race more explicitly into the limelight was the story line in the episode "Where's the Black Lady?" (4.11). The plot twist of Olivia convincing her kidnapper to sell her on the black market to the highest bidder drew much ire from fans who took to Twitter to express their comparisons to slavery (Orley 2015). If color blindness and *Scandal*'s scripts ask us not to recognize race, how could one explain the reception to this plot twist, which was so hotly debated that @shondarhimes, in a Twitter post on February 13, 2015, responded with, "We've been writing about the dynamics of race, gender & power over here at #Scandal for 4 seasons. All Gladiators know that"?

This episode is one of the rare instances where Rhimes has made explicit mention of race, and the intersectionality she highlights in the above tweet runs somewhat in tension alongside the color-blindness framework potently structured in the show, as evidenced in the critiques leveled by fans and scholars (Murphy 2017; Warner 2015). We see in the Olitz relationship that race does not operate in a hierarchy. There is reference neither to Fitz's or Mellie's whiteness nor to Olivia's blackness. So, if in this postracial optimistic vision of a world where, for the "Gladiators in Suits," equality abounds, then where is the problem of race? Has color blindness become *the* framework for understanding race in popular culture in the twenty-first century? Is color blindness the only way to conceptually imagine this televisual racelessness? In his study on Hollywood cinema, Jason Smith offers an alternative reading through "color consciousness," a perspective that would "validate the experiences and perspectives of people of color, . . . name racist practices and . . . point out institutional racism" (2013, 782). It could be posited that Rhimes has complicated the notion of color blindness through this reading, albeit in a veiled manner—for example, in the episode "The Lawn Chair" (4.14), which echoed the real-life shooting of Michael Brown in Ferguson and condemned policing practices, and in the episode "Hardball" (6.02), where Olivia and the director of the Federal Bureau of Investigation briefly share stories of racial discrimination they face as Black women in power. Color blindness and color consciousness exist together in this show in a way that requires "both the seeing and not the seeing of race" (Warner 2015, 644).

Critical studies scholar bell hooks contends that Black female representation in the media "determines how blackness and people are seen and how other groups will respond to us based on their relation to these constructed images" (1992, 5), and the media certainly play a critical role in the construction and reproduction of racial stereotypes. In *Black Feminist Thought* (1991), Patricia Hill Collins furthers this idea by demonstrating how controlling images of Black womanhood are disseminated via social institutions. With this perspective in mind, *Scandal* and the erotic moments of Olitz serve as a space for a continuation of these images, but they also counter hegemonic notions of Black sexuality. Of course, the conclusion drawn as a result of a textual reading of *Scandal* is far from a complete analysis of the picture of Black women's sexuality and representation in television, but it is a part of a much wider conversation on race and sexuality in media. Given that race is on the periphery of the landscape in *Scandal*, it does quietly manifest in the characterization of Olivia Pope and her personal relationships as well as her professional life with female success sketched out in a seemingly gender- and color-blind milieu in which "the language of colorblindness is slippery, apparently contradictory, and often subtle" (Bonilla-Silva 2013, 91). Since a full analysis of the televisual components of color blindness is beyond the scope of this chapter, I have focused on one particular frame of color blindness, which is Olitz, a relationship in which race, gender, and sexuality are paradoxically acknowledged and denied.

The Sex(y) Connection

One of the subtexts in the show is that even in this millennial post-racial, postfeminist fictional world, this couple would face the harsh disapproval of the world, perhaps in material ways, if their relationship was to go public. We get a glimpse of this reality in the episode "Run" (4.10), where Olivia is kidnapped. In a dream sequence, she visualizes herself married to Fitz and living in their house that he built for the two of them in Vermont. In this interlude Fitz is no longer the president but instead a mayor, and she is a housewife, having given up her role at Olivia Pope & Associates. The dream life is indeed a fantasy, but it also reinforces how the possibility of real-life coupledom is so far removed from their reality. Olivia's "hue" has been previously raised as a potential problem for Fitz's political party should they go public, and her parents, at various junctures in the show, remind Olivia of the unattainability of this union, albeit from different perspectives. For example, in "Mama Said Knock You Out" (3.15), Olivia's mother, Maya, says to her, "Cleaning up those people's messes. Fixing up their lives. You think you're family, but you're nothing but the help," a statement that visibly rocks Olivia. When Olivia turns to Cyrus Beene, the chief of staff, to question her role and receive some assurance that she is not merely "the help," she is met with yet another harsh reminder that all their actions are part of a larger purpose, which is ultimately to serve the Republic.

That Olivia, Cyrus, and, to a large extent, Mellie are characters who prop up the White, heterosexual patriarchy embodied by Fitz is a fact that is not lost on both fans of the show and scholars. Indeed, on many digital platforms, fans have expressed their consternation at the lack of engagement with raced politics (Ingram 2014; Maxwell 2013), and the strategy of e(racing) does not resonate a great deal with those individuals who, no longer passive consumers of media, are highly critical of the subtext that "anyone can survive (thrive, even) in the white male patriarchal world" as long as they play their part (Maxwell 2013).

The frameworks, then, of color blindness and (e)racing as deployed in *Scandal* are far from "postracial" in their location of Olivia as negating the norms of White upper-middle-class respectability.

As a result of (e)racing on *Scandal*, new modes of democratically open digital communicative practices have emerged in which fans freely exchange and engage critically with a variety of themes and topics, particularly through re-racing. Olivia's representation of a Black woman in the medium of television has been the subject of much derision and debate on social media. Generally, there is much consensus that her characterization has worked to combat Black women's sexuality on television, a medium that in recent times remains saturated with the "commodification of sex in which sexual desire and desirability are increasingly represented by products and the vocabulary of sex is increasingly derived by commerce and the media" (Attwood 2009, xvi). By showing less commercially driven and more complex lead characters with nonsingular emotions and motivations, and by also refusing to gratuitously showcase sexual acts or offer a singular indication of Olivia's character as the "mistress," "other woman," or "side chick," roles that are frequently maligned and painted as villainous, *Scandal* is careful not to celebrate or condemn her sexual behaviors. It does not provide seamless or linear answers to questions of erotic desire, which we see so strongly in the Olitz encounters.

Conclusion

Throughout this chapter, I underscore that *Scandal* has opened up a matrix of complementary and contradictory perspectives on race and sex in both visual and social spaces. It is evident in the show's narrative (particularly the trajectory of Olitz), which is multilayered, (e)raced, and re-raced at various turns. There are very few manifestations of raced difference between Olivia and Fitz, but those few are at once low-key and loaded. The ebbs and flows, as I elaborated, are what make this on-screen pair so compelling, particularly to Black women. One possible reason is that the show represents a newer example of a critical intervention, signaling a shift in the generic repertoires available to Black women artists and consumers. Though the lines of critique against the (e)racing and color-blindness frameworks are valid and signal the commitment to equality, perhaps it is reasonable to suggest that the sexual-racial identities are not erased in the show but reformed in a way that perhaps resemble deeper, more complex subjective realities. *Scandal* is a galvanizing endeavor to expand public discourses about body politics, sexuality, and power, as well as personal and social freedoms.

For all the labels leveled against the show as racially apathetic and Olivia as a Jezebel, Mammy, or Sapphire (Maxwell 2013)—a cultural analysis that was critiqued for its stark omission of the possibilities of pleasure politics for Black women while re-empowering heteropatriarchy and the politics of respectability (Cooper and Lindsey 2013)—*Scandal* will be one of the definitive shows of the twenty-first century for three reasons: for its casting; for its strategy of (e)racing in media representation that, though problematic, has simultaneously contributed to a national conversation on race and providing a different narrative of blackness; and for its depiction of sexuality through the erotics of Olitz, specifically Black female sexuality in an era that continues to be dominated by pornography, "hip-hop honeys," and "big-booty babes" that reconfirm "the 'butt' as the key marker of Black women's heightened sexuality" (Railton and Watson 2011, 97). The influence of the show and the critical engagement on social media through a raced and gendered lens suggest an increased demand for visual culture that responds to these issues and convenes communities to discern meanings and for the work of critical race theory to continue. To reiterate, while part of Rhimes's color-blind framework is to promote a postracial imagination in which one does not make a huge point about diversity, it is engendered by other vectors of difference that are in turn interrogated by fans and scholars in a plurality of ways.

To revert to the point made earlier about (e)racing and color blindness as a mode of televisual racialization, I offer two other examples, not related to Olitz, that could be forwarded as more direct configurations of raced difference. The first was the adoption of a Black baby by

Cyrus and James, which was an important and deliberate casting move by Shonda Rhimes, as she explains in her tweet posted on February 14, 2013: "FYI: babies with the least chance of being adopted in the US? Black babies. So babies I'm going to show being most adopted? BLACK BABIES." The second example is an interrogation scene in the Pentagon basement between Fitz and Rowan that featured a particularly racially loaded moment where Rowan repeats "You are a boy" to the president at various points in the scene ("A Door Marked Exit" [3.10]). Historically, in American race relations, this word was "common among whites when referring to blacks in the second person. The use of *boy* stressed the White concept that adult Black males were not men, and *boy* increasingly became offensive to African Americans" (Brown and Stentiford 2008, 630). The treatment of the racial subtext through these frameworks may be received with ambivalence from the Gladiators, but it does offer a helpful vantage point for conceptualizing the political and social orientations that produce these sensibilities. It is clear that White privilege as embodied in Fitz does persist, as does racial inequality, but does the access of a Black woman to the upper echelons of power signify that racism is not so widespread that one could be successful solely on merit? There is no tidy answer for this question, as it leads to further questions of how modes of televisual racialization and interpretive practices are sustained. Simply put, there is a long way to go before we can say #It'sHandled.

What we do see in Olitz is that contradiction can also be a convergence so that you can see an aspect of yourself in this space and can see others as well. Whether one loves or loathes the show, or the sexual dynamics of Olitz, it will leave a long-lasting impact on Black women's representation and sexuality of the twenty-first century and will be discussed and debated many years from now for all the reasons illustrated throughout this book. *Scandal* has opened up possibilities for representing Black womanhood in media culture that have not hitherto existed, and for that reason the "white hat" will be tipped to Shonda Rhimes and Kerry Washington for their long-lasting legacy in creating a site for showing the vibrancy of contemporary Black women.

References

Amos, Valerie, and Pratibha Parmar. 1984. "Challenging Imperial Feminism." *Feminist Review* 17(1): 3–19.

Attwood, Feona. 2009. *Mainstreaming Sex: The Sexualization of Western Culture*. New York: I. B. Tauris.

Bonilla-Silva, Eduardo. 2013. *Racism without Racists: Color-Blind Racism and the Persistence of Racial Inequality in America*. Plymouth: Rowman and Littlefield.

Brown, Nikki L. M., and Barry M. Stentiford. 2008. *The Jim Crow Encyclopedia*. Westport, CT: Greenwood.

Collins, Patricia Hill. 1991. *Black Feminist Thought: Knowledge, Consciousness and the Politics of Empowerment*. New York: Routledge.

Cooper, Brittney, and Treva Lindsey. 2013. "Love in a Time of Scandal." *Feminist Wire*, Feb. 11. http://www.thefeministwire.com/2013/02/10180/.

Crenshaw, Kimberlé. 1997. "Color-Blind Dreams and Racial Nightmares: Reconfiguring Racism in the Post–Civil Rights Era." In *Birth of a Nation'hood: Gaze, Script, and Spectacle in the O. J. Simpson Case*, edited by Toni Morrison and Claudia Brodsky LaCour, 97–168. New York: Pantheon.

de Beauvoir, Simone. 2011 [1949]. *The Second Sex*. Translated by Constance Borde and Sheila Malovany-Chevallier. London: Random House.

Ehrenreich, Kelly. 2013. "*Scandal*: The Best and Worst of Feminism in One Show." *Femmillenial*, Oct. 24. https://feministmillennial.wordpress.com/2013/10/24/Scandal-the-best-and-worst-of-feminism-in-one-show/.

hooks, bell. 1992. *Black Looks: Race and Representation*. Boston: South End Press.

Hunt, Darnell M. 2005. *Channeling Blackness: Studies on Television and Race in America*. Oxford: Oxford Univ. Press.

Ingram, Sommer. 2014. "Olivia Pope and the '*Scandal* Effect' on the Image of Black Women." *Georgetown Law Journal of Modern Critical Race Perspectives* (May 13). https://georgetownlawmcrp.wordpress.com/2014/05/13/olivia-pope-and-the-Scandal-effect-on-the-image-of-Black-women/.

Kamp, David, and Jessica Diehl. 2013. "Ms. Kerry Goes to Washington: The First Lady of Scandal Speaks." *Vanity Fair*, Aug. 2013. http://www.vanityfair.com/style/2013/08/kerry-washington-scandal-cover-story.

Levy, Ariel. 2005. *Female Chauvinist Pigs: Women and the Rise of Raunch Culture.* New York: Free Press.

Lorde, Audre. 1984. *Sister Outsider.* New York: Crossing Press.

Mask, Mia. 2015. "A Roundtable Conversation on *Scandal*." *Black Scholar* 45(1): 3–9.

Maxwell, Brandon. 2013. "Olivia Pope and the *Scandal* of Representation." *Feminist Wire*, Feb. 7. http://thefeministwire.com/2013/02/olivia-pope-and-the-Scandal-of-representation/.

Morgan, Joan. 2015. "Why We Get Off: Moving towards a Black Feminist Politics of Pleasure." *Black Scholar* 45(4): 36–46.

Murphy, Caryn. 2017. "'Stand Up, Fight Back': Race and Policing in *The Good Wife* and *Scandal*." In *Politics and Politicians in Contemporary US Television: Washington as Fiction*, edited by Betty Kaklamanidou and Margaret Tally, 47–60. New York: Routledge.

Orley, Emily. 2015. "Some Fans Thought the Latest Storyline on *Scandal* Went Too Far." *BuzzFeed*, Feb. 13. http://www.buzzfeed.com/emily orley/Scandal-olivia-pope-kidnapping-slavery#.oiw6RNkkg.

Railton, Diane, and Paul Watson. 2011. *Music Video and the Politics of Representation.* Edinburgh: Edinburgh Univ. Press.

Rubin, Gayle. 1984. "Thinking Sex: Notes for a Radical Theory of the Politics of Sexuality." In *Pleasure and Danger: Exploring Female Sexuality*, edited by Carol S. Vance, 267–319. Boston: Routledge.

Smith, Jason. 2013. "Between Colorblind and Colorconscious: Contemporary Hollywood Films and Struggles over Racial Representation." *Journal of Black Studies* 44(8): 779–97.

Wadlington, Walter. 2003. "The Loving Case: Virginia's Anti-miscegenation Statute in Historical Perspective." In *Mixed Race America and the Law*, edited by Kevin R. Johnson, 53–55. New York: New York Univ. Press.

Warner, Kristen J. 2015. *The Cultural Politics of Colorblind TV Casting.* New York: Routledge.

Wise, Tim. 2010. *Colorblind: The Rise of Post-racial Politics and the Retreat from Racial Equity.* San Francisco: City Lights Books.

PART THREE

Sisterhood, Feminism, and Female Body Politics

9 | A Sisterhood of Strategic Convenience

Olivia Pope, Mellie Grant, and Their
*Scandal*ous Entanglements

TRACEY OWENS PATTON

OLIVIA POPE is a handler. Whatever the problem, she will be there, as there is no problem too big for her to tackle. To use Olivia's catch-phrase, "It's handled." At three in the middle of the night, who will you call? Olivia Pope. From the late-night sex calls and forbidden, hot and steamy romantic relationship with President Fitzgerald "Fitz" Grant to fighting terrorists and election rigging, it's handled. President Grant was shot, and the vice president, Sally Langston, eagerly awaited her chance to usurp Grant's role as commander in chief. Don't worry . . . It's handled. Olivia wears her superhero cape, her signature white suit, while drinking red wine, beautifully and powerfully.

Not to be outdone is Melody "Mellie" Grant, the president's wife, an organized, intelligent woman who stopped her career as a lawyer to support her husband's bid to win the White House and eventually her own. Both Olivia and Mellie, women who rightfully should hate one another, realize that they need to work collaboratively, particularly if they want to keep Fitz in the White House (seasons 1–6) and keep Mellie in the White House (end of season 6 and season 7). As the seasons progress, the relationship between the women is altered; Mellie and Fitz are divorced, Olivia ended her affair with Fitz (until the end of season seven when they eventually end up back together), Mellie becomes the president of the United States, and Mellie cannot imagine life without Olivia.

> MELLIE: At some point we're going to have to start talking about what happens next. . . . I was thinking we'd do it together.
> OLIVIA: No. Thank you, but no. I think I've spent more than enough time helping people clean up their messes.
> MELLIE: . . . We need you. I need you.
> OLIVIA: Mellie, you don't. You've always wanted to stand on your own two feet, to step up and run this country in the way that you know it needs to be run. I'm not going to get in the way of that. You're gonna be great and I can't wait to watch you do it. ("Over a Cliff" [7.18])

Shonda Rhimes, creator, head writer, and executive producer of *Scandal*, has become part of the ABC "must-watch TV" on Thursday evenings with several hit TV shows. *Scandal* has been nominated for more than fifty different awards (see IMDb.com 2015 for more detail). The show centers on Olivia Pope, a former White House communications director who opens her own private consulting firm. Olivia "handles" many people, including the US president. Because of this handling and managing, particularly as an African American woman, scholars often examine how race is or is not addressed in *Scandal*, thus allowing for arguments to be made that the show, created, written, and produced by an African American woman,[1] is an indication that we are in a postracial society (see, for example, Kay in chapter 8 of this volume). But absent in these conversations is an examination of cross-racial female relationships. Therefore, this paper is focused on the relationship between Olivia Pope and Mellie Grant. The tie that bound these women together initially was a man, but as

---

1. In this chapter the terms *African American* and *Black* are used interchangeably. *African American* specifically refers to people from the United States, whereas *Black* is used as a diasporic term referring to Black peoples worldwide.

the seasons progress their relationship becomes deeper and more complicated. It becomes necessary to ask how "sisterhood," feminism, and cross-racial interactions between these two women are represented. Using standpoint feminism and womanism as theoretical foundations, this chapter draws on problematizing the stereotypical assumptions behind "sisterhood" and female relationships as related to the mediated representations between Olivia Pope and Mellie Grant.

While numerous critical, feminist, and womanist media scholars have written about mediated representations of African American women and men on television and even cross-racial romantic relationships, few scholars have analyzed nonromantic, same-gender, cross-racial relationships, and data regarding this specific type of relationship is limited at best. As will be shown, the relationship between Olivia Pope and Mellie Grant is less a friendship, and their workplace is far from typical. Rather, their lives are integral to one another. Better understanding of cross-racial relationships and communication (both verbal and nonverbal) is important because US workplaces are more gender and racially diverse, and as communication scholars it is important to better understand cross-racial communication and relationships. Further, a better understanding of how feminism may or may not operate in a racially diverse workplace is crucial given that in 2017, 46.9 percent of women aged sixteen years or older were in the workplace (see US Bureau of Labor Statistics 2018). This percentage shows that multigenerational women are in the workplace, thus bringing with them often different expectations for how womanhood and sisterhood are represented. Therefore, two questions guided this research: How is the relationship between Olivia and Mellie shown on *Scandal* as it specifically relates to issues of feminism, womanism, and sisterhood? And does *Scandal* challenge postracist and postfeminist logics through cross-racial female relationships in the twenty-first century?

Black Women in Mediated Representation: A Literature Review

According to David Atkin, "Social changes during the past twenty years . . . may have contributed to changing media images of minorities.

But true parity in representation will remain elusive so long as white cultural ideology—glorifying white norms, mores, and values—works to maintain a status quo for blacks [and other ethnic minority groups] as second class citizens" (1992, 341). Atkin made this observation well over two decades ago, and the same can continue to be said today. Black women still receive problematic media coverage, in large part because of media's failure to adequately and appropriately address the twin oppressions of gender and race that Black women encounter. Despite the ideal of what television and other visual forms of media could portray, the media industry is far from progressive in its portrayal of Black women. Despite early proclamations in the 1940s and 1950s about television being color blind, change for the mediated portrayal of Black people was slow. Black women were often cast in stereotypical roles that ranged from the Mammy to the Jezebel to the Sapphire. Exclusion prevailed in some of the most popular shows in the 1960s and 1970s where there was not one person of color cast: for example, *The Andy Griffith Show* (CBS, 1960–68), *Green Acres* (CBS, 1965–71), and *Hee Haw* (CBS, 1969–86). And while there were notable exceptions of African Americans on television—for instance, *Eastside/Westside* (CBS, 1963–64), *I Spy* (NBC, 1965–68), and *The Jeffersons* (CBS, 1975–85)—the fact was they were the exception and not the norm. Between 1970 and 1983, Fred MacDonald stated, televisual media was "the age of the new minstrelsy" (1992, 155), and the 1999 fall television lineup nearly excluded all people of color (see Braxton 1999).

Black women's televisual representation in particular, as Alexa Harris and Adria Goldman noted, was often a concern. "Once upon a time, the *greatest* debates were about Black women cast in stereotypical roles due to the actions of non-Black Americans in powerful positions. However, we are currently living in a society where White men are no longer the only individuals responsible for the presentation of Black women in popular culture" (2014, 3; emphasis in the original). Black people are now in front of and behind the camera, which allows the possibility for greater power and control of mediated representations of people within the Black diaspora. Understanding how producers and consumers engage with media, whether actively or passively, is particularly important given that media by definition are contested and contradictory spaces, where there are possibilities to resist patriarchal hegemonic hierarchies and stereotypes in favor of foregrounding marginalized identities and their lived realities.

Theoretical and Methodological Perspectives

Theoretical Perspective: Feminism and Womanism

Sandra Harding's feminist standpoint theory, which is associated with second-wave feminism, was used because it advocates the inclusion of all people's perspectives rather than reifying the status quo or inverting the current hegemonic order. According to Brenda Allen, Mark Orbe, and Margarita Olivas, feminist standpoint theory "seeks to expose both acts of oppression and acts of resistance by asking disenfranchised persons to describe and discuss their experiences with hope that their knowledge will reveal otherwise unexposed aspects of the social order" (1999, 409). However, it is worth noting the challenges to the "us-versus-them" binaries that feminism may illicit. While White women may feel the need to address the binaries owing to disparities in gender equality, Black women's twin oppressions of gender and race necessitate a direct challenge to binaries that may not exist for White women. Black women and other women of color must seek to build broader movements and coalitions, as they cannot afford to have a hard line being drawn because of the White supremacist hegemonic power differential that exists.

Thus, the concept of womanism was also used in this study to better include women of color voices and experiences. Alice Walker created the term *womanism*, which focuses on Black feminist or women of color and the interdependence of oppressions like racism and sexism.[2] A womanist or Black feminist critique makes one aware of the

---

2. Walker's definition of *womanism* found in Barbara Smith states that *womanist* comes from the word "'womanish': Opposite of 'girlish,' i.e. frivolous, irresponsible, not serious. A black feminist or feminist of color. From the colloquial expression of

exclusive nature of feminism as it has been popularly articulated by White, educated, middle-class women (Wood 1994). "Womanism recognizes that society is stratified by class, gender, ethnicity, race and sexuality, however, the placement of race, the importance of race, and the experiences ethnic minority women have had to deal with regarding race and racism are central and key points in womanism" (Patton 2001, 242–43). Womanism recognizes that there is a contradiction between the portrayals and stereotypes of Black women and their lived experiences because there is a lack of understanding as to how Black women experience womanhood. Therefore, articulating a type of feminism that shows how the twin oppressions of racism and sexism are interrelated is paramount, and a methodological frame that uses a critical approach to illuminate and center women's voices and experiences was used.

Methodological Perspective

With a total of seven seasons, there are episodes in *Scandal* that exclusively center on the cross-racial relationship between Olivia Pope and Mellie Grant. Previously, the viewer received slices and glimpses of their lives and interactions with one another, with season three providing the greatest insight into Mellie beyond her role as the first lady. A significant interaction between Olivia and Mellie was one that moved beyond a dirty look in the hallway, a smirk, or a snide statement. Conversations that the women had with one another and conversations that they had about each other that moved the dialogue and the pace of the story, in addition to providing greater insight into their relationship, were the focus. For example, in the episode "The Candidate" (5.11), Mellie enlists Olivia's help with her "tell-all book," and

---

mothers to daughters. 'You're acting womanish,' i.e. like a woman. Usually referring to outrageous, audacious, courageous, or willful behavior. Wanting to know more and in greater depth than is considered 'good' for one. Interested in grown-up doings. Acting grown-up being grown-up. Interchangeable with other colloquial expression: 'You're trying to be grown.' Responsible. In charge. Serious" (1983, xxii).

Olivia asks her to dig deeper to address the impact of learning about Fitz's affair with Olivia. "I was devastated when I found out Fitz was having an affair with you. I fell into a deep depression, and the only thing that got me through was thinking that you were just a phase. Fitz and I, we could survive a phase. So I stayed." Using critical analysis to examine the relationship between Olivia and Mellie allowed for an examination of and greater understanding of feminism, womanism, and power as related to cross-racial female relationships.

Scandalous Representation: Feminism, Womanism, and Sisterhood

ELIZABETH NORTH (Chairwoman of the Republican National Committee): There's a special place in hell for women who don't support other women.
OLIVIA: There's a special place in hell for women who spout that tired quote to justify their bad behavior. ("Where the Sun Don't Shine" [4.09])

There is the assumption and history that "sisterhood" is a concept that has solely been occupied by Black women, particularly in terms of vernacular—for example, *sister, sista, sistah, homegirl*. According to Brittany Gardner, sisterhood is a "bond between two or more [women], not always related by blood. They always tell the truth, honor each other, and love each other like sisters" (2003). There is an assumption that all women are bound together simply because they are women. In essentializing moves, politics and media often assume that women will act or behave in ways or support certain causes because of one's gender. In this stereotype of sisterhood, one need only to think of then presidential candidate Senator John McCain's choice for running mate when he selected relatively unknown and novice politician Sarah Palin. News commentators pondered whether McCain would suddenly steal the female voting bloc from then presidential candidate Barack Obama, particularly because he chose White male Joe Biden as his vice presidential choice. Women did not rally around Sarah Palin simply because she was a woman.

Olivia and Mellie are competent, strong women, and Shonda Rhimes successfully cast women in roles that push beyond stereotypes. Rhimes created a "set of heroines who flout ingrained television conventions and preconceived notions about the depiction of diversity" (Stanley 2014). In *Scandal*, Olivia and Mellie are central characters, not only because this is a woman character–centered show, but also because they were sleeping with the same man. Olivia and Mellie were part of Fitz's world and were paramount in ensuring he ascended to and retained the US presidency. Olivia met and began dating Fitz when she worked on his presidential election campaign. The son of a US senator who once joined the navy to make a career and name for himself, Fitz was unhappily married to Mellie and was unable to attain the level of US president without the assistance of Olivia, Mellie, and others on his team who fixed the election vote in Defiance, Ohio, that catapulted him into the White House. In season five Fitz and Mellie divorce, and his affair with Olivia Pope is known. In the episode "Paris Is Burning" (5.03), after Mellie learns that Olivia publicly outs her affair with Fitz, Mellie lashes out:

> MELLIE: I want her to suffer like I have suffered. I want her to suffer so much it makes him suffer. I want to make them bleed. I want their every breath to reek of poison!
> CYRUS (who was called in to help Mellie negotiate the terms of the divorce): What do you want?
> MELLIE: I want the Oval.

And Mellie eventually gets the Oval (end of season six) with the help of Olivia. This relationship between Olivia and Mellie is no stereotypical sisterhood. There is no bonding of these women together simply because they are women.

During the flashback episodes in "Everything's Coming Up Mellie" (3.07), viewers are led to have pathos for Mellie and a greater understanding of and insight into her as related to her career and as she later felt betrayed and wronged by Olivia and Fitz. Like Olivia, Mellie was once a brilliant and successful lawyer who is forced to halt her thriving career in order to prop up Fitz and his political ambitions.

Mellie believes she found a friend, confidante, and sister in Olivia. The narrative Mellie imagines Olivia to have is one where their presumed experiences are similar owing to being women in politics. Part of the same narrative Mellie believes they have to endure is being groped by male politicians, as Mellie did when she was raped by her father-in-law. In the flashback in the episode "Everything's Coming Up Mellie," Mellie catches Fitz and Olivia in a romantic embrace in the elevator. Unbeknownst to Mellie, this elevator encounter is desired and consensual, the beginnings of their romantic affair. Mellie, however, fearing the worst (that Fitz might be like his father and that Olivia might quit the campaign), quickly apologizes and makes excuses about Fitz having had too much to drink. In this face-saving moment, Mellie is hoping that as a woman, friend, and employee, Olivia will understand. Stereotypically, as women we should be understanding and forgiving when our men stray. However, it becomes painfully obvious that Olivia was a willing participant with Fitz, and the viewers see the moment where the bonds of "sisterhood" evaporate between Olivia and Mellie. Olivia was not some unsuspecting sister victimized in an elevator with Mellie's husband, but rather his new "whore," as Mellie once referred to Olivia: "If your whore had died today, brave and strong, protecting a congressman inside the Capitol with a nation watching, honey, the nails, the wood, the cross you would build and hammer her on, the worship you would feel for the rest of your days down on your knees praying to Saint Olivia Pope. That would be . . . I'd lose. Our little war. I'd lose." ("Mrs. Smith Goes to Washington" [3.03]). In a statement that is indicative of second-wave feminism—women versus men as the center of her worldview—Mellie is bound in the binary of us versus them with the context of warfare as the central focus. She projects this analogy onto Olivia initially because she is the reason and blame for the marital discontent, but Olivia violates the codes of second-wave feminist behavior and expectations. Despite being Mellie's enemy and betrayer, the family is unable to function without Olivia as campaign manager. Olivia has a permanent place in their lives, as Mellie says: "He needs you, Olivia. He is tired and broken, and it isn't the job. It's doing the job without you. He's not alive when you're not here. . . . He doesn't have the will to run, much less win, when you're not here, because you, you're everything to him, Liv. He needs you. So I need you. Come back. Come back to us" ("More Cattle, Less Bull" [3.05]). By the end of the series, these "sisters" have to shatter the proverbial glass ceiling in the world of the political boys club. As Mellie says to Olivia, "You've worked so hard to get me here. Two women outran the boys all the way to the Oval. Cyrus doesn't get to steal that out from under us. Cyrus does not get to rewrite the history of women. He doesn't get to erase our climb. Does he?" ("People Like Me" [7.16]). The myth of sisterhood is thus forged by a shared experience of gendered oppression. Not only are Olivia and Mellie strong women, but they are also women who were once committed to making sure their candidate, Fitz, reached the presidential office, and now they are committed to helping Mellie retain her presidency.

So "how is the relationship between Olivia and Mellie shown on *Scandal* as it specifically relates to issues of feminism, womanism, and sisterhood?" Understanding feminism is an important prerequisite in evaluating and understanding the messages of female narratives in order to be more successful in challenging dominant, heteronormative, capitalistic narratives. Feminist scholar bell hooks defined feminism as "the struggle to end sexist oppression. Its aim is not to benefit solely any specific group of women, any particular race or class of women. It does not privilege women over men. It has the power to transform in a meaningful way all our lives. Most importantly, feminism is neither a lifestyle nor a ready-made identity or role one can step into" (2000, 28). hooks's definition of feminism is more akin to womanism, which refuses to engage in the "either/or dualistic thinking that is the central ideological component of all systems of domination in western society" (31). In our patriarchal, hyperindividualistic US culture, women, particularly those women in powerful positions, are taught or led to believe that we are to be enemies, rather than allies. Olivia's affair with the president does not give her additional power; rather, she may have the president's ear and be in his bed, but that relationship is hidden and, therefore, represents a power that she is unable to use to her advantage. In fact, once Olivia makes her affair with the president public in season five, it can be argued that she is reclaiming her power in the relationship by choosing to not stay hidden and silent. Olivia takes on this agency because she does not want her affair with the president to be his Achilles' heel, or her own. Mellie initially received some sympathy and many questions about whether she knew and covered up the affair, but sympathy is not an empowered emotion that can carry an individual very far. For example, in season three Mellie knows she is in a precarious power position when she invites Olivia to lunch at a restaurant to dispel mediated rumors that President Grant is having an affair with Olivia Pope. On the surface and to the media covering their lunch, this looks like a friendly lunch between two powerful women, but really Olivia is being berated by Mellie.

> OLIVIA: What is this?
> MELLIE: A list of men. Eligible bachelors. Prominent, smart. Pick one.
> OLIVIA: Pick one?
> MELLIE: Any one of them. It's an equal opportunity list. Tall, short, Black, White, Republican, Democrat. I don't care who. Just pick one and start dating him. Publicly. So that people can stop thinking that you're screwing my husband. Smile, Olivia. The world is watching. ("Ride, Sally, Ride" [3.11])

When the affair is public and when Mellie is writing her "tell-all book" about her time as first lady and her marriage, Mellie makes this observation about Olivia's affair with Fitz:

> MELLIE: You were a good mistress. Probably a great one.
> OLIVIA: Well, I am an overachiever. ("The Candidate" [5.11])

In the previous examples, the audience sees the relationship through the very second-wave worldview of Mellie, who has certain expectations and assumptions about how women should treat one another and behave. These expectations are violated by Olivia, which creates cognitive dissonance and denial for Mellie, and later we see both women undergo striking transformations in attitude and thought. Mellie is divorced (season five) and has the freedom to pursue her own goals and dreams—for example, becoming the first woman president and enlisting Olivia to run her campaign. In speaking to Abby Whelan, then White House press secretary turned chief of staff, Olivia says, "I guarantee you there is no one on this planet that is as stubborn and as arrogant and as big of a pain in the ass as Mellie Grant. And yet, somehow, I think she'd make a great president. Is that crazy?" ("Pencils Down" [5.15]).

Olivia, on the other hand, sees her freedom taken away when she becomes the first girlfriend. Olivia's life is suddenly tethered to President Fitzgerald Grant. As the first girlfriend, Olivia forfeits the power she has an individual. Olivia seems to be caught in Betty Friedan's world of being trapped, a malaise of which she can name but she cannot speak because she would be seen as ungrateful, and it would be unladylike while holding the unique position of first girlfriend of the United States. From what viewers know of Olivia's past, Olivia is not a silently "stand by your man" kind of woman, but now she has no alternative, as the only power she currently wields is her title as first girlfriend.

Outside of the affair Olivia is having with Fitz, there is a lack of identification that is felt and seen between Olivia and Mellie because there is little understanding of what the other has experienced and is experiencing owing to a lack of intimate communication. As hooks argued, women speaking and understanding their and others' narrative experiences is vital to challenging the patriarchal hegemonic hierarchy. There can be no sisterhood without meaningful dialogue and dyadic exchanges that result in truly seeing one another beyond the confines of social scripts (such as gender, race, and career).

Scandalous Representation: Is *Scandal* Postfeminist and Postracist?

Shonda Rhimes never proclaimed that *Scandal* is a feminist, womanist, postfeminist show, or postracist, yet pundits and scholars have pondered this so-called representative reality. Rhimes said that she is a romance writer, and *Scandal* appears to be traditional romance in televisual form. On its surface, *Scandal* appears to have achieved postraciality in two ways: an African American woman as the lead and central character is beautiful, powerful, and smart, and a White man and an African American woman love each other sincerely. As noted between Mellie and Fitz:

> MELLIE: That is not you cheating on me. That is you . . .
> FITZ: That is me being in love with another woman. ("It's Handled" [3.01])

Simply put, Olivia Pope and Mellie Grant are bonded to one another through the love of the same man. Season three ends with Olivia leaving on a plane with her other lover, Jake Ballard, and leaving Fitz behind. Season four begins with Olivia and Jake returning from a sunny beach locale out of the country, but once again Olivia's heart, actions, and career lead her back into the arms of Fitz no matter how stridently she tries to resist. When forced to choose between her lovers, Olivia says, "I'm choosing me. I am choosing Olivia" ("Where the Sun Don't Shine" [4.09]).

In season five Olivia chooses herself again when she ends her relationship with Fitz. By season seven she and Fitz rekindle their romance, but there is no indication they are officially a couple living together, married, in their imagined Vermont paradise on a farm making jam ("Baby Makes a Mess" [4.07]). However, despite Olivia centering herself (which is a concept found more readily in third-wave feminism as opposed to second-wave feminism or womanism), *Scandal* is not representative of a postfeminist or postracial critique because lead female characters (Olivia and Mellie) do not behave in ways that exemplify a society that is no longer bonded to sexism and racism. "Olivia Pope does not occupy the space of Whiteness; she does not become White in her relationships with others and her access to economic and political resources. Her social and material success do not change the salience of race for her and others, but rather how it is realized experientially" (McKnight 2014, 187). As related to postracism, the silence of racism does not mean that one has surpassed the issue of race, just as maintaining silence about sexism does not mean US society has surpassed the issue of gender. There is no power per se in sharing Fitz, and Mellie did not enter into her marriage with Fitz expecting that there would not be fidelity in this marriage.

In addition to engaging in some tenets of third-wave feminism (for example, destabilizing notions of sexuality), an argument can be made that Mellie's actions once seemed indicative of cultural feminists or domestic feminists from the first wave of feminism (up until her pursuit of the Oval Office). Among other things, cultural or domestic feminists had actions that perpetuated neo-Victorian myths about White women, purity, and protecting the image and spirits of their husbands. Mellie, in her zeal to protect the prestige the presidential office holds before her divorce, is more aggressive about handling the public image of Fitz (and by default her own, since the position of first lady is tied to the president) and the ideal for which the White House stands. She knows that the anathema of the president having sexual relations outside of marriage, and with an African American woman at that, would not be one that resonates well with the majority of Americans.

> SENATOR GIBSON (speaking to President Grant): Sir, next time you decide to go outside your marriage, choose yourself a girl who is a little more palatable to the base.
> PRESIDENT FITZGERALD GRANT: What is *that* supposed to mean? ("Dog-Whistle Politics" [5.04])

If we examine the actions and reactions of Olivia and Mellie over the seasons, what we find are characters who have evolved from some traditional aspects of femininity—for instance, Mellie stopped her vibrant career to help Fitz with his political ambitions—but Rhimes also shows other aspects of femininity, feminism, and womanism that veer from traditionalism. In season four, for example, Mellie seeks advice from a former first lady on how to wield power without the men and Fitz's inner circle having a clue ("The Lawn Chair" [4.14]). Olivia and Mellie show that regardless of what kind of womanhood they are presenting, they are strong, intelligent, and powerful. They control their lives, desires, and sex lives, and in seasons five, six, and seven Rhimes overtly shows that these women are not fully bound by traditional expectations and stereotypes of womanhood.

If the focus is on the perspective of gender and womanism, issues surrounding race and racism do not figure prominently into the series. Olivia, like so many other women of color, has to deal with the double bind (or double consciousness) where one has to address the twin oppressions of race and gender. These issues are some of the very aspects on which womanism centers. Alessandra Stanley argued that "even when [Rhimes's] heroine is the only nonwhite person in the room, [race] is the last thing she or anyone around her notices or cares about" (2014). In the real world, TV viewers are very focused on race. Stanley is incorrect in her assumption that race means nothing simply because no one overtly comments on it. What are at times spurned or naturalized are race and Olivia's handling of it.

Olivia achieves her professional success in spite of her skin color and in spite of the legacies of structural and institutional racism and sexism that would assume that Olivia is the office assistant to a centered White figure. "Olivia's race has not held her back from achieving in her field, it's true, but her race is often explicitly or implicitly commented on, as when a potential client misidentified Olivia as someone's personal assistant because of her race, or in references to the Jefferson/Hemings dynamic between Olivia and the white U.S. president" (D'Addario 2014). Race is real, Olivia's handling of race is real, and race in the relationship between Olivia and Fitz is palpable as well. For example, in season three, episode one, Olivia's father (Eli Pope) tells her, "You have to be twice as good as them [White people] to get what they have" ("It's Handled" [3.01]). Later in the last episode of the final season when Olivia is trying to save Mellie's presidency from impeachment, Eli says: "In the end, they don't care what happens to us. You think because they pat you on the head and tell you that you're smart and pretty that you matter to them?! You are in the light so that they can stay in the dark" ("Over a Cliff" [7.18]). Olivia directly addresses the issue of race when she tries to persuade a reluctant David Rosen (the attorney general of the United States) to issue a subpoena in order to gain access to a videotape of a White male police officer shooting an unarmed seventeen-year-old African American teenager.

> DAVID ROSEN: I can't just go marching into every sensitive situation trying to rush the justice process. There are laws, okay? Ones I'm being paid by the U.S. government to uphold.
> OLIVIA: To protect people who look like you! You talk about fairness and justice like it's available to everybody! It's not! . . . Imagine [living in fear and] feeling like that every single day of your life. ("The Lawn Chair" [4.14])

With reference to narration, Walter Ong (2002) spoke about a "second orality" where televisual media can reintroduce characteristics of storytelling that have the potential to reinscribe stereotypes. These stereotypical aspects reified through storytelling can be absence. Absence, however, does not mean transcendence. Issues involving race, outside of having an African American woman as the lead character, are more naturalized, as there are few overt references to racism. Therefore, rather than perpetuate either-or binaries, *Scandal* has the power to reinscribe and challenge race and racist stereotypes simultaneously.

Fitz, Mellie, and Olivia are entangled in one another's lives, and Olivia acknowledges this dysfunctional relationship, one in which she feels powerless, by also intertwining race and racism:

> OLIVIA: I'm feeling a little, I don't know, Sally Hemings/Thomas Jefferson about all this. . . . I take off my clothes for you. . . . My whole life is you. . . . You own me. You control me. I belong to you.
> FITZ: I'm in love with you. . . . There's no Sally or Thomas here. You're nobody's victim, Liv. I belong to you. ("Happy Birthday, Mr. President" [2.08])

If Fitz is Jefferson, the former president and slave owner, and the White House is the plantation, then that makes Mellie the plantation mistress. Historically, there were no illusions of a loving, supportive, welcoming, and endearing sisterhood between the owner and the owned, the master and the slave. Issues of equality and addressing issues of race and racism were not at the forefront and centered during any wave of feminism. The absence of these conversations does not signal equality or that the United States as a society has moved beyond such notions in the twenty-first century. Rather, the idea of sisterhood superseding aspects of race and racism has created a hierarchy through which women of color remain invisible until issues of race and racism are centered temporarily or at least given a seat at the table until put aside once again in favor of fighting for women's issues in general.

Through the absence of and centering of issues like race, *Scandal*, inadvertently, re-creates the same problematic representation. While one can appreciate that race may not be the consuming and over-arching powerful visible and visual aspect of Olivia's life, the lack of conversation regarding race, even as an underlying metaphor in the relationship between Olivia and Mellie, is one whose absence is at best problematic. In all episodes there has never been a conversation about race between the two women. It is hard to imagine that a lover, let alone the lover's race, would never come up in conversation. The only way this absence may be allowed to pass is if the issue of race is controlled by the White woman, Mellie, who would be able to control and guide such a conversation. As Peggy McIntosh noted in her seminal piece "White Privilege: Unpacking the Invisible Knapsack" (2003), it is White women who are able to access power and visibility as it concerns race and racism. Since Mellie is White and was the president's wife, it is probable that she would be able to control the conversation. Mellie would be the one, through her hegemonic hierarchy and positionality as the first lady, and later as president, who would be able to make the invisible visible (the African American lover—both Fitz's and her own African American boyfriend, Marcus Walker). When race and so-called postracism is viewed from the vantage point of female relationships, *Scandal* may be flattening the experiences of women across racial lines, thereby sneaking in a racial issue through the back door.

The final emotion that keeps Olivia and Mellie intertwined in their cross-racial relationship is respect. The story about forbidden interracial love with the most powerful person in the United States is, in fact, scandalous, but more exciting and less examined is the respect that Olivia and Mellie have for one another. "It is remarkable how both women are developed in the show as self-consciously realizing their lives as connected to each other; Olivia and Mellie need each other repeatedly in the show to control the social and political consequences" (McKnight 2014, 190). This respect is shown before Mellie is called to testify in a hearing about the hijacking of the vice president's Air Force Two plane that was orchestrated by Cyrus Beene in a ploy to impeach Mellie and take over as president. Mellie and Olivia fear they may end up in prison.

> MELLIE: I've already made the biggest mistake I'll ever make not listening to you.
> OLIVIA: If we do this, it may very well be the last thing we ever do together.
> MELLIE: Maybe they'll give us side-by-side prison cells.
> OLIVIA: [laughing and nodding her head] Maybe . . . ("Standing in the Sun" [7.17])

Mellie was the best, the best lawyer in her firm, and now with her sojourn in the White House and her presidential ambitions (the ultimate in power), she wants to be the best here as well, yet she can only do so with help from Olivia.

hooks referenced American author and critic Elizabeth Janeway's 1981 book, *Powers of the Weak*, when she noted the power that women of color hold: "the refusal to accept the definition of oneself that is put forward by the powerful" (2000, 92). It is this very notion, the notion of challenging hegemonic hierarchies, that allows Olivia to respect Mellie and Mellie to respect Olivia. The admiration and respect between Olivia and Mellie over the years extend beyond the confines of a professional relationship and are seen when she laments not having Olivia in her life, after Mellie fired her, but let Olivia publicly announce she was stepping down.

> MELLIE [to Marcus Walker]: She lied to my face multiple times, Marcus. To my face.

MARCUS: I know. But you also miss her, don't you?

MELLIE: . . . I miss having her in my corner. I miss her. I do. ("The Noise" [7.15])

This respect is not based on some kind of antiquated notion of sisterhood because they are both women but, rather, because they are women and because they have had to circumnavigate the rules put before them by men. Therefore, one could argue that the show does not surpass gender and race stereotypes between Olivia and Mellie, but there is respect among these "Gladiators," these rivals, when it comes to desire and pursuit to be the best.

Conclusion: Scandalous Liaison

Arguably, to be in media—whether actor, writer, director, or producer—carries with it a certain level of power and responsibility in representation. The stakes are high with the ways in which women, power, and interracial coupling are represented and shown. It has been argued that *Scandal* reifies stereotypical aspects of feminism and race and racism, thus eliminating the idea that the show is in a postfeminist and postracial landscape. According to civil rights marcher, activist, and congressman John Lewis, "The idea of a post-racial America is more fantasy than reality" (Wright 2014, 22). Further, it can be argued that there is no postracial representation because as McKnight aptly noted, "Switching roles for Mellie and Olivia will not change the intersection of the politics of race and gender in *Scandal*" (2014, 190). Instead, what remains is the racial status quo and hierarchy. As related to the research questions—how is the relationship between Olivia and Mellie shown on *Scandal* as it specifically relates to issues of feminism, womanism, and sisterhood, and does *Scandal* challenge postfeminist and postracist logics through cross-racial female relationships in the twenty-first century?—some viewers and scholars may argue that the show is postfeminist and postracial. The failure to directly address these issues does not mean, however, that US society has transcended issues surrounding gender and race, sexism, and racism.

Shonda Rhimes's *Scandal* is not the first television show with an African American female lead where race and racism were downplayed (for example, the television series *Julia*, 1968–71). However, visually depicting a cross-racial relationship is a deep undertaking because rarely does media show these relationships in ways that push beyond stereotypical depictions. In *Scandal*, Rhimes is offering a unique perspective because she highlights cross-racial same-gender relationships and, at times, pushes the boundaries in which feminism and womanism are often pigeonholed. However, this pushing does not mean that *Scandal* is a postfeminist or postracial show. While it can be argued that the show may infer things that challenge postfeminist and postracial ideologies, the fact is that the "price of equality cannot be the erasure of the historical impact of race [and gender] on social relations in the society, because to do so would mean that there is no way to access [and assess] the impact race continues to have today" (McKnight 2014, 194). Feminist and womanist scholarship and a reading of *Scandal* through these lenses reveal marginalized, disenfranchised, and invisible perspectives that would have otherwise gone unnoticed. *Scandal*, through its characters and story lines, pushes the boundaries of what is possible through an intersectional approach to gender and race that allows aspects of feminism and womanism to shine through whether those systems of hegemonic oppression are overtly addressed or not.

References

Allen, Brenda J., Mark P. Orbe, and Margarita R. Olivas. 1999. "The Complexity of Our Tears: Dis/enchantment and (In)difference in the Academy." *Communication Theory* 9(4): 402–29.

Atkin, David. 1992. "An Analysis of Television Series with Minority-Lead Characters." *Critical Studies in Mass Communication* 9(4): 337–49.

Braxton, Greg. 1999. "TV's Dearth of Diversity Sparks Protest." *Salt Lake City Tribune*, June 28, B7.

D'Addario, Daniel. 2014. "NYT: Shonda Rhimes Should Write Autobiography Called 'How to Get Away with Being an Angry Black Woman': Times TV Critic Alessandra Stanley Gets Things Very Wrong When It

Comes to Race on TV." Salon, Sept. 19. http://www.salon.com/2014 /09/19/alessandra_stanleys_shameful_treatment_of_race_on_tv/.

Gardner, Brittany K. 2003. "Sisterhood." *Urban Dictionary*, Oct. 16. http://www.urbandictionary.com/define.php?term=sisterhood.

Harris, Alexa A., and Adria Y. Goldman. 2014. "Black Women in Popular Culture: An Introduction to the Reader's Journey." In *Black Women and Popular Culture: The Conversation Continues*, edited by Adria Y. Goldman, VaNatta S. Ford, Alexa A. Harris, and Natasha R. Howard, 1–12. Lanham, MD: Lexington Books.

hooks, bell. 2000. *Feminist Theory: From Margin to Center*. 2nd ed. Cambridge, MA: South End Press.

IMDb.com. 2015. *Scandal* Awards. http://www.imdb.com/title/tt1837576 /awards?ref_=tt_awd.

MacDonald, Fred J. 1992. *Blacks and White TV: African Americans in Television since 1948*. 2nd ed. Chicago: Nelson-Hall.

McIntosh, P. 2003. "White Privilege: Unpacking the Invisible Knapsack." In *Understanding Prejudice and Discrimination*, edited by S. Plous, 191–96. New York: McGraw-Hill.

McKnight, Utz. 2014. "The Fantastic Olivia Pope: The Construction of a Black Feminist Subject." *Souls* 16(3–4): 183–97.

Ong, Walter. 2002. *Orality and Literacy*. 2nd ed. New York: Routledge.

Patton, Tracey Owens. 2001. "*Ally McBeal* and Her Homies: The Reification of White Stereotypes of the Other." *Journal of Black Studies* 32(2): 229–60.

Smith, Barbara. 1983. Introduction to *Home Girls: A Black Feminist Anthology*, edited by Barbara Smith, xxii–lvii. New York: Kitchen Table: Women of Color Press.

Stanley, Alessandra. 2014. "Wrought in Rhimes's Image: Viola Davis Plays Shonda Rhimes's Latest Tough Heroine." *New York Times*, Sept. 18. http://www.nytimes.com/2014/09/21/arts/television/viola-davis -plays-shonda-rhimess-latest-tough-heroine.html?_r=0.

US Bureau of Labor Statistics. 2018. "Labor Force Statistics from the Current Population Survey." Bureau of Labor Statistics, Apr. https://www .bls.gov/cps/cpsaat11.htm.

Wood, Julia T. 1994. *Gendered Lives: Communication, Gender, and Culture*. Belmont, CA: Wadsworth.

Wright, Joshua K. 2014. "Scandalous: Olivia Pope and Black Women in Primetime History." In *Black Women and Popular Culture: The Conversation Continues*, edited by Adria Y. Goldman, VaNatta S. Ford, Alexa A. Harris, and Natasha R. Howard, 15–32. Lanham, MD: Lexington Books.

10 | Female Gladiators and Third Wave Feminism

Visualizing Power, Choice, and Dialogue in *Scandal*

LARA C. STACHE AND RACHEL D. DAVIDSON

LESLIE KNOPE, Buffy Summers, Brienne of Tarth, Mindy Lahiri, Leslie Shay, Christina Yang, Annalise Keating: as this short list underscores, strong and dynamic female lead characters are not uncommon on contemporary television, and this set of strong characters represents a positive step forward for representations of women in popular culture. *Scandal*'s Olivia Pope epitomizes this recent trend of female professional leads because she is written as complex and empowered. Writer and producer Shonda Rhimes is responsible for creating and producing many of these strong female characters, all of whom deal with a variety of life issues, in her small-screen hits *Grey's Anatomy* (2005–), *Private Practice* (2007–13), *How to Get Away with Murder* (2014–), and the extremely popular *Scandal* (2012–18). TV shows like *Scandal* are contributing to a popular discourse that features well-rounded and complex female characters who individually and collectively embody femininity, independence, confidence, as well as imperfection.

Given the complexity of contemporary female images on television, third-wave feminist theory offers one possible understanding of the representation of female empowerment that we see with the women on *Scandal*. By interrogating the power of choice and embracing contradictions, third-wave feminist rhetoric addresses female empowerment and femininity, while acknowledging the disparate lives women lead regarding sexuality, race, and socioeconomic status. Roxane Gay's (2014) discussion of "bad feminism" echoes many of these same ideas, where believing a woman deserves equal rights to men is not mutually exclusive from the idea of wanting to be sexy and sexual. Although some radical feminist rhetorics see traditional conceptions of femininity and feminism as antithetical to each other, third-wave feminism embraces this contradiction.

Third-wave feminists argue that we "shouldn't have to make the feminine powerful by making it masculine or 'natural'" (Baumgardner and Richards 2010, 135). The combination of femininity and feminism, or "feminine feminism," is seen as a type of empowerment (Dow 1992). Feminine feminism embraces the idea that traditional markers of femininity such as makeup, high heels, and miniskirts are not signs of subordination, but instead can represent empowerment or be embraced as a feminist statement (that is, slut walks emphasize that the naked body, lingerie-clad body, or short-skirt-wearing body is not asking to be raped). Some feminist scholars have pointed to this type of "feminine feminism" as a reinforcement of patriarchy (Dow 1992; Douglas 2010), but the third wave embraces the fluidity, within a culture of "flux and transformation" that defines gender (Gill 2007, 2). Third-wave feminist theory acknowledges gender inequity as a prevalent problem in society, but also espouses that individuals can be feminist despite contradictory behavior (that is, reappropriating traditional constructions of femininity as signs of feminist empowerment). Therefore, a woman can be trusted to save the president's career, while wearing stilettos and Dior and having sex with him in a closet.

With a show like *Scandal* that has been well received by critics and audience members alike, it is important to analyze the representation of gender showcased by a strong female lead and her fellow female Gladiators. In this chapter, we analyze the intersection of empowerment and femininity for the three female Gladiators in five seasons of *Scandal*. We argue through a critical feminist analysis that the characters of Olivia, Quinn, and Abby illustrate third-wave feminist concepts of empowerment. Ultimately, we critique the image of these empowered women and note some very progressive steps forward by visualizing power through fashion, highlighting tensions in choices between work versus life and man versus self, as well as emphasizing community dialogue between characters in the show. We argue that these three themes can be interpreted as a progressive third-wave feminist narrative, while also highlighting the extent to which these representations of empowerment may function to limit long-term political change. In what follows, we outline the waves of feminism with an emphasis on the third wave and then offer a critical feminist analysis of the female characters in *Scandal*.

Situating *Scandal* within Feminist Waves

Feminist scholars have documented three and, most recently, four waves of feminism. The first wave (approximately 1840–1920) focused on women's suffrage and "the abolition of slavery" (Looft 2017, 894); the second wave (approximately 1960–88) focused on "women's equal rights to education, workplace equality and reproductive freedom" (ibid.); feminist scholarship theorizes the third wave (approx. 1990–early 2000s) as an understanding of cultural discourse about girl power, mediated images of empowerment, and an acknowledgment of the complexity of enacting and understanding gender roles (for example, Baumgardner and Richards 2010; Riordan 2001; Shugart, Waggoner, and Hallstein 2001); and the fourth wave, as described by Looft, is "dated from 2008 onwards, works with the understanding that intersectionality is the common thread between the different communities and groups that link under the term 'feminism.' As noted, a distinctive trait of the fourth wave movement is it[s] reliance and usage of technology and social media to connect and reach populations across cultural and national borders" (2017, 894). In short, the distinction between third-wave and fourth-wave feminism is contained not within feminist goals but rather in fourth-wavers' "savvy use of social media and technology" (ibid.). Though addressing "many of the same issues that third, second and first wave feminists articulated before them" (ibid.), fourth wavers are more concerned with the tools that feminist activists utilize in order to advance the goals of feminism. Third-wave feminism, in contrast, offers a method for analyzing mediated texts, like *Scandal*. As such, the rest of our chapter utilizes a third-wave feminist framework in order to better understand the show at the intersection of empowerment, feminism, and contemporary discourse.

The label of "third-wave feminism" defines a specific conceptualization of female empowerment that focuses on choice and individuality, in ways that are sometimes critiqued as problematic for not creating necessary systemic changes for women (Riordan 2001). In this third-wave context, feminism is defined as embracing "ambiguity" and "individual complexity" when it comes to identifying as a feminist and strives to be inclusive to members from a variety of backgrounds and racial, economic, sexual, and gendered identities (Walker 1995, xxxiii). To be empowered, according to third-wave feminism, is "to be whoever you are—but with a political consciousness" (Baumgardner and Richards 2010, 56–57). A third-wave conceptualization of female empowerment is about making conscious choices in everyday actions in an attempt to confront a gendered oppression, but without denying other identities of race, religion, class, and sexual orientation.

This all-inclusive goal distinguishes the third wave from what is seen by some as the "strictly defined and all-encompassing feminist identity" of the second-wave women's liberation movement (Walker 1995, xxxi). Rising out of the Black feminist and sex-positive movements in the late 1980s, Rebecca Walker (1993) first gave prominence to the term *third wave* in an article for *Ms. Magazine* titled "Becoming the Third Wave." Third-wave feminism is an attempt to be inclusive of women who do not fit the second wave's mold. There have been a variety of stereotypes attributed to the rhetoric of the second-wave feminist movement, which have sometimes created a negative connotation for the word *feminist*. For example, one result stemming from the perceived rigidity of the messages from the second-wave movement is the creation of the cultural stereotype of all feminists as man-hating, antimarriage, business-suit-wearing, angry women

(Baumgardner and Richards 2010). The types of messages from the second-wave movement that provoked this kind of critical stereotype of feminists include a refusal of traditional markers of femininity such as makeup, miniskirts, and high heels, or a maternal drive, which were all viewed as instruments of patriarchal oppression. It is these same markers of patriarchal oppression that some women reappropriate as signs of female empowerment in a third-wave feminist framework, when they are framed as a choice.

The emphasis within third-wave feminism to embrace both traditionally feminine markers of identity and progressive feminist politics can create contradictions when viewed through a second-wave feminist lens. For example, the reappropriation of push-up bras and high heels as signs that a woman is personally empowered by her sexuality creates an ambiguous line between the resulting images of the woman as a sexual subject versus a sexualized object. However, the conceptualization of this type of feminine feminism within the third wave offers an explanation for this contradiction, contending that powerful women should not have to look masculine in order to be taken seriously (Baumgardner and Richards 2010, 135).

This move to embrace both a feminine and a feminist identity is one example of how the third wave pushes back against the perceived rigidity of the second-wave movement. Contemporary feminists have criticized prior mainstream feminist political activists for single-mindedly defining all women via one voice (most predominantly that of a White middle-class heterosexual woman) and instilling strict limitations on empowerment, but "at the same time, [third wave activists] continue to build upon a feminist legacy that challenges the status quo" (Walker 1995, xxxv). A contemporary tenet of third-wave feminism perceives systemic gender inequality as a still prevalent problem, but in response to criticisms of second-wave feminism as too restrictive, a third-wave definition of female empowerment emphasizes individual freedom of choice to look, dress, and act according to feminine standards (Snyder-Hall 2010); doing so becomes a political statement.

The conceptualization of a third wave of feminism is frequently identified with media and celebrity representations of female empowerment at the "intersection of culture and feminism" (Baum-gardner and Richards 2010, 136). For example, the ever-changing personae of Madonna or Lady Gaga are representative of contemporary female empowerment, telling women to "be what you want to be, and then be something else that you want to be" (131). Similarly, "hip-hop diva Missy Elliot, soccer pinup Brandi Chastain, and the movie star Angelina Jolie" have "all parlayed their sexual selves into power in feminist ways" (103). Other contemporary sex icons, like Katy Perry, Jennifer Lopez, and Kim Kardashian, exemplify the idea that to be sexual is feminine, but to be powerful with that sexuality is a feminist choice.

The third-wave movement "draw[s] on the experiences of their predecessors" and recognizes problems within a patriarchal system; however, contemporary feminists that embrace a third-wave ideology also "adapt their rhetorical strategies to new situations and cultural contexts," which includes aligning with powerful female popular culture icons (Sowards and Renegar 2004, 538). In this sense, the empowered woman who emerges within the popular culture narrative offers a reflection and negotiation of these cultural conversations about feminism. Mediated representations of popular female fictional characters on television, like Olivia Pope, can be read as a type of cultural template for female empowerment; they are feminine and feminist, powerful and sexy.

The female Gladiators of *Scandal* are precisely that: complex and sometimes contradictory. Reading them through the lens of third-wave feminism highlights this complexity at the intersection of empowerment and contradiction, but also reveals an articulation of contemporary discussions of female empowerment. The characters do not claim to be feminists, nor does the text reveal itself as an inherently feminist text, although some episodes deal directly with issues of gender inequality (for example, Josie Marcus's speech on sexism in politics in the episode "Icarus" [3.06]). Nevertheless, the women of *Scandal* are clearly empowered in a way that is unexpected based on traditional gender roles. For instance, "Washington plays a powerful political fixer [Olivia Pope] and Goldwyn's president [Fitzgerald

Grant] is emotional and gets into situations that need the fixer's ongoing services. It's a role reversal," which creator Shonda Rhimes contends is "a very interesting gender switch that we purposely have done" (Roberts 2014, 2). These switches that occur throughout the series can be examined as representations highlighting the complexities of gender roles and female empowerment that *Scandal* presents through its powerful female Gladiators.

Feminine Feminism, Choice, and Conversing about Inequality: A Critical Analysis of the Female Gladiators of *Scandal*

The gender politics within *Scandal* are prevalent, but the emphasis in this critique is primarily on the female Gladiators: Olivia, Abby, and Quinn. By conducting a critical feminist analysis of the three women through the lens of third-wave feminism, we discuss how the female Gladiators of *Scandal* offer a progressive illustration of the complexity of female empowerment.

Gladiators in Suits: Feminine Feminism

In this section, we argue that the female Gladiators of *Scandal* convey female strength through their fashion choices and reveal how the series reinforces feminized feminism as a visual representation of female empowerment. A third-wave conception of feminism contends that a woman can be empowered via a feminine identity, including wearing clothes that show off her figure and utilizing makeup to achieve a specific feminine look (Baumgardner and Richards 2010). In a third-wave context, this combination of power and femininity aligns with the concept of feminine feminism, in which a woman can be both politically motivated for gender equality while also embracing her sexuality and traditional markers of femininity (ibid.).

In the first episode of the series, Harrison, one of Olivia's associates, explains to Quinn what it means to work for Pope & Associates by stating, "I'm a Gladiator in a suit, 'cause that's what you are when you work for Olivia" ("Sweet Baby" [1.01]). The phrase "Gladiators in Suits" is the term that Olivia Pope chooses for her staff. They fight on the side of justice, they wear "white hats," they are always ready for battle, and they look good while doing it. We argue that the television show plays with the concepts of masculinity and femininity through the articulation of the female Gladiator and the visualization of power and femininity through fashion.

The show rhetorically aligns power through the feminine dress of the female Gladiators. At the time of writing this analysis, conducting a Google search of the words *Olivia Pope* and *fashion* revealed almost two million results, indicating a cultural obsession with the character's wardrobe. From fan Pinterest boards and articles interviewing the costume designer for the show to the *Scandal* clothing line that was developed in conjunction with the Limited stores during season four of the series, the fashion of the female Gladiators has not gone unnoticed. Lyn Paolo, costume designer for *Scandal*, explains that not only is the fashion of the show carefully chosen for visual appeal, but it also tells a story (La Rosa 2013; Fraser 2017). In an interview with Rachel Weingarten, a writer with the feminist website Jezebel, Paolo contends, "I don't equate femininity with being vulnerable; I see it as a strength and that is, I hope, how my costume design choices for Olivia appear to our audience" (2014). Wide-leg pantsuits, designer handbags, oversize-lapel coats, ball gowns, and gloves all work together to emphasize a specific combination of femininity and power.

Pope's style is a carefully cultivated expression of femininity, with a specifically stated desire to avoid an emphasis on sex. This persona is exemplified in an exchange between characters in the premiere episode of the series, "Sweet Baby" (1.01), when Quinn meets Olivia for the first time:

> OLIVIA (glances briefly at Quinn and looks away): Too much cleavage.
> QUINN (quickly buttoning up her shirt): I'm sorry. I didn't know that I was coming here.

Quinn is visually abashed by Olivia's critique, and within three words Olivia defines the expectation of appropriate dress for women in the Gladiator office. A Gladiator does not need to emphasize her sexuality to be taken seriously, but, even more important, she must actively avoid indicating that she does. In this sense, the women of *Scandal* do not attempt to exert power by appropriating traditionally feminine markers of sexual objectification, like miniskirts and stilettos, as a feminist statement. At the same time, they are not wearing just any pantsuit. Olivia's clothing is Armani, Valentino, Dior; her accessories are Movado and Prada (Elbasha 2013). These are not just clothes; they are expensive and creative designer concoctions. Olivia is powerful and spends much of her day running around DC, and she is also impeccably dressed and frequently in heels, which visually conveys a sense of concern for fashion and style (heels) over practicality (supportive orthotic shoes).

Another prominent example of the visualization of femininity and power in *Scandal* is the transformation of Quinn over the course of the first three seasons of the show. When Quinn first starts working for Pope & Associates, she wears button-down oxford shirts, pencil skirts, and heels. During her character's story arc, Quinn starts working with Huck and finds an affinity for his special skills of torture and killing. As she cycles through the roles of double agent, spy, and loyal Gladiator, Quinn's wardrobe begins to visually juxtapose her ultrafeminine long hair and makeup with tough-girl clothing of tight denim pants and leather motorcycle jackets. This turn coincides with Huck torturing her for information and Quinn coming out alive on the other end. Her narrow escape from death and newfound skills reinforce a feminine feminist persona where Quinn becomes someone who does her own "fixing," without giving up her femininity.

In a time when female news anchors are revealing more cleavage in order to keep their jobs (Newsom and Acquaro 2011), the use of fashion and physical appearance to convey a statement of power and femininity, without sexual objectification is an important step forward for women in prime-time television. Even more important is the opportunity that the writers of *Scandal* take to work these conversations into the characters' dialogue. For example, in "It's Good to Be Kink" (4.16), Abby explains to her boyfriend, Leo, the difference between how the media discusses a professional woman and a professional man.

ABBY: They cover the news, and there are articles about how well I do at my job, but they also write about me. If I wear lipstick, I'm dolled up. If I don't, I've let myself go. They wonder if I'm trying to bring dresses back, and they don't like it that I repeat outfits even though I'm on a government salary. They discuss my hair color. There are anonymous blogs that say I'm too skinny. They have a running joke that I'm on a hunger strike—until I can be liberated by the Democrats.

In this monologue, Abby is specifically comparing how the media treats her versus how they will treat her boyfriend, Leo, who is about to face up to his involvement in a major sex scandal. The emphasis on Abby's appearance highlights the unfair focus of the media when it comes to women, particularly women in power.

The female Gladiators of *Scandal* strike a careful balance between extremes, "combin[ing] power and femininity, strength and seduction, carefreeness and control" (Weingarten 2014). Reading this articulation through a third-wave theory of feminism, the visual images of the female Gladiators of *Scandal* offer a progressive representation of the potential power of the visualization of feminine feminism by emphasizing the characters as sexual subjects *by choice*, as opposed to sexualized objects.

Choice and Individuality: "I Choose Me"

The concept of choice and individuality is important in a third-wave conception of feminism. Choice functions as a symbol of empowerment because "being empowered in the third-wave sense is about feeling good about oneself and having the power to make choices, regardless of what those choices are" (Shugart, Waggoner, and Hallstein 2001, 195). Sometimes this focus on choice aligns with the ideas of feminine feminism, when empowerment is demonstrated by a woman choosing how her body might be displayed to others, or with whom she has sex, rather than having those choices made for her. Hilary Radner describes "the tendency in feminine culture to evoke choice and the development of individual agency as the defining tenets of feminine identity" (2011, 6). In particular, rhetorics of female empowerment that focus on "girl power" are an illustrative enactment of choice because such rhetorics "powerfully [demonstrate] the contradictions of tensions that structure Third Wave feminist politics" (Banet-Weiser 1999, 120). The plotlines and discourse of *Scandal* take up this debate through the illustration of two examples of choice for contemporary women: work versus life and man versus self. We argue that the show presents viewers with tensions in choice along these two dimensions. Instead of resolving the tensions, the show complicates gendered expectations of work versus life and man versus self while emphasizing that the female Gladiators have the individual agency to choose their own path.

Work versus Life

The female Gladiators of *Scandal* are sometimes depicted as grappling with choice and individuality when they must decide whether to focus on their career (work) or their sex drive (life). In season two, Abby is torn between her loyalty to Pope & Associates and her newfound romantic attraction to David Rosen, who—at that time—is an assistant US attorney and someone who is suspicious of the tactics of Olivia Pope. Eventually, she chooses her job, and, more specifically, her friendship with Olivia, but the series uses the tension of her choice to create a dramatic story line.

Similarly, but in a much more complicated story arc, throughout seasons one to four of the series, Olivia is depicted as needing to choose between her love for President Grant/Fitz and her loyalty to her country. Does she allow the man she loves to leave his wife (who is pregnant at one point in the narrative) and his job as president of the United States, or does she do what her job as a fixer would require of her and keep him in office, but without her, because she believes he is the best option for America? While this summary of options is a simplified statement on the obviously much more complicated and nuanced story line, Olivia's battle is frequently depicted as this tension of choice and individuality.

In "The Other Woman" (2.02), Fitz asks her what he can do for her.

OLIVIA: Let me go.

FITZ: Anything but that.

This interchange plays with ideas of choice, with Olivia's dialogue indicating that she has no choice in the matter, when she is not free to go and she has to ask permission. However, in the very next episode, Olivia is furious when Fitz summons her to the woods without her permission: "I am not yours. I don't show up places because you want me. I am not yours" ("Hunting Season" [2.03]). Yet she does show up again and again, because she is powerfully drawn to Fitz, creating not just a plot tension, but also emphasizing the contradiction of choice. Being powerful means acknowledging when your partner has unfair expectations and voicing your displeasure with it, which Olivia does eloquently in the scene in the woods. Regardless, it does not mean that she is not also in love with him and that her choices are both constrained and opened by the choices Fitz makes for himself. *Scandal* frequently complicates concepts of choice, freedom, individuality, and power, with most of the tension found in romantic relationships. We suggest that the show emphasizes the tensions in choice, as opposed to resolving them, which demonstrates a progressive narrative about contradiction in line with third-wave feminist thought.

Man versus Self

As can be expected within a dramatic prime-time narrative, these romantic relationships sometimes become a love triangle, thus shifting the illustration of choice as one between two partners. Starting with the introduction of Jake Ballard in season two, Olivia struggles with her deep attraction to two men. At the end of season three, she seemingly chooses Jake, as she rides off on a plane into the sunset ("The Price of Free and Fair Elections" [3.18]). In season four, Olivia comes back into her role as a fixer and finds both Jake and Fitz asking her to choose between them. It is a familiar formula and one that drives the drama necessary for a prime-time television show like *Scandal*, yet, in "Where the Sun Don't Shine" (4.09), which aired right before the midseason break, we see a revelation of choice and individuality from Olivia that has been missing for most of the season:

OLIVIA: I want Vermont with Fitz.

JAKE (disappointed): Oh. Okay.

OLIVIA: I also want the sun with you.

JAKE: So?

OLIVIA: I'm not choosing. I'm not choosing Jake. I'm not choosing Fitz. I choose me. I'm choosing Olivia. And right now, Olivia is dancing. I'm dancing, Jake. I'm free. Now, you can dance with me or you can get off my dance floor. I'm fine dancing alone.

Through a creative mix of literal action (Olivia dances while she speaks) and figurative metaphor (the dance floor stands in for Olivia's life), Rhimes challenges the plot problem that Olivia Pope's character has been forced to confront throughout the past season and a half: Jake or Fitz? In one thoughtfully constructed speech, Olivia voices the battle cry of "girl power." She chooses herself. She will not be used as a pawn in a game between two men; she will not be forced to choose between two lives, if she is not ready to do so; she chooses herself and, in the process, asks the men to enjoy the dance or get off her floor. This final line links the third-wave feminist concepts of choice and individuality and underscores the fact that we can only choose for ourselves but that this choice will constrain or open up choices to others around us as a result.

Season five continues this theme of choice with two particularly poignant episodes. In "Baby, It's Cold Outside" (5.09), Olivia moves into the White House and plays the role of first lady to the newly divorced Fitz. Throughout the episode, the audience is aware of the ways in which Olivia's new duties are crushing her sense of individuality and choice. She is good at picking place settings for parties and reminding Fitz of important names, but she is also losing her individual identity. During the episode, Olivia finds out she is pregnant and gets an abortion. It is a matter-of-fact and private decision made only by Olivia, but it is clear she is not willing to have a baby that will further entwine her to a life with a man whom she does not want. In the end, she again chooses herself, returning home to her apartment, and embraces her individuality.

Another episode that emphasizes the tensions involved with the concept of choice is the final episode of the fifth season ("That's My Girl" [5.21]). The episode title comes from the line uttered by Olivia's father, Rowan, at the conclusion of the episode. Olivia successfully liberated Jake from Rowan's hold. As Jake prepares to take his place as running mate next to Mellie, who is running for president, he tells Olivia he wants to leave with her. The episode sets the audience up to root for this love affair with Jake, but then Olivia chooses to continue with the campaign and forces Jake to play his role. While this moment appears to be another win for Olivia getting what she wants, the camera then cuts to her father, Rowan, cheering on Olivia's decision, implying that he is pulling the strings all along. This episode was the finale of the season and leaves the viewers wondering what choices Olivia actually makes for herself, if her father (both the literal and the figurative patriarchal figure) is manipulating her all along. The finale of season five reinforces the muddiness of "choice" and the sometimes tenuous connection it has with individuality and power.

The Importance of Dialogue: "Paige Is a Whore!"

It is the dialogue between characters that relates to social conversations about choice, individuality, and power. Nowhere is that more important than in the conversations between the Gladiators themselves. Conversations between characters within a mediated text do more than simply move the plotline forward; the choice of dialogue partners, conversation topic, and differing views between two (or more) individuals indicates the value that the writer of the text is placing on friendship and social issues. We argue that the discourse between the female Gladiators on *Scandal* reveals an emphasis on discourse within their own community as key to problem solving. We demonstrate how these choices are in line with third-wave feminist rhetoric because this dialogue emphasizes tension and gray areas with regard to gender roles and expectations.

Scholars have specifically noted the portrayal of a female community in previous narratives featuring empowered women as a demonstration that "toughness in women does not have to be antithetical to friendship" (Inness 1999, 168). Sharon Ross draws on *Xena: Warrior Princess* (1995–2001) as well as *Buffy the Vampire Slayer* (1996–2003), commenting that both series "break through traditional patterns of heroic toughness that prioritize individualism, isolationism, and emotional withdrawal; these shows offer new visions of women coming together in harmony and community rather than envy and competition" (2004, 248). In contemporary popular culture, similar themes of the traditionally patriarchal prioritization of individualism are seen in characters like Katniss Everdeen and Tris, who function as solitary figures in *The Hunger Games* (2012–15) and *Divergent* (2014–16) film series, respectively.[1] The reliance on female community and discourse between female members is an important tenet of *Scandal*. Having power as a woman should not mean that she has to do it alone, and it certainly should not mean that she relies solely on men for help. The depiction of a community of female supporters in media narratives has been touted as a positive representation of a feminist sisterhood and female empowerment.

Discourse between female characters within a media narrative can articulate larger social issues outside of the issues happening within the smaller plot in the text. Ross comments on media's depiction of the "importance of [female] heroes being flexible about morality and truth" and working through the ethical options together (2004, 240). She cites the play *A Jury of Her Peers*, where a neighbor has been taken in on charges of murdering her abusive husband. The women of the community come together at the accused woman's house, and through "activities as mundane as talking and gossip" the group pieces together the story and "resist what patriarchal law and ethics inform them is true" when they hide evidence of the neighbor's guilt (239). Similarly,

---

1. Both film series are based on hugely popular books, published only a few years earlier.

Sarah Projansky (2001) highlights the conversations between the titular characters in *Thelma and Louise* (1991) as representative of a cultural conversation reaffirming that rape is never the woman's fault. Olivia Pope's conversations with Mellie Grant in the beginning of season five highlight the pressures on women in the spotlight, particularly in political roles, which reflects broader narratives of real-life discourse about and from female politicians. Discourses from previous mediated narratives, where women are united against a gendered system of oppression, have been read as a positive depiction of the benefits of community and sisterhood for achieving feminist goals (for example, Grindstaff 2001; Projansky 2001; Ross 2004).

Unfortunately, a common theme within contemporary narratives that feature a strong female lead is a lack of homosocial friendships (Stache 2014). Frequently, male counterparts or antagonists surround the female lead, but there is little emphasis on female friendships. *Scandal* can be read as a progressive narrative because of the emphasis on discourse between the female Gladiators, and it "is one of the few programs that strives to unveil the ways in which women are undermined in our day-to-day lives with each and every episode" (Putnam 2014). The show's style of quick-paced dialogue and clever, tongue-twisting declarations offers a particularly ripe text for investigation.

The discourse between all the Gladiators emphasizes the value placed on communication and discussion. For example, in the pilot episode, "Sweet Baby" (1.01), there is a moment of meta communication about the community dialogue, when Olivia disagrees with her fellow Gladiators and does what she wants anyway, even when they vote no on a client:

> OLIVIA: We're taking the case.
> STEPHEN: Why do we even bother voting?
> OLIVIA (turns to Stephen): You're pretty and smart. So pretty, so smart.

This dialogue between Olivia and Stephen serves to flip traditional gender roles by utilizing language that might be commonly used when a man talks down to a woman. Men are not typically described as "pretty," unless it is a derisive comment on a feminine handsomeness, and Olivia calls Stephen "pretty and smart" in a playful, condescending tone to indicate that he has asked an ignorant question. She wants to know the Gladiators' opinions, but she is also not going to ignore her own gut.

Utilizing community discourse via the communication with fellow Gladiators, particularly the voices that are in opposition to Olivia, functions to explain the issues they are dealing with as part of a broader social dialogue. Olivia Pope is focused on fixing the problem because that is her job as a "fixer," but the discourse with her fellow Gladiators and the choices she has to make as a result of how the media, government, and public will spin the details of her cases reveal an underlying commentary about the way society handles instances of sexually active women, gay men in politics, and domestic abuse.

This juxtaposition of viewpoints through dialogue is nowhere more prevalent in the show than between the characters of Abby and Olivia when it comes to women, sexuality, and judgment. Abby Whelan is sharp-tongued and most frequently highlights issues of gender politics when it comes to some of the cases the Gladiators take. For example, while looking for the driver of a specific high-end sports car, the list shows up, and Abby declares, "All men [on the list], it turns out, because women don't have embarrassingly small sex organs they need to compensate for" ("Beltway Unbuckled" [2.04]). In the first episode of the series, Abby is charged with finding out more about Pope & Associates' new client, and she comes yelling from her office with good news that the client's girlfriend, Paige, "is a whore" ("Sweet Baby")! In episode 2.01 ("White Hat's Off"), Pope & Associates represents the case of the "finest madame" of DC. Abby, while doing her job and helping with the case, also passes judgment against the men who did business with the madame, including one of her fellow Gladiators, commenting, "She provided whores for him." In the episode "Beltway Unbuckled" (2.04), Abby articulates the upcoming media narrative when the group finds out their client is the anonymous writer behind a sex blog: "Let the slut shaming begin." She is matter-of-fact, representing the voice of public judgment about women and sex.

Although Abby is frequently the voice of judgmental condemnation, her comments are balanced by Olivia's focus on the issues, not the people. *Scandal* consistently articulates the complexity of such situations, sometimes positioning Abby in the right and sometimes Olivia. In the episode "Enemy of the State" (1.04), Pope & Associates is charged with finding the kidnapped wife of a South American dictator. When Abby finds out that the woman was not kidnapped and instead attempted to escape her controlling husband, she tries to help her. Olivia, focused on providing assistance for her client, the husband, reunites the family. The resulting conversation between Abby and Olivia offers an important conversation about morality when it comes to freedom for women from potentially abusive domestic situations:

> OLIVIA: You had no right to do what you did.
> ABBY: No right? No right?!
> OLIVIA: That woman was not our client.
> ABBY: She had one shot, and you took it away.
> OLIVIA: She chose to marry that man. She chose to have children with him. And now, 20 years later, she wakes up and realizes she's sleeping next to a monster and she wants out? She fell in love with the wrong man. She put herself in an impossible position. I did what I had to do for my client. I made a tough call. You don't like it, Abby? Too bad! It is my name on that door, not yours!
> ABBY (speaking over Olivia's line above): Oh, and that makes it your call to decide whether or not . . . Are you kidding me? No, you made the wrong call.

In this case, Olivia realizes Abby is right and makes a new call to help get the woman away from her husband.

Sometimes Olivia serves as the moderator of Abby's judgment. For example, in the episode "The Other Woman" (2.02),

> ABBY: They never leave their wives. What was she thinking?
> OLIVIA (with a reproachful look at Abby): We don't—
> ABBY: Not judging. Just saying.

The discourse between Olivia and Abby, in these moments, reveals a mirroring of social conversations about sexually active women, infidelity, and domestic abuse. Olivia cautions Abby to avoid judgment, but Abby reminds Olivia to focus on the people in addition to the issues. The dialogue between the two women serves to problem-solve and tease out the complexity of issues that are too often framed in black and white, which demonstrates another progressive quality of the show to highlight the in-between-ness of issues instead of a resolution of issues.

A Step Forward (in Heels)

Identifying a feminist media narrative is increasingly difficult with contemporary representations of gender, because the definition of feminism is not unilateral. The complexity and scope of feminism are explained in part by a conception of third-wave feminism and the focus on individuality and not trying to fit all women into the same definitional box. At the same time "television shows and films that feature a tough-woman character may be 'eminently watchable,' to borrow [Bonnie] Dow's phrase, but they still may not embody the feminist values of the viewer" (Stache 2015; see also Dow 1996). *Scandal* does not claim to be a feminist text, but it does claim to represent female empowerment in all its complexity.

Third-wave feminist rhetoric embraces contradiction as a necessary embodiment of the flexibility and fluidity of gender politics in contemporary society. But it is precisely this contradiction that confounds feminists who align with a second-wave conception of feminism. Scholars critical of contemporary representations of feminism and "girl power" caution against allowing rhetorics of power to stand in for necessary political change, arguing that claiming to have a choice is not the same thing as actually gaining social and political rights of equality (Douglas 2010; Riordan 2001). For instance, some critics of third-wave feminism argue that part of the problem with feminine feminism occurs when the individual act of embracing sexuality stands in for necessary political action (Douglas 2010; Dow 1996; Riordan 2001).

Scandal emphasizes femininity as a visual representation of female power, without overemphasizing sexuality; articulates the complexity of understanding choice and agency within contemporary society; and addresses social inequity in the dialogue of the show. While every move that the female Gladiators make may not incite political change in a nonfictional world, the representation of female empowerment on the show offers a valuable glimpse and progressive step forward, as the characters grapple with the boundaries of gender politics in contemporary society. In addition, this analysis offers an alternative for understanding a third-wave conception of feminism and a focus on femininity, choice, and community dialogue as progressive, not in spite of the contradictions, but because of them.

References

Banet-Weiser, Sarah. 1999. *The Most Beautiful Girl in the World: Beauty Pageants and National Identity.* Berkeley: Univ. of California Press.

Baumgardner, Jennifer, and Amy Richards. 2010. *Manifesta: Young Women, Feminism, and the Future.* 2nd ed. New York: Farrar, Straus, and Giroux.

Douglas, Susan. 2010. *The Rise of Enlightened Sexism: How Pop Culture Took Us from Girl Power to Girls Gone Wild.* New York: St. Martin's Griffin.

Dow, Bonnie J. 1992. "Femininity and Feminism in *Murphy Brown.*" *Southern Journal of Communication* 57: 143–55.

———. 1996. *Prime-Time Feminism: Television, Media Culture, and the Women's Movement since 1970.* Philadelphia: Univ. of Pennsylvania Press.

Elbasha, Diana. 2013. "The Enviable Wardrobe of 'Scandal's' Olivia Pope." *Washingtonian,* Jan. 10. http://www.washingtonian.com/blogs/shop around/shopping/gladiators-in-suits-the-enviable-wardrobe-of-scandals -olivia-pope.php.

Fixmer, Natalie, and Julia T. Wood. 2005. "The Personal Is *Still* Political: Embodied Politics in Third Wave Feminism." *Women's Studies in Communication* 28(2): 235–57.

Fraser, Emma. 2017. "'Scandal' Costume Designer Foreshadows Season 7 Ending with Battle-Ready Wardrobe." *Observer,* Feb. 11. http:// observer.com/2017/11/interview-scandal-costume-designer-lyn-paolo -teases-season-7-ending/.

Gay, Roxane. 2004. *Bad Feminist: Essays.* New York: Harper Perennial.

Gill, Rosalind. 2007. *Gender and the Media*. Cambridge: Polity Press.

Grindstaff, Laura. 2001. "Sometimes Being a Bitch Is All a Woman Has to Hold on To: Memory, Haunting, and Revenge in *Dolores Claiborne*." In *Reel Knockouts: Violent Women in the Movies*, edited by Martha Mc-Caughey and Neal King, 147–71. Austin: Univ. of Texas Press.

Inness, Sherrie A. 1999. *Tough Girls: Women Warriors and Wonder Women in Popular Culture*. Philadelphia: Univ. of Pennsylvania Press.

La Rosa, Erin. 2013. "Inside Olivia Pope's Closet." *BuzzFeed*, Nov. 14. http://www.buzzfeed.com/erinlarosa/scandal-secrets-of-olivia-popes-style-kerry-washington#.hf36KQ7MO.

Looft, Ruxandra. 2017. "#girlgaze: Photography, Fourth Wave Feminism, and Social Media Advocacy." *Continuum: Journal of Media & Cultural Studies* 31(6): 892–902.

Newsom, Jennifer Siebel, and Kimberlee Acquaro. 2011. *Miss Representation*. Documentary. Ross, CA: Representation Project, DVD.

Projansky, Sarah. 2001. *Watching Rape: Film and Television in Postfeminist Culture*. New York: New York Univ. Press.

Putnam, Lindsay. 2014. "Is *Scandal* the Most Feminist Show on TV?" *New York Post*, Oct. 31. http://nypost.com/2014/10/31/is-scandal-the-most-feminist-show-on-tv/.

Radner, Hilary. 2011. *Neo-Feminist Cinema: Girly Films, Chick Flicks and Consumer Culture*. New York: Routledge.

Riordan, Ellen. 2001. "Commodified Agents and Empowered Girls: Consuming and Producing Feminism." *Journal of Communication Inquiry* 25(3): 279–97.

Roberts, Robin. 2014. "Shonda Rhimes Talks Strong Women, Weak Men and Setting an Example for Her Daughter." ABCNews, Sept. 14. http://abcnews.go.com/Entertainment/shonda-rhimes-talks-strong-women-weak-men-setting/story?id=25582749.

Ross, Sharon. 2004. "'Tough Enough': Female Friendship and Heroism in *Xena* and *Buffy*." In *Action Chicks: New Images of Tough Women in Popular Culture*, edited by Sherrie A. Inness, 231–56. New York: Palgrave Macmillan.

Shugart, Helene A., Catherine Egley Waggoner, and D. Lynn O'Brien Hallstein. 2001. "Mediating Third-Wave Feminism: Appropriation as Postmodern Media Practice." *Critical Studies of Media Communication* 18(2): 194–210.

Snyder-Hall, R. Claire. 2010. "Third-Wave Feminism and the Defense of 'Choice.'" *Perspectives on Politics* 8(1): 255–61.

Sowards, Stacey K., and Valeria R. Renegar. 2004. "The Rhetorical Functions of Consciousness-Raising in Third Wave Feminism." *Communication Studies* 55(4): 535–52.

Stache, Lara. 2014. "The Avenging-Woman: Man's Best Friend?" *Feminist Wire*, Oct. 27. http://thefeministwire.com/2014/10/avenging-woman -mans-best-friend/.

———. 2015. "When a Man Writes a Woman: Audience Reception of the Avenging-Woman Character in Popular Television and Film." In *Fan Girls and the Media: Creating Characters, Consuming Culture*, edited by Adrienne Trier-Bieniek, 71–83. Lanham, MD: Rowman and Littlefield.

Walker, Rebecca. 1993. "Becoming the Third Wave." *Ms. Magazine.* http:// www.msmagazine.com/spring2002/BecomingThirdWaveRebecca Walker.pdf.

———. 1995. *to be real.* New York: Anchor Books.

Weingarten, Rachel. 2014. "Dressing Olivia: An Interview with Costume Designer Lyn Paolo." Jezebel.com, Oct. 9. http://jezebel.com/dressing -olivia-an-interview-with-scandal-costume-desi-1644446558.

11 | Nimble Readings

Black Women, Meaning Making, and
Negotiating Womanhood through *Scandal*

TIMEKA N. TOUNSEL

DURING THE FIRST DECADE of the twenty-first century when narratives about single professional Black women were rampant in television, there was no Olivia Pope. Instead, there were a host of headlines and story lines that told a mostly agonizing narrative about professional Black women's failure to fulfill their duty of racial uplift—that is, to bolster traditional middle-class Black families through marriage and motherhood. Screenwriter Kriss Turner cinematized the narrative in the film *Something New* (2006), CNN kept the topic front and center in a multipart *Black in America* special (2008–12), national news outlets from the *Economist* to *ABC Nightline* covered the so-called plight of single professional Black women, and megastar Beyoncé made an anthem for "all the single ladies" accented with a hand gesture to showcase an empty ring finger. These media texts ultimately normalized Black marriage as the apex of Black women's romantic and sexual desire and marginalized any alternative ambitions.

While images of Black women dominated television news as the face of single-*doom*, they were virtually nonexistent in the most popular network dramas and sitcoms of the 2012–13 season (Schneider 2013). Thus, when writer and producer Shonda Rhimes, herself an unmarried Black woman at the time, introduced the world to Olivia Pope in 2012, she disrupted the media landscape in at least two critical ways.

First, she placed a Black woman at the center of a dramatic series on network television. In addition, she invited Black women to exchange the yoke of respectable convention for a seemingly more liberated lifestyle absent marriage and motherhood.

Olivia Pope, the lead character in ABC's dramatic thriller *Scandal*, is indeed an unmarried and professionally successful Black woman in her forties. Yet unlike her numerous fictional and nonfictional peers with the same marital status, she is willfully delinquent from the roles imposed on middle-class Black women. Her nontraditional relationship choices and her status as an equal among the world's political elite are packaged in a couture wardrobe that, taken together, represent an alluring new kind of romantic aspiration.

While Olivia may be one part glass-ceiling breaker and one part independent Black woman, she is also one part stereotype. Throughout the early seasons of the series, it was typical to find Pope fielding questions in the White House Press Briefing Room in one scene, while sneaking into the Oval Office for moments of sexual pleasure with the president of the United States in another ("Happy Birthday, Mr. President" [2.08]). She has come to embody the tensions among conflicting visions of Black womanhood: the way a dominant White patriarchal society sees Black women, the way some Black women see (or want to see) themselves, and the way Black communities look upon their women with great expectation.[1]

Indeed, Olivia Pope is aligned with some of the best and the worst images of Black womanhood. Her precarious affairs with the president of the United States and with two Central Intelligence Agency (CIA) operatives situate Olivia as the Jezebel—a Black woman whose insatiable appetite for sex compels her to make irresponsible decisions that carry major (societal) consequences. Specifically, Olivia's judgment is

---

1. The married professional Black mothers in Riché J. Daniel Barnes's ethnographic study demonstrate the ways in which "contemporary women are responding to current portrayals of all Black women as unmarriageable and incapable of parenting" through their career and lifestyle choices (2016, 11).

clouded by her love for the president, causing her to perform criminal acts or to destroy the public reputation of his enemies, all to protect the president's image. Furthermore, once viewers learn more about Olivia's childhood in season three, it is clear that she has been raised by powerful, upper-middle-class Blacks who are also criminals. Her mother is an international terrorist who literally eats through her own flesh to escape from prison. Olivia's father commands a secret subdivision of CIA operatives who will kill anyone, even the president's teenage son, to maintain the status quo. Despite her elite boarding-school education and Ivy League law degree, Olivia is a bad seed—a Black woman who struggles every day to suppress the evil within ("Where the Sun Don't Shine" [4.09]).[2]

Nevertheless, writers have noted that Black women think of *Scandal* as a "guilty pleasure" and a commentary on Black female gender roles in the new millennium.[3] For example, television critic Richard Prince described Olivia Pope as "the ideal for so many black women, a successful career woman who didn't just reach the so-called 'glass ceiling,' but smashed through it," while also noting that what makes Olivia especially compelling are her "tremendous flaws" (2014). On the one hand, Olivia Pope is a shining Black female character who is well educated, well paid, and well liked among her employees and her clients—the most powerful people in the world. On the other hand, she is a twenty-first-century rendition of the damsel in distress, constantly being outstrategized by the men in her life who fight, kill, and scheme to keep her firmly within their grasp. Given the collective memory of pejorative tropes that characterize dominant representations of Black women, how does a character who simultaneously acts

---

2. Olivia's father repeatedly emerges in the series when the flawed heroine is at her worst. He positions himself as a mirror of truth eclipsing her performance of goodness. He functions as a reminder to Olivia and to the audience that she "cannot be normal" because she has "no comprehension of love" ("Where the Sun Don't Shine" [4.09]).

3. Television critic Mary McNamara called *Scandal* "a social-media phenomenon and a test case for TV networks trying to navigate new media" (2013).

as a top-tier political consultant and mistress manage to hail a large Black female audience? Furthermore, what does their engagement with *Scandal* reveal about Black women's modes of meaning making?

In this chapter I contextualize the appeal of *Scandal* through the voices of seven Black women who have watched the show and used it to negotiate their understandings and lived performances of Black womanhood in their everyday lives. The interview data presented here yield three key findings about the ways in which the series compels a nimble interpretive practice among Black female viewers. First, interviewees reject the ratchet-respectable binary imposed on Black women through their reading of Olivia Pope. They allow her flaws and her glory to coexist, rather than allow one set of traits to eclipse the other. By refusing to see Olivia as just a mistress or just a highly educated professional, they make room for a more complex understanding of Black female humanity. Second, the shared kinship of Black female experience informs the way that Black female viewers interpret media texts created by other Black women. Study participants see themselves as part of the same interpretive community as Shonda Rhimes and Kerry Washington, the content creators who produce *Scandal*, and they make sense of the show from within this shared space of Black womanhood. Finally, the interpretive process is often guided by personal aspiration. The interviewees read the female characters of *Scandal* and other media texts through the lens of their own personal desires and ambitions. Through aspirational readings a character like Olivia Pope interrupts imposed scripts of Black womanhood and transcends beyond trope to become a radical imagining of what a study participant believes is possible for herself.

Importantly, these nimble interpretive strategies are not reserved for *Scandal* and suggest that Black women's meaning-making practices function as more than filters for negative and positive images. This study demands serious consideration for the ways in which Black women engage media texts through a constructive hermeneutics whereby deeply personal visions of the Black female self are imagined and realized.

Studying *Scandal* through a Womanist Framework

The research that informs this chapter is born out of a five-year qualitative womanist inquiry into the ways that Black women engage media texts through their interpretive work and through content creation.[4] As a school of thought, womanism values Black women's intersectional identities (for example, race, gender, class, sexuality, religion), yet honors their shared struggles for wholeness through intimacy with God (Hamlet 2000). Researchers have used womanism as a lens through which to take account of the multifaceted experiences of oppression that impact Black women in ways that do not register in Black nationalist and White feminist frameworks (Williams and Wiggins 2011). Furthermore, womanism validates Black women's meaning making strategies shared through intergenerational woman-to-woman networks (Cannon 1988).

In order to fulfill the aim of the project, I gathered data through individual in-depth interviews with a total of thirty adult Black women. As an interpretive community, this group interacts in a model similar to that enacted by the classic audience.[5] According to James Anderson, "Classic audiences were not aggregates of isolates but were interacting, interconnected social memberships" (1996, 75). In my effort to capture the interpretive processes of Black women in a natural social state, I recruited participants already a part of preformed collectives including college-based peer networks, a book club, and a

---

4. This chapter includes data collected from a previous project titled "The Black Woman That Media Built." All quoted material is taken from interviews with adult women who agreed to participate in this study under the provisions of informed consent. Names and other identifying factors of each participant have been changed to protect their identities.

5. Stanley Fish (1976) used the concept of the interpretive community to explain the shared cultural assumptions that inform particular readings of a literary text. In this chapter I use Jacqueline Bobo's conception of interpretive community to speak to the "bond of collective concern" that connects Black female content creators and audiences (1995, 59).

church. By targeting women already part of a social group, I was better able to capture their everyday interpretive networks.

The seven voices highlighted in this chapter represent those women who spoke at length about *Scandal* in their interviews and who affirmed the salience of the show in their personal lives as they make sense of what it means to be a Black woman in twenty-first-century America. Each study participant is represented with a pseudonym in order to maintain the agreement of confidentiality.

Black Women's Meaning Making in Context

As they discussed Olivia Pope, it became clear that interviewees sift through a long media memory in order to grapple with cultural misrepresentations of themselves. That is to say that study participants bring past media figures into the present in order to piece together a script for Black womanhood that fits their values, experiences, and aspirations. The data indicate that these Black women are practicing the womanist strategy defined by Karen Baker-Fletcher as making do. "In the midst of scarcity, this ethic functions as a power of material survival and spiritual thriving." When very few diverse representations of Black womanhood exist in contemporary media, Black women are forced to "make something out of nothing" (1994, 197). The study participants have enacted complex strategies that enable them to embrace and denounce the same media text all at once. These ways of reading reveal a mode of interpretation whereby Black women stretch between oppositional points of view in an effort to keep their own personal understanding of Black womanhood intact.

In negotiating their interpretive strategies, the interviewees are also negotiating their beliefs about the gender roles, the public and private behaviors, and the desires that are appropriate for Black womanhood. Interpretation is a process not simply of evaluating a text, but also of making sense of and constructing one's identity as a Black woman. As defined by Joke Hermes, "Identity construction [is] a process of meaning making whereby individual identities are formed as a result of social interaction based on or making use of cultural sources of meaning production" (1999, 71). Study participants tend to approach media texts and media figures as potential scripts, or "cultural resources," that can be used to inform how they perform Black womanhood in their own lives. Thus, their interpretive processes are never just about whether a media text is satisfying or enjoyable. Rather, their engagement with mediated scripts for Black womanhood is always a negotiation toward an intimate understanding of the Black female self.

Reading Olivia Pope beyond a Ratchet-Respectability Binary

In their discussions of *Scandal*, study participants reveal that they are not ignorant about the problems that a character like Olivia Pope embodies. Nevertheless, they are looking beyond these issues to be able to enjoy the media text and to uphold Olivia as a role model of sorts. Cocoa, a twentysomething professional working in the health care industry, spoke of a complicated relationship with Olivia Pope in her attempt to manage the gap between Olivia's presentation of Black womanhood and her own understanding of what it means to be a good Black woman.

> INTERVIEWER: What appeals to you about [Olivia Pope]?
> COCOA: She's in control. She is still vulnerable, even though I just talked bad about her being a strong Black woman stereotype. I remember now, she cries. And, what else is good about her? She's very smart. She's usually the smartest person in the room. She's driven. She knows what she wants. She inspires others. You know, she's got a gang of followers that do whatever, whatever she needs because they trust her even though she's a politician, kinda, so she's not very honest sometimes. She's on the good side of things. Even if things that she does aren't 100 percent honest, she still has good intentions, I think.

Earlier in the interview, Cocoa stated that she did not think of Olivia Pope as an ideal Black woman because of her association with the strong Black woman stereotype. This stereotype is based on the idea that Black women are expected to be all things to all people—sexually appealing and available wives, family and community nurturers, and stellar professionals in the workplace. Understanding the physical and emotional strains of fulfilling an image as impossible as the strong Black woman, Cocoa further explained that the stereotype "could be a good thing, but can also be a bad thing." While it is honorable that Olivia cares for the people in her life and assumes a nurturing role with many of her clients, her external output of care leaves her internal reserves empty. Nevertheless, Cocoa's statements indicate a hesitancy to categorize Olivia Pope with any one overarching label. Over the course of the interview, Cocoa shifts perspectives, considering representations of Black womanhood through various lenses. Rather than reject Olivia altogether, Cocoa pivots, listing the character's preferable attributes just as easily as she discusses Olivia's flaws.

Sara, a woman in her late twenties, also resists categorizing Olivia as either "positive" or "negative." Furthermore, she explains that the tendency to place Olivia Pope in a single category is born out of the limited number of popular Black female portrayals. "I think that the problem is that we have so few roles like Kerry [Washington's] on *Scandal*. That's kind of like the one example that a lot of people look at, or one of the few examples that a lot of people look at, as opposed to there being, like, a variety. So a lot of people nitpick on the fact that she is having an affair with a White man." According to Sara, the scarcity of Black female representations compels some viewers to cling to an ideal of perfection and therefore obsess over Olivia's many glaring flaws. Rather than seeing Olivia through the lens of her affair, Sara suggests a more comprehensive reading of Olivia where viewers also take into account that she is "a hardworking woman" who excels in her career and in at least some of her personal relationships. By rejecting a dichotomous analysis where Olivia must either be all good or all evil, Sara makes room for a fuller and more human understanding of Olivia as a Black female subject.

In yet another example of nuanced interpretation, Ashley, a graduate student in her twenties, also negotiates the tensions embodied in Olivia Pope through simultaneous appreciation and resistance. Ashley describes her interpretive practice as a switch that she turns on or off depending on the type of media content she engages. She credits her years of experience in academic environments, and the challenge of one professor in particular, with helping her develop a critical lens that now causes her to question the motives behind media content. "I think now [the critical lens] is more on than off . . . It is so turned on that even though I love *Scandal*, I'm like, dang, Olivia! Why you gotta be the sidepiece and telling everybody that it's okay to be the sidepiece? I'm like, it's so on, and I see it's so on that sometimes it determines what I can and cannot, will and will not, engage with." Like many other study participants, Ashley believes that her experiences in higher education, specifically with women's studies courses, give her a more critical edge that she wields within and outside of the classroom during her time of leisure media engagement. She can enjoy a show like *Scandal* while also challenging the show's depiction of Black womanhood. Specifically, Ashley disagrees with a glorification of the "sidepiece"—the idea that the role of mistress or the woman on the side is a viable and even appealing alternative for Black women in romantic relationships.[6] Nevertheless, Olivia's political acrobatics continue to draw her into the series. Ashley's mode of meaning making allows her to derive pleasure from the show without compromising her critical instincts.

Cocoa, Sara, and Ashley each embrace an interpretive practice that rejects binaries and allows for an understanding of Black womanhood that is as messy and complex as their own humanity. They do not require that Olivia fully meet the terms of respectability in order to win their affection; neither do they feel compelled to turn a blind eye to Olivia's flaws or betray their own understandings of acceptable

6. Kerry Washington, the actress who portrays Olivia Pope, once stated that the categorization of Olivia Pope as a sidepiece is "debatable" during a visit to *The Wendy Williams Show*. She explained, "I don't like the expression sidepiece because I think when you call a woman a 'piece,' it objectifies her. But I think also: the president has said to her 'I will leave my wife for you' and she said no. Is she a sidepiece or is she just somebody who's afraid to be all in? I don't know" (see Carter 2013). When Olivia has the opportunity to transition from mistress to wife and mother in season five, she ultimately rejects both, seemingly proving Washington's point.

behavior. They read Olivia Pope for all that she is without compromising who they are as Black women. Cocoa, Sara, and Ashley's way of making sense of *Scandal* shatters the thinking that Black women must choose between ratchet or respectable representations, that they must either love a text or hate it.

Interpretation as an Expression of Intimacy

Another motivation that undergirds a dexterous mode of meaning making in relation to *Scandal* is the sense of community that links Black female content creators to their Black female audiences. As Sammy Jo, a retired mother in her sixties, describes, she finds value in the show despite its troubling elements because it enriches her participation within a larger group of interconnected Black women all seeking to co-construct the Black female self.

SAMMY JO: I will watch episodes four or five times. I don't care how many times I've watched an episode, I always get something new. . . . Now, there were a couple of episodes where I turned the TV off totally upset with what had taken place. Um, and *upset* isn't the correct adjective. I felt betrayed. I felt that Shonda Rimes had betrayed us, meaning Black women, in what had taken place in the episode, and I felt, even though I knew that was her job, that Kerry Washington had disappointed me in allowing this scene itself to take place.

INTERVIEWER: Mm-hmm. Is there . . . Do you remember one particular episode or particular scene that made you feel that way?

SAMMY JO: Definitely. When everyone was at the christening ceremony, [Olivia] turned around and walked out, and Fitz followed her down the hall and dragged her into this little equipment closet. And after their little tryst was over, he said something like, "That was just my loins longing for you." In other words, I just used you; that's all I wanted. And, I was like, how could you do this?

INTERVIEWER: So, what keeps you watching? Given that there are those moments where you are into the political thrill of the show, but then there are those moments where you feel betrayed?

SAMMY JO: I think there is a community, and that community is those friends of mine that watch also, and we can have hours and hours of discussion about what took place and the nuance. I belong to two online *Scandal* discussion groups.

Sammy Jo's words reveal the intensity of her engagement with media texts that speak directly to the limitations and possibilities of Black womanhood. As a self-proclaimed "political junkie," she does not engage *Scandal* the same way she engages nonfictional narratives about power and government, such as *Morning Joe* (MSNBC). Rather, there is an intimacy established between Sammy Jo and the fictional characters that inhabit the story world of *Scandal*, as well as the individuals who write and perform the narrative. The social, or interactive, quality of Black female media interpretation is therefore dual in nature—existing among audience members and between producers and interpreters. Within this union built on a shared identity of Black womanhood, Sammy Jo has established her connection to *Scandal* and its Black female leads as a mutual exchange where she invokes her rights as a media citizen.

Sammy Jo expects a particular treatment of Black womanhood as a return on her investment of viewing and supporting *Scandal*. Although the show does not always meet her standards, Sammy Jo is no more compelled to dismiss the text than she would be compelled to dismiss a friend over a disagreement. She maintains her commitment to the show but, more important, to Shonda Rhimes (creator and executive producer of *Scandal*) and Kerry Washington as the Black women behind the show. In Sammy Jo's mind, these women are just as much a part of her interpretive community as the friends and the members of the online community with whom she collaboratively interprets the series.

Sammy Jo's willingness to continue making do with the show and grappling with its content, that which she appreciates and that which she rejects, is in part owing to her loyalty to Black female content creators in the midst of a scarce media landscape of Black womanhood. Jacqueline Bobo describes the relationship between Black female content creators and their Black female audience as one based on an "instant intimacy" constituted by a common body of codes and symbols that make Black women particularly attuned to implicit connotations of texts produced by Black women (1995, 59). This quality of intimacy distinguishes Black female interpretive communities from Stanley Fish's original definition, because it speaks directly to shared experiential *and* cultural-linguistic referents. Thus, Sammy Jo's connection to Shonda Rhimes and Kerry Washington/Olivia Pope is not a parasocial relationship based in fantasy, but rather a psychosocial link (re)produced through the broad commonalities embedded in living in a Black woman's body. Indeed, Sammy Jo's nimble reading of *Scandal* is also a product of her being able to understand Rhimes's interplay between real and imagined issues of blackness, womanhood, and power.

Similar to Sammy Jo, Lena, a counselor in her late fifties, also spoke about her relationship to Olivia Pope as one of mutual understanding. Hence, where other people misread Olivia's intentions, Lena sees something she can relate to, another imperfect Black woman just trying to make do:

> Now this might strike you as weird, but to me Olivia is not a manipulator. She is a fighter. She always does what's necessary. When people come to her with issues, she kind of operates in grace; she's kind of wicked with it. And I don't agree with her tactics, but what you need to do is look at the big picture. . . . She's not lazy, and she works. She has a purpose. And her purpose is, here we go again, everybody on her team, she saw something in them, and she said come and work with me. She's a leader and she's a rescuer, but also codependent. And I can relate to that.

Lena's interpretation of Olivia invokes the common gender role of family and community nurturer that many Black women assume at some point in their lives. By reframing Olivia Pope as someone who supports an entire team of people, and not just another devious woman in power, Lena is actively rejecting the trope of the Black bitch and exchanging it for the symbol of the Black woman as nurturer. Her response goes beyond empathy and reflects the kind of intimate understanding that can only be born out of shared experience. Ultimately, Lena sees herself as someone who is able to see Olivia beyond the rough edges and understand her at the core of her truest self, as another Black woman walking in her purpose. In much the same way that close relatives may engage in intense arguments without completely destroying their relationship, Sammy Jo and Lena can feel betrayed by Olivia Pope yet remain loyal in their viewership each week because they connect to her through a mutual understanding of Black womanhood.

Scandal as a Building Block: Co-constructing the Black Female Self

Of all the study informants, those interviewees who described the most intense relationships with Olivia Pope and other female characters on *Scandal* were those women who used these cultural resources to build the Black woman of their dreams. These interviewees are women in their late twenties who are focused on fulfilling their own personal checklists of what it means to be an ideal Black woman, and therefore rely on media figures such as Olivia Pope to embody their ideals. When Olivia Pope falls short of meeting their full list of expectations, these women stretch their understanding of Olivia rather than reject her altogether.

For example, Skylar, a corporate professional in her late twenties, makes sense of media texts in collaboration with fellow Christian women whom she trusts and admires. When she engages shows like *Scandal* that fail to meet her personal standards of lifestyle and behavior, she pivots and shifts her perspective in order to better appreciate the aspects of the show that do align with her personal aspirations. "You know, it's so funny because my aunt, somebody who I really admire and respect her opinion, she actually had been telling me, 'Hey, you've got to rent and watch *Scandal*.' She's like, 'Hey, you gotta watch it, like it will even help you in your career.' And you know she was really touting the show, if you will. So, during Christmas break I spent time on my iPad on *Netflix*, and I caught up on seasons 1 and 2. So, yes, I am watching *Scandal* now." Skylar's relation to the

Olivia Pope character is somewhat contextualized in fantasy. She uses Olivia Pope to think about ways of confronting dilemmas that are common to Black women in high-stress professional environments. The fact that Skylar's aunt advised her to treat *Scandal* as a career playbook of sorts suggests that she, too, has evaluated the show as a fantastical exploration of Black women in corporate America.

Ien Ang argues that in order to understand the significance of female media citizens' appreciation of media subjects that embody disempowering characteristics, analysts must resist conceptualizing fictional characters as "realistic images of women" and instead approach these characters as "textual constructions of possible modes of femininity" (1996, 78). Skylar's reading of Olivia Pope can thus be analyzed as an effective way of thinking through versions of the Black female self in the imaginary, without risking the consequences of a disempowered Black female subjecthood in real life.

Given Skylar's Christian convictions, however, it is impossible for her to be completely swept up in the imaginary world where a Black woman can soar beyond every limit of political power that would realistically become a hindrance to someone of her age, race, and gender. She will not allow herself to fully embrace a character who, for the first four seasons of the show, engages in an affair with a married man.

> Like I said, my aunt was somebody who really wanted me to watch Kerry Washington's character and see how she handles herself in different situations and her temperament, and you know how her confidence is a good thing, and that would kinda, you know, be used as a navigator for me at this point, especially in my career. However, the spiritual side of me knows that a lot of the things that happen on this show aren't right—being the fact we are glorifying a woman who is having an affair with a married man. I mean, that is not something that sits well with me, even though, the way that it's portrayed, and it's mixed in well, and it is pretty riveting watching that affair unfold. But at the end of the day, you're like, wow, like you know, that's not right. And it's not something that I should be supporting because I sure wouldn't want it happening in my own household.

At the core, Skylar's reading of Olivia Pope and *Scandal* hinges on the tension between the pleasure of fantasy and the responsibilities and values that shape everyday experience. As long as Skylar treats the show as a work of fiction that is entertaining, informative, and a source of connection between herself and her aunt, then her enjoyment is maximized. When Skylar reflects on the real-world implications of a woman like Olivia Pope living out a script of Black womanhood that diverges from Skylar's values and personal aspirations to become a wife and mother, her connection to the show and her relation to the character are weakened.

The definition of Black womanhood that Skylar holds in heart and mind is the measure by which she ultimately evaluates *Scandal*, Olivia Pope, and media texts in general. Still, it is necessary that Skylar's interpretive practice be nimble. She must be able to pivot perspectives in order to map the script for Black womanhood presented in *Scandal* onto her own aspirations. Skylar can make sense of Olivia Pope through her aunt's eyes and benefit from the professional role playing and career motivation that the character offers. In this way, Olivia Pope can inform the part of Skylar's Black female self that is the most professionally ambitious. Skylar can also make sense of Olivia Pope through the lens of her faith and create distance between her own relationship choices and those glamorized in *Scandal*. In this way, Olivia Pope does not sully the part of Skylar's Black female self that is focused on living a life in tune with Christian principles.

Importantly, when Skylar considers *Scandal* within the context of her own aspirations and values, she aligns herself with a very different kind of role model, Mellie, who is the wife of Olivia's lover for the first four seasons of the series. Since Mellie is a White female character, Skylar's responses suggest that when she pivots her perspective as an interpreter, she may be repelled away from Black female characters altogether.

Melanie was another interviewee drawn more to Mellie than to Olivia when she read each female character within the context of her own lifestyle goals. Olivia's nontraditional professional life and chaotic romantic life are far from the kind of life to which Melanie aspires.

MELANIE: I think [Olivia] has an interesting job. I mean, Mellie, by far, is my favorite character on the show, so I'm not gonna say I watch the show for, like, for Olivia per se. She's not my favorite, but she has an interesting job. She definitely helps people. It's an interesting career, something I would've never thought of if it wasn't on TV.

INTERVIEWER: What about Mellie attracts you to her character?

MELANIE: She's living the American dream. I mean, she's the first lady of the United States. She's married. She has children, and she's educated, and she has some power. I mean, you literally have everything I would want. I just think I relate more to Mellie than I do to Olivia. I mean, Olivia is just a single person sleeping with someone's husband.

Mellie is a White character with a law degree who traded her law career for the role of political wife when her husband decided to run for governor (and later for president). Although Mellie and the president divorce in the fifth season of the series, she has leveraged her personal brand to transition from first lady to US senator to eventually president herself.

As a young Black woman who also holds a professional graduate degree and longs for the day when she will be able to trade her health care job for a career as a wife and homemaker, Melanie reads the former first lady as a role model. Many viewers, including myself, might read Mellie Grant as a character who miserably makes do with a life that has cost her more than she imagined having to pay. Melanie, however, views the character as having the most desirable lifestyle of any other woman on the show. The fact that she and Mellie do not share the same racial identity is superseded by the fact that Mellie Grant has lived the type of life to which Melanie aspires. Since Melanie's understanding of Black womanhood deviates from some of the most popular mediated scripts, she is often drawn away from Black female media characters.

While many of the study participants, some of whom are also friends of Melanie, reference fictional Black female figures like Clair

Huxtable as their media role models, Melanie describes Alicia Florrick of the CBS drama *The Good Wife* (2009–16) as her favorite female media character.[7] Alicia Florrick, similar to Mellie Grant in *Scandal*, is a White law school graduate and mother of two who spends fifteen years as a homemaker after marrying a politician, Peter Florrick. The contrast in favored media characters among Melanie and her friends is symbolic of the contrast in their life aspirations. Within her interpretive community, there are different ideas of the gender roles and lifestyle choices that will lead to the most happiness.

> MELANIE: I have probably six really, really good friends who have told me that they want their husbands to be stay-at-home dads. . . . That's the way they are. I don't want to be like them. I still believe it is important to have a parent home, but I would want to be the one at home. I'm not that supergirl. I respect those girls. I understand where they're coming from. I see it. I see they want it. They're working hard for their education. They want to work, but they want someone to be at home with their kids. So we kind of have the same . . . we have the same thought process. It's just I want to be the one staying at home, and they all want to go to work.
>
> INTERVIEWER: Hmm. And so why would, why do you want to be the one to stay at home?
>
> MELANIE: Because I think, I think I can be a really good wife. I think staying at home is more than just taking care of your kids. I think it's promoting your husband, promoting your family, promoting your brand, what makes you money. If your husband is an attorney, that means you going out there, when you're going to lunch, you're mentioning your husband's name, like, hey, maybe you should talk to him. Or, maybe, I think I could add just as much value working as I can if I stay at home. I think I could promote my husband. I think I could add. I think I could make our family

---

7. Alicia Florrick is portrayed by the Emmy Award–winning actress Julianna Margulies.

money in a whole totally different way that'll be more enjoyable and allow me to be with my kids more.

Melanie's description of the life that she imagines for herself and the agency and power she ascribes to the role of wife-mother are reflective of a more nuanced reading of the dutiful wife role than is typically understood in relation to such fictional characters. Her reading is informed neither by the dominant understanding of wife-mother nor by the meaning of wife-mother that members of her interpretive community uphold. Rather, Melanie interprets characters like Mellie Grant and Alicia Florrick within the realm of her interior logic of the advantages of fulfilling traditional gender roles. Melanie can therefore see strength, efficacy, and joy, where others might read weakness, inadequacy, and pain. She demonstrates that the interpretive practices of Black female media citizens fall along a continuum that may be more or less in line with imposed gender norms depending on their personal aspirations and desires.

Melanie's connection to White female media figures is a unique response among the interviewees who look to cultural resources as they are building the Black female self. The more common practice, exemplified through Cocoa, is to create a hybrid ideal of Black womanhood based on the best attributes of multiple characters. Thus, Cocoa reads Olivia Pope in pieces, grasping the parts of the character that align with her personal values and life goals, and releasing those fragments that do not align. She uses other media figures to fill in the gaps of the insufficient script for Black womanhood that Olivia embodies.

INTERVIEWER: How do you try to emulate those traits of your favorite characters in your day-to-day life?

COCOA: Okay, let's start with Clair [Huxtable]. Even though I'm not a wife and mother, like you said, she has a very good work-life balance, so basically I kinda try to do it all. I know that's not a very good thing, but I try to have a, you know, be good at my job and at school, and also keep up home, so keep my place nice, you know, cook every now and then for my boyfriend, you know, stuff like that. Olivia Pope, I use her, like, confidence. I just, I was promoted at my job over a lot of people that have higher degrees than me and that have been there a lot longer, so that confidence when she walks into a room like she knows her stuff. You know, she's about that professional work life, and I like that about her, so I try to emulate that too, so her professionalism and her control.

Cocoa finds points of relation that allow her to map her own daily performances of Black womanhood at work, at home, and at school onto the performances of various Black female characters. Importantly, rather than narrow her focus to one character, Cocoa's expansive interpretive practice compels her to weave traits from multiple characters together in order to achieve a comprehensive model of Black womanhood that will fit the scope of the life she aspires to live.

Conclusion

The Black women who participated in this study have demonstrated that an appreciation for a character like Olivia Pope does not make one a cultural dupe or a passive audience member. On the contrary, these women have exhibited a capacity to choose when and how to activate the multiple lenses that shape their nimble interpretive practices when engaging a text like *Scandal*. Rather than feign ignorance of pejorative tropes, interviewees deploy reading techniques whereby they twist and stretch a text until it fits the definition of Black womanhood that offers them the most satisfaction. Importantly, this mode of meaning making is a radical way of making do. It is a technique developed out of the scarcity of Black female representations and a desire to imagine one's own ideal Black womanhood.

The intensity with which study participants engage and read *Scandal* supports the theory that meaning making only minimally concerns the enjoyment or basic reception of a media text. Interpreting mediated scripts of Black womanhood is also a profound practice of co-constructing what it means to be a Black woman. The Black women involved in this study survey the media landscape, past and present, to create a mosaic of Black womanhood that reflects the traits they believe are necessary for achieving their own ideal. This effort is both deeply internal and collaborative, as interviewees move back and forth between their own conceptions of Black womanhood and those valued within their diverse and overlapping interpretive communities.

Ultimately, the data presented in this chapter advance that Black women are quite reflective about their media engagement habits and must therefore be taken seriously as the experts of their own experience. Understanding and defining that experience accurately require a framework where passive absorption and vehement resistance are not the only descriptions of meaning making. The complicated readings presented in this chapter are better accommodated within a continuum of interpretive strategies that allow for a matrix of overlapping desires, motivations, and belief systems. Anything less would fail to capture the sophistication of all of the mechanisms that are at work as Black women make sense of a text like *Scandal*.

In the lives of Black women, media interpretation is the capacity to, as Katie G. Cannon describes it, "decipher the various sounds in the larger world, [and] to hold in check the nightmare figures of terror" (1988, 125). This approach to media interpretation reflects the power of making do. In other words, Black women's practice of negotiating media texts like *Scandal* to arrive at affirmative readings that hold intact their personal definitions of black womanhood is made possible by their possession of a particular psychosocial dexterity. Such a strength helps Black women to thrive in the midst of an often depressing media landscape.

Still the question remains of why Black women are forced to make do at all. At a time when corporations have broad access to audience opinions and experiences through social media platforms, why do so many Black women still report that they do not see their experiences reflected in dominant media? Why does Olivia Pope—one of the few foils to the professional Black women plagued by single-*doom*—spend so many years as a mistress? Although stretching a character like Olivia Pope demonstrates a kind of resilience, perhaps it would be preferable if media engagement did not demand such intense labor from Black women. Perhaps the ideal media landscape is not one where tropes and derogatory images are nonexistent, but rather an environment with such an abundance of Black female representations that no one image or small set of images must bear the weight of so many diverse values and aspirations.

References

Anderson, James A. 1996. "The Pragmatics of Audience in Research and Theory." In *The Audience and Its Landscape*, edited by James Hay, Lawrence Grossberg, and Ellen Wartella, 75–93. Boulder, CO: Westview.

Ang, Ien. 1996. *Living Room Wars: Rethinking Media Audiences for a Postmodern World*. London: Routledge.

Baker-Fletcher, Karen. 1994. *A Singing Something: Womanist Reflections on Anna Julia Cooper*. New York: Crossroad.

Barnes, Riché J. Daniel. 2016. *Raising the Race: Black Career Women Redefine Marriage, Motherhood, and Community*. New Brunswick, NJ: Rutgers Univ. Press.

Beyoncé. 2008. "Single Ladies." Columbia Records, digital download.

Black in America. 2008–12. Live broadcast. Produced by Soledad O'Brien. New York: CNN.

Bobo, Jacqueline. 1995. *Black Women as Cultural Readers*. New York: Columbia Univ. Press.

Cannon, Katie. 1988. *Black Womanist Ethics*. Atlanta: Scholars Press.

Carter, Kelley L. 2013. "Kerry Washington Launches a Debate: Is Olivia Pope a Sidepiece?" CocoaFab, May 15. http://cocoafab.com/kerry-washington-launches-debate-is-olivia-pope-a-sidepiece/.

Fish, Stanley. 1976. "Interpreting the Variorum." *Critical Inquiry* 2(3): 465–85.

The Good Wife. 2009. Live broadcast. Performed by Julianna Margulies. New York: Columbia Broadcasting System.

Hamlet, Janice D. 2000. "Assessing Womanist Thought: The Rhetoric of Susan L. Taylor." *Communication Quarterly* 48(4): 420–36.

Hermes, Joke. 1999. "Media Figures in Identity Construction." In *Rethinking the Media Audience: The New Agenda*, edited by Pertti Alasuutari, 69–85. London: Sage.

McNamara, Mary. 2013. "'Scandal' Has Become Must-Tweet TV." *Los Angeles Times*, May 11. http://articles.latimes.com/2013/may/11/entertainment/la-et-st-scandal-abc-social-media-20130511.

Prince, Richard. 2014. "Why 'Scandal' Ranks No. 1 with Black Viewers." Maynard Institute, Jan. 8. http://mije.org/richardprince/scandal-no-1 -black-viewers.

Schneider, Michael. 2013. "America's Most Watched: The Top 25 Shows of the 2012–2013 TV Season." *TV Guide*, June 10. http://www.tvguide .com/news/most-watched-tv-shows-top-25-2012-2013-1066503/.

Something New. 2006. Directed by Sanaa Hamri. 2006. Los Angeles: Focus Features. DVD.

Williams, Carmen Braun, and Marsha I. Wiggins. 2011. "Womanist Spirituality as a Response to the Racism-Sexism Double Bind in African American Women." *Counseling and Values* 54(2):. 175–86. doi: https:// doi.org/10.1002/j.2161-007X.2010.tb00015.x.

12 | Good Black Girls Wear White

Olivia Pope and Conflicted Constructions
of Black Female Personhood

KIMBERLY ALECIA SINGLETARY

IN SOME WAYS, in that first season of *Scandal* (2012) it seemed impossible to disentangle the fictional life of Olivia Pope from the reality of lived Black womanhood. For Black audiences, and in particular Black women, to see a Black woman on-screen who was not a caricature of Black femininity was a breath of fresh air. It might be said that by dint of her blackness, a Black person is automatically politicized, socially, racially, or sexually. So to see Pope kicking butt and taking names, being sexual but not sex crazed, and empathetic but not weak, all while being professionally successful, replicated the complex lives of Black women outside of a mainstream media that relies on worn-out tropes of Black dysfunctionality to make a story line work. Shonda Rhimes's character also resonates beyond the Black community. Pope, for women of all colors, is the embodiment of a professional insider wielding the kind of power of which many of us can only dream. That she is Black is icing on a cake that is normally baked and served with White audiences in mind.

Olivia Pope's arrival on the televisual scene set American (and global) audiences on fire, with *Scandal* roundtables at conferences, debates on blogs, and potentially millions (a healthy number of which were provided by yours truly) of real-time tweets, texts, and posts on social media reacting to the show's plot twists, sex scenes, and crisp one-liners. The show has inspired quizzes testing the depths of one's fandom, clothing lines, and the use of the term *Gladiator*, however divorced from the original function of the word, in everyday parlance. In creating a vehicle for the first Black woman to lead a prime-time network drama since Teresa Graves in *Get Christie Love!* in 1974–75, and making her both unapologetically and unmistakably Black, Rhimes has forced viewers to not only grapple with the complexities of Black female personhood but also challenge the notion that the man who wears the white hat, one, is not a man, and, two, is not White.

There is an understanding of heroism in the media that presents an equation of worthiness that has at its core the requirement of whiteness. As Hernan Vera and Andrew Gordon argue, "The ideal White American self . . . is constructed as good-looking, powerful, brave, cordial, kind, firm, and generous: a natural-born leader worthy of the loyalty of slaves or subordinates of another color" (2003, 2). In order to create a vision of the best, however, there must be one who represents the worst. Televisual and filmic history has relied on an antagonistic binary of White and Other. In making Pope a woman flush with cultural, economic, and political capital, Rhimes challenges the ideal White self presented to us in popular culture and demands that audiences expand their conception of what a "real" hero looks like. Yet Pope, for all of her white-hat wearing, doing-it-for-the-Republic saving, and don't-my-hair-look-fly-today being, still reinscribes some notions of flawed Black womanhood even as she rewrites narratives about the place of Black women in popular culture and society at large.

As a televisual vehicle, *Scandal* reflects and refutes stereotypes about Black sexuality and identity that long have locked Black women into what Patricia Hill Collins calls "controlling images" that have allowed others to justify their subordination of Black women (2000). Instead of the asexual Black Mammy who puts others before herself, or the bad Black Jezebel whose desire for sex and power directs her behavior, Pope is both the caring matriarch and the sexually desirable power player. Her character blasts away assumptions about what it means to be Black, female, and desirable, a topic of consideration also discussed in Harris, Washington, and Akers's chapter 13 of this book.

Pope's character makes it clear that conversations about *Scandal* must make central the very controlling images critics are trying to subvert.

It is impossible to see Olivia Pope's historic character apart from the controlling images that always already structure the popular conception of Black women. She is the personification of mythical tropes of Black femininity that are refracted and reified through a White gaze that all viewers are forced to acknowledge in order to discuss how the show rejects those tropes. That acknowledgment runs the risk of being tacitly accepted as a societal truth that must be refuted rather than a blatant falsehood that must be ignored. This chapter will examine Pope's debut in season one as well as her evolution as a character in season five, asking the following questions: What would critics gain or lose from discussing Pope's role without referencing race? How might culturally solidified understandings of Black femininity and sexual identity subvert viewers' ability to see Pope as a deeply complex woman who happens to be Black? In what ways does *Scandal* make it impossible to see Olivia Pope outside of the controlling images that she seemingly refutes?

More and more Americans are choosing to believe the misconception that if they embrace color blindness, racism will magically disappear and structural racism will become a distant memory without our having had to do any of the heavy lifting. The United States is in a cultural moment that embraces the false positive of color blindness and postracialism. The number of stories circulating in the media about racial violence inflicted on people of color, and in particular Black people, however, seem to be more numerous, not less. In the first five months of 2015, for example, the *Washington Post* reported that there were more than 385 people shot and killed by police, with two-thirds of unarmed victims being Black or Hispanic. In 13 cases, the victims killed were carrying toy guns, such as Tamir Rice, a twelve-year-old boy from Cleveland, Ohio, who was shot within seconds of officers' arrival at the park where he was playing. The *Post* found that Black people "were killed at three times the rate of Whites or other minorities when adjusting by the population of the census tracts where the shootings occurred" (Kindy 2015). The Black Lives Matter movement was inspired by the acquittal of George Zimmerman, who attacked and killed seventeen-year-old Trayvon Martin in Sanford, Florida, in 2012. Since Martin's death, there have been numerous other reports of Black men, women, and children killed at the hands of neighbors, law enforcement officials, and strangers. The United States has proved time and again that while race may be a fictional construct, there are real-life challenges and indignities that those individuals who are raced must endure. As Eduardo Bonilla-Silva argues, "Discrimination affects almost every aspect of the lives of people of color. It affects them in hospitals, restaurants, trying to buy cars or hail a cab, driving, flying, or doing almost anything in America. Indeed, 'living while black [or brown]' is quite hard and affects the health (physical and mental) of people of color tremendously, as they seem to always be in 'fight or flight' mode" (2014, 259). The fact of one's blackness, whether it is deemed real or theoretical, makes it impossible for one who is identified by such a marker to exist apart from it, particularly in spaces in which Black mobility is treated as a threat to economic, political, and social structures that rely on Black subordination to prosper. As Michael Omi and Howard Winant have argued, "Race has been a *fundamental axis* of social organization in the U.S." (1994, 13). What *Scandal* does so beautifully, in many respects, is tilt the axis. Unlike other televisual vehicles that hire minorities as supporting players, in *Scandal*, power and race are inextricably combined and wielded by those persons who have been historically marginalized by their gender, race, or sexual orientation. The standard-bearers of power are not so standard after all.

Although hopeful citizens may argue otherwise, the United States is so far behind in terms of racial equality that despite centuries of racial and ethnic diversity, it has been only within the past sixty years that people of color were granted equality under the law in terms of schooling and voting rights. Citizens were so frightened that the first Black US president, Barack Obama, would be killed before the business cards were dry that prayer cards were circulated in Black churches across America—and in particular on the South Side of Chicago—for the first family. As Anthony Anderson's character in *Black-ish* (ABC,

2014–) declared in the episode "Hope" (2.16): "Obama ran on hope. Remember when he got elected? And we felt like maybe, just maybe, we got out of that bad place and made it to a good place. That the whole country was really ready to turn the corner. . . . And we saw him, get out of that limo, and walk alongside of it, and wave to that crowd. Tell me you weren't terrified. . . . Tell me you weren't worried that someone was gonna snatch that hope away from us like they always do." Anderson's character was relaying the fear not of existence but in existing that many Black Americans grapple with on a daily basis. Pope's character refuses to be terrified in the face of often insurmountable odds. She offers a bold-faced "I dare you" for audiences to treat racial diversity as business as usual, without acknowledging that this diversity has often reflected a racial hierarchy that still places whiteness at the very top of the pyramid.

Scandal's sophisticated use of color also extends beyond the level of the skin. Pope's arrival onto the scene in variations of white-hued outfits, meant to signal her status as the "good guy," would also seem to indicate that power balances have shifted. Not only is Pope a Black woman who single-handedly reenergized a flagging presidential campaign, but the president she helped get elected is so besotted with her, he cannot sleep without speaking to her on a regular basis. Pope is a Black woman whom Morris Elcott, the security guard in charge of the White House's front gate, calls "the big guns" ("Grant: For the People" [1.07]). Pope is a Black woman with such a loyal group of employees that they regularly flout the law on her behalf and, without hesitation, clean up crime scenes, harbor fugitives, and torture informants. Pope wields a power that one would expect only the president of the United States to have, not a Black civilian unknown to most of America. On its face, Pope is not just able to compete with the boys—she is the Man. What is more, her preferences toward a white fashion palette signal not only a purity of action and thought, but also a desire to be invisible. In the United States, whiteness is erroneously understood as the standard skin color; its normalization has meant that those persons not possessing it are registered as foreign or Other. Whiteness allows one to blend in, to be unremarkable. Much of Pope's work was behind the scenes; she become known only after the country discovered she was the president's mistress. Shrouding herself in the color of racial normalcy can also be read as a way to claim whiteness and power and, by extension, a way to hide among the masses. In season five, however, Pope shifts to a more colorful palette. She throws off the white hat, literally and figuratively. Much of her new wardrobe employs colors in various hues of red and orange, indicating not only a willingness to be seen but a desire to stand out. No longer is Pope simply content in helping others attain and retain power. She is on the hunt for what her father has called "1600 Pennsylvania Avenue power" ("It's Hard Out Here for a General" [5.10]). Pope's adoption of bright clothing, however, has not resulted in a change to how she frames herself racially and politically.

Pope seems to be a part of a community that Roopali Mukherjee, citing Angela Dillard, discusses as Black and Brown "multicultural conservatives," in other words: "Political converts disillusioned by 'identity politics' who aligned themselves with the New Right and the Republican Party . . . abdicating historical solidarities founded on race and ethnic lines, zealously promoted the redemptive possibilities of colorblindness, individualism, assimilation, and neo-liberal standards of entrepreneurial responsibility. . . . [T]hese voices read ongoing disarticulations of the 'end of race' itself" (2011, 179). Pope would seem to fit in well within this category, although her political affiliation remains unknown in season one. She represents the rich, powerful Republican with a tenacity that would imply she is firmly in their camp. As the Republican vice president's chief of staff, Billy Chambers, says about Pope after questioning presidential chief of staff Cyrus Beene's decision to revoke Pope's access to the White House, "Since when are you two on opposite sides? Liv's one of us" ("Dirty Little Secrets" [1.02]). Given that the show takes place in the present day, it would be absurd to assume Pope was not aware of the injustices lobbied at the Black community by members of the conservative bloc of elected officials, the least of which have been voter disenfranchisement, Jim Crow, redlining, and job discrimination. As a multicultural conservative, Pope would recognize her blackness and the challenge it presents while also refusing to articulate an affinity with others based on race.

Pope is visibly divorced from any kind of Black communal fellowship either at the beauty salon (she has to get that sew-in done *some-where*); on the streets of "Chocolate City," as DC is nicknamed for its high percentage of Black residents; or even at work. Harrison Wright, her employee, and Elcott interact with her as friendly Black subordinates. She is on equal footing with a majority of DC's White power players, while Black urbanites in DC seem to exist as the support staff. In the season finale of season one, Pope has been called in to manage a scandal relating to President Fitzgerald Grant's seemingly serial marital infidelity. As Pope walks to the checkpoint at the front gates of the White House, Elcott implores her to do her best to save Grant's reputation and job: "In all my years here, he's the only president who's made a point to ask about my wife and kids. You do your best, Ms. Pope" ("Grant: For the People" [1.07]).

Having worked for Grant for two years and having served as White House communications director, one would expect a high level of familiarity between Pope and Elcott that on some level acknowledges their place as one of few Black faces on the White House grounds. While shared blackness does not require Black people to treat one another with more warmth or familiarity than with others, it is telling that the conversations between Elcott and Pope never progress beyond the formal, that Pope never implores him to call her by her first name. Both are in service to the state, but only one is allowed inside the Big House. Differences in social station become exacerbated by Elcott's admission that despite being employed in a position that requires a high level of trustworthiness for at least two presidencies, only one saw him as a person with a family and life outside of his job. In season five, Marcus Walker becomes the team's newest Gladiator, but the relationship between him and Pope is also one-sided. Walker and Pope met after the death of a young Black man—the son of Walker's friend—at the hands of police; Walker called Pope for help just months after first meeting her and questioning her loyalty to the Black community. Walker refused an initial job offer to work at Pope

& Associates because of his aversion to what he saw as their embracing of a seedy side of political maneuvering. Yet when Walker heard how everyday Americans were describing Pope after she was confirmed as the president's mistress—as falsely coming from an impoverished background, as being greedy, crafty, and dishonest—he accepted the offer out of disgust with the way non-Black Americans were labeling Pope's actions according to an assumed deficiency of character that relied on anti-Black stereotypes. It was Walker who orchestrated a blitz that took the media to task for its racial dog whistling and, for all intents and purposes, saved Pope's business ("Dog-Whistle Politics" [5.04.]). Still, Pope and Walker barely seem to interact as boss and coworker, much less as Black woman to Black man. The Black men throughout the series seem to work to protect Pope out of, in part, a loyalty to a good Black woman, while she seems to regard their effort as loyalty to a good boss. It is in the modes of familial interpretation that we see how Pope's multicultural conservatism fails her.

Blacks are a group historically tied by bonds of fictive kinship, which Melissa Harris-Perry defines as "connections between members of a group who are unrelated by blood or marriage but who nonetheless share reciprocal social or economic relationships" (2011, 102). Although Elcott's political affiliation or beliefs on race are never defined, his having a family connects him automatically to a larger Black populace outside of the job. Walker is a local kid with friends and family in the District. Pope, on the other hand, is a woman unto herself. She lives alone, she has no Black friends outside of her job, nor does she have what seems to be a connection to a larger Black community. Pope's visual distance from blackness not only reflects the definition of a multicultural conservative, but also makes it easier for audiences to deracialize her, disregarding her race as they watch her accomplishing heroic feats as a Black woman in service of the nation.

There is an act of disassociation that happens with Pope's blackness being separated from her *blackness*. The dissociation between one's color and its perceived meaning has played out in other televisual venues, such as in the February 2016 *Saturday Night Live* skit "The Day Beyoncé Turned Black," in which White Americans reacted with fear and inconsolable sadness after R&B singer Beyoncé Knowles produced a song that referenced her daughter's natural hair, Black Lives Matter, and police brutality. On-screen, Pope's race reflects the criticism Barack Obama received during his first presidential campaign—and throughout his presidency—that his blackness was palatable to White voters because he did not often focus on it (Harris 2012). Not focusing on her unique status as a *Black* DC insider does not render Pope's blackness less of an issue—it merely helps viewers avoid discussing why that status remains unique this far into the twenty-first century. Sidestepping issues of race also helps viewers avoid discussing how Pope's status as a Black woman may impact how we understand her personal and professional relationships, particularly in regard to sex and desirability.

Black female personhood has long been represented as deviant or deficient in US popular culture. Black women, Harris-Perry argues, have long had to deal with a crooked room in which popular media representations of Black female personhood are so "warped" that they struggle to "figure out which way is up," sometimes replicating the very stereotypes they wish to refute (2011, 29). Being misrecognized as deficient, unproductive, or morally abject hampers Black women's ability to act as citizens (40). One means by which women have been included as members of the citizenry is by their ability to be seen as pious mothers, daughters, wives, and sisters. The "Cult of True Womanhood," as outlined by Barbara Welter, described femininity with pillars of piety, purity, submissiveness, and domesticity in antebellum America (1985, 21) and, as I have argued elsewhere, could be understood as instrumental in distinguishing American White female personhood from American Black female personhood (Singletary 2011). Ideal femininity could not be inhabited by Black women in the popular imagination because stereotypes about their sexual voracity, licentiousness, and immorality created a binary in which Black and White women were placed at either end of a femininity spectrum. The enduring stereotypes of Black women as "mammies, matriarchs, welfare recipients, and hot mommas," in Patricia Hill Collins's phrasing, not only perpetuates Black women's Othering, but also makes it less likely that non-Black women would actively identify with Black women, thus creating problems for coalition building or deeper understandings of the intersection of oppressions related to class or gender or race or sexuality or any such combination. As Hill Collins argues, "Women are differentially evaluated based on their perceived value to give birth to the right kind of children, pass on appropriate American family values, and become worthy symbols of the nation. African-American women encounter differential treatment based on our perceived value as giving birth to the wrong race of children, as unable to socialize them properly because we bring them into bad family structures, and as unworthy symbols for U.S. patriotism" (2000, 230). With her educational pedigree and her father's position as the head of a venerable public institution, Pope could naturally be seen as pushing back against existing racial stereotypes. Her actions that flout the law are done in service of a greater national good. Her employment of people who would be dismissed as mentally unstable, ethically challenged, or morally bankrupt speaks to her understanding of the power of forgiveness and redemption. Her affair with a married man is out of a deep yearning for love. Olivia is an everywoman who, ostensibly, reflects the ideals and desires of every woman. The avoidance to locate Pope as explicitly Black, however, provides one less instance in which to reinforce Black women's status as equal participants in American citizenship and also as complicated, complex figures. First Lady Mellie Grant later challenges that equality, throwing into relief the tenuous hold Pope has—and by extension Black women have—in transcending racial stereotypes.

It is not until the final episode of season one when Pope learns that Mellie turned a blind eye to Pope and Fitzgerald's affair and blames Pope for Fitzgerald's sexual indiscretion with a White House aide who, after claiming to be carrying the president's baby, is found dead: "You fell down on the job! You broke his heart, and you left him open and vulnerable and helpless. I do my job. Why couldn't you do yours?" ("Grant: For the People" [1.07]). Although race is not explicitly mentioned, Mellie's accusation that Pope does not play team ball positions her as an outsider incapable of coalition building.

As Catherine Squires notes in the opening chapter of this book, Mellie pulls rank on Olivia, reinforcing Olivia's role as an employee, if not a servant. The job is to keep the president happy so that he might run the nation effectively. But Pope, the "bad" Black woman, did not show up for her shift. Although she was ultimately unsuccessful in her attempt to reclassify Pope's job from communications director to that of concubine, Mellie's words indicate her subconscious understanding of Pope as a Mammy. The Mammy, Hill-Collins argues, "symbolizes the dominant group's perceptions of the ideal Black female relationship to elite White male power" (2000, 80). In that scene, Pope's patriotism and socioeconomic belonging are inextricably tied to her ability to keep the president sexually satisfied. Pope was reduced to being a servant to the White patriarchy ("Hell Hath No Fury" [1.03]). Unlike the Mammy who knows her subordinate place in the White "family," by walking away from the White House and starting her own consulting business, Pope declared her equivalency. Mellie's rage at Pope's ignorance of the unspoken contractual agreement between her, Pope, and Fitz indicates the degree to which Mellie expected Pope to perform the sexual and emotional functions of a wife without expecting reciprocation. For Mellie, Pope should have known her place and acted accordingly. Or, as Pope put it in season two, "I'm feeling . . . a little Sally Hemings/Thomas Jefferson about all this" ("Happy Birthday, Mr. President" [2.08]). With or without the explicit mention of race, Pope has been reduced to and treated as the help. Harris-Perry opines that shaming is used to delineate hierarchies of power in that only the inferior can feel ashamed and that shame is a social phenomenon that Black women, in particular, are "structurally positioned" to experience chronically (2011, 107). Pope's unapologetic sexuality and her refusal to feel ashamed of her relationship with the president indicate an understanding that she sees herself as an equal to the Grant family rather than as its subordinate. In effect, her actions ultimately reject a dominant narrative in US race relations that assumes blackness exists to serve whiteness.

For all of the ways Pope's race is alluded to, mentioned, or ignored, audiences are supposed to understand her capability, her competence,

and her sex appeal apart from her blackness. Her blackness is coinci-
dental to her success, not the cause for it. She is a postracial, color-
blind dream. One might argue that the avoidance of references to
Pope's race can potentially be positive. Empathy, or the ability of a
person to identify with another, can sometimes be in short supply
when White audiences are asked to apply it to Black characters or people. For example, the backlash that ensued when British actor Idris
Elba was tapped to play Heimdall in the Marvel film based on Norse
mythology *Thor* (2011) was most often related to White viewers' resistance of seeing a Black man in the *fictional* role they believed should
have been reserved for a White man (Khouri 2010). White audiences
also were angry with the casting of teenage actress Amandla Stenberg
as Rue in *The Hunger Games* (2012); some Internet *Hunger Games*
fans argued that Stenberg's blackness "ruined" the film, despite her
character being described as Black in the original book series (Riffe
2011). If accomplished actors tapped to play characters in intergalactic
or postapocalyptic worlds could create such a furor among audiences,
it would seem that a Black woman playing a character with unparal-
leled access to national secrets would send them into a blind fury, but
by and large audiences have embraced Olivia Pope.

Scandal's evasion of how race would necessarily impact a real-life
DC fixer who had an affair with the sitting US president and broke
federal law in the pursuit of a personally defined justice allows non-
Black audiences to identify with Pope, not because she is Black but in
spite of it. The fact of Pope's blackness, therefore, is rendered a foot-
note. Yet the fact of US race relations is such that audiences cannot
help but notice and are hard-pressed to ignore Pope's race. In many
ways, the collective desire to sidestep or transcend race is understand-
able and contributes to what Carrie Crenshaw describes as a fantasy
escape. "The promise of transcendence is the ability to elevate oneself
and others to a level of existence above the contradictions and complexities of the human world," she writes (1998, 246). To transcend
race, then, is to be able to escape having to deal with it outside of
the theoretical realm. If we transcend race, we also transcend situ-
ational racism, race-based crimes, racially biased laws, and the like. We

can, therefore, avoid challenging our racial privilege and our racially inflected social position because we have moved on, positioning those individuals who still want or need to have a meaningful conversation about race as stuck in the past and unwilling to look toward the future. On its face, Pope seems to be a living contradiction to narratives of Black female personhood that locate Black womanhood firmly within the categories of powerlessness, suffering, or wantonness. Her character represents those women of color whose professional and personal lives require them to compartmentalize how their race may or may not impact their treatment at the office. In the refusal to explicitly name the moments when race and racial disregard dovetail with her professional and personal interactions, however, Pope implicitly condones silence in the face of injustice, leaving audiences to wonder if she extends the same desire to fix what is wrong in others' lives to herself.

References

Black-ish. "Hope." 2.16. Directed by Beth McCarthy-Miller. Written by Kenya Barris. ABC. February 24, 2016.

Bonilla-Silva, Eduardo. 2014. *Racism without Racists: Color-Blind Racism and the Persistence of Racial Inequality in America*. 4th ed. Lanham, MD: Rowman and Littlefield.

Collins, Patricia Hill. 2000. *Black Feminist Thought: Knowledge, Consciousness, and the Politics of Empowerment*. 2nd ed. New York: Routledge.

Crenshaw, Carrie. 1998. "Colorblind Rhetoric." *Southern Communication Journal* 63(3): 244–56.

Harris, Fredrick. 2012. "Still Waiting for Our First Black President." *Washington Post*, June 1. https://www.washingtonpost.com/opinions/still-waiting-for-our-first-black-president/2012/06/01/gJQARsT16U_story.html.

Harris-Perry, Melissa. 2011. *Sister Citizen: Shame, Stereotypes, and Black Women in America*. New Haven, CT: Yale University Press.

Khouri, Andy. 2010. "Racists Totally Freak Out over Idris Elba Playing Norse God in 'Thor.'" *Comics Alliance*, Dec. 16. http://comicsalliance.com/racists-thor-idris-ebla-racism/.

Kindy, Kimberly. 2015. "Fatal Police Shootings in 2015 Approaching 400 Nationwide." *Washington Post*, May 30. https://www.washingtonpost

.com/national/fatal-police-shootings-in-2015-approaching-400-nation
wide/2015/05/30/d322256a-058e-11e5-a428-c984eb077d4e_story
.html.

McNamara, Mary. 2013. "*Scandal* Has Become 'Must Tweet' TV." *Los Angeles Times*, May 11. http://articles.latimes.com/2013/may/11/entertain
ment/la-et-st-scandal-abc-social-media-20130511.

Mukherjee, Roopali. 2011. "Bling Fling: Commodity Consumption and the Politics of the 'Post-racial.'" In *Critical Rhetorics of Race*, edited by Michael G. Lacy and Kent A. Ono, 178–98. New York: New York Univ. Press.

Obenson, Tambay A. 2012. "38 Years before 'Olivia Pope' There Was 'Christie Love,' and She Made History." *Shadow and Act*, Apr. 12. http://www.indiewire.com/2012/04/38-years-before-olivia-pope-there-was
-christie-love-and-she-made-history-146470/.

Omi, Michael, and Howard Winant. 1994. *Racial Formation in the United States: From the 1960s to the 1990s*. 2nd ed. New York: Routledge.

Riffe, Shannon. 2011. "Why the Casting of *The Hunger Games* Matters." *Racialicious*, Mar. 25. http://www.racialicious.com/2011/03/25/why
-the-casting-of-the-hunger-games-matters/.

Saturday Night Live. 2016. "The Day Beyoncé Turned Black." NBC, Feb. 13.

Singletary, Kimberly Alecia. 2011. "Opposing Blackness: Black American Women and Questions of Citizenship in the U.S. Media." In *REAL: Yearbook of Research in English and American Literature*, edited by Winfried Fluck, Katharina Motyl, Donald E. Pease, and Christoph Raetzsch, 27:199–216. Berlin: Narr Verlag.

Vera, Hernan, and Andrew M. Gordon. 2003. *Screen Saviors: Hollywood Fictions of Whiteness*. Lanham, MD: Rowman and Littlefield.

Welter, Barbara. 1985. *Dimity Convictions: The American Woman in the Nineteenth Century*. Athens: Ohio University Press.

PART FOUR

Race, Gender, and the Politics of Respectability

13 | "It's Handled!"

Critiquing the Politics of Respectability at the
Intersection of Race and Gender in *Scandal*

TINA M. HARRIS, MYRA WASHINGTON,
AND DIAMOND M. AKERS

THE ABC POLITICAL DRAMA *Scandal* debuted in the spring of
2012. Along with it came public debate about the hypersexualization
of African American women in mainstream media. This public furor
surrounding lead character Olivia Pope (played by Kerry Washington)
rearticulated for many a long-standing issue regarding the intersectionality of race and gender. The critically acclaimed show by African
American screenwriter and executive producer Shonda Rhimes was
one of several popular shows that she introduced to mainstream and
racially and ethnically diverse viewing audiences around the world.
Despite her use of a color-blind casting approach, Rhimes's complex,
overlapping story lines in *Scandal* were ultimately overshadowed by
the controversial images and subtexts enacted by Olivia. Judy Smith,
"real-life crisis management pro," was the inspiration for Olivia (Begley 2014). As a "one-time special assistant to former President George
Bush," Smith serves as a consultant for the show. Smith explains that
the profound difference between her and Olivia is the sexually charged
affair that Olivia has with President Grant (ibid.). While both women
represent strength and intelligence in a White male–dominated political world, Olivia's reputation as *the* political fixer of the world was
"sullied" by Rhimes's decision to weave an adulterous relationship

between Olivia and the US president, Fitzgerald Grant, a married family man who happens to be White, into the fabric of the show. The unbridled, forbidden passion between the two characters took precedence over all other story lines centered on the original premise of the show: Olivia, the powerful, smart, and intelligent woman "handling" the political nightmares—murder, blackmail, affairs, and espionage—haunting her wealthy, elite clients.

This seismic shift created two different camps among *Scandal* fans (known as Gladiators): those viewers who critiqued Olivia for participating in her own objectification and those fans who viewed her as a symbol of (Black) feminist empowerment (see also Tounsel in chapter 11 of this volume). As an intelligent, powerful, and independent single African American woman in an industry dominated by White Republican males, an undue burden was placed on the shoulders of this character that symbolized a historic moment in television history. Olivia is the first lead African American female character of a multiracial or predominantly White cast on a major network drama series since Teresa Graves played an undercover police detective in *Get Christie Love!* (1974–75). While Olivia is to be lauded for making the invisible Black body visible by intersectionally addressing the underrepresentation of race and gender in mass media, her character is also an excellent site for critiquing the discourse surrounding the hypersexualization or liberation (or both) of African American women in the twenty-first century. This dialectical tension speaks to a larger issue of respectability politics, which we will address at length in this chapter, and how it is negotiated through this groundbreaking character. Unlike other characters of color on Rhimes's *Grey's Anatomy* (2005–), *Private Practice* (2007–13), and *How to Get Away with Murder* (2014–), Olivia challenges, perhaps forces, audiences to engage critically with the socially and culturally imposed double standard inextricably linked to the Black body. While Rhimes's character Annalise Keating on *How to Get Away with Murder* introduces audiences to an equally complex and compelling African American lead female character, our focus in this chapter will be limited to Olivia. Like Olivia Pope on *Scandal*, Annalise has evolved into a morally and ethically flawed protagonist on *How to Get Away with Murder.* She is a revered lawyer who wields an immeasurable degree of power over her colleagues, clients, and underling interns. Despite the revelation of her numerous flaws as a ruthless arbiter, Annalise possesses myriad qualities such as intelligence, strength, vulnerability, depth, and sexuality that conform to the typical characteristics of an antagonist in entertainment. Thus, because of her equal level of complexity and richness, we exclude her from critique here, as she is worthy of attention in a separate essay elsewhere.

To better grasp the complexity of this phenomenon regarding the representation of African American women in television through the lens of Olivia Pope, we use Patricia Hill Collins's (2005) Black feminist thought (BFT) as the theoretical framework guiding this chapter. We limit our attention to seasons one and two because they played a significant role in setting the stage for the development of this pivotal character. We will demonstrate how the intersection of race and gender vis-à-vis Olivia Pope is reflective of the larger, public critique of the racialized sexuality of African American women that has existed since slavery (Collins 1989; Begley 2014; Crais and Scully 2009). More specifically, we argue that the Gladiator archetype that is overtly and covertly embraced and promoted through *Scandal* presents audiences with a counterimage of African American female identity that subtly deviates from the historical images of the Mammy, Jezebel, Sapphire, and Tragic Mulatto (Collins 1989; Begley 2014). As we will demonstrate, Olivia is held to the unreasonable standard of being an asexual, intelligent, and attractive moral compass in how she is expected to single-handedly represent race and gender; thus, we advance the argument that African American women are beautifully complex beings who should not be restricted to antiquated notions of otherness in an ever-changing world.

African Americans and the Sexual Gaze: An Oppositional Stance

The relentless scrutiny to which Black bodies have been and continue to be subjected dates back to slavery, as exemplified through the horrific account of former slave Saartjie "Sara" Baartman (the Hottentot Venus) by colonists in Denmark and Paris (Crais and Scully 2009). Saartjie was sold into slavery for the sole purpose of entertaining audiences with her "unusual physique." Both her race and her gender were problematized, framing her as an anomaly to be gazed upon and critiqued. Saartjie was treated like a caged animal while being showcased as a human oddity for the amusement of Europeans. She was eventually sold to a scientist. As Crais and Scully explain, "Many believed the Hottentot Venus was more ape than human, or that she represented a fifth category of human, *a Homo sapiens monstrous*, a kind of Frankenstein's monster scarcely capable of emotion and intelligence yet also a reminder of the primitive living deep within the self" (2009, 2; emphasis in the original). This mistreatment, abuse, and subjugation of Africans through slavery set the stage for how women and men of African descent were (and are) to be treated. Not only have Africans and African Americans been viewed and treated as being less than human, they have also been treated as sexual objects with no value or worth.

According to Patricia Hill Collins, chattel slavery, or the "buying and selling of human beings of African descent formed a template for the economic and racial oppression of Black Americans" (2005, 55). Collins further noted that "this process of objectification, commodification, and exploitation took different forms for African American women. Black women were workers like men, and they did hard manual labor. But because they were women, Black women's sexuality and reproductive capacity presented opportunities for forms of sexual exploitation and sexual slavery (ultimate submission of the master/slave relationship)" (55–56). African American men and women were equally devalued, yet a greater burden was placed on women because of their ability to reproduce and fulfill the sexual needs of their masters. Despite qualities that should have increased their worth, African American women experienced greater exploitation and abuse than the men. This cruelty was further exacerbated by the fact that their White female cohorts were treated as "pure" and "virginal," which ultimately functioned to create yet another dualistic approach to conceptualizing and understanding their raced and gendered identities.

This fixation and perpetual mistreatment remain a part of contemporary perceptions of the Black body. The body shaming of North American tennis star Serena Williams during her 2015 Wimbledon victory is a prime example of the staying power of the chattel slavery mentality (Collins 2005; Rothenberg 2015; Newman 2015). Rather than celebrating her historic wins at Wimbledon and her record twenty-one Grand Slam single titles at the time, Williams is unfairly subjected to harsh racialized and gendered criticisms that have too often plagued African American women. She is critiqued as the antithesis of the ideal athlete, framed as having the least desirable and least attractive physique for a female tennis athlete (Newman 2015). This objectification, not surprisingly, is reflective of mainstream ideals of Black femininity, which are in direct opposition to the universally accepted but highly contested Eurocentric standards of beauty and (perceived) normalcy (Rothenberg 2015).

In order to reclaim our bodies, it is imperative that African American women, and men, assume an oppositional gaze (hooks 1992), a stance that "resists intended and embedded ideologies that are based on racist and internalized racist views" (Boylorn 2008, 414). As a collective, we combat the objectification of the Black female body by "assert[ing] agency by claiming and cultivating 'awareness' [that] politicizes looking relations—one learns to look a certain way in order to resist" (hooks 1992, 116). This oppositional stance requires that African Americans as an interpretive community, or oppositional readers, acknowledge and understand that dominant interpretations exist regarding the Black body that must be rejected because they "[do] not resonate with their experience of reality" (Boylorn 2008, 414). As Boylorn further explained, "Black women viewing audiences can use their gaze and personal experiences to both resist and relate to media representations, finding both commonality and contradictions" (ibid.).

The Politics of Respectability, *Scandal*, and the Gladiator Archetype

Assuming an oppositional gaze requires African American audiences to become critically engaged with the mediated controlling images that have long been associated with the historically marginalized community. The stigmatized controlling images of the Jezebel, Mammy, Tragic Mulatto, and Sapphire (Fuller 2011; Sewell 2013; Adams-Bass, Bentley-Edwards, and Stevenson 2014) have been largely contested; however, they have been replaced with other troubling images that continue to objectify African American women. "These historical caricatures have been transformed into contemporary distortions: the welfare queen, who is sexually promiscuous and schemes for money; the video vixen, a loose woman; and the gold digger who schemes and exploits the generosity of men" (Adams-Bass, Bentley-Edwards, and Stevenson 2014, 80–81). A more recent and equally troubling image is the "angry Black woman" (Brooks 2004) caricature, which refers to the "aggressive, flamboyant behavior [of the upwardly mobile Black person] that emphasizes their racial Otherness" refusing to assimilate to dominant culture (Kretsedemas 2010, 155). Sadly, this caricature has evolved into the "angry Black girl" (Workneh 2015). This archetype is applied to young African American girls who actively speak out against mainstream society's efforts to "devalue black women by reducing their emotions and labeling them erratic and irrelevant when they're everything but" (ibid.).

Reactions to cultural appropriation (ibid.) and misrepresentations in the media are excellent examples of a renegotiation of the original definition of respectability politics (Bowen 2013). As Gross (1997) explained, politics of respectability have been historically considered a "form of resistance to the negative stigmas and caricatures about their morality." This resistance involved the adoption of manners and morality as a form of agency designed to redefine blackness against the backdrop of prevailing racist discourses in mainstream society and within the African American community (ibid.). This strategic resistance is an ideology that has essentially purposely yielded to societal values constructed by mainstream society. The "self-imposed adherence" to respectability politics by African Americans has dominated the lives of the women and the culture as a whole. Scholars note that respectability politics eventually emerged in African activism and the scholarship of African American studies. As a form of self-policing, the politics of respectability ultimately functioned to have an adverse effect on the very community it was supposed to empower.

Efforts to reframe and reconceptualize how African Americans are (and should be) perceived must involve critical engagement with mass-media representations that simultaneously resist and conform to mainstream definitions of Black identity. Toward that end, we challenge fans and nonfans alike to critique Olivia and her embodiment of blackness as the very complex character that she is. Although the character was inspired by real-life crisis-management professional Judy Smith, Olivia Pope can conceivably be a new archetype that deconstructs the controlling images associated with African American women. Olivia's reputation as *the* ultimate fixer speaks to her political clout and social power. *Scandal* has introduced us to an ever-evolving character who is very complex. Her sexual identity has become central to her identity. While this shift from her public to her private life is arguably a natural progression of the show's story line and character development, it also reflects the tensions surrounding the politics of Black sexuality in mass media. Olivia clearly has the clout, skill, and staff necessary for averting all manner of political calamities, yet audiences are forced to acknowledge her as a raced and gendered woman. The image of the successful political fixer who is an African American woman that embodies sexuality and professionalism is a controverted normalcy with which mainstream audiences are forced to deal. Rather than accepting her as an "oxymoron," audiences are forced to critique her as a fatally flawed woman dealing with her forbidden love of or infatuation for the highly unattainable, unavailable Fitz, the commander in chief of the United States. African American women are typically depicted in media as either asexual (Mammy) or hypersexual (Jezebel), and because Olivia conforms neatly to neither, mainstream audiences, and some segments of the African American community, resist accepting an image that does not comport with long-held perceptions of raced and gendered bodies. Instead, they are forced to reconceptualize Black femininity in a very new and textured way.

Scandal has garnered critical acclaim for its creator and producer Shonda Rhimes, an African American woman, and her team of writers, the cast, and lead actress; however, Olivia Pope has emerged as an incredibly complex woman who appears to reflect the virgin-whore tension in her gender identity, which is largely attributed stereotypically to her race. *Scandal* also has a flaw that was evidenced in *Julia*, where a relatable character was created "by eliminating any references to black culture and by isolating her from the black community," which has functioned "as a precursor to the current era of colorblind racial discourse" (Kretsedemas 2010, 153). Although Olivia's racial standpoint has been occasionally addressed in the show's story lines, her physicality as a raced and gendered character is an appropriate site, per se, for examining how African American women are depicted in a show with crossover appeal. This new iteration of the Black female body occupies a space in a profession that is typically reserved for White males. With the introduction of the trope of the Gladiator, we argue that this counterimage challenges understandings of the intersection of race, gender, and sexuality in contemporary society. It is through the main character of "political fixer" Olivia Pope that we will deconstruct the visual representations of Black female identity by directing our attention to the four controlling images historically associated with African American women and the extent to which Olivia is believed to perpetuate them despite her fierce independence and seemingly feminist identity. More important, we introduce a new counterimage that potentially reframes African American women and takes to task the controlling images that have become all too familiar.

The Story of a Scandal

The April 2012 premiere of *Scandal* set the stage for a groundbreaking political thriller drama for the network and the show's creator, Shonda Rhimes. Rhimes is also recognized as the "sole prominent black female showrunner in television" (Nussbaum 2012). Audiences from all demographic backgrounds were drawn into the political narrative centered on lead character Olivia Pope, a "facilitator to the elites" (McKnight 2014, 186). We were introduced to an intelligent, fiercely independent, and politically savvy woman who was the command center for resolving an array of political crises in the nation's capital. As McKnight explained, "It is not therefore that she is an African American woman that makes her important to viewers, but that she offers the possibility of stabilizing the status of Black women professionals" (ibid.) who are complex, heterosexual beings. Her elite clients seek assistance from the "fixer," the woman with an impeccable reputation for solving incomprehensible problems owing to morally and ethically questionable actions while preserving their public personae. Olivia "handles" whatever dramatic situation she is contracted to make disappear.

The first season was dedicated to understanding how Olivia and her cadre of self-appointed "Gladiators" collectively work together to solve these various cases. We witnessed the investigators use less than scrupulous means to protect the image problems of their clients (McKnight 2014). Olivia's "no-holds-barred" approach is critical as she deals with her clients with sanctimonious attitudes and behaviors that call into question whether they are deserving of highly sought-after services and redemption. Nevertheless, Olivia engenders gratitude, respect, and loyalty from her clients and employees alike, despite her often ethically questionable approaches. This somewhat contradictory tension in her character reminds audiences of her humanity, which is best understood through a critique of her "white-hat" personae of a legal arbiter. Though flawed and compromising, regularly forced to choose between the lesser of two evils, Olivia is established as a successful and strong woman in a leadership position "without using the potential racial dynamic as a central trope" in the show (ibid., 184).

During season one, Olivia established her identity as *the* Gladiator who is leading her team of investigators in their journey towards social justice. The Gladiators define themselves as "empowered individuals who take pride in their ability to maneuver the US political and legal system in order to serve their clients' best interests during public crises" (Monk-Payton 2014). It is through their team meetings, client consultations, and crisis-resolution plans that the team at Pope & Associates forge a bond, an undying allegiance to their formidable leader and her vision for managing the troubles of Washington, DC's elite. Audiences were presented with numerous eloquent monologues by characters such as Huck and Harrison who articulated their unwavering support of Olivia, no matter the cost. While she is an excellent professional committed to her craft, she also revealed a vulnerability that has emerged as a site of contention for many aiming to understand the respectability politics at play on *Scandal.*

The counterimage of a Gladiator emerged early on in the first season. Fans began to adopt the moniker in an attempt to connect and identify with their newfound heroine. This parasocial relationship with Olivia is questioned when we learn she is the mistress of the president of the United States, Fitzgerald "Fitz" Grant (Tony Goldwyn). Rhimes introduces a "carnivalesque reversal of roles for a Black woman" that "recalls the roles of the Black slave woman as a jezebel and mammy, roles that were central to the operations of the plantation superimposed on contemporary descriptions of Black social mobility" (McKnight 2014, 186). Olivia's stellar reputation in the political world, and among viewers, is problematized by her sexual indiscretions with a married man who also happens to be the most powerful man in the world. She ends her career as White House communications director to sever her relationship with Fitz. Later, Olivia and Fitz are even confronted by First Lady Melody "Mellie" Grant (Bellamy Young), and despite the obvious inappropriateness of this affair, the trio ultimately enters into an unspoken agreement that allows clandestine meetings between the two. Mellie remains complicit in this arrangement in order to protect the political legacy she is trying to build as she aspires for the presidency herself.

While Rhimes capably draws audiences into the entertainment element of the show with sex, betrayal, and infidelity, she introduces the race trope in very difficult, fascinating, and complex ways. For some, Olivia embodies a contemporized version of the controlling images inextricably linked to African American women (Brooks 2004; Collins 2005). Others would argue that Olivia is a feminist, a woman fighting for equality and justice. She is proactively independent, while negotiating her identities as a single, sexual professional woman with choices, in charge of her own destiny (Ulen 2014).

Regardless of which camp one occupies, it is arguably the case that this character is "reifying and dispelling stereotypes simultaneously" (Boylorn 2008, 418). It is a burden to which all images of African American women are subjected, and in order to reclaim our bodies, we must critique the body politics and self-policing that censure the ways in which the intersectionality of Black womanhood is portrayed in mass media. While ambitious, this goal can be achieved through the application of Patricia Hill Collins's (2005; 1989) Black feminist thought. This theory will be used to articulate how the oppositional gaze (Brooks 2004) fixated on the racial and sexual politics (Shabazz 2008) of African Americans is the most productive response to the politics of respectability. By extension, we argue that a reworking of the politics of responsibility is essential in the effort to affirm the diversity of identities and experiences inherent within African American female interpretive communities.

Using Black Feminist Thought to Critique Intersectionality

Developed by Patricia Hill Collins (1996a; 1996b), Black feminist thought is a theoretical lens that provides an excellent framework for understanding the intersectionality or double consciousness (Andrews 2003) that is unique to African American women. It was born out of the continued marginalization perpetuated in and by the feminist movement (Spitzack and Carter 1987). Much like other women of color, African American women simultaneously experience racism and sexism, and their experiences with systemic oppression have largely been ignored by the feminist movement (hooks 1995), which essentially adopted a color-blind approach to addressing systemic sex-based oppression (Hartsock 1983). BFT was born in response to their socially imposed invisible status. This framing of Black womanhood was also an extension of the chattel slavery ideology that set the foundation of the marginalized treatment of African American women in North America. Thankfully, BFT has emerged as an eloquent means by which to articulate the valuable experiences of African American women in a patriarchal and racist society (Collins 1996b). More important, BFT is critical in providing an understanding of the everyday communicative experiences of African Americans that are diverse, yet similar in their responses to double consciousness (Bell et al. 2000).

BFT is fundamental to our efforts to address the body politics that continue to play out in mainstream media. It is even more critical to do so with "popular discourses such as film and television" (Childs 2005, 544). As Collins (1996a; 1996b; 1989) argued, being a racialized individual calls for the embodiment of a stream of consciousness and awareness of oneself as the proverbial "Other." Thus, BFT is a tool of empowerment that gives voice to a self-defined collective Black women's standpoint about Black womanhood (Collins 1996a). This effort can be enriched by critiquing the politics of respectability that is censuring the expression of African American womanhood vis-à-vis intersectionality in television and film (Childs 2005). Indeed, these images and depictions are salient for all interpretive communities or audiences. As such, we must recognize and act upon "the importance of a specific Black feminist criticism in defining strategies for both improving the politics of representation of Blacks in television and when resolving the politics of respectability" (McKnight 2014, 183).

Politics of Respectability and Black Sexuality

Olivia Pope alludes to the Jezebel trope, which is in direct opposition to the fundamental arguments of the respectability politics. As a form of resistance, this ideological framework functioned to combat these caricatures by identifying manners and morality to be adopted as agency against racist discourses (Gross 1997). Self-imposed adherence to a respectability politics by African Americans has evolved into a very narrow view of the rich diversity that lies within this community. In an effort to distance themselves from the Jezebel stereotype, African Americans meticulously scrutinize expressions of sexuality that feed into this long-standing image. While it is imperative that this type of objectification be critiqued and dismantled, it is also important to recognize that sexuality is in fact a part of African American identity, and to ignore this reality and to restrict visual representations of this intersectionality is troubling. Moreover, doing so reflects a subconscious desire to be demarcated by mainstream definitions of African

American womanhood that are markedly different from understandings of womanhood for European Americans. Cartier describes this dialectical tension as follows: "My problem with Pope is her wholesale utilization of the politics of respectability despite her being a whore, a mistress. As black female audiences, we sublimate this fact because we are so desperate for black female images to do so much ideological work for us: each image has to be everything to every black woman, when that always leads to frustration and disappointment. We elide the Jezebel trope in which she is enmeshed and focus only on her positive traits of power, both sexual and economic" (2014, 155).

We acknowledge that Olivia has "successfully" navigated the politics of respectability as dictated by African American mores and her (treacherous) African American parents; however, we question how harshly she is to be scandalized, and subsequently vilified, for her sexuality. We agree that her complicity in an adulterous affair is questionable, but to instinctively mark her with the Jezebel trope we are made privy to her other sexual escapades introduces a process of censure in how African American women with diverse sexual histories are to be reinscribed and depicted in mass media by both the consumer of these images as well as the creator.

A tremendous burden is placed on this character, one that further marginalizes a systemically oppressed community. Much like the women she represents, Olivia has her strengths and her Achilles' heel. She embodies the image of the "strong Black woman," which is "a long-established image in U.S. society placing pressures on Black American women to maintain a façade of strength, self-sufficiency, and resilience" (Davis 2015, 20). She caters only to high-end clientele and uses discretion regarding whom she will save from certain political calamity. This message of being fiercely independent, to the point of insularity, coupled with an idealism of self-sufficiency is a lesson frequently taught to African American women. Not surprisingly, this strong Black woman trope is embraced by a collective of African American viewers. As Davis explained, the idea of a "Strong Black Woman Collective" is "a developing standpoint framework for analyzing the complexities associated with embodiment, communication, and regulation of strength among groups of Black women" (ibid.). To that end, we argue that in the case of *Scandal*, the Gladiator metaphor is the equivalent of a strong Black woman.

As we advance our argument regarding the layered identity of Black womanhood embedded within Olivia, it is imperative that we acknowledge, at the very least, the collective of African American women who embrace a counternarrative that tells a different story about race and gender. Anecdotal evidence from social media posts and informal conversations with other African American women who are either fans, former fans, or refuse to watch the show feel disenfranchised by this brand of woman that is being lauded by media critics, viewing audiences, and society as a feminist with significant power in a largely White male political culture. Without fail, Olivia repeatedly gives in to her sexual and emotional desires for forbidden fruit, despite the consequences of going against societal mores. While she is not the only character whose morals and values are oftentimes lacking, a double standard exists to which Olivia is held to a greater extent than President Grant, his adulterous wife, and myriad other characters who engage in similarly troubling behaviors. Olivia's intersectionality (for example, race and gender) presents a conundrum whereby people believe she is culpable in perpetuating the very images that her adoring fans believe she is challenging. Indeed, implicit and explicit messages within the show are open to interpretation; however, Olivia's portrayal of race and gender continues to function as an excellent site for critiquing representations of Black womanhood in popular culture.

Conclusion

As our critique argues, Olivia the fixer has an unprecedented expertise in crisis management, is an advocate for social justice, and is fully in charge of her own destiny (Ulen 2014). As a Gladiator, for her clients, she is a spin doctor, strategically crafting public and private narratives about her clients that ideally function to save face from impending political calamity. The protagonist in this visual narrative is also a protector of her well-meaning clients and her morally and ethically flawed investigators. As the character Harrison once stated, she is a "bad guy in the name of national security." All of these characteristics are fueled by Olivia's loyalty, or unwavering support and acceptance of her "team," in her pursuit of truth and social justice. Granted, she compromises her ethics and morals in nearly all of her decision making; however, that trait contributes to her complicated humanity. Olivia is much like the rest of us: inherently flawed.

Despite the strength that she embodies as a Gladiator, Olivia's sexuality and sexual indiscretions with the president always emerge in public critiques of what she represents or reflects as it relates to African American women. As Boylorn (2008), Cartier (2014), and Davis (2015) demonstrated, she simultaneously reifies and dispels familiar stereotypes. Regardless of the possible reification of the Jezebel stereotype (Collins 2005), we also challenge audiences to closely examine the character that simultaneously embodies strength, intelligence, beauty, and vulnerability. Admittedly, because of her "blackness" and the perpetual gaze upon the Black body, Olivia will inextricably be linked to her sexuality. It is our hope that the trope of the Gladiator will challenge viewers to critically engage with these complex representations of inherently flawed human characteristics, thus de-essentializing contemporary notions of blackness and Black female identity.

As we argue, the politics of respectability are in desperate need of redefinition. They are counterintuitive to the diversity that exists within the African American community. This ideology ultimately functions to define for everyone what constitutes Black culture, requiring "Black people [to] live positively" (Dolberry 2013). Unfortunately, this positions us as a monolithic community, lacking any racial, ethnic, or cultural diversity (Adamo 2010). This means that as we challenge ourselves as African American women, and mainstream society, to become critical consumers of the ways in which our experiences and realities are reflected in all genres of television and mass media (Cartier 2014), we must also question the self-imposed restrictions we place on ourselves regarding story lines that engage contemporary iterations of Black sexuality.

As critical readers of media texts such as *Scandal* where African Americans figure prominently, African American and mainstream audiences are afforded the unique opportunity to be entertained by intriguing plots and story lines that pique our interests and sensibilities. Unfortunately, body politics is at play that informs the politics of respectability (Dolberry 2013; Gross 1997; McKnight 2014), ultimately restricting the ways in which Black womanhood is represented and performed. Thus, a speculative gaze of these dynamics must be adopted as we reconceptualize Black female identity via the new counterimage of the Gladiator.

References

Adamo, Gregory. 2010. *African Americans in Television: Behind the Scenes.* New York: Peter Lang.

Adams-Bass, Valerie N., Keisha L. Bentley-Edwards, and Howard C. Stevenson. 2014. "That's Not Me I See on TV . . . : African American Youth Interpret Media Images of Black Females." *Women, Gender, and Families of Color* 2(1): 79–100.

Andrews, Vernon L. 2003. "Self-Reflection and the Reflected Self: African American Double Consciousness and the Social (Psychological) Mirror." *Journal of African American Studies* 73: 69–79.

Begley, Sarah. 2014. "Real Life Olivia Pope Reveals What President George H. W. Bush Thinks of *Scandal.*" *Time*, Sept. 24. http://time.com/343 3338/scandal-george-h-w-bush/.

Bell, Katrina E., Mark P. Orbe, Darlene K. Drummond, and Sakile Kai Camara. 2000. "Accepting the Challenge of Centralizing without Essentializing: Black Feminist Thought and African American Women's Communication Experiences." *Women's Studies in Communication* 23(1): 41–62.

Bowen, Sesali. 2013. "*Scandal* and Respectability Politics: Olivia Pope Is Not Setting Her Race or Gender Back by Having an Affair." *Feministing*, Oct. 26. http://feministing.com/2013/10/16/scandal-and-respectability -politics-olivia-pope-is-not-setting-her-race-or-gender-back-by-having -an-affair/.

Boylorn, Robin M. 2008. "As Seen on TV: An Autoethnographic Reflection on Race and Reality Television." *Critical Studies in Media Communication* 25(4): 413–33.

Brooks, TaKeshia. L. 2004. "We Have a Hottentot History to Consider: The Black Female Sex Symbol from Josephine to Tina to Kim." Conference Papers, International Communication Association.

Cartier, Nina. 2014. "Black Women On-Screen as Future Texts: A New Look at Black Pop Culture Representations." *Cinema Journal* 53: 150–57.

Childs, Erica Chito. 2005. "Looking behind the Stereotypes of the 'Angry Black Woman': An Exploration of Black Women's Responses to Interracial Relationships." *Gender and Society* 19: 544–61.

Collins, Patricia Hill. 1989. "The Social Construction of Black Feminist Thought." *Signs: Journal of Women in Culture and Society* 14(4): 645–773.

———. 1996a. "Sociological Visions and Revisions." *Contemporary Sociology* 25: 328–31.

———. 1996b. "What's in a Name: Womanism, Black Feminism, and Beyond." *Black Scholar* 26(1): 9–17.

———. 2005. *Black Feminist Thought: Knowledge, Consciousness, and the Politics of Empowerment.* New York and London: Routledge.

Crais, Clifton, and Pamela Scully. 2009. *Sara Baartman and the Hottentot Venus: A Ghost Story and a Biography.* Princeton, NJ: Princeton Univ. Press.

Davis, Shardé M. 2015. "The 'Strong Black Woman Collective': A Developing Theoretical Framework for Understanding Collective Communication Practices of Black Women." *Women's Studies in Communication* 38(1): 20–35.

Dolberry, Maurice E. 2013. "'I Hate Myself!': What Are Respectability Politics, and Why Do Black People Subscribe to Them?" *A Line in the Sand,* Sept. 5. http://alineinthesand.com/respectability-politics/.

Fuller, Jennifer. 2011. "The 'Black Sex Goddess' in the Living Room: Making Interracial Sex 'Laughable' on *Gimme a Break.*" *Feminist Media Studies* 11(3): 265–81.

Gross, Kali N. 1997. "Examining the Politics of Respectability in African American Studies." *Almanac* 43(28). http://www.upenn.edu/almanac/v43/n28/benchmrk.html.

Hartsock, Nancy C. M. 1983. "The Feminist Standpoint: Developing the Ground for a Specifically Feminist Historical Materialism." In *Discovering Reality: Feminist Perspectives on Epistemology, Metaphysics,*

Methodology, and Philosophy of Science, edited by Sandra Harding and Merill B. Hintikka, 283–310. Boston: D. Reidel.

hooks, bell. 1992. *Black Looks: Race and Representation*. Boston: South End Press.

———. 1995. *Killing Rage: Ending Racism*. New York: Henry Holt.

Kretsedemas, Philip. 2010. "'But She's Not Black!': Viewer Interpretations of 'Angry Black Women' on Prime Time TV." *Journal of African American Studies* 14(2): 149–70.

McKnight, Utz. 2014. "The Fantastic Olivia Pope: The Construct of a Black Feminist Subject." *Souls: A Critical Journal of Black Politics, Culture & Society* 16(3–4): 183–97.

Monk-Payton, Brandeise. 2014. "The Sound of *Scandal*: Crisis Management and the Musical Mediation of Racial Desire." *Black Scholar: Journal of Black Studies and Research* 45(1): 21–27.

Newman, Elizabeth. 2015. "No Room for Body Image Criticism in Serena Williams' Grand Slam Chase." *Sports Illustrated*, July 14. http://www.si.com/tennis/2015/07/14/serena-williams-body-image-wta-tennis.

Nussbaum, Emily. 2012. "Primary Colors: Shonda Rhimes's *Scandal* and the Diversity Debate." *New Yorker*, May 21. http://www.newyorker.com/magazine/2012/05/21/primary-colors.

Rothenberg, Ben. 2015. "Tennis's Top Women Balance Body Image with Ambition." *New York Times*, July 11. http://www.nytimes.com/2015/07/11/sports/tennis/tenniss-top-women-balance-body-image-with-quest-for-success.html?ref=sports&_r=0.

Sewell, Christopher J. P. 2013. "Mammies and Matriarchs: Tracing Images of the Black Female in Popular Culture 1950s to Present." *Journal of African American Studies* 17(3): 308–26.

Shabazz, Demetria. 2008. "Racializing 'the Male Gaze': Images of Black Women in American Cinema and the Limits of Feminist Film Theory." Paper presented at the International Communication Association, Montreal, Quebec, May 22–26.

Spitzack, Carole, and Kathryn Carter. 1987. "Women in Communication Studies: A Typology for Revision." *Quarterly Journal of Speech* 73(4): 401–23.

Ulen, Eisa Nefertari. 2014. "Sisters Are Doing It for Themselves: Onscreen and Behind the Camera, Online, on the Streets and in the Corridors of Power, Black Women Continue to Create a Liberating Space." *Crisis* 121(1): 18–21.

Workneh, Lilly. 2015. "Amandla Stenberg and the Sad Reality of the 'Angry Black Girl' Stereotype." *Huffington Post*, July 16. http://www .huffingtonpost.com/entry/amandla-stenberg-and-the-sad-reality-of -the-angry-black-girl-stereotype_55a5384de4b0b8145f73a3ad.

14 | Advocacy and Normalcy

The Politics of Same-Sex Marriage in *Scandal*

WILL HOWELL

"IT'S SUNDAY." Olivia Pope stands on James Novak's doorstep, and he is displeased. "He doesn't work on Sunday unless there's a war. Is there a war?" "Somewhere in the world, there's always a war," she retorts. "When my husband's dead, I'm blaming you," he replies. The camera cuts away, and pans up through flowers and greenery to reveal Cyrus Beene in his garden, enjoying a brief respite from his work ("Enemy of the State" [1.04]).

This is how ABC's political drama *Scandal* "outs" Cyrus to viewers. They meet Cyrus in the show's first episode and learn that he is the president's hardworking chief of staff. Over the first three episodes, viewers get to know Cyrus's character; this scene, which begins the fourth episode of season one, introduces viewers to his sexuality and marital status. As this scene begins, viewers do not know the identity of the man in the doorway. In the span of fifteen seconds, viewers learn that this man is "James," that he is friends with Olivia, that he is shielding a man from Olivia, that the shielded man is James's husband, and finally that James's husband is Cyrus Beene. At no point here are Cyrus or James labeled "gay": as Jeff Perry, the actor who plays Cyrus, puts it, "a man answers the door and says, my husband doesn't work on weekends. So oh, Cyrus is gay" (Starr and Newman 2013).

Over the program's next three seasons, Cyrus and James's complicated relationship becomes a crucial subplot for the series. Flashbacks show a younger Cyrus ending his heterosexual marriage, accepting his homosexuality, beginning his relationship with James, and making their relationship public. While the program does not show either their marriage or their engagement, it does portray them adopting a daughter and the subsequent struggle to balance work and parenting. But as they adjust, James learns that Cyrus's realpolitik sensibility led him to steal a presidential election and sanction several murders. James wrestles with these truths, and their relationship gradually destructs in a series of escalating betrayals. At the end of the third season, these escalations culminate in James's jarring murder.

In creating these two characters, Shonda Rhimes (*Scandal*'s creator) demonstrated her commitment to more-representative television. Rhimes has received praise for "crafting complex, original characters unconstrained by such singular definitions as 'black,' 'Asian' or 'gay'" (Rose 2014). Scripting Cyrus and James meant writing the characters to "live in a world where there is no closet" (Willmore 2013). Across mainstream media, there is critical consensus that her shows are "groundbreaking" (Fallon 2014). Perry proposes that *Scandal* operates in a useful tension between "methodically pushing this agenda" and "not [shoving] it in your face every second" (Prudom 2014). While not using the term *agenda*, Rhimes powerfully characterized her motivation: "There's a box you get put in. My goal is to blow that box wide open" (Hess 2013). Rhimes's comment begs two critical questions about Cyrus and James: What was "the box" circumscribing how they might be represented? And how did *Scandal* blow the box "wide open"?

For decades, heteronormativity has been a significant box limiting representations of gay and lesbian couples. Heteronormativity unites heterosexual prevalence with normative force. It both presumes that people are heterosexual until they admit (or are outed) to be otherwise and pushes people to adopt heterosexual traits and behaviors (Adams 2010, 236). It presumes common, stable gender roles—that men and women behave in distinctly gendered ways; heteronormative men, for example, might fix cars, and heteronormative women might cook. Despite their sexuality, gay men or lesbians can participate in this network when they adopt "decidedly conventional heterosexual signifiers" (Shugart 2003, 72). Those signifiers stabilize gay men and lesbians for heterosexual audiences, while those individuals who eschew heteronormativity are labeled as "outsiders," "unreasonable," or "controversial" (Cherney and Lindemann 2013, 15). Larry Gross aptly notes that a heteronormative force "limits the ways lesbians and gay men . . . are depicted in the media" (2001, 13).

Those limitations began taking shape during twentieth-century gay and lesbian activism. Early gay and lesbian activists fought total exclusion and began seeking inclusion in dominant (heterosexual) institutions. By the 1980s, this activism meant engaging mainstream media for more regular representation. Gay men and lesbians were being represented more and more often—but those representations took a heteronormative form. Heteronormative signifiers marked both news and entertainment media and were particularly present in the campaign for same-sex marriage.

That campaign unfolded in the years preceding *Scandal* and during its first several seasons. Between *Scandal*'s April 2012 debut and its season-three finale (April 2014), America more than doubled the number of citizens who could legally marry someone of the same gender; by its fifth-season premiere, same-sex marriage was legal nationwide (Silver 2013). The actors playing James and Cyrus advocated for marriage equality by invoking their fictional same-sex marriage. In accepting a Creative Arts Emmy, for example, Dan Bucatinsky (who plays James) "got choked up because we're living in a time when I can say to everybody that I'm thanking my onscreen husband and my real-life husband" (Rabinovitch 2013). Bucatinsky's on-screen husband, Jeff Perry, recorded a video for the Human Rights Campaign in which he criticized people's obsession with Cyrus being gay and married. Perry felt that the show had made Cyrus's sexuality secondary to more plot-related character traits (Human Rights Campaign 2014).

Perry's belief correlates with scripting choices that mirror the strategy of same-sex marriage advocates: represent a same-sex marriage using heteronormal signifiers. This happened in two rhetorical moves: first, *Scandal*'s writers characterized James and Cyrus in familiar, heteronormative tropes; those tropes were then accepted by heterosexual protagonists and, simultaneously, disdained by heterosexual antagonists. Unlike many prior television shows, *Scandal* did not go out of its way to present the couple's sexuality "as an anomaly that must be explained," but it did package their sexuality in familiar terms that needed no explanation (Gross 2001, 16). Some popular press critics suggested that *Scandal* helped some wary Americans accept same-sex marriage, and I do not disagree. Nonetheless, I contend that *Scandal*'s contribution—a heteronormatively modeled same-sex marriage—was actually so familiar that it safely reinforced the box increasingly forming around same-sex couples rather than breaking it open.

But this argument has a dark side: at moments when the box cracked open, and James and Cyrus drifted to nonheteronormative territory, the relationship and partners were diegetically punished. Each significant moment in James and Cyrus's descent is spurred by a prior moment when the husbands challenged heteronormativity: they cheated, balked at parenting, or undermined another marriage. Scripting muddles the cause of these moments, presenting them as individual failings rather than as flaws in heteronormativity as a foundational concept. Despite this veneer of individual failing, *Scandal* delivers a hard lesson about deviating from heteronormativity: don't. This lesson actually takes clearest form after James is dead, when Cyrus takes up with a prostitute. Cyrus's nonnormative same-sex relationship ultimately cannot survive without being reinscribed into heteronormative terms.

Heteronormativity's Imprint on Media and Political Advocacy

Heteronormativity's force in *Scandal* stems in part from the late-twentieth-century gay rights movement. Early advocates sought rights and respect from dominant heterosexual society, dividing over whether inclusion or separatism was the better course. Media was a crucial front in this debate: Should activists encourage community-driven entertainment and news or lobby for mainstream, heterosexually dominated media to represent same-sex individuals and couples as they wanted to be represented? The latter impulse carried the day, and the movement expended significant effort to influence mainstream media representations. While doing so ultimately resulted in more, and increasingly positive, representations, it also meant those representations took heteronormative form.

Before advocating for specific forms, though, gay men and lesbians had to fight total exclusion by heterosexual-controlled society. "Exclusion" often meant "out" people could not work or survive. Preceding, during, and after World War II, for example, the government presumed that gay government employees were vulnerable to blackmail by foreign agents. Morris contends this presumption caused enormous "pressure to pass the muster of heteronormativity," so that gay individuals would not lose their livelihoods (2002, 231). Such negative presumptions were further reinforced by psychologists, whose *Diagnostic and Statistical Manual of Mental Disorders* classified "homosexuality" as a mental disorder. Jakobsen notes that such policing created a "network of norms," sustaining heterosexual superiority in the process (1998, 518). Groups like the Mattachine Society and the Daughters of Bilitis formed to challenge such thinking. They reasoned that if psychologists stopped treating their sexuality as a disease, or the federal government stopped indiscriminately firing "out" employees, broader institutional acceptance would follow (Marotta 1981, 50–54).

Even as they fought exclusion, though, these early activists fought internally about whether acceptance was desirable. The radicals who began the Gay Liberation Front (GLF) in the late 1960s objected that these same institutions were "impos[ing] sexual roles and definitions of our nature . . . through a system of taboos and institutionalized repressions" (ibid., 88). They alleged that organizations like the Mattachine Society and the Daughters of Bilitis were beholden to heterosexist institutions, pursuing what Ron Becker calls a "politics of access" to those institutions (2006, 42–44). The GLF's agitation fueled the decline of both the Mattachine Society and the Daughters of Bilitis, but not the goal of access. A new organization—the Gay Activists Alliance (GAA)—formed to advocate for access "grounded in the fact of our common humanity," rather than in adherence to heteronormativity (Marotta 1981, 144).

Establishing "common humanity" meant shaping how media represented same-sex couples. GAA and its successor, the Gay and Lesbian Alliance Against Defamation (GLAAD), formed committees to work with news and entertainment media. These committees pushed first for regular representation of gay men and lesbians, and second for positive representations. In general, they sought to displace dominant "[framing of] heterosexuality and opposite-sex desire as better than homosexuality and same-sex desire" (Adams 2010, 236). To that end, some gay and lesbian activists rejected the discriminatory mainstream media entirely and created their own institutions—newspapers, radio, blogs, and, more recently, podcasts.[1] While supporting these efforts, GAA and GLAAD kept pushing mainstream media to offer "pictures of gay life designed to be acceptable to the gay community and still palatable to a mass audience" (Gross 2001, 50). "Mass audience," though, meant a predominantly heterosexual audience.

As the 1980s gave way to the 1990s, supportive members of the media began representing gay life more often and more positively— but through a heterosexual lens. Stories had heterosexual people validate gay and lesbian people, for example, or praise gay and lesbian people for their heteronormative characteristics (Goltz 2013). A well-known example from this period is the simultaneous coming-out of Ellen DeGeneres and her sitcom character, "Ellen Morgan." Bonnie Dow argues that it was "geared toward gaining the approval of mainstream, heterosexual Americans," rather than creating a moment of identification for gay and lesbian viewers (2001, 128). Larry Gross places blame with mainstream media's need for advertising revenues, but also sees heteronormative representations as "the great American bargain, offered to successive minorities . . . add your flavoring to the

---

1. Larry Gross has provided an excellent, exhaustive accounting of these outlets in *Up from Invisibility* (2001), and Toby Marotta addresses GAA's early work most clearly in *The Politics of Homosexuality* (1981, 182–84).

national stew, but keep it subtle enough not to threaten the dominance of white, middle-class, Christian, hetero-normativity" (2001, 262). As a result of this bargain, Shugart argues, twenty-first-century gay and lesbian representations have remained largely bounded by heteronormativity (2003, 68).

Advocating for Marriage

Since the 1990s, the gay and lesbian movement has increasingly become the gay, lesbian, bisexual, transgender, and queer (GLBTQ) movement—but it remains split over whether, and how, to pursue equal access to marriage. Some activists had previously pushed marriage equality, but other issues had always taken precedence (for example, HIV/AIDS, police and employment discrimination, antigay violence). Gay men and lesbians found themselves thrust into the political spotlight when homophobic politicians introduced preemptive legislation to limit their already-nonexistent marriage rights. Some believed that other issues remained more pressing than engaging marriage politics, or that gay men and lesbians should reject marriage as an exclusionary heterosexist institution. Marriage-equality proponents countered that "avoiding the issue would hinder progress on a wide variety of LGBT issues" (Moscowitz 2013, 32). Heteronormative aspirations won out, and activists engaged conservatives in a years-long battle for the right to marry.

Within this battle, the mainstream movement gravitated to familiar markers. Moscowitz found that movement leaders strove to "present themselves as 'normal'" to heterosexual audiences whose political power was needed to win marriage equality (ibid., 41). These audiences, it was assumed, would recognize and respond to heteronormative signifiers: "poster couples" were "suburban, middle to upper class, Caucasian, nonthreatening in demeanor and appearance, anchored to appropriate depictions of femininity and masculinity, and already a part of a long-lasting, monogamous, child-rearing partnership" (73). These couples were also completely "out" to their communities, and activists publicized this idea to demonstrate acceptance by heterosexual family and friends (40, 48–50).

The movement's decision to frame same-sex marriages in heteronormative terms generated much debate. Suzanna Danuta Walters disparages the decision as "gay mimesis," suggesting that gay men and lesbians were trying to "[show] straight America that they are just the same as them" (2001, 189–90). But scholars question whether activists had much agency. After all, as Gross argues, both news and entertainment media "reflect the biases and interests of those powerful people who define the public agenda" (2001, 4). Moscowitz interviewed GLBTQ activists and found that they actually preferred that marriage was *not* on the public agenda during the 1990s and early 2000s (2013, 28). They knew, try as they might to develop alternative framing, news and entertainment media would inevitably emphasize heteronormatively modeled same-sex marriages—representing some, but certainly not all, same-sex couples and individuals.

Heteronormative Gayness and Diegetic Acceptance in *Scandal*

Scandal's portrayal of James and Cyrus seems to justify activists' concerns about heteronormative representation. Like the same-sex couples in marriage-equality coverage, Cyrus Beene and James Novak are in a committed relationship; unlike those couples, they are married. They own a home together, and that home infuses their marriage with middle-class domesticity. When the show begins they are childless, but they eventually adopt a daughter. Preceding and during parenthood, James is the dominant parent, while Cyrus plays a supportive parenting role. The show's heterosexual protagonists accept their marriage, while the show's antagonists denigrate it.

Irrespective of marriage, though, the show establishes the couple's deep commitment to each other. In season three, viewers are transported back in the show's timeline to the moment when James and Cyrus met on the campaign trail, nearly four years before James's death. A subsequent scene shows the two after several months of dating; Cyrus was still "not ready to tell the president of the United States what I do when I go home at night," and James felt that Cyrus was treating him like "some dirty, little secret." This conflict resolves when Cyrus acts boldly, out of love, and asks James to dance with him publicly at the inaugural ball. These flashbacks unfold in the episode following James's murder, and Cyrus works through his grief by recalling these earlier moments ("Kiss Kiss Bang Bang" [3.14]). Viewers, though, learned of and saw these key scenes for the first time in this episode. Cyrus recalls these moments with fresh eyes, then, thereby mirroring the reaction of dedicated viewers who are only now able to appreciate the depth of the relationship. As their relationship ebbs within the diegesis, *Scandal* leaves viewers with these scenes and with a strong sense that the couple loved each other deeply, despite the bad moments.

Those moments aside, Cyrus and James's relationship is often the most stable among *Scandal*'s volatile opposite-sex romances. Three romantic relationships span the show's first three seasons: the president's marriage to the first lady, the president's affair with Olivia Pope, and Cyrus's marriage to James. The first lady knows about the president's affair but declines to discuss it with Cyrus, saying, "We can't all be you and James, Cyrus. We can't all have a perfect marriage" ("Molly, You in Danger, Girl" [2.18]). Cyrus and James's marriage involves no infidelity, and both the first lady and Cyrus affirm James and Cyrus's commitment to each other ("Snake in the Garden" [2.17]; "Vermont Is for Lovers, Too" [3.08]). When Cyrus lectures the president about the president's infidelity, Cyrus begins with references to his own marital stability.

Their domesticity further nudges the couple on to heteronormative territory. In the third episode that includes both James and Cyrus, viewers learn that James wants "a fat, drooling, smushy baby" and that Cyrus has "been fighting him on it" ("Grant: For the People" [1.07]). Viewers later learn that Cyrus's marriage proposal to James—unseen, but recounted in detail—promised "a wedding and a baby—and a house in Georgetown with a garden" ("Happy Birthday, Mr. President" [2.08]). Recall that viewers first meet James on the porch of that house, protecting his family's domestic space from the intrusion of public affairs. After the adoption finalizes, James stays home with baby Ella. When Cyrus asks about James's day, James speaks of "the new graph paper I bought for Ella's poop log" and "the riveting conversation I had" about the neighbor's sprinklers ("Vermont Is for Lovers, Too" [3.08]). In these fragmentary moments, James and Cyrus are rhetorically constructed in a way that mirrors the real-life, home-owning, middle-class couples from the marriage-equality movement.

And like those couples, Cyrus and James's parenthood is constructed in heteronormative tropes. At their engagement (if not sooner), they were already planning to have a child ("Happy Birthday, Mr. President" [2.08]). Once they are married, Cyrus gets cold feet because he takes great pride in his work, and "once you have a kid, your life's no longer your own" ("Grant: For the People" [1.07]). To alleviate that concern, Cyrus and James divide responsibilities: Cyrus tells James, "You'll have to quit your job because one parent should be at home," and James obliges ("Blown Away" [2.09]). James becomes the dominant parent, while Cyrus assumes a supportive but reduced parenting role. These roles coalesce as soon as baby Ella becomes a part of the plot: Cyrus arranges the adoption, but James goes by himself to get the girl ("One for the Dog" [2.10]). Cyrus comes home for lunch occasionally with his stay-at-home husband and their daughter, but often forgets the baby when making plans ("Blown Away" [2.09]). When Ella cries at night, Cyrus grumbles and keeps sleeping; James responds, sleeps in her room, and thinks first of her as he lies on the ground dying ("Nobody Likes Babies" [2.13]; "Kiss Kiss Bang Bang" [3.14]). As Cyrus grows into his parental role, though, the show emphasizes both parents' commitment to their child by showing them baptizing their daughter in elaborate fashion ("Whiskey Tango Foxtrot" [2.14]).

James and Cyrus may be the show's best heteronormative parents when juxtaposed with the heterosexual parents. Over the first three seasons, *Scandal* offers three other parenting story lines: the president's father, Olivia's mother and father, and the president and first lady. The script aligns James with the two mothers and tasks them with nurturing their children and playing a more active role in the children's lives. Like Cyrus, all three fathers work (or worked) long hours and are (or were) removed from the lives of their kids. The first lady speaks about how the president "always had problems with his father," and one of Olivia's colleagues remarks on her "daddy issues" ("A Criminal, a Whore, an Idiot, and a Liar" [2.11]; "It's Handled" [3.01]). The first children disparage their parents throughout; in a particularly stark example, the first son starts an anonymous Twitter account to criticize his father ("Mama Said Knock You Out" [3.15]). The president, first lady, Olivia's father, and Olivia's mother each criticize his or her spouse on camera and at length for poor parenting. All of these fragments assemble into a fictional setting that accentuates James's attentive parenting and Cyrus and James's commitment to Ella's well-being.

Scandal also creates a diegetic atmosphere in which heterosexual characters seamlessly accept Cyrus and James without belaboring their sexuality. While many examples could demonstrate this point, their relationship with the first family illustrates it most clearly. When James visits Cyrus at the White House, the first lady invites the husbands to "dinner in the residence, just the four of us" ("All Roads Lead to Fitz" [2.05]). In a national broadcast, one of James's reporter colleagues notes that James "know[s] the [president's] family intimately" ("White Hat's Back On" [2.22]). When James and Cyrus decide to baptize baby Ella, they ask the president and Olivia to become her godparents ("Whiskey Tango Foxtrot" [2.14]). Indeed, James and Cyrus are "practically family" to the Republican first family at a time when the nonfictional Republican Party vehemently opposed marriage equality ("Vermont Is for Lovers, Too" [3.08]). In a particularly telling flashback, Cyrus enters the president's office with the intention of coming out to him:

CYRUS: I'm s-seeing someone.
PRESIDENT: That's wonderful. Is this the first person you've started seeing since the divorce?
CYRUS: It is.
PRESIDENT: And it's serious?
CYRUS: It is.

PRESIDENT: Well, good for you, Cy. Do you . . . want to tell me anything else about this person?

CYRUS: It's . . . a journalist.

PRESIDENT: A journalist?

CYRUS: A very . . . opinionated journalist. [President chuckles.] Is that going to be a problem?

PRESIDENT: Of course not.

CYRUS: Good. Okay. That's a-all I wanted to say.

PRESIDENT: Cyrus. Are you in love?

CYRUS: I am, sir . . . in love. They . . . make me happy.

PRESIDENT: Then that's all that matters. ("Kiss Kiss Bang Bang" [3.14])

The absence of the word *gay* from this and other scenes is not insignificant (nor the absence, in this scene, of a gendered pronoun). In searching through the first three seasons, I found only eight episodes out of fifty-one in which *gay* or a similar term is used to identify Cyrus or James.[2] By omitting these markers—words that would set Cyrus and James apart—*Scandal* creates a fictional world in which same-sex attraction is normalized.

In *Scandal*'s diegetic world, homophobia is one of the characteristics used to build opposition to some of the show's antagonists. Hollis Doyle, a sleazy oil lobbyist who facilitated the stealing of the presidential election, is identified by Cyrus as a "racist, sexist, homophobic son of a bitch" ("Spies Like Us" [2.06]). When James writes a newspaper exposé, Doyle complains to Cyrus about "what I hear is your boyfriend":

CYRUS: We're married, actually.

DOYLE: Your wife then.

2. I limited my search to the first three seasons since James is killed toward the end of season three. The episodes are "Spies Like Us" (2.06), "Defiance" (2.07), "Nobody Likes Babies" (2.13), "Icarus" [3.06], "Vermont Is for Lovers, Too" (3.08), "YOLO" (3.09), "A Door Marked Exit" (3.10), and "Kiss Kiss Bang Bang" (3.14).

CYRUS: Husband.

DOYLE: Oh. Sorry. I assumed you were the, you know, fella in that deal. ("Spies Like Us")

Hollis Doyle's disrespect flies in the face of the respect other characters have shown James and Cyrus and brands him as an antagonist. The socially conservative vice president, Sally Langston, locates herself in a similar discursive place when she sanctimoniously tells Cyrus, "I have never once mentioned how I feel about your godless homosexual lifestyle and that poor . . . baby that you have dragged into it" ("It's Handled" [3.01]). In similar vitriolic fashion, Cyrus calls Vice President Langston a "pro-life, homophobic, raging bitch" ("Ride, Sally, Ride" [3.11]). Cyrus gives voice to *Scandal*'s perspective: homophobia—not homosexuality—is unacceptable and undesirable.

What *is* desirable is the kind of domestic stability found almost exclusively in Cyrus and James's relationship. Among *Scandal*'s protagonists, Olivia is engaged in an ongoing affair with the president. The president loves Olivia and not the first lady. The first lady was raped by her father-in-law and eventually falls in love with the president's friend. Parental characters are distant from their children, and children hate their parents. Physical domestic spaces also reflect *Scandal*'s unstable diegetic world: the first family temporarily lives at the White House, yet the first children do not regularly reside there. Olivia and the members of her organization live in apartments, and the show regularly depicts Olivia as never having food in her cupboards. In contrast, James and Cyrus live in a home that they own, actively raise their daughter, eat meals together, and (until James's final episodes) are committed monogamists. Their fictional marriage demonstrates that a same-sex couple can enact heteronormativity as—or more—completely than a straight couple, with slight discursive adjustments for gender.

Breaking from Heteronormativity

But James and Cyrus do more than just enact heteronormativity: they suffer when they challenge it. Cyrus's hesitance to adopt a child puts his career, his friends, and his marriage in peril. When Cyrus undermines another couple's commitment—the vice president and her husband—he sets off a string of escalating crises that envelop both him and James. One such crisis, which in turn begets more suffering, is a further rebuke of heteronormativity: James betrays monogamy and cheats on Cyrus. Cyrus and James's acts undermine and question heteronormative stability, and the outcome is pain and suffering, including James's murder. When it comes time to assign blame, however, *Scandal* points the finger—through James, no less—at Cyrus's individual character defects. An opportunity is lost to discuss whether heteronormative pursuits played a role in the chaos and whether the characters had alternative paths.

Cyrus and James, for example, might have collaboratively crafted a relationship without child rearing, rather than having Cyrus passive aggressively avoid adoption. His ambition and commitment to his job leave no room for raising a child; initially, his career matters more to him than domestic happiness. James leaves his job to raise their child, but in lieu of that child, he returns to his work: investigative reporting. He warns Cyrus that because "I'm childless, . . . I got plenty of time to give it my all" ("All Roads Lead to Fitz" [2.05]). In the course of his work, James discovers that Cyrus—and everyone around him—helped steal the presidential election, and James obfuscates to cover up his research ("Defiance" [2.07]). Cyrus interprets James's demeanor as cover up for an affair. When Cyrus eventually discovers James's research, Cyrus blames himself and traces it all back to his obstinacy over adopting a baby. He immediately arranges the adoption so that James will leave his reporting job ("Blown Away" [2.09]). The ploy works, and stability returns to James and Cyrus's relationship.

Their lives destabilize again when Cyrus undermines the vice president's marriage. Vice President Sally Langston planned to oppose the president's reelection, and Cyrus will stop at nothing to stop her. He orchestrates circumstances in which her closeted husband, Daniel Douglas, thinks that James wants a sexual rendezvous. Cyrus then sets up a private meeting between Daniel Douglas and James, knowing that Daniel Douglas will act on his mistaken belief. In undermining their marital commitment, Cyrus risks his own, confident that "my husband will refuse said pass, slap his closeted face, and then when James wants to write about it—to expose the hypocritical lie that is their marriage—I will tell Sally that she can either fall in line or she can continue to run for office as an independent and read James's sordid account in the *Times* along with the rest of the world" ("Vermont Is for Lovers, Too" [3.08]). This plan assumes that a long-term, committed marriage—a heteronormative institution—can be easily infiltrated with the promise of unencumbered sex. Cyrus behaves as though he does not have to respect such an institution, such a commitment, even as he banks on his own husband respecting it. In doing so, Cyrus assumes that each will continue to fulfill the heteronormative gender roles that manifest in other aspects of their life: Cyrus will be the traditional domineering husband, telling James what to do, and James will oblige. Of course, none of it would be possible if heternormativity did not *also* cause Daniel Douglas to feel he needed to suppress his sexuality in order to be accepted. But instead of exploring those problematic gender and sexuality dynamics, Daniel Douglas disappears (3.09) as quickly as he appeared (3.05), and the show hums along. Viewers are instead encouraged—as Jeff Perry said they should be—to contemplate Cyrus's evil masterminding.

Plot as he might, though, Cyrus could not foresee that James would also challenge heteronormativity by betraying their monogamy—and that James's act would reverberate until their relationship implodes. When James realizes that Cyrus set him up with Daniel Douglas, James sees it as evidence that Cyrus does not respect their commitment to each other. He decides to behave as though they were not committed to each other to punish Cyrus and has sex with the vice president's husband. When Cyrus learns of it, as James knew he would, Cyrus immediately invokes the stability promised by heteronormativity: "I trusted you," he cries, "that you'd honor our marriage." James snidely retorts that the fling was a "pleasant surprise," but viewers get the sense that he's trying to hurt Cyrus more than genuinely expressing his pleasure with the fling. Before that nonnormative pleasure can be considered, though, James has moved on to tell

Cyrus that he is leaving and "taking our baby" and that Cyrus "broke our family" ("YOLO" [3.09]; "No Sun on the Horizon" [3.13]).

As tensions escalate from this betrayal, James becomes the vessel through which the show cements blame with Cyrus. James labels Cyrus "the devil" and tells him that he has "ruined us" and "ruined everything" ("YOLO" [3.09]). James tells him that he is "sick"; in turn, Cyrus professes, "I'm still the same man you married. You just maybe never noticed the '6-6-6' on my forehead before . . . I'm hoping you'll love me anyway" ("A Door Marked Exit" [3.10]). In this oddly touching moment, Cyrus accepts James's condemnations: he accepts that he is evil and that it is something unchangeable in his character. In these last scenes between Cyrus and James, *Scandal* positions Cyrus—and his inherent character defects—as being responsible for James's murder. Lost are numerous chances along the way to delve more deeply into the character's choices and motivations and critically evaluate them. One such motivation—heternormativity—shares in the blame throughout these crucial scenes, but generally gets a pass.

Reframing Cyrus?

If *Scandal*'s first three seasons did not provide the narrative space to blow open the heteronormative box surrounding James and Cyrus, the fourth season holds greater promise. Following James's murder, Cyrus dives deeper into his work and moves further from actively parenting baby Ella. Indeed, as the season begins, Cyrus behaves as though Ella were no longer even a part of his life. Cyrus's husband and daughter are heteronormative attachments, but without them, *Scandal* can redefine Cyrus in nonheteronormative terms. Yet by the end of season four, the potential of such a Cyrus closes once again.

As the season begins, James's memory is a significant impediment to Cyrus taking nonheteronormative form. Despite their last days together, James's murder has "broken" Cyrus ("The State of the Union" [4.02]). In the season's first few episodes, revenge motivates Cyrus's actions, and he envisions the day Olivia will "find me dancing on [the] grave" of James's killer ("The Key" [4.05]). Four episodes later, he reminds viewers that he "only ever slept with two men," and one of them was James, "the love of my life" ("Where the Sun Don't Shine" [4.09]). Between such comments, melancholy and grief over James become the defining characteristics of the new Cyrus Beene. Cyrus remains monogamous to James, emotionally and sexually committed to a man who is not, and will not be, physically present.

When Cyrus eventually breaks this monogamy, the plot disciplines him back to heteronormativity. A political opponent hires a prostitute named Michael to tempt the lonely Cyrus and collect sensitive political information ("The State of the Union" [4.02]). After initial fear and hesitation, Cyrus begins sleeping with Michael. Cyrus acknowledges that this relationship is "a terrible decision on my part," but he still becomes infatuated. When their relationship becomes public knowledge, Cyrus resigns as the chief of staff—but Olivia Pope charts a course for his return. "America loves a love story," she tells Cyrus and Michael; if they get married, America will forgive their nonnormal relationship. Cyrus resists, but Olivia pushes him by saying, "The Cyrus Beene I know doesn't hide in his half-empty closet" ("Where the Sun Don't Shine" [4.09]). In the end, Michael and Cyrus get engaged and then married ("Put a Ring on It" [4.17]).

Cyrus and Michael's story line temporarily disrupts—but ultimately affirms—the power of heteronormativity. *Scandal* repeatedly captures Michael and Cyrus either before or after sex. They meet in bedrooms, but these bedrooms are not domestic spaces: they are spaces for sex, and Cyrus gets angry when Michael enters the domestic space of Cyrus's house. There is no sense that either man desires the heteronormative stability that Cyrus had with James. Whereas James and Cyrus fought, Cyrus and Michael are happy and happy to continue without any deep commitment. But when society's heteronormative expectations intrude, Cyrus and Michael have no choice but to adhere to those expectations.

Conclusion

Does this adherence to heteronormativity "simultaneously [contradict] or [undercut] a progressive premise," as Bonnie Dow argued *The Mary Tyler Moore Show* did in its representation of feminism (1990,

263)? A gay Republican politician, a leading gay journalist, and a gay prostitute meeting heteronormative expectations on prime-time television is certainly a meaningful degree of progress. Eighty years ago, when gay men and lesbians were being indiscriminately fired from government jobs, the budding movement spent no energy on getting more, and more positive, media representations. Organizations did not prioritize same-sex couples on the silver screen or even on television news or entertainment: they fought to not be classified as diseased or seen as threats to American society. As those issues ameliorated, later generations of activists fought for more regular, and better, media representation—which, in turn, further ameliorated conditions. This process compounded until, by 2012, a heteronormative gay couple could safely anchor a prime-time drama without diegetic disruption.

Yet that progress remains checked, even when media personalities would use their platform to move society farther. *Scandal* is representative: even with showrunner Rhimes intent on "blow[ing the] box wide open," the show is unable to sustain a nonnormative relationship within its plot. Rhimes's boldest attempt—Michael and Cyrus—stands out for its inability to survive even *fictional* heteronormative scrutiny. Indeed, as a piece of fiction, *Scandal* created its own diegetic limits based in, but not bound by, the nonfiction world. Michael embodies *Scandal*'s capacity to push this reality-based fiction to the limits: he is a political operative and spy who prostituted himself so he might wheedle his way to sleep with the president's chief of staff, only to fall in love and abandon his mission. It strains logic, but such is the nature of fiction: to go where nonfiction cannot. But even with its malleable reality, *Scandal* reins Michael in to a familiar representation. Michael becomes Cyrus's husband and moves safely within heteronormative diegetic boundaries, the world stabilized—and then Michael more or less disappears from the plot.

Yet Michael is more than just a compromise: he is also a shot across society's bow. For three seasons, *Scandal* establishes Cyrus and James as a baseline for representing a same-sex couple. Such an intradiegetically low baseline allows *Scandal* to easily push upward with characters and story lines like Michael. Those story lines are not (yet) sustainable beyond the diegesis (or, perhaps, within it), but they temporarily model what alternative representations might look like. In this way, American society can progress as storytellers use their malleable, fictional rhetoric to set progressive limitations, pose challenging questions, and momentarily question dominant social forces like heteronormativity.

References

Adams, Tony E. 2010. "Paradoxes of Sexuality, Gay Identity, and the Closet." *SYMB Symbolic Interaction* 33(2): 234–56.

Becker, Ron. 2006. *Gay TV and Straight America*. New Brunswick, NJ: Rutgers Univ. Press.

Cherney, James L., and Kurt Lindemann. 2013. "Queering Street: Homosociality, Masculinity, and Disability in *Friday Night Lights*." *Western Journal of Communication* 78(1): 1–21.

Dow, Bonnie J. 1990. "Hegemony, Feminist Criticism and *The Mary Tyler Moore Show*." *Critical Studies in Mass Communication* 7(3): 261–74. doi:10.1080/15295039009360178.

———. 2001. "Ellen, Television, and the Politics of Gay and Lesbian Visibility." *Critical Studies in Media Communication* 18(2): 123–40.

Fallon, Kevin. 2014. "How to Get Away with Gayness: Shonda Rhimes Kills TV's Sex Stereotypes." *Daily Beast*, Sept. 25. http://www.thedailybeast.com/articles/2014/09/25/how-to-get-away-with-gayness-shonda-rhimes-kills-tv-s-sex-stereotypes.html.

Goltz, Dustin Bradley. 2013. "It Gets Better: Queer Futures, Critical Frustrations, and Radical Potentials." *Critical Studies in Media Communication* 30(2): 135–51. doi:10.1080/15295036.2012.701012.

Gross, Larry. 2001. *Up from Invisibility: Lesbians, Gay Men, and the Media in America*. New York: Columbia Univ. Press.

Hess, Amanda. 2013. "How Shonda Rhimes Triumphed over Clueless 'Older Guys' at ABC." *Slate*, Nov. 8.

Human Rights Campaign. 2014. *Jeff Perry for HRC's Americans for Marriage Equality*. https://www.youtube.com/watch?v=kYxocuYJ27w.

Jakobsen, Janet R. 1998. "Queer Is? Queer Does? Normativity and the Problem of Resistance." *GLQ: A Journal of Lesbian and Gay Studies* 4(4): 511–36.

Marotta, Toby. 1981. *The Politics of Homosexuality*. Boston: Houghton Mifflin Harcourt.

Morris, Charles E., III. 2002. "Pink Herring & the Fourth Persona: J. Edgar Hoover's Sex Crime Panic." *Quarterly Journal of Speech* 88(2): 228–44.

Moscowitz, Leigh. 2013. *The Battle over Marriage: Gay Rights Activism through the Media*. Urbana: Univ. of Illinois Press.

Prudom, Laura. 2014. "'Scandal' Preview: Jeff Perry Talks Cyrus' 'Catastrophic' Choices." *Variety*, Nov. 13. https://variety.com/2014/tv/news/scandal-preview-jeff-perry-talks-cyrus-catastrophic-choices-1201355649/.

Rabinovitch, Simona. 2013. "'Scandal' Star Dan Bucatinsky on the Highlight of His Career." *Gotham*, Nov. 14. https://gotham-magazine.com/scandals-dan-bucatinsky-on-same-sex-marriage-meeting-oprah.

Rose, Lacey. 2014. "Shonda Rhimes Opens Up about 'Angry Black Woman' Flap, Messy 'Grey's Anatomy' Chapter and the 'Scandal' Impact." *Hollywood Reporter*, Oct. 8. http://www.hollywoodreporter.com/news/shonda-rhimes-opens-up-angry-738715.

Shugart, Helene A. 2003. "Reinventing Privilege: The New (Gay) Man in Contemporary Popular Media." *Critical Studies in Media Communication* 20(1): 67–91.

Silver, Nate. 2013. "Same-Sex Marriage Availability Set to Double in One-Year Span." *FiveThirtyEight*, June 26. https://fivethirtyeight.blogs.nytimes.com/2013/06/26/same-sex-marriage-availability-set-to-double-in-one-year-span/.

Starr, Liane Bonin, and Melinda Newman. 2013. "Interview: Jeff Perry Talks about Cyrus' Heartbreak on 'Scandal.'" *Uproxx*, Dec. 4. https://uproxx.com/hitfix/interview-jeff-perry-talks-about-cyrus-heartbreak-on-scandal/.

Walters, Suzanna Danuta. 2001. *All the Rage: The Story of Gay Visibility in America*. Chicago: Univ. of Chicago Press.

Willmore, Alison. 2013. "Dan Bucatinsky on 'Scandal,' 'Web Therapy' and the Evolution of Gay Characters on the Small Screen." *IndieWire*, Feb. 13. http://www.indiewire.com/article/television/dan-bucatinsky-talks-scandal-web-therapy-and-the-evolution-of-gay-characters-on-the-small-screen.

15 | "He Exists Because I Say He Exists"

The (Un)Making of Fitz's Manhood and the
Enduring Adaptability of Hegemonic Masculinity

DAVID PONTON III AND
KELLY WEBER STEFONOWICH

FITZGERALD GRANT is a man forlorn. He grimaces, overindulges in alcohol, expresses himself in bouts of anger and self-pity, and seems always on the brink of losing control. As president of the United States, however, he is supposed to epitomize modesty, orderliness, and power. Indeed, Fitz is the closest approximation to hegemonic masculinity on *Scandal*, yet, rather than exuding power, he is coerced into performances and positions by others who have learned to wrest power for themselves in a heteropatriarchal society by exploiting the symbol of manhood—in this case, most immediately visible in Fitz's status as man-as-president to their advantage.

Men like Fitz learn to prize manhood, but they also learn that manhood needs to be recognized by others to be considered valid. Far from being transcendent of their societies, men stand at risk of misrecognition and, to avoid the loss of gender validation, struggle to be "men" as others expect them to be. Men, then, are formed out of vulnerability and taught to believe that they made themselves. However, as Mellie asserts, "I did all the work! . . . I made him. He exists because I say he exists!" ("Truth or Consequences" [2.12]). Thus, the president frequently finds himself vulnerable, manipulable, unsure, and dependent. Quite often, his loved ones remind him just how short of manhood he falls.

Reading *Scandal* offers opportunities to think critically about the (dis)connections between masculinity, power as domination, and power conceived as agency. We explore Mellie's declaration that Fitz exists because she made him through Fitz's relationships with five characters that impact his masculine identity and performances. Cyrus misrecognizes the president by infantilizing him, thereby manipulating Fitz into proving his manhood by following Cyrus's lead. Mellie coerces Fitz into impregnating her by placing his sexual and political virility on the line. Big Jerry undermines Fitz's notion that he can be self-made, indicating that Fitz's success is a consequence of Jerry's genes, wealth, and influence. Rowan too disrupts Fitz's sense of agency, suggesting that White masculinity's claim to agency—to Self-Made Manhood—is the discursive curtain behind which White supremacy's exploitations of people of color hide. Olivia provides Fitz the opportunity to escape these coercions because it is his desire for her that exposes masculinity as a cultural deception. However, Fitz is pulled into multiple directions at once, and instead of imagining a way out, he draws on racialized gender tropes to Olivia's detriment, even if subconsciously, to salvage what he can of his sense of dominance and control in his relationships.

Fitzgerald Grant's masculinist dominance might be fixed within the institution of the presidency, but his status as a "man" is far more ephemeral. Craig defines masculinity as "what [our] culture expects of its men" (1992, 3). This definition is helpful insofar as the category "men" is treated as a stable one. However, masculinity is a fairly recent cultural notion; it is immeasurable, "always local and subject to change" (Brittan 2001, 51–52), multiple in its manifest performances (Connell 2005), and characteristically unattainable. The cultural assumption that masculinity is an innate, biological trait of "men" cannot be overstated. It is through this relationship that the volatility of masculinity renders the category "men" unstable. Indeed, groups of male-bodied people throughout American history have been denied access to recognition as "real" men and have found the social and economic privileges associated with the political category of "men" inaccessible (Shenk 1997; Tragos 2009; Hine and Jenkins 2001). That is, "men," rather than being synonymous with male-bodied people, constitute a political category dependent on the recognition of others.

Scholars have also begun using assemblage and affect theories to make the similar argument that gender or, more specifically for our purposes, "manhood," "masculinities," and "men" are emergent subjectivities (Day 2016, 122–27; Puar 2012; Thompson, Kitiarsa, and Smutkupt 2016). Rather than there being individual men, the category "men" is recognized as a consequence of sociopolitical subjectification. This distinction is an important one. There are at least two ways constructivists think of "men." One is as an "identity," defined by what a person *"does,* an active corralling of practices, events, desires, contingencies, and regulating semiotic and material operation" (Ferguson 1993, 159). In this sense, manhood is all about identity, even though, as constructivists understand, identity is itself a consequence of social forces rather than a prediscursive self that emanates from within the body (Butler 1999; Gannon, Gottschall, and Pratt 2013; Bourdieu 2001). We take no theoretical issue with this understanding of the category "men" or the topic of identity. However, our analysis focuses on a second way of thinking about "men," which is not centrally about identity but rather the processes of becoming that give social and political weight to identity. It is one thing to identify as a man and another thing to be recognized as such.

For us, then, men are structured consequences of social processes rather than ontological atoms. Therefore, we understand "men" as that group of people who are conferred all of the privileges accorded to that category in society, the most important of which is the power to dominate and to avoid being dominated (Hurtado 1996, 96; Lemons 2010, 207; Mosher and Tomkins 1988). Yet, as an assemblage, the status of being a man (that is, "manhood") is vulnerable to stabilization and destabilization, and because it is a political position rather than a biological trait, immediate and local power relations are the site through which to understand where and when men become men and to identify when their gender-political status is destabilized. We ask, then, when does a man cease to be a man, and what do the processes of (de)stabilization that produce such a change stand to teach scholars about masculinities?

Scandal's Fitzgerald Grant and his varied relationships present multiple opportunities to explore this question. Power struggles between President Grant and Cyrus, Big Jerry, Mellie, Rowan, and Olivia evince surpluses of emotional expression from Fitz, including frustration, anxiety, fear, and powerlessness. The flows of affect between Fitz and others often destabilize his sense of self-control and his capacity to dominate, rendering him vulnerable in ways that do not honor his identity as a man. In these moments, Fitz *unbecomes* a man—not in terms of his identity, but in terms of how he is recognized, politically, by the opposition he is at that moment sparring with. Ironically, it is Fitz's identity as a man that renders him vulnerable to this "misrecognition" (Fraser 1995; Fraser and Honneth 2003). For him, masculinity is, among other things, the earned right to dominance conferred to self-made men. Those individuals closest to him constantly reminded Fitz that he is not self-made and that he deserves no such honor. Although masculinists view manhood as embodied agency, we highlight the irony of such a claim: since men are subjects rather than self-made individuals, they can never attain what they perceive as agency and therefore, as long as they vest their identities in masculinity, are always at risk of being exposed as fraudulent men.

We read Fitz's relationships with Cyrus, Mellie, Big Jerry, Rowan, and Olivia attending to the ways the struggles over power between them expose Fitz's fragile grasp of his own sense of manhood and how his masculinity gets manipulated by others attempting to wrest power for themselves. Throughout the series, these characters have the greatest impact upon the construction and deconstruction of Fitz's manhood. Men such as David Rosen or Huck, although presenting masculinities that contrast Fitz's performance, do not engage him in ways that brings his identity to crisis. We conclude with a few thoughts about the character of Fitzgerald Grant as a critique of patriarchy while it may, unwittingly perhaps, reinforce masculinist ideologies.

Masculinities, Fragility, and Fraudulent Men

Masculinities, like the gender order of which they are constitutive components, tend toward crisis—iterative historical moments when it appears that men cease to be "men," failing to live up to the contemporary paradigm of manliness (Connell 2005; Gilbert 2005; Kimmel 2012). Masculinity, as a symbol in a gender system, is cultural chicanery—a "discursive . . . means by which 'sexed nature' or 'natural sex' is produced and established as 'prediscursive'" (Butler 1999, 10). In a quite circular and paradoxical way, masculinity is a culture's suggestion that men are inherently, yet must strive to be, "masculine," a "natural" and universal state of manly being. But as scholars have shown, allegedly immutable masculine traits mutate throughout history to adjust to structural and institutional transformations.

Until the late nineteenth century, manhood was understood as an internal quality that men possessed. It was the natural outgrowing of childhood for males; a boy became a man by becoming older and conquering the market. But when others could ostensibly enter and conquer the market too, already anxious White American men began looking to outward cultural characteristics to pacify their unease, and the language of masculinity was born. As opposed to manhood, masculinity "referred to a set of behavioral traits and attitudes that were contrasted now with a new opposite, *femininity*" (Kimmel 2008, 89). Instead of the urge to prove that one was a man, the new impetus became proving that one was not a woman. This fear of feminization led to new cultural forms in that manliness could be physically displayed as the power that emanated—and innately so—from the physical bodies of "men."

By analyzing gender as a system of symbols in historical context, we aim to avoid what might be a reductionist formulation that reinscribes masculinity as innately powerful and socially transcendent. We conceptualize the power that appears to accompany masculinity more acutely as access to tools of domination and echo Schippers's argument that the "significance of masculinity and femininity" is that their relationship "provides the legitimating rationale for social relations ensuring the ascendancy and dominance of men" (2007, 91). In a self-fulfilling way, patriarchal cultures view masculinity as inherently powerful in relation to feminine and feminized others because masculine subjects are proffered, through these gendered symbols, socially legitimated positions through which to subjugate and delegitimize the feminine.

But all masculinities are not created equal. After the transition from a discourse of manhood to one of masculinity, American men internalized the traits of masculinity so as to make it synonymous with manhood (Kimmel 2012). Now both manhood and masculinity were considered innate characteristics, and the challenge of American manhood became even more daunting. Connell describes "hegemonic masculinity" as the most ascendant, "culturally exalted" content of masculine performance at a given time in relation to other masculinities (2005, 38). This status, a "position" (I. M. Young 2003, 13), is one that grants certain men access to tools of coercion and control. In this sense, hegemonic masculinity appears as the most powerful symbol in the gender system. It allows for some men to subjugate other men and for all men to benefit from the subjugation of women—and for all these men to do so with the impression of "natural" legitimacy (Lorber 2001).

Yet even as hegemonic masculinity grants some men status positions in important institutions that allow them to make subjects out of others, these men do not themselves escape subjection. The gender system makes subjects out of sexed people, functioning as a "form of power [that] applies itself to immediate everyday life which categorizes the individual, marks him by his own individuality, attaches him to his own identity, imposes a law of truth on him which he must recognize and which others have to recognize in him" (Foucault 1982, 781). The masculine subject's gender is an identity that he believes is his "own," but that is, actually and invariably, an inherited, learned, performative sociohistorical subjectivity (Bourdieu 2001; Butler 1993). Therefore, even while hegemonic masculinity provides for the ascendancy of some men over other men and over women in general, the privileges it provides these men are given only within the system of gender and, in turn, compel men to perform "masculinity" to uphold the charade of gender itself. If power is "an action upon an action" (Foucault 1982, 789), the hegemonically masculine subject is himself dominated by the gender system, forced into compulsive (Pascoe 2011) and compulsory (Rich 1983) gendered performances even as he coerces others.

In patriarchal societies, masculinity is both the promise and the achievement of independence, individualism, authority, and control for and by men (Messerschmidt 1993). But "independence," "self-mastery," and "transcend[ence]" (Floyd 2009, 87) prove elusive, and men find themselves both incapable of incarnating hegemonic masculinity and powerless to escape their crippling fear that they will be "exposed as fraudulent men" (Kimmel 2008, 43). The identity "man," like all identities, "is a process involving an intensification of habituation" (Puar 2012, 62). That is, gender is a "conditioned subjectivity" shaped by socialization, the result of which is a disciplined sense of "self" that signifies to the subject and the society in which they live that their self is naturally occurring rather than socially constructed (and, as is often the case, socially mandated) (Schwalbe 2015, 64). While Fitz's words and behaviors fail to evince that he is aware that "manhood" is not a naturally emanating quality from his male body, his most intimate political interlocutors are not only mindful of the constructed nature of manhood, but also willing to target its pressure points to manipulate the president and thus assume some of the power of his position as their own. In the next section, we discuss the vulnerabilities in Fitz's identity and the implications it has for our understanding of masculinity as a position of power relative to other gender systems—namely, that it is not *always* powerful. The symbol of hegemonic masculinity within *Scandal* privileges men like Fitz to make decisions, give orders, and demand attention. However, these privileges do not grant Fitz the power to avoid coercion. Indeed, his privileges comes with debts to others. Because Fitz remains oblivious to the constructed nature of his manhood, Cyrus, Mellie, and Big

Jerry are able to routinely destabilize the president's identity by challenging his presumptions about himself.

Manhood as a Pressure Point in the Construction of the Self

As a gay man in American society, Cyrus faces a mismatch between his sexual and gender identities—specifically, no matter his gender performance, his masculinity is subordinated. Gay men have adapted to this subordinate position in many ways in American history, and many have taken the road Cyrus takes: hypermasculinity (Levine 1998). Yet as thoroughly masculine as he may be, Cyrus is not president. He tells James, "I would have been a great president. But guess what? I'm fairly short. And I'm not so pretty. And I really like having sex with men, so . . . I get to be the guy behind the president of the United States" ("Nobody Likes Babies" [2.13]). Cyrus's body and his sexuality are incompatible with the current articulation of hegemonic masculinity, so Cyrus exists in a liminal gendered space. He is a White man, but he does not have access to the office that he aspires to—the office that a person like Fitz can vie for. Instead, he becomes a "monster," a word he (and others) often uses to describe himself ("It's Handled" [3.01]; Benshoff 1997).

Cyrus and Fitz's gendered relationship is one between the monstrous and the man-child: Cyrus effectively locates Fitz's vulnerability and scares him into action while he also masks himself as Fitz's guardian and protector. He repeatedly misrecognizes Fitz as a child to shape the president's desires and to keep him grounded (in both senses of the word), and he does all of it to "steer the country" ("Nobody Likes Babies" [2.13]). When he learns that Fitz spent the night with Olivia, Cyrus lectures the president: "What did you do, throw pebbles at her window? Hide under her bed while her mom and dad came by her room, said good night?" Before Fitz learns of the election-rigging cover-up in "Defiance," Cyrus lectures him: "You were a flyboy with a good head of hair and a pushy dad. . . . You don't deserve this job" ("Grant: For the People" [1.07]). In Cyrus's estimation, Fitz looks the part but is still haunted by the destructive forces of his adolescent sexual desires and his father's emotional manipulations. As Cyrus frankly notes to James, "I already have a baby, and his name is President Fitzgerald Grant" ("The Other Woman" [2.02]). As a hypermasculine, predatory monster of sorts, Cyrus contrives a discursive strategy that grants him access to power. He manipulates Fitz, purposefully misrecognizes him as a child, justified, he feels, by Fitz's failures to fulfill his obligations as an adult man. Their relationship reveals that hegemonic masculinity is subject to manipulation through misrecognition, namely, because Fitz's identity is at risk of unraveling. What could be more frightening? The mandates of Fitz's gender identity as an adult man are the pressure points through which Fitz can be manipulated to fulfill the desires of others.

Mellie notices this vulnerability as well. In the context of his marriage, Fitz finds himself compelled by multiple options of masculine performance: he can practice honorable fidelity to his wife, he can demonstrate his manhood by touting his sexual access to women, or he can demonstrate his manly maturity and self-discipline by being "true" (Kimmel 2008, 8) to himself and his heart. Mellie exploits the vulnerability created by her husband's indecision and competing desires. She uses his desire for a masculine image suitable to his position as president to force him into a sexual relationship with her. This scheme serves the dual purpose of salvaging Fitz's political career by making him appear to fulfill the honorable masculinity associated with the presidency while punishing his marital infidelities by robbing him of sexual choice. To ensure that he rises to the occasion, Mellie publicly announces that she is pregnant before she conceives. This move makes Fitz the reactionary partner in the relationship, stripping him of the dominant position and illustrating that masculinity is not necessarily power. Although Mellie's sexual manipulation of Fitz proves his literal procreative virility, it renders his masculinity impotent by making him the subordinate partner in the relationship ("Grant: For the People" [1.7]).[1]

---

1. Of course, Mellie's manipulations do not free her from masculine dominance; she is compelled to her actions precisely because of her own subjection as

Thus, as a "man," Fitz is compelled to certain behaviors—required to reject his own fantasies and libidinal desires to reproduce in the interest of "the Republic," though probably just in the interest of maintaining his identity. And while Mellie and Cyrus surreptitiously manipulate Fitz's sense of self in order to wrest some power in an uneven system of gender for themselves, Big Jerry, already powerful, explicitly exposes the fiction of Fitz's manhood so as to make his own demands of the president. In season three, Jerry accuses Fitz of "run[ning] away to the Navy to get away from his daddy," something that a "real man" would never do. "You're a senator's son! You had a trust fund. You're a damn Grant!" Jerry roars, implying that Fitz owes his potential to the Grant family name and to Jerry's political success specifically. Jerry suggests that like status, wealth, and political power, masculine power is a racial, gender, class, and sexual inheritance. He stresses that in order to maintain that power Fitz must honor and submit to his family's legacy. "That's all you are," he bellows, "My son, not as smart, not as interesting, but my son just the same. I made you! I could destroy you. So you'll do what you're told, and that's an order" ("Everything's Coming Up Mellie" [3.07]).

Masculinity, rather than liberating Fitz, comes with the obligation of filial deference. Fitz chafes at this requirement, partly because he had no choice and partly because of his hatred for his father and his desire to establish his masculinity independent of Jerry's shadow. Fitz admits his frustration with his father's status affecting his ability to act on his of his own accord: "I aced flight school, top of my class, and because of you, they had me raising flags and shaking hands. They had me on a desk" ("Everything's Coming Up Mellie" [3.07]). Rejecting Jerry's concept of masculinity as *grant*ed and debt ridden, Fitz seeks to define his own manhood (Remmo 2009), but this attempt is precisely his folly. By failing to fully consider the implications of Jerry's proposal that manhood is constructed and therefore not necessarily

---

a woman. She exclaims to Olivia, "I have been destroyed while I have *made* him president" ("Flesh and Blood" [3.17]).

essential to his identity, every challenge to Fitz's manhood leads him to a crisis. And no one is as equipped to manipulate this threat to White-male identity as is Eli Pope—the selfsame manipulation that Rowan ultimately uses to end the series ("Over a Cliff" [7.18]).

The Deconstruction of White Masculinity's Alleged Agency

Eli Pope, known as Rowan to B613 and to Fitz, performs a Black masculinity in opposition to Fitz's hegemonic masculinity. Scholars of Black masculinities have convincingly argued that in racialized societies, men's gender performances are also racial performances (V. Young 2011; Carby 2000; Alexander 2006; Plath and Lussana 2009). Some have argued that Black masculinity is not merely a reaction to or a "parallel" of White masculinity, though they have cautioned, as is true in the case of Rowan, that it may be difficult to ascertain the ways Black men and Black women who identify as masculine understand themselves because they often maneuver their gender performances for public consumption in ways that may not reflect what gender means to them in private (Ross 2004, 6–9; Whitehead and Majors 2001; Neal 2013). That said, we understand Black masculinities to be multiple and may materialize in competing ways (Johnson 2003; Carby 2000; Rosengarten 1974; hooks 2004; Pelzer 2016; Harris, Palmer, and Struve 2011). Therefore, to speak of a singular Black masculinity, even in media, would be misleading (Harper 1998; Wallace 2002). Thus, Rowan performs *a* Black masculinity, and consciously so, in opposition to the White hegemonic masculinity that he detests in Fitz's character.

Rowan demonstrates an ability to assimilate within the existing racial-gender order, yet he consistently addresses structural racism in explicit and implicit terms, unsatisfied with the status quo as it denies recognition of his racialized manhood. Such invisibility angers him, for, as he argues, the Republic survives because of his labor— the unacknowledged, dirty, difficult, but necessary work performed through his Black body that makes "democracy . . . possible" ("It's Handled" [3.01]). Rowan's unspoken experiences have disadvantaged him in a White supremacist order and shape the ways he socialized Olivia as a child and how he continues to train her as an adult. Rowan repeatedly argues that his hard work has made both the life of the nation and his own manhood possible. His claim to Self-Made (Black) Manhood functions as a biting critique of the worth of White manhood in a society where hegemonic status is heritable and protected by White supremacist structures. Rowan deconstructs Fitz's masculinity, demonstrating it as a shield behind which Fitz's "manhood" hides. The relationship between Rowan's and Fitz's masculinities, then, is defined by Rowan's ability to perceive whiteness and hegemonic masculinity as co-constructed, though his critique somewhat mediated by both men's investment in racialized patriarchy.

Rowan's Black masculinity is a "hustle" (Schwalbe et al. 2000, 426) that reflects one way that marginalized masculine subjects cobble together recognition in a society that does not always value them. Despite the ugly nature of his work, Rowan is a proud man— "man" being an acquired status that, in a long monologue pervaded by racialized language, he defines for Fitz: "I have worked for every single thing I have ever received. I have fought and scraped and bled for every inch of ground I walk on" ("A Door Marked Exit" [3.10]). Rowan, ever attuned to the machinations of White supremacy, sees himself as a Self-Made Black Man and Fitz's manhood as pretense.

When Fitz attempts to use his sexual dalliances with Olivia to provoke Rowan, Rowan reminds Fitz that not only does sexual access to women fail to qualify him for status as a man, his position as president also fails to do the same: "You're a boy. You've been coddled and cared for, pampered and hugged. For you, it's always summertime and the livin' is easy. Daddy's rich! And your mama's good-lookin'. You're a Grant! You've got money in your blood! You are a boy" ("A Door Marked Exit" [3.10]). Like Cyrus and Jerry, Rowan reduces Fitz's successful approximation of hegemonic masculinity to his physical and economic inheritances. Skin color, height, hair, culture, and wealth have made Fitz appear to be a man, but unearned status, Rowan intimates, doth not a man make. Rowan exposes hegemonic masculinity as a cornerstone of White supremacy and identifies it as a weakness characterized by a lack of will, gratitude, and work. For Rowan it appears manhood is not nature's gift to all males; it must be achieved, not granted, to be worthy of respect.

Despite Fitz's insistent declarations that he is the "most powerful man on the planet" ("Crash and Burn" [1.05]), Rowan reminds Olivia, "He is never in charge. Power is in charge" ("White Hat's Back On" [2.22]). Rowan's philosophy reflects a paradox inherent in hegemonic masculinity: it is weakness masquerading as power, but when performed it grants certain men access to positions of privilege that afford them the power to dominate others. Thus, Rowan is not afraid to acknowledge Fitz as "a man with too much power" ("White Hat's Back On" [2.22]), even as he maintains that Fitz "never had any at all" ("A Door Marked Exit" [3.10]). Hegemonic masculinity, then, is powerful because, in the context of its relationship to other symbols of gender, race, class, and sexuality, it is able to grant its performers access to positions of privilege. But because, from Rowan's perspective, it is heritable rather than earned, those individuals who perform hegemonic masculinity fail to become Men—and Men, perhaps, are the only legitimate wielders of power in Rowan's world.[2] Rowan's seething contempt for Fitz is rooted in this critique of hegemonic masculinity, which exposes the symbol as a palimpsest of centuries-old White supremacy, White power, and White privilege, the performance of which allows "boys" to pretend to be agents constructing their own manhood. Hegemonic masculinity assures that men like Fitz will always be "coddled and cared for" by the labors of gendered others, even as the status of hegemonic dominance acts as a veil behind which those labors go unseen. The hegemonically masculine subject appears to be a Self-Made Man, but he is still merely a historical consequence, "an apple . . . never too far from the tree,"

---

2. Though we do not have the space to expound further, we would be remiss if we did not mention that Rowan's manhood is built against the interest of Black women's freedom—specifically his exploitation of Olivia's sexuality through Jake Ballard and his enslavement of Maya Lewis.

declaring his autonomy while being "pampered and hugged" ("A Door Marked Exit" [3.10]).

Exploiting Black Female Sexuality, Avoiding the Denaturalization of Gender

In contrast with his other relationships, Fitz represents himself as powerless in his relationship with Olivia, drawing on two well-established patriarchal tropes. The first trope naturalizes female inferiority. However, Fitz's relationship with Olivia disrupts the cultural narrative that men are born with traits considered to be "masculine." Troubled by his lack of self-control concerning Olivia, Fitz experiences many crises concerning his masculinity, but his love for her ostensibly provides Fitz a "door marked 'exit'" from the burden of proving his "natural" masculinity ("A Door Marked Exit" [3.10]). Yet instead of deconstructing gender ideology and its symbols of subjection, Fitz uses Olivia's Black sexuality as the foil to his White masculinity and effectively reinscribes the second, long-standing, trope: the hypersexualization of Black women. Far from eliding hegemonic masculine embodiment, Fitz resurrects, consciously or subconsciously, a White masculine construct that forgives its own shortcomings by "shift[ing] responsibility" for "the White man's infidelity" onto Black women's "passionate" sexuality (Jordan 1968, 151).

When Fitz and Olivia are together, viewers watch Fitz initiate frequent and passionate sexual interludes that show him as the dominant partner, mostly absent from his relationship with Mellie following her rape. Many of these intimate encounters have an air of recklessness to them. Fitz behaves as though he cannot control himself around Olivia; her sexuality is so spellbinding that he must have her regardless of the consequences. Even when he is furious with her over Defiance, his sexual attraction for Olivia remains. At Cyrus and James's house, Fitz pulls Olivia into a closet, and the two engage in an explicit tryst. As they exit the closet and Olivia expresses regret for her role in Defiance, Fitz refuses her apology and says, "I may not be able to control my erections around you, but that does not mean I want you. We are done" ("Whiskey Tango Foxtrot" [2.14]). Fitz's insistence that his "erections" are not indicative of his actual desires destabilizes the naturalness of male-female dualism. These so-called feminine traits— irrationality, concupiscence, and imprudence—seem constitutive of Fitz's self-identity in the context of his relationship with Olivia. To manage the masculine-feminine dissonance in this relationship, Fitz traffics in paradox.

Therefore, although Olivia represents an opportunity to do away with masculine-feminine dualism, her sexuality can also be exploited to explain away the realization that no natural relationship exists between expected gendered behaviors and sexed bodies. For example, Fitz's predicament exposes that self-control is not an innate masculine quality. This destabilization provides Fitz an opportunity to admit not only that he has failed to be a man, but that he does not want to be a man as it is socially defined. Instead, Fitz shirks personal responsibility, blaming his sexual practices and romantic desires on Olivia and on his body, as if his body were not him. He intimates that there is an inner, "honorable," and shameless man that exists prior to and despite his actions and that his failure to realize his allegedly true self is Olivia's fault. As he explains to her, in what he meant as a declaration of love, "You own me! You control me" ("Happy Birthday, Mr. President" [2.08]).

Love notwithstanding, Olivia's reference to Thomas Jefferson and Sally Hemings, which prompted Fitz's above confession, is fitting. Like Jefferson, Fitzgerald Grant's "libidinal desires, unacceptable and inadmissible to his society and to his higher self, [are] effectively transferred to others and thereby drained of their intolerable immediacy" (Jordan 1968, 459). Evidence suggests that Jefferson believed, as did many White Americans, that Black women's bodies were sites of sexual sin (Brown 2009; Gross 2006) and that the "ardent" and "animal" impulses (Jordan 1968, 459) contained within those bodies could supercharge the passions of honorable White men. Fitz feels self-disgust and disappointment for failing to resist Olivia—feelings of revulsion not unlike the ones that English colonists and early White Americans expressed when they succumbed to the alleged magnetism of Black sexuality (Jordan 1968).

As in his relationship with Jerry, Fitz tries to subvert the hegemonic masculine ideal that he dislikes by pursuing a path that he believes will release him from the gender structure. Unhappy in his marriage with Mellie and his responsibilities as president, Fitz seeks to "be a better man" in his love affair with Olivia ("Happy Birthday, Mr. President" [2.08]). Rather than finding his escape in Olivia's sexuality, however, Fitz once again remains bound to a conception of manhood and masculinity that, in its deployment, subjugates women's freedoms to the desires of men. By remaking the sexual subjugation of a Black woman, using her sexuality as the excuse for his infidelity, and disassociating mind (his desires) and body (his erections), a practice with such a lurid history in the United States, Fitz reasserts a hegemonic legacy that harks back centuries. Although Olivia represents the possibility for a refashioning of race and gender, Fitz remains invested in, and subjected by, the gendered order.

Indeed, as Catherine R. Squires describes in this collection's first chapter, rather than providing an escape out of White supremacist, heteronormative nationalism, "love" functions to discipline Fitz, Olivia, and others into subjecthoods that justify that selfsame nationalism and the impulses of imperialism. Fitz's love for Olivia does not valorize Black women's lives or their dignity; she is a symbol of liberal multiculturalism whereby Fitz and the nation appear tolerant and inclusive. Ultimately, however, both Fitz and "the Republic" would rather nullify their own freedom dreams than challenge the racist, sexist, and heterosexist structures that work to make Black people invisible and Black lives fungible. It is precisely this love for nation masked as a love for Olivia (and full democracy)—where the nation is conceived as a composition of White people and White power—that Rowan calls out, subverts, but also reinstates in the series finale ("Over a Cliff" [7.18]).

The Subjection of Fitz and the Restabilization of Masculinity

With Olivia seemingly out of reach at the end of *Scandal*'s fifth season, Fitz believes that his fail-safe, his "exit," is finally gone. All of the other relationships that have defined, constrained, and manipulated Fitz's identity as a man have changed as well: his father is dead, his son is dead, Mellie divorces him, Cyrus joins the political opposition by appending himself to another presidential candidate, and Rowan is the puppet master of nearly all this despair. So Fitz, unable to see any other possibilities, relents to his subjection as a hegemonic masculine figure in the gender system and decides that his access to power, with all its concomitant obligations and costs, must "mean something" ("No Sun on the Horizon" [3.13]). The presidency proved an effective seat from which to dominate others and coerce them into submission, exhibited most violently in the torture of Jake Ballard, Olivia's new beau and Fitz's old friend, but it failed to prove powerful in itself. It, like masculinity, was simply not a vehicle for realizing agency. Fitz's defeat echoes his realization in the first season that his position is at least as personally restrictive as it is politically liberating, when he says to his Secret Service agents, "I am the most powerful man on the planet." "Yes, sir," they answer. "But I can't leave my house," Fitz replies in disbelief. "No, sir" ("Crash and Burn" [1.05]). There he stood, a symbol in a system of hierarchy, most powerful, yet without agency.

Trapped in a gender system he did not create, but to which he actively contributes, Fitz is a subject forlorn. Mellie captures this crisis in manhood that troubles Fitz throughout his presidency and, indeed, his whole life:

> MELLIE: You are standing up here thumping your chest, reeling off your stats, chiseling yourself onto Mount Rushmore. Like you didn't stand on my back to get there—on Olivia's back, on Cyrus's, and your daddy's. I didn't have a $100 million trust fund, a political legacy. I didn't go to the best boarding schools on the planet, and I am not a White man. . . . You talk about what a great president you are, and yet you whined and cried about how much you hate the job every chance you got. . . . How privileged and entitled do you have to be to think of the most powerful office in the world as a prison? ("That's My Girl" [5.21])

Made and remade by those around him and historical circumstance, Fitz finds that the symbol he has come to embody, rather than freeing him, enslaves him. Payoffs, including wealth, status, and sexual access to women and other men, often appear to outweigh hegemonic masculinity's costs in ways that could perhaps only be dramatized in an artistic genre like television. Granted, Fitz is the most privileged person on *Scandal*. Thus, this is not an exercise in lamenting hegemonic masculinity, but rather an opportunity, especially for privileged persons, to imagine the freedom possibilities in a yet unseen society that disinvests in racial and gender subjection.

The writers of *Scandal* thereby expose the fragility of masculinity and the ways "men" are inevitably bound in the process of becoming and unbecoming men through interpersonal power struggles. In some ways, this is the kind of art that feminist scholars might hope for—the persistent destabilization of definitions of masculinity and the exposure of gender as a socially constructed caste system devoid of any so-called objective justification (Lorber 2001). Yet even as *Scandal* might be working to expose yet another historical crisis in masculinity, it may also be participating in the "hegemonic process" of redefining masculinity to render it "more adaptable to contemporary social conditions and more able to accommodate counter-hegemonic forces" (Hanke 1992, 197). Namely, Fitz's character, as troubled as he is, is still a hero, and his masculinity is still perhaps the most noble on the show.

Like the other characters, he has his own share of blood on his hands, but unlike them he is remorseful, finds no pleasure in killing, and makes no habit of it. His rejection of his father's and Hollis Doyle's abrasive masculinity of yesteryears, his embrace of a homonationalist Cyrus (Puar 2007; Hopkins 1996), and his willingness to sacrifice prestige for love configure him not as feminine but rather as redeemable. He is the antihero that the audience can love to hate but ultimately admire. He is "ironic," "fallible," and "antimasculine," though still a hero—a "new man" who consciously rejects the "executive aspiration" (Benwell 2002, 57). His fragility, rather than being a weakness, is merely a reflection of what it is like to be a real man—the man who watches on the other side of the television screen. Fitz's struggles, in this way, are less unsettling and more affirming. One thing remains clear: though Fitz suffers multiple crises involving his masculinity, even the writers never fail to mark him as a "man"; his sexuality is never ambiguous, and his status as president is never fully lost. Fitz's character lends flexibility to the way our culture defines and consumes masculinity, which might in turn make it less prone to such devastating crises as often (Kelley 2016; Mosse 1998, 191). Indeed, hegemonic masculinity itself remains firmly pitted in a system against the racialized and femininized other, and however malleable masculinity becomes, Fitz still gets to be president of the United States, with all its attendant privileges.

References

Alexander, Bryant Keith. 2006. *Performing Black Masculinity: Race, Culture, and Queer Identity*. Lanham, MD: AltaMira Press.

Benshoff, Harry M. 1997. *Monsters in the Closet: Homosexuality and the Horror Film*. Manchester: Manchester Univ. Press.

Benwell, Bethan. 2002. "Elusive Masculinities: Locating the Male in the Men's Lifestyle Magazine." In *Windows on the World: Media Discourse in English*, edited by Antonia Sánchez Macarro, 41–62. Valencia, Spain: Universitat de València.

Bourdieu, Pierre. 2001. *Masculine Domination*. Stanford, CA: Stanford Univ. Press.

Brittan, Arthur. 2001. "Masculinities and Masculinism." In *The Masculinities Reader*, edited by Stephen M. Whitehead and Frank J. Barrett, 51–55. Malden, MA: Polity.

Brown, Kathleen M. 2009. *Foul Bodies: Cleanliness in Early America*. New Haven, CT: Yale Univ. Press.

Butler, Judith. 1993. *Bodies That Matter: On the Discursive Limits Of "Sex."* New York: Routledge.

———. 1999. *Gender Trouble: Feminism and the Subversion of Identity*. New York: Routledge.

Carby, Hazel V. 2000. *Race Men*. Cambridge, MA: Harvard Univ. Press.

Connell, R. W. 2005. *Masculinities*. Berkeley: Univ. of California Press.

Craig, Steve. 1992. "Considering Men and the Media." In *Men, Masculinity and the Media*, edited by Steve Craig, 1–8. Newbury Park, CA: SAGE.

Day, Keri. 2016. *Religious Resistance to Neoliberalism: Womanist and Black Feminist Perspectives*. London: Palgrave Macmillan.

Ferguson, Kathy E. 1993. *The Man Question: Visions of Subjectivity in Feminist Theory*. Berkeley: Univ. of California Press.

Floyd, Kevin. 2009. *The Reification of Desire: Toward a Queer Marxism*. Minneapolis: Univ. of Minnesota Press.

Foucault, Michel. 1982. "The Subject and Power." *Critical Inquiry* 8(4): 777–95.

Fraser, Nancy. 1995. "Recognition or Redistribution? A Critical Reading of Iris Young's Justice and the Politics of Difference." *Journal of Political Philosophy* 3(2): 166–80.

Fraser, Nancy, and Axel Honneth. 2003. *Redistribution or Recognition? A Political-Philosophical Exchange*. London: Verso.

Gannon, Susanne, Kristina Gottschall, and Catherine Camden Pratt. 2013. "'A Quick Sideways Look and Wild Grin': Joyful Assemblages in Moments of Girlhood." *Girlhood Studies* 6(1): 13–29.

Gilbert, James. 2005. *Men in the Middle: Searching for Masculinity in the 1950s*. Chicago: Univ. of Chicago Press.

Gross, Kali N. 2006. *Colored Amazons: Crime, Violence, and Black Women in the City of Brotherly Love, 1880–1910*. Durham, NC: Duke Univ. Press.

Hanke, Robert. 1992. "Redesigning Men: Hegemonic Masculinity in Transition." In *Men, Masculinity and the Media*, edited by Steve Craig, 185–98. Newbury Park, CA: SAGE.

Harper, Phillip Brian. 1998. *Are We Not Men? Masculine Anxiety and the Problem of African American Identity*. New York: Oxford Univ. Press.

Harris, Frank, III, Robert T. Palmer, and Laura E. Struve. 2011. "'Cool Posing' on Campus: A Qualitative Study of Masculinities and Gender Expression among Black Men at a Private Research Institution." *Journal of Negro Education* 80(1): 47–62.

Hine, Darlene Clarke, and Ernestine Jenkins, eds. 2001. *A Question of Manhood: A Reader in U.S. Black Men's History and Masculinity*. Vol. 2, *The 19th Century: From Emancipation to Jim Crow (Blacks in the Diaspora)*. Bloomington: Indiana Univ. Press.

hooks, bell. 2004. *We Real Cool: Black Men and Masculinity*. New York: Routledge.

Hopkins, Patrick D. 1996. "Gender Treachery: Homophobia, Masculinity, and Threatened Identities." In *Rethinking Masculinity: Philosophical*

Explorations in Light of Feminism, edited by Larry May, Robert Strikwerda, and Patrick D. Hopkins. Lanham, MD: Rowman and Littlefield.

Hurtado, Aída. 1996. *The Color of Privilege: Three Blasphemies on Race and Feminism*. Ann Arbor: Univ. of Michigan Press.

Johnson, E. Patrick. 2003. *Appropriating Blackness: Performance and the Politics of Authenticity*. Durham, NC: Duke Univ. Press.

Jordan, Winthrop D. 1968. *White over Black: American Attitudes toward the Negro, 1550–1812*. Chapel Hill: Univ. of North Carolina Press.

Kelley, N. Megan. 2016. *Projections of Passing: Postwar Anxieties and Hollywood Films, 1947–1960*. Jackson: Univ. Press of Mississippi.

Kimmel, Michael S. 2008. *Guyland: The Perilous World Where Boys Become Men*. New York: Harper.

———. 2012. *Manhood in America: A Cultural History*. 3rd ed. New York: Oxford Univ. Press.

Lemons, Gary L. 2010. "Learning to Love the Little Black Boy in Me: Breaking Family Silences, Ending Shame." In *African Americans Doing Feminism: Putting Theory into Everyday Practice*, edited by Aaronette M. White, 189–211. Albany, NY: SUNY Press.

Levine, Martin P. 1998. *Gay Macho: The Life and Death of the Homosexual Clone*. Edited by Michael Kimmel. New York: New York Univ. Press.

Lorber, Judith. 2001. *Gender Inequality: Feminist Theories and Politics*. 2nd ed. New York: Oxford Univ. Press.

Messerschmidt, James W. 1993. *Masculinities and Crime: Critique and Reconceptualization of Theory*. Lanham, MD: Rowman and Littlefield.

Mosher, Donald L., and Silvan S. Tomkins. 1988. "Scripting the Macho Man: Hypermasculine Socialization and Enculturation." *Journal of Sex Research* 25(1): 60–84.

Mosse, George L. 1998. *The Image of Man: The Creation of Modern Masculinity*. New York: Oxford Univ. Press.

Neal, Mark Anthony. 2013. *Looking for Leroy: Illegible Black Masculinities*. New York: New York Univ. Press.

Pascoe, C. J. 2011. *Dude, You're a Fag: Masculinity and Sexuality in High School*. Berkeley: Univ. of California Press.

Pelzer, Danté L. 2016. "Creating a New Narrative: Reframing Black Masculinity for College Men." *Journal of Negro Education* 85(1): 16–27.

Plath, Lydia, and Sergio Lussana, eds. 2009. *Black and White Masculinity in the American South, 1800–2000*. Cambridge: Cambridge Scholars.

Puar, Jasbir K. 2007. *Terrorist Assemblages: Homonationalism in Queer Times.* Durham, NC: Duke Univ. Press, 2007.

———. 2012. "'I Would Rather Be a Cyborg than a Goddess': Becoming-Intersectional in Assemblage Theory." *PhiloSOPHIA* 2(1): 49–66.

Remmo, Clyde J. 2009. "Understanding Masculinity: The Role of Father-Son Interaction on Men's Perceptions of Manhood." PhD diss., Univ. of Denver.

Rich, Adrienne. 1983. "Compulsory Heterosexuality and Lesbian Existence." In *Powers of Desire: The Politics of Sexuality*, edited by Ann Snitow, Christine Stansell, and Sharon Thompson, 177–205. New York: Monthly Review Press.

Rosengarten, Theodore. 1974. *All God's Dangers.* New York: Knopf Doubleday.

Ross, Marlon Bryan. 2004. *Manning the Race: Reforming Black Men in the Jim Crow Era.* New York: New York Univ. Press.

Schippers, Mimi. 2007. "Recovering the Feminine Other: Masculinity, Femininity, and Gender Hegemony." *Theory and Society* 36(1): 85–102.

Schwalbe, Michael. 2015. *Manhood Acts: Gender and the Practices of Domination.* New York: Routledge.

Schwalbe, Michael, Sandra Godwin, Daphne Holden, Douglas Schrock, Shealy Thompson, and Michele Wolkomir. 2000. "Generic Processes in the Reproduction of Inequality: An Interactionist Analysis." *Social Forces* 79 (2): 419–52. doi:10.2307/2675505.

Shenk, Gerald E. 1997. "Race, Manhood, and Manpower: Mobilizing Rural Georgia for World War I." *Georgia Historical Quarterly* 81(3): 622–62.

Thompson, Eric C., Pattana Kitiarsa, and Suriya Smutkupt. 2016. "From Sex Tourist to Son-in-Law: Emergent Masculinities and Transient Subjectivities of *Farang* Men in Thailand." *Current Anthropology* 57(1): 53–71.

Tragos, Peter. 2009. "Monster Masculinity: Honey, I'll Be in the Garage Reasserting My Manhood." *Journal of Popular Culture* 42(3): 541–53.

Wallace, Maurice O. 2002. *Constructing the Black Masculine: Identity and Ideality in African American Men's Literature and Culture, 1775–1995.* Durham, NC: Duke Univ. Press.

Whitehead, Stephen M., and Richard Majors. 2001. "Cool Pose: Black Masculinity and Sports." In *The Masculinities Reader*, edited by Stephen M. Whitehead and Frank Barrett, 209–18. Malden, MA: Polity.

Young, Iris Marion. 2003. "The Logic of Masculinist Protection: Reflections on the Current Security State." *Signs* 29(1): 1–25.

Young, Vershawn A. 2011. "Compulsory Homosexuality and Black Masculine Performance." *Poroi* 7(2): 1–20.

16 | "I Can't Fix This"

Reflections on *Scandal*'s Racial Commentary
in the "Lawn Chair" Episode

RONALD L. JACKSON II, KIMBERLY R.
MOFFITT, AND SIMONE ADAMS

THE INTERNATIONALLY ACCLAIMED television show *Scandal*
has always made a point not only to serve as a fictional hyperdrama
for its fan base (Paskin 2014), but also about the political reality
of the United States with its story lines of art imitating life (Puff
2015). One of the most discussed and controversial moments in the
show's history was the "Lawn Chair" episode, which aired on March
5, 2015, during its fourth season. This episode appeared within
months of a release of reports documenting nationwide police brutality that led to the death of more than one hundred unarmed
Black people in 2015 alone ("Mapping Police Violence"). With that
regularity, Black people have gone beyond disenchanted and frustrated to express complete distrust and heightened anger against law
enforcement. The Black Lives Matter (BLM) movement began with
a hashtag in July 2013, after the acquittal of George Zimmerman, a
private citizen acting as a neighborhood watch coordinator who had
shot and killed unarmed Black teenager Trayvon Martin in 2012.
The hashtag and the movement quickly spread across the country,
turning its focus from state-sanctioned violence against Black people
in general to the endemic problem of police brutality against Black
men and women as well as Black trans and gender-nonconforming

people. Among other things, the BLM movement gripped the country between January 2014 and August 2015, serving as a catalyst to more than one hundred university antiracist campus protests ("The Demands"). This rising discontentment was at a fever pitch on campuses and in local communities, and there was no sign of relief for Black people across the United States. Even after this episode of *Scandal* aired in March, the conditions only worsened, with subsequent police-involved shootings such as the killing of Sam DuBose on July 19, 2015, by a University of Cincinnati campus police officer. This kind of horrific violence represents a climate that has continued to set the conditions for activists' responses across the country. Given this climate, the authors thought it was critical to engage in an open dialogue about the episode and its connection to contemporary racial discourses.

RON JACKSON: What is the "Lawn Chair" episode really about, and what are they trying to teach us or show us?

SIMONE ADAMS: I'm going to go with what Shonda Rhimes said in a tweet the night the episode aired. She said: "In the end, we went with showing what fulfilling the dream SHOULD mean. The idea of possibility. And NOT the despair we feel now." If we take this statement, I think the episode is about restoring the ideals of the American dream in a sense, the idea that everyone has access to the same rights and opportunities. It's the Jeffersonian ideal of life, liberty, and the pursuit of happiness and that justice will be served in the end. But of course, as we all know, this dream is nothing but a romanticized version of American history. And I think for far too many Black and Brown folks in this country, the American dream has rather turned into the American nightmare, as Malcolm X famously said.

So, for me, the episode is in many ways simplifying the issue of a Black male teenager shot by a White police officer with an ending where everything is resolved with poetic justice. We even find that the cop turns out to be this hideous racist, this bigot who is held accountable for his actions. On the flip side, the teenager is exonerated, even if only posthumously, and his father's grief is acknowledged by the president of the United States. I remember the final scene where President Grant (played by Tony Goldwyn) embraces the father Clarence Parker (played by Courtney B. Vance). There's a tear-jerking moment for the audience—but we all know that reality doesn't look like that. But overall, I believe that when we look at Shonda Rhimes's tweet, what she is saying to us is what the dream should look like.

RON JACKSON: It's interesting that you say that because I also thought about that moment where you see the Courtney Vance character being embraced by the president. And as he's being embraced, one of the things that he does is he leans in and says to the president, "His name was Brandon." I think that this episode really tried to acknowledge the work around naming. I think that that's probably one of those little small interstitial dynamics that we can kind of overlook in the episode because what it does is disallow us from forgetting the fundamental act of naming victims while simultaneously acknowledging the violence done to them. Like, for example, with the Michael Brown case, that became known as Ferguson. People slipped and forgot the name of the person whose life was taken while the media circulated the name of a city where it happened. There is further violence done to the victim, their family, and their community when we fail to somehow remember the name.

This reminds me of the campaign or movement that was launched by the African American Policy Forum. They've actually called this movement #SayHerName because it's really about trying to reclaim the names of these victims and their lives as something that is really special, and we can't take away the humanity of this person's life by trying to make it seem like their lives are just objects or generic pinpoints in history. Critical race theorist Kimberlé Crenshaw is one of the founders of this movement and talks about how important #SayHerName is as a way of memorializing individuals like Sandra Bland, Rekia Boyd, Miriam Carey, Mya Hall, Shantel Davis, Shelly Frey, and all the other women whose lives were lost through anti-Black police brutality. Their stories often don't get told in narratives on police brutality and racism, which historically have focused on Black and Brown men, hence the focus on gender and saying "her" name.

So I think that the importance of naming is one thing that this episode is about, and I also think that it is about a way in which we have to challenge our own sense of moral and social agency. It suggests that in a time when we collectively imagine ourselves as indignantly righteous around issues of social justice, we also are paralyzed around the state apparatus. We don't know how to advance our social justice imperatives. We do it through various means, but in many ways, we are like the extras during this episode who stand around watching as though we are voyeurs rather than citizens who, in defense of OUR collective community, are obliged to act.

We oftentimes don't know what to do when the state apparatus doesn't want to acknowledge or value us as marginalized beings. In the same way the Trump administration is currently pursuing its agenda around issues of immigration, and many other issues, most people are complaining in little private coffee-side conversations, but they're not really doing the work of trying to gather together and push against the apparatus in a way that really moves toward change.

I think this episode highlights this tragically interesting epidemic where we've seen people like Sandra Bland, Trayvon Martin, Tanisha Anderson, John Crawford, and hundreds of other people who were unarmed Black folks lose their lives since 2012. This particular episode tries to explore how we actually make sense of this in a country that's supposed to be about democracy, fairness, equity, and justice.

And so I agree with you, Simone, that this is really, in many ways about the American ideals and how we retrieve custody over those meanings associated with what it means to be ideally American. I think that the "Lawn Chair" episode is really about the crisis of moral turpitude and social agency. It basically says to us that there is this time in which we imagine ourselves to be postracial, yet we have this stain of patriarchy called racism that remains and is manifested via racial profiling and police brutality against Black men. Police brutality and its almost singular focus on Blacks are what conspicuously reveal the racist underpinnings of these sanctioned acts of violence. This episode of *Scandal* tries to help us grapple with the complexity of and tragedy in this very real national concern.

KIMBERLY MOFFITT: What I find interesting about this episode is I still feel like even though it turns out the way that I personally would like it to, I feel as though it is Shonda Rhimes's attempt to show us the level of complexity that exists in these cases, recognizing that there are multiple sides to the story. This affords us the chance to slow down the frame and be able to hear and see what the experience of a police officer may be versus that of a parent versus that of, in this case, a victim who was presumed to be the culprit.

I also find it interesting that Rhimes attempted to strike a balance, recognizing who her audience is. She could have taken an approach that sounded as though it was more in line with how Black America might look at this issue, but she understood it was not the only way that she could do so. I felt like she needed to show greater complexity—because she recognized that there were a number of other members of her audience that didn't look like the victim and his family and recognized that there needed to be an understanding of what might be the possibility for us to see it in a different vein.

Now even though I felt like she attempted to strike that balancing act, I also recognize in terms of how social media responded to her, that a number of people were angry she brought this particular political issue into the entertainment realm. Perhaps that segment of her audience would have preferred to see Olivia Pope on the couch with her popcorn and glass of wine processing her day of saving the world inside the Beltway. But here was a real-life issue that Americans are dealing with that was brought into their homes in ways that I feel like some of her audience had a visceral reaction to. They seemed to respond like, "Why is she doing this to us? Why is she messing with the reality that we've created?"

Going back specifically to the episode, I felt like what was given to us was this hour of suspended reality rather than the true reality we have all experienced in which we continue to think about all of these other victims who have lost their lives as a result of police brutality.

But, in this one hour, Shonda Rhimes allows us to imagine this American ideal or this American dream that we aspire to.

I also think it's interesting to revisit the final moment between the two dads, because I think that's what has to be remembered, even though we're talking about the father of the victim and the president of the United States. In that moment, we're also talking about two dads. And in that moment, we're also talking about two dads who have experienced a loss of a child, in different ways, clearly, but it's still a form of loss. They as men are finding a way to grapple with or deal with that loss.

I suspect Shonda Rhimes decided to have that as part of this episode as a way to link with Barack Obama's comments about the fact that Trayvon Martin could have been his child. And so just like what Barack Obama did in making the comments about Trayvon Martin, here we have President Grant also coming into this space to offer commentary about what he feels and believes is the experience of this particular dad's grief.

RON JACKSON: If this episode is about police brutality, then let's talk about why the focus has been on Black masculinity. I mean, why not talk about people like Sandra Bland? I guess the question here really is about what is so special or peculiar about Black masculinity in America, and maybe we can talk a little bit about characters that this particular show tries to unveil for us and why Black masculinity matters in America.

From my standpoint, the episode is about police brutality, but it's about something greater than that. It's about our collective responsibility. It's about how we all have a sense of humanity that needs to be acknowledged and valued, regardless of our race, culture, or gender.

So, I do think that the episode kind of reaches more broadly, but I do understand as well that it takes advantage of the zeitgeist that is about what happens when we look at cases like Michael Brown's death or that of Eric Garner or any of the many other individuals that were high-profile police brutality cases, most of whom were Black males. I think what's so peculiar or special about Black masculinity as it relates to *Scandal* is that each of its characters who are Black and who are male seem to have a very interesting set of conflicts, dualities, and flaws that are very peculiar to that particular person.

Let's just start, for example, with Papa Pope (played by the actor Joe Morton). He is essentially the boogeyman of the entire series. Every time we see him we know that he's up to something. We know that he's done something. We know that he is in control or at least imagines himself to be and that there is probably violence involved. We also know that we are to essentially fear him.

We are intrigued by him, yet we must also fear him because we know that he is able to rationalize his malignant behavior as something that has been stimulated by the noble goal of protecting the state. He is always trying to protect either Olivia, the White House, or both at all times and at all costs. This presents an interesting conflict or duality as it relates to what we imagine in the public in real life, which is that the Black male works or operates independently except in gangs, and does not care much at all about the state. In fact, the public narrative is that Black males tend to be constantly in direct rebellion against the state; hence, police brutality is warranted to keep their volatility in check.

As I stated, each of the characters who are Black and who are male seem to have this very interesting dynamic, with maybe the exception being Edison Davis (played by Norm Lewis), who is the senator who seems to be all in for the state. There is the character named Marcus Walker (played by Cornelius Smith Jr.) who is an activist that in later seasons becomes a Gladiator on Olivia Pope's team and then eventually serves as Mellie's chief campaign confidant and fling before taking a post as press secretary under Fitz's presidential administration. It's interesting that in each part we see him strongly resisting, but always in search of more power. It's kind of fascinating to think about how stereotyping of Black masculinity gets revealed through these characters. And it's also clear that Shonda Rhimes's signature is that she makes sure we understand the human complexity of all these characters.

KIMBERLY MOFFITT: I think that's what I like most about how the characters who are Black and male on the show are represented. We do get to see a level of complexity of how they can be. Even in unpacking police brutality, Rhimes allows us the space to explore that complexity because so much attention has been placed on the victims who are Black and male. Her focus on police brutality via *Scandal* gives us the chance to show the humanness of those victims, and she does a great job of that in this particular episode. She shows how the police and political officials' PR plan pertaining to the slain victim is to portray him as a typical street thug who has to be reeled in or confined. The sad part is that this narrative has been told so much by media that it is now believable. In this episode, the reality is Brandon Parker turns out to be an upstanding citizen who was stereotypically profiled.

I think in many instances, Black men are "enemy number one" for the state, and so here we have an opportunity in this episode, but also in the show in general, to see just how complex Black men can be. Yes, you can have someone like Papa Pope, who clearly is the boogeyman. When I think of him, I always go back to your work, Ron, in *Scripting the Black Masculine Body* when you write about the voice-over in a toothpaste commercial that warns against the "evil plaque man," where clearly the plaque man is also being represented as a Black man and signifies something that is duplicitous and has to be done away with before he brings us to ruins.

But here it is, we've got Papa Pope who seems to be that same type of boogeyman, but he also evokes so much compassion and commitment to those that are important to him. He relentlessly loves while also embodying much of what he sees to be negative in nature.

SIMONE ADAMS: I agree with what you both have said in terms of the complexity of the Black male characters on this show. I want to push back on something that Ron said earlier, and maybe I misheard that, but Ron you were saying when we talk about police brutality most of the victims were Black males, right? But that reminded me of your earlier reference to Kimberlé Crenshaw and the #SayHerName campaign. I think historically we've never heard as much about Black women in either their victimization by racism or their fight against it, so the voices that were centered were always those of Black men. This practice continues to this day.

And so to return to the earlier part of the question regarding why the focus is all about Black masculinity, even with this episode that centers on police brutality, I think it occurs because Shonda Rhimes reflects on this lack of understanding of the intersections of race, gender, class, and sexuality and how structural oppression oftentimes multiplies based on what intersections we inhabit. For example, when we think about the numerous transgender people of color who are victims of institutionalized racism, we might realize we don't ever hear from them. That's why we need campaigns like #SayHerName and #BlackTransLivesMatter to shed light on this.

I appreciate all of the TV shows that have picked up on this issue of police brutality and the Black Lives Matter movement. The ABC sitcom *Black-ish*, for example, also did an episode on police brutality and the illusion of a postracial America and explored how difficult it is to discuss this as a Black family, let alone as a broader multicultural community. To my knowledge, the show *Being Mary Jane*, which ran on BET, was the only show that so far featured a Black female character who experienced unjust and excessive violence at the hands of law enforcement, and they explored that from a woman's point of view, even if only briefly.

In other words, I think what we're seeing on television is reflecting what's happening in real life. By that I mean that the voices of Black women and Black trans folk are not often centered in either place. *Scandal* is one of the exceptions here: while the victim of police brutality is still a Black man on the show, with the focus on Olivia Pope we see the agency of a Black woman as the center of the resistance, and I agree with Ron that that is one of the reasons it has successfully compelled so many viewers.

RON JACKSON: Great point. I think you're exactly right, and my comment about police brutality was that these are the high-profile cases. But I agree with you entirely that it is in fact this sort of oversight, really recognizing that this violence happens across gender, race, and cultures, that further entrenches the problem. In fact, we'd like to believe it's only happening to Black males, yet the reality is it's happening to Black and Brown peoples all over the country. Yet I think at this moment in time, what episodes like this one seem to be pointing out to us is that for our country, to be Black and to be masculine is to always be the perennial target, the endangered species, and that seems to not really be going away. It gets reflected even in the outcomes of these cases where uneven sentencing leads to overcrowding of the prison system. And, of course, we know about Michelle Alexander's work on *The New Jim Crow* and how she really documents it. These inequitable kinds of treatment really become a reverberation of structural inequalities we see every day.

So thinking about that, what is your personal reaction to this episode?

SIMONE ADAMS: Well, I commend Shonda Rhimes and the *Scandal* cast for essentially going there and bringing these difficult and important conversations on race into our living rooms. Yet I will say that I was disappointed how simplistic the story line turned out to be in the end.

What this episode boils down to is that a racist White cop shoots an unarmed, honest Black teenager, and Olivia Pope swoops in, uncovers all the racism and bias, and saves the day and posthumously the teenager's reputation. She makes sure that justice is served, but a life has still been taken.

At some point in the episode she says, "I can't fix this." This is when I was hoping there would be more of a complex take on this issue because it's not easily fixed. Yes, we have a sense of what Kimberly mentioned earlier, a suspended reality, and I guess that works for an hour of television, but at the same time, she handles it just like she handles all her other cases. And I do understand that the idea behind this episode was to get people talking about it, and, as Kimberly mentioned, Rhimes had to take into account the racially diverse audience on ABC. I mean, this isn't a show that airs on BET. But at the same time, I still think that the episode could have portrayed a more nuanced image of structural racism in law enforcement. It doesn't take an openly bigoted police officer to engage in racial profiling or to make somehow racially motivated choices when it comes to interacting with Black and Brown people in this country. We all know from recent law enforcement reports and official investigations that came out in cities like Ferguson, Baltimore, and Chicago, structural bias and systemic racism exist on a larger scale, particularly against African Americans, all the way from policing to what happens in the courts.

So for me, while I was moved at the end, and, I guess, most of the fan base was, I couldn't help but feel the sense of frustration because I know of too many instances when the media dug up the victim's conflicted pasts in an attempt to somehow justify the person's killing. It happened to Michael Brown. It happened to Eric Garner and to Freddie Gray, and so many others. None of them were any different from this fictional Brandon Parker, but we didn't get that aspect on the screen. And that's where my frustration was in the end. That it was just all too easy, that Olivia Pope fixed it, after all.

KIMBERLY MOFFITT: I hear Simone's point loud and clear, and I think there is significant validity to what you're saying. I wonder, however, thinking of this through the lens of media studies, whether anyone would be able to convey the subtleties of racial bias in a one-hour program that is established for entertainment. I feel like in the entertainment sphere, it is much more difficult to demonstrate or highlight those nuances in ways we might experience on a daily basis.

That's because the three-dimensional character of these experiences helps us as marginalized beings to see how each links to the other. In this hour-long program Rhimes had to account for a diverse audience that might not understand all of those nuances. Simone, I'm wondering if that's why she decided to take the approach she did in this episode instead of trying to reflect the sordid reality. Perhaps it was just too difficult to convey in an hour-long program.

I can easily imagine an audience viewing this episode and saying it is more of the same and wanting to reread it as something different or wanting to suggest that particular populations (in this case, those persons of African descent) are reading too much into something rather than allowing alternative explanations.

In this case, because you've got a racist cop, the situation is so much more apparent. Consequently, that allows showrunner Shonda Rhimes to justify the actions that are taken in the episode, whereas if it were more subtle, I don't know if it would have been as well received or understood by her diverse audience.

When I think about programs like this I almost immediately think about my thirteen-year-old son. Despite his age, as a Black mother, I worry about him more now than I did when he was three years old. At three years old, he was so adorable. Everyone wanted to be in his midst. It didn't matter what particular race or background that someone was, everyone wanted to embrace my child. But as he's aged, which is exactly what the research tells us, things have changed dramatically. I mean the American Psychological Association study back in 2014 revealed to us that Black children in this country essentially lose that idea of childhood innocence at the age of nine, that their childhood innocence gets taken from them very early because society starts to look upon these children as more adultlike or having actions that are more adultlike, and we engage them in that way instead of as a nine-, ten-, or eleven-year-old child. And so for me, as he's grown, I worry more and more because I think about how that same three-year-old that was so adorable to everyone has now become a thirteen-year-old that segments of our population are suspicious of, that may render him guilty without even recognizing the context for whatever situation might have emerged. He is not given the benefit of the doubt but instead is typecasted and considered a threat just by the sheer presence of his body, his Black skin.

That is what kept coming up for me as I watched the program. I find myself worrying about how this episode might work to change the way in which we view the world for our boys because it becomes a part of their reality and not something that is just on-screen for us to digest in an hour-long program.

RON JACKSON: I think you both make very compelling points, and to be quite frank, as I watch this episode I feel like it is asking me to engage in a willing suspense of disbelief. Although I am enticed to imagine it as real, it looks quite artificial to me. I mean that I've seen plenty of cases, even in the past couple of years, where a White male walks on a college campus or walks out in public with a gun and waves it around, and the police talk with him politely, approach him with a sense of humanity, and ask him to settle down and leave the premises. But I have never seen a case where a Black male waves a shotgun around in a downtown area or a very busy street, and the police just sort of surround him and ask him to please put it down and subsequently try to have a rational conversation.

In fact, our collective experience has shown us quite the opposite. We have been socialized to expect the result to be more like what happened to Amadou Diallo in 1999, who was shot at forty-one times, with nineteen bullets hitting him, by four New York City police officers, all of whom were later acquitted of all charges. So the episode plays with an alternative world where Black males are privileged to be treated as ordinary citizens who deserve rights.

My willing suspension of disbelief is intercepted by thoughts of John Crawford, the Black male killed at Walmart for supposedly waving a gun at children when in fact he was simply talking on a cell phone. The gun he had was one he was ready to purchase at Walmart, and it didn't even have any bullets in it, yet he was shot to death. The *Scandal* "Lawn Chair" episode seems to artistically play around with the idea of equitable treatment to bring the dramatic point that these police brutality cases are complex and come with different angles. For example, we get to see the perspectives of a parent who is fed up, Olivia Pope as the PR fixer, the federal government and state apparatus and their political worries, and we get to see how all these different angles come to bear in this particular situation.

After watching the episode, I was left feeling empty about the possibilities for racial progress because I did not feel that it helped me to address what's real, and so I wanted to know what resources

I can reasonably use in a real-life situation. I'm not going to have an Olivia Pope standing there. There's not going to be this activist who gets somehow in this direct conversation with Olivia Pope. The police department is not always going to easily agree to stand down and publicly put one of their officers on the line as a racist.

First of all, in real life I'm going to be shot if I publicly wave a gun on a busy street, so I can't even have a gun and I can't just set a chair in the middle of the street to seek justice. The cops are going to get me off the street first. I'm going to be swept away quickly, and it will have been a relatively quick and meaningless kind of activity in a very short period of time. So I just find the episode's premise to be incredulous. Nonetheless, when I am truly willing to simply watch the episode as the fiction it is, I find it to be an interesting portrayal. I think that it made some really good points. I think that if the viewer is willing to suspend their disbelief, it had value. But that's asking a lot of viewers who experience this systemic violence on a daily basis, especially Black males.

KIMBERLY MOFFITT: Yes, but you know what's interesting, I think it is a lot to ask of Black males, but I think it's also something Black males desired. Because even as adults who are dealing with this issue, we're looking for ways to process our own trauma. And even if in that suspended reality for only an hour, I think so many of us were appreciative to say, "Finally, there is something that shows this is a reality for us, and it can have an ending that shows our worth does mean something to the state apparatus and there can be consequences for it." I feel as though in that moment, so many of us were appreciative of this outcome so that we could have our moment to exhale, even if it was just for that moment.

RON JACKSON: The situation comedy *Black-ish* did a much better job, in my mind. I felt like they at least made it real; they spoke to the real issues. I guess there is some value in authenticity especially with the situation being so dire. It really has consequences around life and death. I agree people want reprieve, and they want to be heard and represented properly. They wanted to see a treatment like this one. They wanted to hear conversations. They wanted to heighten the conversation to something broader that goes beyond a "Black Lives Matter" movement. It's a significant act. I just don't know that we can say that any action is substantial action.

So let me ask you this: From your understanding, how did people react to the episode? I mean, at the same time it was released, what was happening? We know, for example, people were having watch parties, forming marches, and so on. There were Facebook conversations, and I guess people were asking about what sort of license, or set of risks, this particular episode tried to take and whether it was art imitating reality. What are your thoughts about it?

SIMONE ADAMS: I know from some of the conversations I saw on Twitter that night, that for some viewers it felt like too much too soon, but there were also a large number of viewers who said they felt validated.

I think for some viewers it was too much too soon because, as you may recall, this episode aired in March 2015 and, we had seen so many high-profile cases in the media since the police killing of Michael Brown. This graphic image of the dead Black boy lying in the street, similar to how Mike Brown's body was lying dead in the street for hours in Ferguson, seemed in a way too close to reality for some. And at the same time, I also remember a lot of praise for the episode based on the fact that, up until that point, the character of Olivia Pope had rarely engaged with her blackness on the screen. We only got brief glimpses into Olivia's racial politics before. It was, as one of you said earlier, this ideal of a "postracial" world, but with the "Lawn Chair" episode, her character literally and figuratively changes sides, if only briefly. She moves from working for the state and the predominantly White establishment to joining ranks with the Black protesters and Marcus Walker as a community activist. Meanwhile, there is this very real backdrop of protesters demanding an end to police brutality and racial profiling by chanting on the streets of Washington, DC. She's literally crossing the police tape in that scene. She even goes so far as to defend the people's rights to protest and to free speech and assembly. I recall that one scene when she speaks to the White DC police department chief and explains that the fact that protesters stand in groups and say things the police do not like doesn't make them a mob; it makes them American. That's a great line!

Therefore, as critical as I was earlier of some of the episode, I hear Kimberly's point, and I do see a lot of value of the episode in the way it complicates Olivia's character, in the sense that it gives us this moment where she gets to engage more fully with her blackness. And with her making that stand it made the episode even more powerful for me.

RON JACKSON: I think that after reading all kinds of reactions from *Washington Post*, *PopSugar*, and a variety of different popular Internet websites, what I remember most is the mixed reaction. Some people were praising the episode. Other people were saying, "I can't watch this junk." Some people were saying things like, "When are they going to deal with the reality of the inequity in our country, the way in which we're being treated, versus other individuals who always seem to exist above the radar around issues of racial injustice?" My frustration with this episode, in part, is that it seems to present police brutality as an isolated incident, as though it is something we need to deal with on a case-by-case basis. It suggests to us that it's not something that actually happens in a very real and rampant way that leads to a heightened anxiety within Black families across the entire nation.

I can't tell you how many times I have heard that when a Black child is born, many Black parents have reported that they have a significant amount of anxiety about that child's future and about that child being able to survive something as simple as a traffic stop. The public narrative is that as long as the child does not commit a crime and stays in school, they will enjoy life success, but then we see young lives eclipsed through police violence, as in the case of Tamir Rice.

And so I think that there is so much more to be said about the bloodshed that has become expected and has become ordinary in a society that presumes that it is still embracing a democracy that values everyone. I'm deeply troubled by the episode, and I think that

I've seen other people's commentary as being reflective of something that is not playful for any of us. It is so very real, and so very devastating to our communities, that we can't afford to speak about it or to represent it in a way that is any way insubstantial. I don't want to say the episode was lighthearted, but it certainly felt somewhat light on its commentary as another episode where Olivia fixed some incident that, in many ways, for many families feels like something that's unfixable. The Black community is in search of very real solutions. We turn to our faith in God to help us through it all. We turn to our families for comfort. We turn to elected officials for accountability. Yet, we are left with the stain of racial hegemony that has taken so many Black lives.

KIMBERLY MOFFITT: I was most intrigued by and disturbed by social media commentary that suggested not only that it was too soon, but also that it was odd that Shonda Rhimes was dealing with this issue in the first place. There were a number of *Scandal* audience members who were angry about Rhimes's decision to grapple with sensitive topics that are very much a part of our collective American social reality.

And what I find really interesting about that reaction is it feels as though there's still a segment of the American population that has constructed that American ideal that does not actually look like or reflect what American realism is. What is the reality happening here in America?

The fact that this topic is such a major issue and it doesn't seem to pervade into all communities is unfathomable. It seems to become something that America wants to turn away from and pretend as though it is not as rampant as it is. It's simply not a reality that all people are having to deal with personally.

And in fact, what many audience members felt is that Rhimes needs to stick with what's happening inside the Beltway and what's going on between Olivia and Fitz. She has done it for four seasons so well, and many people in her audience felt that's where her focal point should be. But it was bold to actually engage in commentary of real-life social tragedy, then suggest to viewers that they have to deal with what our status quo really is, even though they don't want to have to deal with it.

RON JACKSON: What do you imagine the complexities would be that are unraveled via these characters within the episode, from the father to the activist, to the president's office to Olivia?

I can start us off here: There was an interesting article that was done on March 6, 2015, by an author named Brittney Stephens, where she mentions there are several reasons everyone's talking about *Scandal* the week the episode aired. In this *PopSugar* article she explained that one of the things that happened was that the actors of this episode watched it together for the first time while it was being aired live, and they found themselves blown away by it. Even Kerry Washington is quoted as saying that she found herself weeping as if she hadn't read it and didn't act in it. She said she felt proud to be a part of the episode. Shonda Rhimes indicated that the last image really affected her because that child is just like others' children. She felt this guttural instinct to empathize that that child was someone's baby.

I think that gives you a little insight into what the director and actors were thinking. But it also is about the complexities and what the characters are supposed to represent. They're supposed to represent Black folks in their quintessentially human form. The activist Marcus is simply trying to advocate for this father's right to grieve his child and fight on behalf of his child even at a time when everyone is trying to say that this kid had something on him and that's why the police had to kill him.

And the father believes in his son to the last moment, to the point of being willing to put his life on the line to stand firmly with rifle in hand and proclaim, "My son would not do that." And I think that that moment struck a chord for many parents out there that are saying, "I know my child, and I know what my child is capable of, and what my child would or would not do."

So there was this very deeply penetrating sense of emotion that cuts to the core of this episode with each line being delivered. I would imagine it doesn't feel like acting anymore. It feels real. I thought that's part of the complexity of it, just hearing from the father and seeing the activist's representation.

I'll let you all comment on the rest of it. But I just think that those two characters for me delivered a certain kind of complexity that represents the Black man's burden in America.

KIMBERLY MOFFITT: I'll just say very quickly, I think Simone's early point about Olivia Pope being brought into a Black space for the first time demonstrates her own complexity. So we see her in terms of her complexity as this well put together woman who is able to fix everything but then has this complicated love situation going on with the president of the United States, even though he's a married man. There's a lot that has been raised about that as a complexity to her character that she is this well put together woman, yet she allows herself to continue to be the "side chick"?

But we also have the opportunity to see another aspect of her complexity by seeing her in a space that requires her to acknowledge and to verbalize what it means to be a person of color in this country and how that impacts the experience of the victim, the dad, Marcus, all of these men who she is surrounded by in that moment. Here we see that she is very much a Black woman. You get to see in that instance, even if she is not always articulating it in the hour-long episode. Her willingness to take a stand, to stand with Marcus and start shouting with the crowd, to walk into the police station and say, "I am not doing that" all speaks to this. In all of these instances, she asserts herself. It gives us the opportunity to see her operating in a Black space, in a Black body, in ways that we haven't seen in other episodes.

SIMONE ADAMS: I think we touched on a number of these aspects in an earlier question. I'm also thinking about Fitzgerald Grant as the president and his position as the father figure, and when these two fathers meet at the end, in this moment where he is no longer the president so much, he is a private individual. He's a parent, and the two of them share the grief of both having lost, under different circumstances, their sons. I think we see Fitz from a different perspective there as well. He is shown as being able to empathize, being able to share that moment with Clarence, the father, in a joint role that transcends racial lines.

I find it interesting that Marcus is introduced in this episode as an activist, yet he later becomes a part of the system he was just fighting against by working for Olivia Pope & Associates and after that even serving as White House press secretary. Then again, during the one hundredth episode in season six, we see him in this alternative *Scandal* universe where both Olivia and Marcus are activists and where they're working for a criminal justice reform bill that gets passed.

Of course, we don't see much of that complexity in Marcus in the "Lawn Chair" episode yet, but it's interesting that they're introducing this character in this way to replace Harrison Wright, the "Alpha Gladiator" who left the show earlier, as another loyal Black man working for and with Olivia Pope.

I think overall the episode gives us a moment to see different sides that are more political on *Scandal* than we've seen before.

RON JACKSON: So let me ask you this question, which is our final question here. What does this episode say to us about contemporary social movements and their protagonists? In other words, what does it say about the extent to which Black lives matter? And you can take that question figuratively or literally as it relates to Black Lives Matter.

KIMBERLY MOFFITT: One of the points that is made in the introduction of the volume Regina Spellers and I coedited, *Blackberries and Redbones: Critical Articulations of Black Hair/Body Politics in Africana Communities,* is this whole notion of Black bodies being the spaces that are both revered and reviled at the same time. And so when I think about this particular episode, but even many of the other social movements that we are experiencing, it's in the similar vein. We recognize these bodies as having value, yet it depends on what those bodies are doing that ultimately allows us to see their humanity.

But there are also those same bodies that we revile in negative ways especially when it's not doing the things that we want it to do and so we can have someone like a Black Lives Matter activist DeRay McKesson who is college educated and well spoken and has been in the community. All of his work has been around public school education and has seemingly, at a very young age, thrived in that space. And as a result, he was able to catapult himself to a particular space where people did revere him as being a voice that should be heard on social justice issues, particularly around public school education.

But he is also a body that is reviled. So it's the same body that is being uplifted as this voice that makes sense to us and wants to take a stand on public education for young children. But that body also becomes reviled because people see him as trying to push to change the system and alter the way in which we do business as usual, which means that it has to require inviting other parties to the table to participate in what it means to be or to have justice in this country.

Because he is willing to push, and push in ways that don't necessarily work for the state apparatus like we talked about earlier, then he is villainized. We've seen the images of him protesting and being arrested or protesting and being handled roughly because people see his body as one to revile because of what he is willing to speak out against.

So for me, I see it in a similar vein, even in a contemporary movement like Black Lives Matter.

RON JACKSON: You know, I am deeply conflicted by the Black Lives Matter movement. When I think of this episode, I think that it honestly reveals some of the same complexities of Black Lives Matter. Clearly, Black Lives Matter is a faceless movement that has been designed in a way that invites those people who agree with its principles to become like its brand ambassadors. So, technically, anyone can say they're a part of Black Lives Matter.

When the Black actor Jesse Williams got up at the BET Awards and talked about Black Lives Matter, and that whole speech went viral, I don't think he had a conversation with anyone from the Black Lives Matter "headquarters." I don't think that he really even knows anybody

376 | JACKSON, MOFFITT, AND ADAMS

from Black Lives Matter "headquarters." He was just speaking from his heart and was able to invoke the essence of Black Lives Matter, and right after that they claimed him, and he embraced their agenda.

We had a similar situation, I don't know if you know that in 2015–16 there were more than a hundred college campuses that protested against campus racism in the United States and that even among those hundred or so college campuses, people also invoked Black Lives Matter because they needed a language. They needed a term to attach themselves to that people might understand or resonate with and this is such a popular thing that it was almost like saying, "I'm down with the hip-hop movement."

But it didn't necessarily have the kind of force that was necessary to hold individuals accountable for the social injustices that were being rendered against Black and Brown peoples.

This point is really frustrating for me because this episode does the same thing. The accountability is seemingly individual and not systemic or institutional. We're not holding institutions responsible; we're holding these individuals one by one responsible. So what I'm saying is that we need institutional reform. Whether it's at the level of the state police and local police to college campuses and universities and beyond.

I feel like that the presumption is that social justice activists talk loud and get momentary results and very minimal rewards that do not solve the problem of institutional injustice. I think this episode is like a flash point in the conversations around race in America, and we can't expect it to solve all racism in America. And so its commentary is special and unique and important, and I think the same is the case for Black Lives Matter. Yet it feels that there is something tragic and something that is quite indefinite about the violence being presented around police brutality, and the presumption is that we can't do much about it, so we remain paralyzed. I think this episode just kind of pulls out more of that frustration.

KIMBERLY MOFFITT: I wonder if that is reflective of a generational gap that exists between ourselves and even folks like Simone, who fits in with the millennials, in terms of how they believe in handling and carrying out social movements when so much of what we're familiar with is what our parents talked about.

The kind of struggle and activism our parents and grandparents talked about was more aligned with what we know as the civil rights movement, and it seems to be the possible disconnect because this newer version of activism doesn't have this very formal or hierarchical structure to it, but it does have a mass following all around the country and around the world. It just doesn't align with what we're most familiar. Its approach to strategic structural change to systems seems to place more energy on the immediate issues.

And then I also wanted to say very quickly that I was very excited to respond to this particular question about how the Black body is being revered and reviled at the same time, especially since Marcus's character had a lot of venom spewed at him in this episode. Only with Olivia's presence did we have the opportunity to see his complexity and to understand why he should be revered and not just reviled as that typical activist on the street causing a ruckus and blocking our street.

SIMONE ADAMS: Let me react to something that both of mentioned. What Kimberly said actually reminded me of how I wanted to phrase this generation gap. Let's not forget that Black Lives Matter really started as a hashtag on social media. It was three Black queer women who, after the death of Trayvon Martin, decided to express their frustration with this hashtag. These women were Alicia Garza, Opal Tometi, and Patrisse Cullors. And this moment was before a formal organization by the name of Black Lives Matter was even created. I think a lot of what this initial idea is about is to find digital spaces that allow the younger generations to come together and to quickly react to things that are happening.

If we think back to the first nationwide protests as a response to what was happening in Ferguson, it was within hours that people would find out about yet another hashtag of somebody gunned down by the police. And within hours of that moment, you had thousands of people connected through social media gathering in public spaces. It didn't need a leader for them to organize them. All it needed was this idea of the shared hashtag to meet in a shared deliberative space online that served as a vehicle for people to take to the streets. I think there is something to this difference in how this "new" civil rights movement is playing out in the sense that it is actually "leaderful." It's not leaderless, as it is sometimes criticized for, it's leaderful, but it is true that it is often not hierarchically organized. Some individuals do stand out, but overall I think it allows more people to join, and participate and I think that is part of the appeal to people.

I hear Ron's frustration. I hear that it seems like there are all these isolated incidences and protests, but if we really think about what has happened over the past few years, representatives of Black Lives Matter rallies have been able to assemble a national platform for solidarity that has been mediated on an international scale. The multiplied voices have a significant impact on institutions that would rather not be blasted on this scale.

I remember in the spring of 2015 I was in Austria teaching this American studies class called "From Selma to Ferguson: The Cultural Politics of Protest." We were so far removed in the center of Europe and obviously didn't have all the access to firsthand news accounts based on limited availability with our own television networks. But because of social media, it felt like we were able to connect to the struggle and participate in this dialogue.

We continue to see these solidarity movements spread around the globe, with hashtags and with other forms of digital activism. I see a lot of potential in that. Syracuse, New York, has a Black Lives Matter chapter. I'm sure all of your cities have Black Lives Matter chapters that are focusing on local issues. In Syracuse, for example, they are focusing on police mistreatment on a local level, things you would never hear on a national platform but things that are being addressed. Mostly young people are involved, and many of these young people have no previous experience in organizing, no previous experience in social justice activism, but it gave them a space where they felt welcomed, and it gave them a space where they felt that their voice mattered. So I think that there are many differences between what social justice movements used to look like and what they look like today. And even though contemporary movements have not yet been able to change things on a larger scale, there is so much happening locally that I hope will make an impact in some way or another.

"We Need to Fix This": Reflecting on Reflections

When terms such as *civil unrest* are appended to any discussion of racism and police brutality in the United States, the statement presupposes that we have once rested. The reality is that there has been no respite for Black and Brown peoples in the United States. They have been under attack since entering the country. If it wasn't slavery, then it was Black codes, or civil rights, or the "new Jim Crow" (Alexander 2012), or the ongoing assault on Black and Brown men, women, and children by local law enforcement and hate groups. As Viola Davis's character, Annalise Keating, highlights in her impassioned speech to the Supreme Court during the second part of the *Scandal* and *How to Get Away with Murder* crossover in March 2018, "Racism is built into the DNA of America. And as long as we turn a blind eye to the pain of those suffering under its oppression, we will never escape those origins" ("Lahey v. The Commonwealth of Pennsylvania" [4.13]).

It is baffling that anyone could, in the present day, say they do not know what White privilege is or what racism looks like. Even more baffling is that the mere talk about racism in this country, whether individual or systemic, brings about immediate charges of "reverse racism," "race baiting," and "playing the race card." The July 2017 advertising campaign by Procter and Gamble (P&G) called "The Talk" is a case in point. While the company's goal was to spark a #TalkAboutBias and the video went viral within hours, many quickly took to social media to accuse the company of being racist themselves (Callender 2017). Yet P&G simply portrayed the realities of Black and Brown parents who are forced to have "The Talk" with their children when it comes to the very real impacts of race in their lives. As Toni Morrison said in a 2014 appearance on *The Colbert Report*, "There is no such thing as race. None. There is just a human race—scientifically, anthropologically. Racism is a construct, a social construct. . . . [I]t has a social function, racism"; in other words, race as a meaningful category is not real, but racism very much is a reality (Dickerson 2014). Not seeing this point is the epitome of what Peggy McIntosh (2012 [1988]) talked about when she introduced the "invisible knapsack" metaphor of white privilege in the 1980s.

This chapter on "The Lawn Chair" seeks to do more than simply report what occurred in an episode of *Scandal*. It seeks to do more than point out social inequities and personal idiosyncrasies. It is about having a "talk" on how racism tragically interrupts, contaminates, and does violence to democracy as it has been articulated in the US Constitution.

In fact, racism in all its manifestations has left marginalized group members feeling that once again the only protections and freedoms that are ensured by the US Constitution are that of White people. How else are we to interpret the paralyzing terror with which Black families are left when they see hundreds of Black males dying at the hands of police over the course of just a few years? What are people of color, who are taxpaying citizens, to think when a jury of peers is 90 percent White for a White police assailant who is acquitted in virtually every case?

It is simplistic to say that these are complicated times or that the person of color must have provoked their own murder or bodily harm. Black and Brown families are not guaranteed equal treatment. And despite their best efforts to raise their sons and daughters to live with integrity, they often feel compelled to prepare their children for the reality that they will one day be discriminated against for no other reason than the color of their skin—in other words, have "The Talk." Meanwhile, White kids are taught about discrimination as an historical instance that is now far gone. As a result, White adults grow old thinking racism does not exist or that the only possibility for racism to have occurred is that Black and Brown people deserved it.

Racism, police brutality, racial discrimination, redlining, gentrification, and all the other means of discrimination based on skin color still exist. Television shows like *Scandal* are just art imitating reality. We need this reality to stop! We need to fix this!

References

Alexander, Michelle. 2012. *The New Jim Crow: Mass Incarceration in the Age of Colorblindness*. Rev. ed. New York: New Press.

Callender, Samantha. 2017. "A Lot of White People Are Mad about Procter and Gamble's 'The Talk' Video." *Essence*, Aug. 3. http://www.essence.com/procter-and-gamble-the-talk-reactions.

"The Demands." 2015. "Campus Demands." Compiled by *We the Protesters*. http://www.thedemands.org/.

Dickerson, Jessica. 2014. "Toni Morrison Breaks Down the Reality of Race on *The Colbert Report*." *Huffington Post*, Nov. 21. http://www.huffingtonpost.com/2014/11/21/toni-morrison-colbert_n_6199402.html.

How to Get Away with Murder. 2018. "Lahey v. The Commonwealth of Pennsylvania." 4.13. Created by Peter Nowalk. Directed by Zetna Fuentes. Written by Morenike Balogun and Sarah L. Thompson. ABC. Mar. 1.

Jackson, Ronald L., II. 2006. *Scripting the Black Masculine Body: Identity, Discourse and Racial Politics in Popular Media*. Albany, NY: SUNY Press.

"Mapping Police Violence." N.d. "Police Killed More than 100 Unarmed Black People in 2015." https://mappingpoliceviolence.org/unarmed/.

McIntosh, Peggy. 2012 [1988]. "White Privilege: Unpacking the Invisible Knapsack." In *White Privilege: Essential Readings on the Other Side of Racism*, edited by Paula S. Rothenberg, 121–25. New York: Worth.

Paskin, Willa. 2014. "How to Get Away with Hyperdrama." *Slate*, Sept. 25. http://www.slate.com/articles/arts/television/2014/09/how_to_get_away_with_murder_review_viola_davis_show_is_the_latest_shonda.html.

Puff, Simone. 2015. "Another *Scandal* in Washington: How a Transgressive, Black Anti-heroine Makes for New 'Quality TV.'" In *Transgressive Television: Politics and Crime in 21st-Century American TV Series*, edited by Birgit Däwes, Alexandra Ganser, and Nicole Poppenhagen, 103–26. Heidelberg, Germany: Universitätsverlag Winter.

Rhimes, Shonda. 2014. "Shonda Rhimes '91, Commencement Address." Dartmouth College Commencement, June 8. http://www.dartmouth.edu/~commence/news/speeches/2014/rhimes-address.html.

Spellers, Regina E., and Moffitt, Kimberly R., eds. 2010. *Blackberries and Redbones: Critical Articulations of Black Hair/Body Politics in Africana Communities*. Cresskill, NJ: Hampton Press.

Stephens, Brittney. 2015. "4 Reasons Everyone Is Talking about *Scandal* This Week." *PopSugar*, Mar. 6. https://www.popsugar.com/entertainment /Scandal-Lawn-Chair-Episode-37025405.

Appendix

Contributors

Index

Complete Episode List, *Scandal*

(2012–2018, created by Shonda Rhimes)

Season One

1.01: "Sweet Baby." Directed by Paul McGuigan. Written by Shonda Rhimes. ABC Broadcasting. April 5, 2012.

1.02: "Dirty Little Secrets." Directed by Roxann Dawson. Written by Heather Mitchell. ABC Broadcasting. April 12, 2012.

1.03: "Hell Hath No Fury." Directed by Allison Liddi-Brown. Written by Matt Byrne. ABC Broadcasting. April 19, 2012.

1.04: "Enemy of the State." Directed by Michael Katleman. Written by Richard E. Robbins. ABC Broadcasting. April 26, 2012.

1.05: "Crash and Burn." Directed by Steve Robin. Written by Mark Wilding. ABC Broadcasting. May 3, 2012.

1.06: "The Trail." Directed by Tom Verica. Written by Jenna Bans. ABC Broadcasting. May 10, 2012.

1.07: "Grant: For the People." Directed by Roxann Dawson. Written by Shonda Rhimes. ABC Broadcasting. May 17, 2012.

Season Two

2.01: "White Hat's Off." Directed by Tom Verica. Written by Jenna Bans ABC Broadcasting. September 27, 2012.

2.02: "The Other Woman." Directed by Stephen Cragg. Written by Heather Mitchell. ABC Broadcasting. October 4, 2012.

2.03: "Hunting Season." Directed by Ron Underwood. Written by Matt Byrne. ABC Broadcasting. October 18, 2012.

2.04: "Beltway Unbuckled." Directed by Mark Tinker. Written by Mark Fish. ABC Broadcasting. October 25, 2012.

2.05: "All Roads Lead to Fitz." Directed by Steve Robin. Written by Raamla Mohamed. ABC Broadcasting. November 8, 2012.

2.06: "Spies Like Us." Directed by Bethany Rooney. Written by Chris Van Dusen. ABC Broadcasting. November 15, 2012.

2.07: "Defiance." Directed by Tom Verica. Written by Peter Noah. ABC Broadcasting. November 29, 2012.

2.08: "Happy Birthday, Mr. President." Directed by Oliver Bokelberg. Written by Shonda Rhimes. ABC Broadcasting. December 6, 2012.

2.09: "Blown Away." Directed by Jessica Yu. Written by Mark Wilding. ABC Broadcasting. December 13, 2012.

2.10: "One for the Dog." Directed by Steve Robin. Written by Heather Mitchell. ABC Broadcasting. January 10, 2013.

2.11: "A Criminal, a Whore, an Idiot, and a Liar." Directed by Stephen Cragg. Written by Mark Fish. ABC Broadcasting. January 17, 2013.

2.12: "Truth or Consequences." Directed by Jeannot Szwarc. Written by Peter Noah. ABC Broadcasting. January 31, 2013.

2.13: "Nobody Likes Babies." Directed by Tom Verica. Written by Mark Wilding. ABC Broadcasting. February 7, 2013.

2.14: "Whiskey Tango Foxtrot." Directed by Mark Tinker. Written by Matt Byrne. ABC Broadcasting. February 14, 2013.

2.15: "Boom Goes the Dynamite." Directed by Randy Zisk. Written by Jenna Bans. ABC Broadcasting. February 21, 2013.

2.16: "Top of the Hour." Directed by Steve Robin. Written by Heather Mitchell. ABC Broadcasting. March 21, 2013.

2.17: "Snake in the Garden." Directed by Ron Underwood. Written by Raamla Mohamed. ABC Broadcasting. March 28, 2013.

2.18: "Molly, You in Danger, Girl." Directed by Tom Verica. Written by Chris Van Dusen. ABC Broadcasting. April 4, 2013.

2.19: "Seven Fifty-Two." Directed by Allison Liddi-Brown. Written by Mark Fish. ABC Broadcasting. April 25, 2013.

2.20: "A Woman Scorned." Directed by Tony Goldwyn. Written by Zahir McGhee. ABC Broadcasting. May 2, 2013.

2.21: "Any Questions?" Directed by Mark Tinker. Written by Matt Byrne. ABC Broadcasting. May 9, 2013.

2.22: "White Hat's Back On." Directed by Tom Verica. Written by Shonda Rhimes. ABC Broadcasting. May 16, 2013.

Season Three

3.01: "It's Handled." Directed by Tom Verica. Written by Shonda Rhimes. ABC Broadcasting. October 3, 2013.

3.02: "Guess Who's Coming to Dinner." Directed by Allison Liddi-Brown. Written by Heather Mitchell. ABC Broadcasting. October 10, 2013.

3.03: "Mrs. Smith Goes to Washington." Directed by Jeannot Szwarc. Written by Matt Byrne. ABC Broadcasting. October 17, 2013.

3.04: "Say Hello to My Little Friend." Directed by Oliver Bokelberg. Written by Mark Fish. ABC Broadcasting. October 24, 2013.

3.05: "More Cattle, Less Bull." Directed by Randy Zisk. Written by Jenna Bans. ABC Broadcasting. October 31, 2013.

3.06: "Icarus." Directed by Julie Anne Robinson. Written by Peter Noah. ABC Broadcasting. November 7, 2013.

3.07: "Everything's Coming Up Mellie." Directed by Michael Katleman. Written by Peter Nowalk. ABC Broadcasting. November 14, 2013.

3.08: "Vermont Is for Lovers, Too." Directed by Ava DuVernay. Written by Mark Wilding. ABC Broadcasting. November 21, 2013.

3.09: "YOLO." Directed by Oliver Bokelberg. Written by Chris Van Dusen. ABC Broadcasting. December 5, 2013.

3.10: "A Door Marked Exit." Directed by Tom Verica. Written by Zahir McGhee. ABC Broadcasting. December 12, 2013.

3.11: "Ride, Sally, Ride." Directed by Tom Verica. Written by Raamla Mohamed. ABC Broadcasting. February 27, 2014.

3.12: "We Do Not Touch the First Ladies." Directed by Oliver Bokelberg. Written by Heather Mitchell. ABC Broadcasting. March 6, 2014.

3.13: "No Sun on the Horizon." Directed by Randy Zisk. Written by Matt Byrne. ABC Broadcasting. March 13 2014.

3.14: "Kiss Kiss Bang Bang." Directed by Paul McCrane. Written by Mark Fish. ABC Broadcasting. March 20, 2014.

3.15: "Mama Said Knock You Out." Directed by Tony Goldwyn. Written by Zahir McGhee. ABC Broadcasting. March 27, 2014.

3.16: "The Fluffer." Directed by Jeannot Szwarc. Written by Chris Van Dusen and Raamla Mohamed. ABC Broadcasting. April 3, 2014.

3.17: "Flesh and Blood." Directed by Debbie Allen. Written by Severiano Canales and Miguel Nolla. ABC Broadcasting. April 10, 2014.

3.18: "The Price of Free and Fair Elections." Directed by Tom Verica. Written by Shonda Rhimes and Mark Wilding. ABC Broadcasting, April 17, 2014.

Season Four

4.01: "Randy, Red, Superfreak, and Julia." Directed by Tom Verica. Written by Shonda Rhimes. ABC Broadcasting. September 25, 2014.

4.02: "The State of the Union." Directed by Allison Liddi-Brown. Written by Heather Mitchell. ABC Broadcasting. October 2, 2014.

4.03: "Inside the Bubble." Directed by Randy Zisk. Written by Matt Byrne. ABC Broadcasting. October 9, 2014.

4.04: "Like Father, Like Daughter." Directed by Paul McCrane. Written by Mark Fish. ABC Broadcasting. October 16, 2014.

4.05: "The Key." Directed by Paul McCrane. Written by Chris Van Dusen. ABC Broadcasting. October 23, 2014.

4.06: "An Innocent Man." Directed by Jeannot Szwarc. Written by Zahir McGhee. ABC Broadcasting. October 30, 2014.

4.07: "Baby Made a Mess." Directed by Oliver Bokelberg. Written by Jenna Bans. ABC Broadcasting. November 6, 2014.

4.08: "The Last Supper." Directed by Julie Anne Robinson. Written by Allan Heinberg. ABC Broadcasting. November 13, 2014.

4.09: "Where the Sun Don't Shine." Directed by Tony Goldwyn. Written by Mark Wilding. ABC Broadcasting. November 20, 2014.

4.10: "Run." Directed by Tom Verica. Written by Shonda Rhimes. ABC Broadcasting. January 29, 2015.

4.11: "Where's the Black Lady?" Directed by Debbie Allen. Written by Raamla Mohamed. ABC Broadcasting. February 5, 2015.

4.12: "Gladiators Don't Run." Directed by Randy Zisk. Written by Paul William Davies. ABC Broadcasting. February 12, 2015.

4.13: "No More Blood." Directed by Randy Zisk. Written by Heather Mitchell. ABC Broadcasting. February 19, 2015.

4.14: "The Lawn Chair." Directed by Tom Verica. Written by Zahir McGhee. ABC Broadcasting. March 5, 2015.

4.15: "The Testimony of Diego Muñoz." Directed by Allison Liddi-Brown. Written by Mark Fish. ABC Broadcasting. March 12, 2015.

4.16: "It's Good to Be Kink." Directed by Paul McCrane. Written by Matt Byrne. ABC Broadcasting. March 19, 2015.

4.17: "Put a Ring on It." Directed by Regina King. Written by Chris Van Dusen. ABC Broadcasting. March 26, 2015.

4.18: "Honor Thy Father." Directed by Jeannot Szwarc. Written by Severiano Canales. ABC Broadcasting. April 2, 2015.

4.19: "I'm Just a Bill." Directed by Debbie Allen. Written by Raamla Mohamed. ABC Broadcasting. April 16, 2015.

4.20: "First Lady Sings the Blues." Directed by David Rodriguez. Written by Paul William Davies. ABC Broadcasting. April 23, 2015.

4.21: "A Few Good Women." Directed by Oliver Bokelberg. Written by Severiano Canales and Jess Brownell. ABC Broadcasting. May 7, 2015.

4.22: "You Can't Take Command." Directed by Tom Verica. Written by Shonda Rhimes and Mark Wilding. ABC Broadcasting. May 14, 2015.

Season Five

5.01: "Heavy Is the Head." Directed by Tom Verica. Written by Shonda Rhimes. ABC Broadcasting. September 24, 2015.

5.02: "Yes." Directed by Tony Goldwyn. Written by Heather Mitchell. ABC Broadcasting. October 1, 2015.

5.03: "Paris Is Burning." Directed by Jann Turner. Written by Matt Byrne. ABC Broadcasting. October 8, 2015.

5.04: "Dog-Whistle Politics." Directed by Zetna Fuentes. Written by Shonda Rhimes and Mark Fish. ABC Broadcasting. 15 October. 2015.

5.05: "You Got Served." Directed by Kevin Bray. Written by Zahir McGhee. ABC Broadcasting. October 22, 2015.

5.06: "Get Out of Jail, Free." Directed by Chandra Wilson. Written by Chris Van Dusen. ABC Broadcasting. October 29, 2015.

5.07: "Even the Devil Deserves a Second Chance." Directed by Oliver Bokelberg. Written by Raamla Mohamed. ABC Broadcasting. 5 November, 2015.

5.08: "Rasputin." Directed by John Terlesky. Written by Paul William Davies. ABC Broadcasting. November 12, 2015.

5.09: "Baby, It's Cold Outside." Directed by Tom Verica. Written by Mark Wilding. ABC Broadcasting. November 19, 2015.

5.10: "It's Hard Out Here for a General." Directed by Tom Verica. Written by Severiano Canales. ABC Broadcasting. February 11, 2016.

5.11: "The Candidate." Directed by Allison Liddi-Brown. Written by Alison Schapker. ABC Broadcasting. February 18, 2016.

5.12: "Wild Card." Directed by Allison Liddi-Brown and Tom Verica. Written by Mark Fish. ABC Broadcasting. February 25, 2016.

5.13: "The Fish Rots from the Head." Directed by Sharat Raju. Written by Heather Mitchell. ABC Broadcasting. March 10, 2016.

5.14: "I See You." Directed by Paris Barclay. Written by Matt Byrne. ABC Broadcasting. March 17, 2016.

5.15: "Pencils Down." Directed by Regina King. Written by Chris Van Dusen. ABC Broadcasting. March 24, 2016.

5.16: "The Miseducation of Susan Ross." Directed by Scott Foley. Written by Raamla Mohamed. ABC Broadcasting. March 31, 2016.

5.17: "Thwack!" Directed by Tony Goldwyn. Written by Zahir McGhee. ABC Broadcasting. April 7, 2016.

5.18: "Till Death Do Us Part." Directed by Steph Green. Written by Paul William Davies. ABC Broadcasting. April 21, 2016.

5.19: "Buckle Up." Directed by Oliver Bokelberg. Written by Michelle Lirtzman. ABC Broadcasting. April, 28 2016.

5.20: "Trump Card." Directed by Jann Turner. Written by Severiano Canales and Jess Brownell. ABC Broadcasting. May 5, 2016.

5.21: "That's My Girl." Directed by Tom Verica. Written by Shonda Rhimes and Mark Wilding. ABC Broadcasting. May 12, 2016.

Season Six

6.01: "Survival of the Fittest." Directed by Tom Verica. Written by Shonda Rhimes. ABC Broadcasting. January 26, 2017.

6.02: "Hardball." Directed by Allison Liddi-Brown. Written by Matt Byrne. ABC Broadcasting. February 2, 2017.

6.03: "Fates Worse Than Death." Directed by Scott Foley. Written by Mark Fish. ABC Broadcasting. February 9, 2017.

6.04: "The Belt." Directed by Tom Verica. Written by Paul William Davies. ABC Broadcasting. February 16, 2017.

6.05: "They All Bow Down." Directed by Millicent Shelton. Written by Zahir McGhee. ABC Broadcasting. March 9, 2017.

6.06: "Extinction." Directed by Tony Goldwyn. Written by Chris Van Dusen. ABC Broadcasting. March 16, 2017.

6.07: "A Traitor among Us." Directed by Tom Verica. Written by Alison Schapker. ABC Broadcasting. March 23, 2017.

6.08: "A Stomach for Blood." Directed by Oliver Bokelberg. Written by Severiano Canales. ABC Broadcasting. March 30, 2017.

6.09: "Dead in the Water." Directed by Nicole Rubio. Written by Michelle Lirtzman. ABC Broadcasting. April 6, 2017.

6.10: "The Decision." Directed by Sharat Raju. Written by Johanna Lee. ABC Broadcasting. April 13, 2017.

6.11: "Trojan Horse." Directed by Jann Turner. Written by Jess Brownell and Nicholas Nardini. ABC Broadcasting. April 20, 2017.

6.12: "Mercy." Directed by Nzingha Stewart. Written by Severiano Canales and Ameni Rozsa. ABC Broadcasting. April 27, 2017.

6.13: "The Box." Directed by Steph Green. Written by Austin Guzman and Raamla Mohamed. ABC Broadcasting. May 4, 2017.

6.14: "Head Games." Directed by Zetna Fuentes. Written by Juan Carlos Fernandez and Chris Van Dusen. ABC Broadcasting. May 11, 2017.

6.15: "Tick Tock." Directed by Salli Richardson-Whitfield. Written by Zahir McGhee and Michelle Lirtzman. ABC Broadcasting. May 18, 2017.

6.16: "Transfer of Power." Directed by Tony Goldwyn. Written by Mark Fish Matt Byrne. ABC Broadcasting. May 18, 2017.

Season Seven

7.01: "Watch Me." Directed by Jann Turner. Written by Shonda Rhimes. ABC Broadcasting. October 5, 2017.

7.02: "Pressing the Flesh." Directed by Tony Goldwyn. Written by Matt Byrne. ABC Broadcasting. October 12, 2017.

7.03: "Day 101." Directed by Scott Foley. Written by Zahir McGhee. ABC Broadcasting. October 19, 2017.

7.04: "Lost Girls." Directed by Nicole Rubio. Written by Austin Guzman and Ameni Rozsa. ABC Broadcasting. October 26, 2017.

7.05: "Adventures in Babysitting." Directed by Oliver Bokelberg. Written by Severiano Canales and Tia Napolitano. ABC Broadcasting. November 2, 2017.

7.06: "Vampires and Bloodsuckers." Directed by Jann Turner. Written by Chris Van Dusen and Tia Napolitano. ABC Broadcasting. November 9, 2017.

7.07: "Something Borrowed." Directed by Sharat Raju. Written by Mark Fish. ABC Broadcasting. November 16, 2017.

7.08: "Robin." Directed by Daryn Okada. Written by Juan Carlos Fernandez. ABC Broadcasting. January 18, 2018.

7.09: "Good People." Directed by Nzingha Stewart. Written by Shonda Rhimes, Jess Brownell, and Nicholas Nardini. ABC Broadcasting. January 25, 2018.

7.10: "The People v. Olivia Pope." Directed by Kerry Washington. Written by Ameni Rozsa. ABC Broadcasting. February 1, 2018.

7.11: "Army of One." Directed by Allison Liddi-Brown. Written by Austin Guzman. ABC Broadcasting. February 8, 2018.

7.12: "Allow Me to Reintroduce Myself." Directed by Tony Goldwyn. Written by Raamla Mohamed. ABC Broadcasting. March 1, 2018.

7.13: "Air Force Two." Directed by Valerie Weiss. Written by Severiano Canales. ABC Broadcasting. March 8, 2018.

7.14: "The List." Directed by Gregory T. Evans. Written by Jess Brownell and Juan Carlos Fernandez. ABC Broadcasting. March 15, 2018.

7.15: "The Noise." Directed by Darby Stanchfield. Written by Raamla Mohamed and Jeremy Gordon. ABC Broadcasting. March 29, 2018.

7.16: "People Like Me." Directed by Joe Morton. Written by Chris Van Dusen and Nicholas Nardini. ABC Broadcasting. April 5, 2018.

7.17: "Standing in the Sun." Directed by Jann Turner. Written by Mark Fish and Matt Byrne. ABC Broadcasting. April 12, 2018.

7.18: "Over a Cliff." Directed by Tom Verica. Written by Shonda Rhimes. ABC Broadcasting. April 19, 2018.

Contributors

Simone Adams (PhD, University of Klagenfurt, Austria) is an American cultural studies and communication scholar as well as an instructional design and educational technology specialist, currently working at the Center for Digital Teaching and Learning at the University of Graz in Austria. Previously, she taught in the Departments of Women's and Gender Studies and African American Studies at Syracuse University and in Departments of American Studies across Austria and Germany. Adams (née Puff) has published on topics such as colorism and skin-color politics in African American literature and culture, on representations of the Black feminist movement in the media, and on teaching with technology to foster diversity and inclusion. Other research interests are in contemporary protest cultures and the use of social media, representations of race and gender in popular culture, and critical whiteness studies.

Diamond M. Akers is a proud alumna of the University of Georgia. While attending the University of Georgia, she had the pleasure of working with Harris throughout her undergraduate career on various research projects. She is currently pursuing her Juris Doctorate at Mercer University School of Law. Ms. Akers is involved with many organizations within her law school. She is a member of the Black Law Students Association, Association of Women Law Students, and a cadet through Mercer University Army Reserve Officers' Training Corps. Upon graduation from law school, Ms. Akers plans to commission into the Army Judge Advocate General Corps and serve her country.

Sean Eversley Bradwell (PhD, Cornell University) is the director of the Center for IDEAS (inclusion, diversity, equity, and social change) as well as the director of the MLK Scholar Program at Ithaca College. He has published on the impact of racialized local histories, and his research focuses on critical race theory, educational policy, and hip hop culture. He is currently serving his fourth term as an elected member of the Ithaca City School District Board of Education.

Shantel Gabrieal Buggs (PhD, University of Texas at Austin) is an assistant professor of sociology and African American studies at Florida State University. Her research interests center on how race and ethnicity, gender, and sexuality shape the ways that people build and negotiate family, and pursue and maintain romantic intimate relationships (particularly interracial relationships). She has published on these topics in journals such as *Identities, Journal of Marriage and Family*, and *Sociology of Race and Ethnicity*, and her research has appeared in popular outlets like *Bitch Magazine* and *The Stoop* podcast. Through her research, she illustrates how interpersonal relationships structure and reify identities and social inequalities. She also writes about the representation of race, gender, and sexuality in popular culture and how social media platforms are utilized to build intimate relationships or to create community.

Rachel D. Davidson (PhD, University of Wisconsin–Milwaukee) is an assistant professor of communication at Hanover College. Her research broadly addresses rhetoric and public culture with interest in motherhood, caregiving, and social advocacy. In particular, her research explores the implications of the ways in which values embedded in issues assumed to be private (that is, mothering and caregiving) are manifested in a broad range of diverse texts from film and television to online public advocacy efforts. Rachel's research has appeared in *Communication Quarterly*, *Women and Language*, *Disability Studies Quarterly*, and *Gender, Education, Music, and Society*.

Ernest L. Gibson III (PhD, University of Massachusetts–Amherst) is associate professor of English and codirector of Africana studies at Auburn University. He is the author of *Salvific Manhood: James Baldwin's Novelization of Male Intimacy* (2019). An interdisciplinary scholar by training, his research lies at the intersections of literary, cultural, and queer theories and often pivots on questions of manhood, masculinity, and vulnerability. He is currently at work on his second book project, "Between Ritual and Rebellion: Black Male Joy and Vulnerable Masculinities."

Tina M. Harris (PhD, University of Kentucky) is a professor of communication at the University of Georgia. Her primary research interest is in the area of interracial communication. She is the coauthor of the textbook

Interracial Communication: Theory into Practice (2015, with Mark P. Orbe). Other research interests include communication and pedagogy, diversity and media representations, and race and ethnic disparities and religious frameworks in health communication. She has published many articles and book chapters on race and communication, served as reviewer for top-tier communication journals, and fulfilled many service roles within the discipline, the National Communication Association, and the Southern States Communication Association. The University of Georgia awarded her the 2017 Engaged Scholar Award by the Office of Public Service and Outreach and the title of Distinguished Josiah T. Meigs Teaching Professor (highest teaching honor). She has been recognized by the University System of Georgia Board of Regents with the Scholarship of Teaching and Learning Award for her research on pedagogy and race. Her commitment to translating research from theory into practice is evidenced in her continued service to the department, university, discipline, and community through work that facilitates critical engagement with the issue of race.

Christopher A. House (PhD, University of Pittsburgh) is an associate professor of communication studies and affiliated faculty member in communication and culture and the MLK Scholar Program at Ithaca College. He has published academic articles and book chapters that examine intersections of race, religion, and rhetoric in his research areas of Black church studies, neo-Pentecostal rhetoric, rhetorical theology, critical media and digital studies, rhetorics of race, and African American rhetoric. He is currently completing his first book, *Touch Your Neighbor and Say Black Lives Matter: Black Neo-Pentecostal Social Action in the Age of #BlackLivesMatter.*

Will Howell (MA, University of Maryland, College Park) is a rhetoric doctoral candidate in the Department of Communication at the University of Maryland. Originally from Salem, Oregon, he graduated from Macalester College in 2008 with a BA in political science. He spearheaded outreach for political campaigns and nonprofits in Minnesota and Oregon and continues to advise local candidates. He studies entertainment's impact on political participation, political identity, and perceptions of political issues and actors.

Ronald L. Jackson II (PhD, Howard University) is a professor of communication and previous dean of McMicken College of Arts & Sciences at the University of Cincinnati. Jackson is one of the leading communication and identity scholars in the nation. Jackson is past coeditor (with Kent

Ono) of *Critical Studies in Media Communication*. His research explores empirical, conceptual, and critical approaches to the study of masculinity, identity negotiation, whiteness, and Afrocentricity. He is the author of fourteen books, including *Scripting the Black Masculine Body in Popular Media* (2006), *Interpreting Tyler Perry* (2014, with Jamel Bell), and the 2014 Comic-Con Eisner Award finalist, *Black Comics: Politics of Race and Representation* (2013, with Sheena Howard).

Kavyta Kay (PhD, University of Leeds, UK) is a cultural sociologist and a qualitative researcher who engages in critical work from academic, popular culture, and digital platforms. Currently, she is a University of London associate fellow at the Institute of Commonwealth Studies and a senior lecturer at Leeds Beckett University. In her research, teaching, and writing, she has drawn on intersectional feminism, gender, postcolonial studies, and critical race theory. Her work, so far, has focused on the body, the politics of beauty and skin color, and South Asian cultural studies.

Nicholas Manganas (PhD, University of Technology, Sydney) is a lecturer in international studies at the University of Technology, Sydney. He is the author of *Las dos Españas: Terror and Crisis in Contemporary Spain* (2016). He has published extensively in various disciplinary areas, including contemporary Spanish studies, cultural studies, and queer studies. His research interests include narratives of terrorism, contemporary Spanish cultural studies, and necropolitics.

Kimberly R. Moffitt (PhD, Howard University) is a media studies scholar and chair of the Language Literacy and Culture PhD program at the University of Maryland–Baltimore County. Her teaching interests include culture, media studies and criticism, Black hair and body politics, sports and media, and popular culture. Her research focuses on mediated representations of marginalized groups as well as the politicized nature of Black hair and the body. She has published three coedited volumes, including *Blackberries and Redbones: Critical Articulations of Black Hair and Body Politics in Africana Communities* (2010), *The Obama Effect: Multidisciplinary Renderings of the 2008 Campaign* (2010), and *The 1980s: A Transitional Decade?* (2011). Her current research focuses on the representations of children of color in Disney programming.

Tracey Owens Patton (PhD, University of Utah) is a professor of communication in the Department of Communication and Journalism and adjunct professor in African American and diaspora studies in the School of Culture, Gender, and Social Justice at the University of Wyoming. She also served as the director of the African American & Diaspora Studies Program from 2009 to 2017 at the University of Wyoming. Her area of specialization is critical cultural communication, rhetorical studies, and transnational studies. Her work is strongly influenced by critical theory, cultural studies, womanist theory, and rhetorical theory. She has authored a number of academic publications on topics involving the interdependence between race, gender, and power and how these issues interrelate culturally and rhetorically in education, media, memory, myth, and speeches.

David Ponton III (PhD, Rice University) is a historian and an assistant professor in the School of Interdisciplinary and Global Studies at the University of South Florida. His research traces the varied consequences of racial residential segregation and the criminalization of racialized spaces for Black Americans in the twentieth century—consequences that include police brutality, intimate-partner violence, and environmental racism. His teaching interests include Black American history, Black feminist genealogies, critical race theory, and race and society.

Kadian Pow is a Jamaican American ex-pat and assistant lecturer in Sociology at Birmingham City University. She is also an honorary research associate in the digital humanities at the University of Birmingham and a member of Britain's Black Studies Association. Ms. Pow's topics of interest include Black women and desire in US TV, queer formations of blackness, the intersectional politics of Black hair, and Tumblr as a media geography space, to name a few. Prior to pursuing her PhD, Kadian spent more than a decade as a museum education specialist for such places as the US Holocaust Memorial Museum and the Smithsonian's National Museum of Natural History, as well as served as a community engagement consultant for the Barber Institute and the Wolverhampton Art Gallery. She is the owner of Bourn Beautiful Naturals, a boutique natural hair and skin-care line of products created for Black women that was launched in January 2017. Kadian Pow received her BA in anthropology from Vassar College and her MA in languages and cultures of Asia from the University of Wisconsin–Madison.

Ryessia Jones Russell is assistant director of the Greg and Lisa Smith Global Leadership Scholars program in the Haslam College of Business at the University of Tennessee–Knoxville. She is also a doctoral student at the University of Texas at Austin in the Department of Communication Studies with a focus on rhetorical and language studies. Her research interests include portrayals of African Americans in reality television, specifically in the areas of Black fatherhood, Black motherhood, and masculinity. Furthermore, she has taken an interest in examining media representations of police brutality victims, specifically Black males.

Kimberly Alecia Singletary (PhD, Northwestern University) received her MA from Georgetown University's Communication, Culture, Technology program and her BJ from the Missouri School of Journalism. She was awarded the Gerald R. Miller Outstanding Doctoral Dissertation Award from the National Communication Association in 2014. She has received DAAD and Fulbright fellowships to Germany and Austria, respectively. She was a JET scholar and taught in rural Japan directly following her undergraduate degree. Her work on blackness in the global public sphere has been published and featured in various journals and online forums. She writes about race, visuality, and popular culture on her blog, *Melancholy and the Infinite Post-Blackness.* After ten years in the classroom at universities in the Midwest and Pacific Northwest, she made the leap to working in the educational technology field.

Catherine R. Squires (PhD, Northwestern University) is a professor of communication studies at the University of Minnesota. She is the author of multiple books, including *Dispatches from the Color Line* (2007), *African Americans & the Media* (2009), and *The Post-racial Mystique* (2014). Most recently, she edited the collection *Dangerous Discourses: Feminism, Gun Violence & Civic Life* (2016), which was a finalist for the Tankard Award. Squires has published articles on media, race, gender, and politics in many journals, including *Communication Theory, American Quarterly,* and the *International Journal of Press/Politics.* Squires is also engaged in a long-term partnership with Gordon Parks High School and the Hallie Q. Brown Community Center in St. Paul, Minnesota. She collaborates with youth and elders to create publicly oriented media that explore the history and future development of the Rondo neighborhood. Her undergraduate degree in politics is from Occidental College, which is where she discovered her passion for media research and critical studies in the midst of the Los Angeles uprising that followed the not-guilty verdict for the policemen who beat Rodney King. Squires was awarded a Bush Fellowship for 2017–19, which will support her explorations of intergenerational learning and healing practices.

Lara C. Stache (PhD, University of Wisconsin–Milwaukee) is an assistant professor of communication and the program coordinator for the gender and sexuality studies program at Governors State University. She has written one book, *"Breaking Bad": A Cultural History* (2017), academic articles, and book chapters focused on popular culture, rhetoric, and gender.

Kelly Weber Stefonowich (PhD, Rice University) completed her dissertation, "The Ideology of White Southern Daughterhood, 1865–1920," which examined woman's perpetual status as daughter and how White southern women used daughterhood to claim leadership roles in the politics of memory after the Civil War. She lives in Virginia Beach, Virginia, with her husband and two dogs.

Timeka N. Tounsel (PhD, University of Michigan) is an assistant professor of African American studies and media studies at Pennsylvania State University. Her research considers Black women's media engagement practices and identity work. Her article on race, gender, and faith-based social media discourses is forthcoming in the *Journal of Media and Religion*. Tounsel is currently completing her first book, "Tangled Visions: Black Women and the Search for Self in Popular Culture."

Patricia Ventura (PhD, University of Florida) is an associate professor of English at Spelman College in Atlanta. Her research and teaching center on American studies, cultural studies, critical theory, and film and media studies. She has been awarded the Woodrow Wilson National Fellowship Foundation Career Enhancement Fellowship and a Marion L. Brittain Fellowship. Among other publications, she has written the monograph *Neoliberal Culture* (2012, reprinted 2016). Her most recent article in the field of TV studies is "Dystopian Eating, Queer Liberalism, and the Roots of Donald Trump in HBO's *Angels in America*" in the *Journal of Popular Culture* (2018). She is currently coediting two collections on race and utopia, one a book titled "Race and Utopian Desire in American Literature and Society" and the other titled "Race and Utopia" for the journal *Utopian Studies*, both forthcoming.

Myra Washington (PhD, University of Illinois at Urbana–Champaign) is associate professor of communication and journalism at the University of New Mexico. Her research is situated in the areas of cultural studies, critical media and digital media studies, comparative ethnic studies (with a focus on African American and Asian American studies), critical rhetorical studies, gender and sexuality studies, and the emerging field of critical mixed-race studies. The critical focus of her work examines the ways power enhances or elides the way meta-narratives of identity like race, gender, class, sexuality, and nation are understood.

Index